American Commissar

Then Nahash the Ammonite came up, and encamped against Jabesh-Gilead: and all the men of Jabesh said unto Nahash, Make a covenant with us and we will serve thee.

And Nahash the Ammonite answered them, On this condition will I make a covenant with you, that I may thrust out all your right eyes . . .

. . . and they fled every man into his tent: and there was a very great slaughter: . . .

I Samuel

American Commissar

By SANDOR VOROS

CHILTON COMPANY · BOOK DIVISION
Publishers
PHILADELPHIA *and* NEW YORK

FOR THOSE
> Whose recollections of the violent events that presaged
> The Shape of Things to Come
> Have grown rather dim.
> More particularly

FOR THOSE
> Born during and after World War II;
> The New Generation, confused by the distorted claims of
> The wicked Righteous, and
> The righteous Wicked—
> Who find it difficult to distinguish
> Which is which, and
> Which is worse,
> Yet who are fated to determine whither mankind.

FOR THEIR
> Clearer comprehension of the
> Vision and Despair which motivated so many in the
> Era (not yet at an end), this
> Leftward trail in pursuit of a
> Better World has been retraced from memory
> and
> Faithfully recorded.

Transcript:

REPUBLICA ESPANOLA
BRIGADAS INTERNACIONALES
(*International Brigades*)

LIVRET MILITAIRE (*Military Book*) No. 41,986

NOM: Voros
PRENOMS: Sandor
Date de naissance (*Date of birth*): 1 VII 1900
Lieu de naissance (*Birthplace*): Hongrie (*Hungary*)
Nationalite: Americaine
Domicile: U.S.A.
Ville: Cleveland, Ohio   Rue: 1500 S. Taylor Road
Parti Politique (*Political Party*): Antifasciste
Date d'entree dans les B. I. (*Date entered I. B.*): 2 VI 1937
Profession: Journaliste
Etat Civil (*Marital Status*): Celibataire (*Single*)

NOMINATIONS (*Appointments*):
Grade: Comisario de Compania (*Company Commissar*)
Fonctions (*Functions*): Jefe del Comisariado XV Brigada (*Chief
of the Commissariat of the XV Brigade*)
Ayudante al Comisario de Brigade (*Ad-
jutant to the Brigade Commissar*)

AFFECTATION (*Assignment*):
le: 2 VI 1937
a: Almansa Artilleria (*To Almansa Artillery*)

MUTATIONS (*Transfers*):
le: 18 VI 1937

a: Section Politique (*To Political Section*)

le: 1   VII   1937

a: Section Historique (*To Historical Section*)

le: 8   XII   1937

a: XV Brigida Estado Mayor Comisariado (*To Headquarters of the XV Brigade Commissariat*)

le: 10   IX   1938

a: Comisariadio de las BB.I.I. (*To Commissariat of all the International Brigades*)

SERVICE AU FRONT (*Front Service*):

du: 31 XII 1937   au: 16 V   1938   Front: Aragon and Ebro
du: 23 VII 1938   au: 10 IX 1938   Front: Ebro and Gandesa

OBSERVATIONS DU COMMANDANT:

Si este documento es un honor el llevarlo es doblemente para las camaradas como Voros, que abandonó su profesión periodista olvidando su tranquilad del despacho para asistir a nuestro mando, en los combates de Pandols y Gandesa.

Salud Camarada Voros! La XV Brigada te recordará con cariño.

JOSÉ VALLEDOR
Jefe Mayor XV Brigada Mando

(*Translation:*)

OBSERVATIONS OF THE COMMANDER:

If this document is a bestowal of honor, it is doubly so for comrades like Voros who abandoned his profession of journalism and in disregard of the tranquillity of his pursuits, hastened to assist our command in the battles of Pandols and Gandesa.

Greetings, Comrade Voros! The XV Brigade will remember you with affection.

(signed)

JOSÉ VALLEDOR
Commander in Chief, XV Brigade

PART I

1 It could have been eleven in the morning or one in the afternoon, it was hard to tell which by the hot Spanish sun. The last glimpse I'd had of the map was two nights before, too long ago to do me much good. Besides, our maps were not too dependable. I tried to recall where due north was but couldn't. I had lost my orientation in the last bombardment and one mountain top looked very much like another. It felt still early and a long day lay ahead.

The road below had been cut. Nothing had come through past the bend to the left for hours, since I saw that camion blown up. That was accurate shooting, three shells landing short, three shells right on target. That couldn't have been Franco artillery. It must have been one of those new Nazi automatic batteries Captain Smirčka had described to me which the Nazis were trying out for the first time in Spain. I had never seen them in action before.

The Stukas were dive-bombing to the right—roar, flash, burst —ripping black columns of smoke out of the heaving ground.

Enriquez, the battalion *enlacé,* was dead and so was the other new Spanish runner whose name I hadn't caught. The Spanish company, most of them stragglers we had managed to round up during the night and placed here in reserve, had bolted with the first shelling, giving away our position. It takes good training to hold troops under prolonged artillery fire. The Spaniards we had been getting as replacements lately were raw green recruits with only rudimentary training. Thrown in as fast as they arrived, they never had a chance. They did not do us much good either.

Mortars were now landing on top of the mountain where our Spanish 24th battalion was holding and the sound of machine guns was heavy. It was high time for me to get up there to check with the battalion commissar. I started up. Then it dawned on me that there was something wrong with the sound of that machine-gun fire. I listened intently and then I knew. Our answering fire was lacking. The battalion must have withdrawn— evidently somewhere to the right. That would account for the dive-bombing over that spot, for we had positioned no troops there.

The Fascist artillery opened up again, exploding at random along the mountainside. Although I found fairly good cover in a hollow I was beginning to get jittery. Bombing and strafing I could take, the suspense was usually over before there was time to work up panic, but artillery fire was different. I feared shelling more because I knew something about artillery. Fortunately for me, Franco's artillery had been rather poor when I was first exposed to their fire so I was never bothered much by it. I was familiar with his field guns, archaic, pre-First World War models with rifle gun-sights, designed more for coping with domestc uprisings than for action in the field. The training of his artillerymen was poor, they did not have many shells, and they usually quit after firing a couple of dozen rounds.

This time it did not look as if they were about to quit. The bombardment grew in intensity and I discerned a definite pattern in it. It was developing into a regular area shelling in gridiron pattern, which definitely bespoke Nazi artillery. It meant the Fascists were getting ready to attack and this shelling was aimed at an interdiction of our reserves.

But we had no reserves. I was the only one alive on that mountainside. That made me the reserves.

4

Name: Sandor Voros.

Age: 37.

Arms: One Belgian automatic pistol, not official issue but a present from Joe Dallet, a former commissar and friend, long dead.

Ammo: One extra clip of bullets; one hand grenade for strictly personal use—to avoid being captured alive and to take a few of the enemy with me.

There it was, that was the list. I was the reserves to hold that mountainside for the Loyalist Army. Now the thought, which I had persistently refused to recognize during all those days of the nightmarish Fascist offensive in Aragon in that spring of 1938, boldly emerged for the first time from behind the threshold of suppressed consciousness. It sprang forth stark and startlingly frank. This was death. The end of the trail, personally, for me. The artillery was beginning to box me in. "Correction fifty meters ahead. Fire!" Four more shells. BINGO! Sic transit . . .

I felt the beginning of panic, the almost irresistible urge to bolt, but I fought it down quickly. I was not under direct observation, by staying put I still had a chance. Four more shells . . . There is no one-hundred per cent killing zone, only a ninety-five per cent one. That five per cent margin, that five per cent chance. The shells might be duds . . . That was Nazi artillery firing Nazi shells. That *Inprecor* article a little while back describing the sabotage in Nazi munition factories by the Communist underground . . . I smiled wryly. I wouldn't want to be taken in by our own propaganda. God! Please God. It was no go. I was a nonbeliever. Faith . . . Lord, it would be most comforting to believe in miracles, in the supernatural, to have You reach out . . .

Four more shells and it would be over, a matter of two minutes or less. I was going to die. I was going to be killed right here. I was going to die all alone, in faraway Spain, on a mountainside the name of which I did not even know.

5

My parents! They had no idea where I was. They would be spared grief. They would expect me to turn up as usual every few years or so. My brothers, my sisters, my girl, my friends . . . they would grieve. They would be waiting for news for a long time and then they would guess, give up hope.

The *Daily Worker,* the *Uj Elore* Hungarian Communist daily —to them it would be welcome news, one of their own killed in battle, fighting Fascism in Spain. My death would identify the Party press with me. That would be a good issue to tie in with their next campaign for subscriptions and contributions . . . So what! Were I in their place I would exploit the situation the same way.

It was a shame to have to die before our triumph over Fascism! Come on Sandor, cut that stuff out. Face it. What's so terrible about death? Let's reverse it. Suppose I were to come out alive, what then? What's so precious about me? I have lived a full life. I have eaten my fill, have drunk my share, have known love. I have laughed and I have grieved, have walked in the lead and have followed in turn. I have fought and I have argued, I have won and I have lost. I have read what others have published and I have been published for others to read. I have tasted applause and suffered slander. I have lived and now I would die. So what if I lived on! Life would be a repetition.

Why cry about it when it was a natural, logical progression for me to die here within the next few moments. Cause and effect. I was born in a certain era; developed ideas in a certain direction; adopted a certain code of conduct which led inevitably here, to this mountainside. Since I was here at this moment, it was logical that I should die. Saul Mills was right when he told off the demoralized Lincoln Battalion men: "What if it cost the international proletariat a hundred thousand lives to stop Fascism in Spain!" Of course Mills had only been visiting here and went right back home, yet I upheld his position to the men who bitched and protested.

6

"Why does it have to be us? Why not the lives of some other international proletarians?"

"Because you have volunteered to come here and because you are here," I lectured them, giving them no comfort. I had also volunteered to come here, I was here, and now it was my turn to die.

I had come a long way to be here. The trail began on that hot summer day in July, 1914, in Hungary when I, still in knee pants, was among the marching crowd cheering the Austro-Hungarian Declaration of War against Serbia, which initiated World War I. That trail eventually led to this mountain on the Aragon front where I, a one-time humanist and liberal, late of Cleveland, one of the leading members of the Communist Party in Ohio, presently Chief of the Commissariat of War of the XV International Brigade, was about to die because of my consistent sympathies with the underdog.

A wave of self-pity rushed over me and now I felt infinitely sad yet mentally at peace beneath the convulsively mounting muscular tension as the screaming shell roared home. Concussion squeezed me till all was black, my lungs choked, the ground heaved, my eyeballs swelled to bursting, my nose was burning, my eardrums were clanging anvils, my throat was seared, falling earth was burying me. I was gagging and choking and struggling and gasping and alive. THE . . . NINETY-FIVE . . . PER . . . CENT . . . KILLING . . . ZONE ran like the *Times'* illuminated news ribbon before my blinded eyes. By the time I finished digging the earth off my head and neck only to duck back again, the next shells exploded safely offside.

It was approaching sunset. I sat up, already organizing in my mind the best place to set up a field kitchen, if I could locate one, for luring the scattered men out of their hiding places with the smell of hot food. My mind was on the problem of how to feed those men and hold them around the kitchen until we could get them back into the new line which would be improvised dur-

7

ing the night. For that was the kind of war we were reduced to fighting and that was the way it was done.

Resolutely I cut my thoughts off from circling back to their previous channel, and it worked, but with one curious side effect. From that afternoon on I became indifferent to my fate. Not because of fear or the lack of it, but because I simply stopped caring. If I stayed alive, fine. If not, so what!

That indifference to my own fate, however, set up an unanticipated subconscious reaction. I found myself growing more concerned with the welfare of human beings in the singular instead of the abstract "masses." Subsequently this led to my reappraisal of Communist theory in the light of its practical application as I had witnessed it, especially in Spain.

That was the turning point. It had been a long road from a soft humanist to a hard-boiled Communist although the signposts had been clearly marked and I had many eager guides to beckon me on. The road back was uncharted and lonely, the tracks faint and uncertain.

It has been rough going, not without its perils. I am still being barred from reaching my objective—nor can I tell for how long.

2 IN the summer of 1936 when I drove up to Madison Square Garden from Cleveland as a member of the Ohio delegation to the National Convention of the Communist Party in New York, I found the place humming. There was a festive, welcoming, even carnival air about the Garden; the sidewalks were crowded with cheerful comrades hawking party literature, shouting welcome, clustering eagerly around the entrances to greet the Party leaders. Even the "Cossacks," the mounted police assigned to keep order, looked friendly.

That transformation amazed me. In 1931, when I was transferred by the Party to Cleveland, the streets of New York were barred to the Communists. They were then living in a sort of semilegality hounded by the police; most Communists were fearful to reveal their identity in public. I surveyed the changed scene approvingly and my spirits soared.

I had reason to be elated. A new venture lay just ahead. I had been picked by Comrade Roberts, the American representative of the Comintern, to manage the 1936 presidential election campaign for Earl Browder on the Communist Party ticket.

As I entered the lobby of the Garden the transformation seemed even greater. The New York Party evidently succeeded in making converts even in the advertising profession. Huge graphic charts adorned the lobby depicting the progress of the various Party activities. One of those charts featured the growth of Party membership and I stopped to examine it. To my astonishment the total membership figure was still incredibly low, not quite 50,000 exclusive of the Young Communist League. More than half of the total were new members less than two years in the Party. The bottom line gave the numbers of the oldest members who had been in the Party for six years or more. That figure was somewhat under 3,000.

I looked at that last row incredulously. Familiar as I was with membership fluctuations, I had not expected to find that figure so low. I turned to Mac, a fellow delegate from Ohio, and pointed to the bottom row.

"I'm in that group. Imagine that, less than six per cent."

Mac, a tall, upstanding, dignified Scotsman, long-time president of one of the most exclusive local AFL craft unions in Cleveland, looked at me approvingly.

"Of course you are. We all know in Cleveland you're one of the Old Bolsheviks."

"I an Old Bolshevik?" I asked him, amused.

"Sure. From 'way back. Weren't you in the Hungarian revolution?"

"Yes, but . . ."

"Weren't you in the Red Army?"

"Yes, but . . ."

"So don't be so modest! Let's go out and have a drink."

From Mac's reply it was evident that I had been given the "build-up" without my knowledge. I did not want to pursue it further then, nor to analyze it. We went out to Jack Dempsey's and had our drink.

3   EIGHT years before that convention, I, the "Old Bolshevik," had little interest in politics. I was then living in Greenwich Village right in back of the Sheridan Theater, in a four-room railroad flat, drawing down a hundred dollars a week as a foreman in a fur shop. I was single, had more than enough for my needs, luxuriating in what for me was comfort, and spending my free time perfecting my English in preparation for a career as a playwright.

By then I had come a long way from that 21-year-old immigrant boy who had landed in New York in the summer of 1921, eager to shake off his last ties with Hungary. I was bursting with enthusiasm for the new way of life, for the humanitarian and democratic ideas America represented for the people of Europe. The first time I had a weekday off and the required extra dollar in my pocket I went downtown to apply for my first citizenship papers. Two of my replies to that lengthy questionnaire still linger in my mind.

The first one called for renunciation of every and all affiliation, allegiance, and submission to all foreign dynasties and foreign governments, to which my emphatic reply was:

"With the greatest of pleasure."

The other simply asked: "Complexion?"

That word baffled me. Neither my Latin nor my smattering of Greek managed to evoke any etymologically clear meaning. It definitely seemed to have something to do with complexity but

I could not guess what. After careful consideration I decided on a somewhat guarded answer.

"In general, yes!" I wrote.

Both of these answers were subsequently corrected by an officious court attendant and I emerged triumphantly, only a few months after my arrival, as an American citizen, almost.

I was proud of that status and could hardly wait for that day five years later when my final papers would be granted and I would become a citizen with full rights to vote. So innocent was I in politics that after I had been sworn in, beaming with pride and happiness, I immediately hastened over to the Democratic Club in my neighborhood.

That Democratic Club occupied a dingy one-time store in the Village, its plate glass covered with flaky orange paint. It was early afternoon and the two young fellows there eyed me with distrust. They were in the back room playing cards.

"Whatcha want?" asked one of them.

"I want to join the Democratic Party," I told him.

"Whaffor?"

"Because I just got my citizenship papers." The reply did not appear to make much sense to them. They kept looking at me impassively. I waited. There was silence. Finally the second guy asked:

"What are you, a Bohunk?"

"No, a Hungarian. I mean I was. Now I am an American. I just became a citizen."

He turned away from me and told the other chap, as if I obviously did not rate a direct answer from him:

"Tell him to come back tonight and see Murphy."

The first fellow so told me and I left.

That same evening, around nine o'clock, I was back. Although the lights were now on the place looked even more dim and run-down. Three groups of people were playing cards in the back room, clustered around different tables. As I was making my way in, a young man with a stiff straw hat tilted way back on his head who was standing in the doorway separating the front from the back room and chewing on a toothpick, stopped me.

"Whered' ya think you're goin'?" he wanted to know.

"I was told to see Mr. Murphy tonight about joining the Democratic Party," I told him.

"Hey, Murphy! Some squarehead here to see yah!" he called into the back room, still barring my way.

A few minutes later Murphy came out, hitching up his pants. He was the man I had observed sitting at the head of the table where the largest group of players and kibitzers were centered. He was squat, medium height, a man in his fifties. His face was florid, his stomach bulged, and it was girdled by a black belt with a silver buckle well below his waistline. He wore a yellow striped silk shirt, the long sleeves held back by yellow elastic bands.

He shuffled over, his eyes measuring me slowly up and down. He shifted his half-chewed cigar and said:

"Well?"

I explained my just having been made a citizen and that I wanted to become a Democrat. He did not say a word, just kept looking at me. I felt additional explanations were in order.

"I have given this a great deal of thought, Mr. Murphy," I assured him. "I am opposed to kings. I became a republican already in Hungary and I am still a republican. As a matter of fact, at first I thought of joining the Republicans. But in Hungary all republicans were democrats while here in the United States the Republicans are not Democrats. I want to be a Democrat and still be a republican because I am for a republic. Since the Democrats here stand for the republic also, I have decided to become a Democrat instead of just a plain Republican."

Murphy just stood there without the slightest change of expression. Finally he spoke.

"Where do you live?"

13

I told him.

"Yeah, that's in my Assembly District. When did you become a citizen?"

"Today."

"That's no good. This is August 17. You are two weeks too late. You can't vote in this election. You gotta be a citizen for three months and with that sonofabitch in the registration I can't fix that now. Why didn't you come to me before? I'd seen to it that you became a citizen in time."

I told him I was sorry but I really did not know.

"Do you know any other Hunkies who live here who can vote?"

Again I did not.

"Well, come around next year, when we'll have the presidential elections. You'll be able to vote then." He was evidently finished with me.

"Wait a minute, Mr. Murphy. Can't I join now anyway?"

"Yeah. You can do that. You can sign the book."

He went to his desk, pulled out a book, and I signed my name. Now I was a Democrat.

"Maybe I can do something anyway, even this year?" I volunteered expectantly. "I can type, I can also write English better than I speak it. Maybe I can help you with some money."

Murphy seemed to turn that last one over in his mind.

"Yeah. Maybe you can help with that."

I pulled out my wallet and handed him twenty dollars. That left me with only two dollars, but I didn't mind. I wanted to help. Murphy reached into his pants pocket, pulled out a fat bankroll, took the rubber band off, added my twenty to it, and put the band back on. He did not thank me. He was thinking.

"You working?" he asked.

I told him I was a foreman in a fur shop.

"You play poker?"

I told him I did.

14

"Any time you feel like a game, just come around and meet the boys." I was grateful for that and thanked him. But just so we wouldn't have any misunderstanding, I added: "I don't play for money, only for matches."
That was a fatal sentence. It terminated right there and then whatever my future association might have led to in the regular Democratic organization. Murphy jerked his thumb upward, signaling the end of the interview, and returned to the back room.

It did not matter. I was a Democrat. And when the 1928 elections rolled around I duly voted for Al Smith and the entire Democratic ticket. Thus I kept my faith with republicanism and democratism as well.

4 It was the summer of 1928, and I was starting on a new play dealing with some events of the 1918 October Revolution in Hungary. I had been an ignorant participant in those events and much to my chagrin I discovered that this ignorance, despite the intervening years, still persisted.

To turn them into a good play those incidents had to relate to universal experience and I found myself beyond my depth. The background was a historical one.

In the late spring of 1918, having graduated 14th in my class from the Infantry Officers School in Hungary at the age of seventeen, I was unexpectedly assigned to the artillery for further training as an artillery officer. That transfer gave me my first glimpse of the great class differentiation as it existed in Hungary.

Service in the artillery in the positional warfare of the First World War was incomparably safer than in the Infantry.

The artillery officer lived in the lap of luxury. Billeted in comfortable quarters well behind the trenches, he ate good food well prepared, he was warm and clean, and his access to the official officers' bordello was limited only by his own libido.

This privileged branch of service became the refuge for the scions of the aristocracy, the wealthy, and those with political and social influence, no matter how ignorant.

As a result, by 1918 the Army found itself in desperate need of competent junior artillery officers in the field. To remedy the situation, it adopted a policy of picking out the cream of the

16

young plebeian graduates from the Infantry Officers School, transferring them to the artillery, giving them accelerated training, and sending them to the front. I was one of the cadets so transferred.

Curiously, I was rather unhappy over the transfer. I was romantic, full of patriotism and loyalty, looking forward impatiently to front service, to assuming command of a platoon, to distinguishing myself in action, to taking over a company, maybe to reorganizing under fire the remnants of several companies into a battalion, and then who knows . . .

Because of my army indoctrination I was completely blind to the war weariness of the population, although I should have had at least an inkling of that because of one incident.

Shortly before graduation, we had been suddenly alerted and called into readiness to put down a threatening antiwar strike and demonstration in a near-by town, scheduled to begin on May 1. Along with the other cadets I repeated with outraged vehemence those sections of the Articles of War the Colonel read to us as we were drawn up in ranks ready to depart, armed with rifles, hand grenades, mortars and machine guns. In essence it ran:

"I will remain loyal to my Emperor and King. I will execute all my orders in blind obedience, shooting down my father, my mother, my own brothers and sisters without a moment of hesitation, if so ordered. . . ."

It was a grim order and I would have carried it out, too, such was the strength of loyalty inculcated in me. I consoled myself with the fact that it was most unlikely for my father or mother to engage in treasonable activities, and that my brothers and sisters were far too young. Had that demonstration not been called off I know we would have aimed well and shot to kill men, women, and children without hesitation until ordered to cease fire.

That episode meant nothing to me at that time, nor did I guess that it foreshadowed events soon to come—the end of the war, revolution. Going on the presumption that the war would go on forever I was impatient to leave for the front, disappointed by this transfer which disrupted my plans.

I reported to the Artillery Officers School in Kobanya, outside Budapest, with considerable misgivings. Artillery officers had to supply their own uniforms and the cost of these was greater than a man like me, without private means, could afford from his pay. I also knew I would be out of my social element among those wealthy scions.

My apprehensions proved justified. Out of four hundred-odd cadets in that school there were only about thirty like me who had been transferred from the infantry. The rest of the cadets looked upon us "proletarians," although that term was not familiar to me then, with that total disinterest that is akin to contempt. We were not ignored, we were simply not noticed except during the performance of our official duties.

Represented among them were many historically prominent names which were familiar to every Hungarian schoolboy. I myself was amazed to find that a count or a baron with a legendary name was as often as not a commonplace, often pimply, gangly youngster, sometimes handsome and robust but more often not, exactly like the kids I had known at home.

It was easy to tell us apart. Most of us still wore our infantry uniforms with artillery patches sewed on. As an added hardship the school had neither a mess nor sleeping quarters for officers, only for enlisted personnel. I was obliged to rent a cheap furnished room and worry about providing my meals. The other cadets lived in their own private apartments, two or sometimes three together, complete with cook and sometimes even a valet, frequented good restaurants and clubs in Budapest.

Even the training program had been devised to suit their convenience. Classes started at eight, adjourned at eleven; afternoon classes started at two, finished by five. No classes were held over the week ends. Having just come from the grueling Infantry Officers School with its Spartan discipline, I found myself lost in this new sybarite environment.

I was also lonely. One would expect that we, "the brains," as our instructors referred to us in a half-condescending, half-derogatory manner, would be drawn to each other. But that was not the case. In that environment we ourselves were ashamed of our pitifully small means and tried to hide it from one another. In addition, since we outranked the other cadets, we were loaded up with duties as Officer of the Day, Officer of the Guard, Officer of the Stables, etc. This was unfair and against regulations but we did not object. When on duty we got our meals free.

I spent most of my free time in my miserable furnished room rented from a poor family not far from the school, subsisting mostly on food sent by my family at great self-denial to themselves. The man sitting next to me in one of my classes was Keresztessy, the scion of an old landholding family. He was a broad-chested, very strong, dark-visaged young man with a very low hairline who seemed always to be scowling. He walked in a hunched, apelike manner, his hands practically at a level with his knees. Aside from formal nodding and greeting, we had never talked. He would come in at the last minute, nod to me, and then say in a polite, formal manner:

"May I see your papers, please."

He would then copy them and return them to me with a quiet "Thank you" as one thanks a waiter for bringing a glass of water.

One day we were coming back from the riding school when Keresztessy rode up to me and said:

"Sandor, are you off duty this Saturday?"

"Why?" I asked in surprise. This was the first time he had spoken to me outside of the usual routine or called me by my first name.

"Would you care to come to Five O'clock Tea tomorrow?"

I was totally dumbfounded. No man in Hungary, to my knowledge, would ever drink tea unless he was sick or eccentric. I had never tasted tea in my life. The Hungarians I knew would drink coffee, and wine, and beer, and slivovitz and plenty of it. But tea! It was hard for me to visualize Keresztessy, that scowling hunk of a man, sipping tea delicately as depicted in those few English romances I had read in Hungarian translation. The Hungarian aristocracy was known for their aping of English and French customs, so I could easily conceive of Five O'clock Tea having been adopted by them. But tea and Keresztessy simply did not go together.

"Tea?" I asked, bewildered.

Keresztessy explained. He was in love with a cousin of his, a second cousin, Elizabeth, who was sixteen. Elizabeth had an English governess whose job it was to be both companion and chaperon to her. Nancy, the governess, was very broadminded about her duties and would leave them alone as much as possible at her home, but there were too many interruptions. Elizabeth would love to visit his apartment but Nancy was balking at that. Nancy's reasons were personal. As an Englishwoman she was an enemy alien technically in internment, released in custody of Elizabeth's parents; she was lonesome and pining for a boy friend. Elizabeth told Keresztessy if he could only provide another man to keep Nancy company her objections to the visit would disappear. So he thought of asking me.

I was flattered and eager to go. After all, a cup of tea couldn't kill me. But I was a bit suspicious.

"Just how old is Nancy? What does she look like?"

Keresztessy was vague.

"She is old, sort of skinny and blondish." When he saw my dismay he hastened to add:

"But not wrinkled old and she has sort of a nice face."

I agreed to go, what the hell! I had never seen an Englishwoman, nor an Englishman for that matter. I might as well come face to face with one of those perfidious Albions I had heard so much about. There was, however, one doubt in my mind.

"Wouldn't I be violating the Articles of War by having contact with the enemy?"

Keresztessy just waved his hand in dismissal.

"Why, everybody knows Nancy. All the ministers and generals who come to Elizabeth's house. After all, she is only a governess."

When I got to Keresztessy's apartment punctually at five the next afternoon, Elizabeth and Nancy were already there. Elizabeth was a buxom, cherry-ripe girl with undulating hips and coquettish brown eyes, radiant with vitality.

Nancy *was* old. She must have been at least twenty-six, maybe even twenty-eight. For a woman that age she had a very nice face that was almost transparently pale, but it wasn't really, she had rosy spots on her cheeks. She had a beautifully chiseled profile and a rather subdued smile. Her movements were smooth, she did not bustle around like Elizabeth, and she was much taller than the average Hungarian girl, nearly as tall as I. Nor was she quite as skinny as Keresztessy had described her, although she certainly was far from buxom.

Keresztessy's apartment was furnished simply. Its most conspicuous features were a large mounted elk's antler on the wall over the bed and a thick Hungarian hard salami, at least a yard long, hanging by a string from the ceiling above the center of the table—a real mark of luxury in that starved country, then in its fifth year of war.

The huge table was piled high with food: a country smoked ham, dry sausages, jars of jam, a huge cartwheel of home-baked rye bread, a large nut *rollade,* another *rollade* filled with poppy seeds, bottles of wine and liqueur. The table was in disorder, a new pair of knee-length boots nestling against the bread. The table had not been set and there were no signs of plates, cups, or silver.

The introductions and greetings over, Keresztessy picked up

a huge bread knife, reached up and hacked off three thick slabs of salami for Elizabeth, Nancy, and himself, and then handed the knife to me to help myself. I did and we all ate, Keresztessy and I drinking wine, Elizabeth and Nancy sipping apricot brandy. There was little conversation while we ate and Nancy said nothing.

I was still chewing on my salami when Keresztessy got up and told Elizabeth to ask Nancy to show me the other room. Elizabeth laughed and started to talk with Nancy in English, which neither Keresztessy nor I understood. Their speech sounded very fast. It must have been funny, too, because they both giggled a lot.

Finally Nancy rose, took me by the hand, and said in her broken Hungarian. "Come, I will show."

She led me to a door, Elizabeth following us. There was a key in the lock. No sooner did Nancy and I enter than I heard the door close, the key turn, and the lock click. Elizabeth had played a joke on us and locked us in.

The room was of fair size, furnished with a large bed and a hard chair alongside to throw clothes on. It held a sunken bathtub, a pipe from a coil gas heater on the far wall led to the tub to supply instantaneous hot water. This invention was entirely new to me. I went over and examined it at length. Nancy, in the meantime, had seated herself on the bed. After I had studied the diagram and all the printed instructions I sat down gingerly on the chair near the bed. I wasn't at all at ease.

Nancy was sitting with her legs drawn up, her arms enfolding her legs, her chin resting on her knees. She was looking at me and I was looking straight ahead at the hot water heater, although by then I was so familiar with it I could have lectured on it in class.

"Why you no speak?" asked Nancy in her broken Hungarian. "Is it because I am enemy?" Now I had to look at her directly.

"Women and children are not considered enemies unless they

22

are caught bearing arms," I answered. I knew my Articles of War.

"Perhaps is it you not like Englishwomen?" she persisted.

I assured her I liked Englishwomen very much. I did not consider ourselves sufficiently well acquainted to reveal to her certain intimate personal facts about myself, such as my extremely meager experiences with Englishwomen—or with other women for that matter.

She slid forward on the bed, closer to my chair, her feet dangling right by my face. She had nice slender legs.

"Perhaps is it you not like me?" Her voice was pleasant, although pitched much higher than that of the throaty Hungarian girls.

"No, I do like you," I protested but because of my embarrassment it did not sound emphatic.

"Perhaps you not like me because I haven't many breasts?" she complained in her curiously high voice. Her Hungarian was assuredly very poor. I felt impelled to correct her.

"You do have two. Two is all that Hungarian girls have." This lesson in grammar must have pleased her for she laughed and laughed. But I was feeling more and more uncomfortable and suddenly started perspiring.

"Hungarian language so difficult to learn. I always mix 'much' with 'many.' I wanted to say my breasts small, not much like Hungarian girls have. Regard!" She straightened up, linked her fingers behind her neck, inhaled and threw her chest out. Considering she was only a woman she had quite a chest expansion.

I was conscious of a deep blush spreading all over my face. It was most embarrassing to regard, yet I regarded. They did not seem small. I so told her and added that she seemed to be in fine physical condition.

She laughed again. But she appeared to be flushed also. She leaned down, took my hand, lifted it, pressed it to her blouse, and asked:

23

"Feel how little?"

That demonstration did not bear out her contention nor seemed there to be any direct ratio between volume and sensation. Her breasts, although small, felt fully adequate—size seemed to have no bearing on the subject. I realized that the initiative had now been passed to me.

I rose and sat down on the bed next to her, putting my arm clumsily around her shoulders. Obviously the situation called for kissing. Then I realized I had committed a tactical error; I had moved without having reconnoitered the terrain in advance for the required operation and my deployment was all wrong. I had taken up position sitting on the edge of the bed, side by side, with my right arm around her shoulders. It was a most disadvantageous embarking point from which to turn her flank and maneuver her into the face-to-face position which, in my experience, was essential to kissing. It was quite a problem and I was brooding over the solution.

Nancy, although she had not attended two Officers Training Schools as I had, proved to be the better tactician. She hit upon the Macedonian evolution. She reached out her right arm, turned my flank by pivoting my left shoulder, put her left arm around me, and there we were, face to face. The most elementary maneuver in the book. She then kissed me. Then I kissed her. We then both kissed, and kissed again. And once more. Then she said,

"You warm. Your collar hurt. Take jacket yours off."

It was uncanny how right she was. I was more than warm, I was burning. I was very much inclined to take my tunic off but doubted the propriety of it. It was a most uneasy situation. I looked at my watch. It was way past five o'clock, nearer to six.

"What about the tea?" I asked.

Nancy burst into loud laughter.

"Geza not have tea. He not have even pot and cups. Tea only

for invitation was. Come." She helped me off with my tunic, we kissed again and then we both undressed.

It was nearly eight o'clock when we heard knocking and the door was unlocked. The three hours had really flown. It was high time for Nancy to chaperon Elizabeth back home.

Five O'clock Tea had been an all-around success. It was agreed that we would have tea together as often as possible. To assure my availability as chaperon for Nancy, Keresztessy invited me to share his flat with him.

For weeks thereafter my supper often consisted of a chunk of hard salami, a hunk of bread, and Five O'clock Tea. It was a well-balanced repast and agreed with me fine.

5 ▦ Toward the end of September, 1918, our allies manifested signs of treachery; the Turks and Bulgarians were negotiating for a separate peace. Worse still, trouble was brewing among the population right in Hungary itself.

Budapest was placed under summary law under General Lukasits. To stop the alarming rate of desertions, soldiers guilty of repeated desertions were ordered to be hanged.

Thousands upon thousands of Hungarian prisoners of war in Russia who had escaped from prison camps following the Bolshevik revolution and painfully made their way on foot thousands of miles back to Hungary, were being kept in "decontamination camps" to purge them of the "bacilli of Bolshevism." A number of those considered to have been "infected by the disease" were summarily hanged.

Rigid censorship kept most of these developments secret. My information came from Keresztessy's friends. They heard it discussed in their family circles to which many high-ranking army officers, members of the Upper House, and high government officials belonged.

The evil mind behind all these horrible developments, as they discussed it, was Count Michael Károlyi, owner of the largest landed estate in Hungary, a member of the oldest aristocracy. Back from his internment in France, he took up his old tricks of rabble rousing. Count Károlyi advocated the formation of a separate Hungarian Kingdom and negotiation of peace with the Allies. This was high treason. But he did not stop there. He was urging land reforms, the division of the large landed estates which constituted the largest percentage of all the land in Hungary. From what I gathered, this proposal to divide the land among the peasants far transcended treason to Emperor and Country; it violated the divine order of the Universe itself.

As I listened to the conversations around me with the uncritical ears of my youth and ignorance, I became utterly fascinated by the evil character of Count Károlyi as it was unfolded to me. He was said to be syphilitic, his brains softened by paresis, the last stage of syphilis. He couldn't even talk normally because his larynx and his upper palate had rotted away due to that disease. The brother-in-law of one of the cadets was a first cousin of Michael Károlyi, and he personally knew that to be a fact.

(Eighteen years later, during the 1936 presidential campaign, I was to hear the very same accusations in almost identical terms, except that they were spoken in English then. This time these slanders were leveled against another man—the President of the United States, another great man who had the compassion to dissociate himself from the narrow interests of his own social class in order to advance the welfare of the entire nation.)

The last days of October, 1918 found our artillery base in a "state of alarm." We were standing by day and night as the only troops absolutely loyal to King and Country the Budapest authorities could depend on to suppress the threatening disorders in the capital. We were cadets and each and every one of us was greatly outraged by the treasonable activities going on in Budapest. We were equipped with both field guns and howitzers and itching to put them to use.

On October 30, we received orders to march. As gun commander of a 75-mm. fieldpiece I was swelling with pride and responsibility. We were briefly told that Budapest was in danger of being taken over by the rabble. We were to draw up with our guns in front of the Parliament and other public buildings and, if the mob would not disperse, fire on them at point-blank range. Those orders excited and pleased us. We recalled Napoleon and expected to do even better than he.

We left our barracks under the command of a newly assigned general. Our artillery was horse-drawn and as our column moved out officers and gun commanders were mounted, artillerymen were seated on their caissons. I was elated. I pictured myself with my gun saddling an avenue, giving an order to fire, the mob fleeing in disorder, falling to the ground like wheat being mowed, just like in the heroic paintings. It did not enter my mind that what I was so eagerly anticipating was the butchery of my own fellow citizens. What I saw in my mind's eye was the "mob," an abstract concept of traitorous rabble.

By ten in the morning we reached the outskirts of Budapest and there was a long halt. It was a sunny, cheerful, unseasonably mild fall day, the kind especially ordered by the gods for the kind of heroic action we were about to perform, yet, inexplicably, we were just standing still. Our horses were getting restless and we too were getting bored.

The general and his staff were huddled in a council of war about a hundred yards ahead. There was a constant coming and going, staff officers were constantly being dispatched to the city, others were arriving from there. Emissaries of all kinds, including high-ranking artillery and infantry officers, were coming and going, but in general there seemed to be a desultory air about all that traffic. Something appeared to be lacking which puzzled me until I discovered what it was—there was no "snap to" in it. We sensed that the Command was hesitant, indecisive, unduly cautious, even timid. The staff officers passing along our column looked preoccupied, slouching down in their saddles forgetful of their military bearing. There was no vehicular traffic on that very broad cobblestoned road. The few civilians on the sidewalks appeared to have a festive air about them, many were in their Sunday best hastening toward the heart of the city.

Time was stretching out. The artillerymen, without orders to permit it, got off their hard, uncomfortable iron seats and lounged around their guns and ammunition wagons, whispering to each other. One of the cadets dismounted, also without orders, on his own initiative. The other cadets, myself included, frowned on this breach of discipline. Minutes later, when nothing happened to him, other cadets followed his example. Soon all dismounted, including me.

After a while our own colonel passed by, riding slowly toward the rear of the column. We all stiffened, scared, but he did not appear to see us; that hard disciplinarian and martinet failed to notice the definitely sloppy appearance of that previously proud martial column, even though by now, to use his own favorite expression, we definitely looked like a "bunch of civilian whores lolling under a red light, awaiting their pimps."

Shortly afterward there was a commotion up front. An automobile from the city came to a halt there. Some civilians alighted and went up to the general. They talked a while with him and then the general stepped aside, called over his staff, and they went into a short consultation. Afterward, the general got into the car with two of his aides and drove off toward the city. The rest of the officers gathered around the two civilians who had remained behind and there was an animated conversation.

Time became an unmoving vast cloud, dull, unstretching, and never ending. I was getting hungry and so was everybody else. Since we hadn't hitched up our food wagons, there was no promise of either food or fodder. The horses were getting very restless standing there in harness.

After an eternity of just standing around listlessly, I became aware of people in the distance, civilians approaching from the city, moving toward us. They were walking down the center of the road in small groups, but as the first groups advanced the road behind them filled up with more and more people. They were shouting as they approached but it sounded friendly, more like cheering. Then an automobile came weaving through the crowd with its horn blowing constantly, followed by about six other autos. They reached us before the people did. The cars pulled up in front of our column. A civilian jumped out and said something to our colonel who immediately jumped into the car. The other officers all came running. They crowded into the cars, a few of them even stood on the running boards. The cars turned around and headed back to the city. A captain who had reached there too late rode alongside me on his horse. We were on friendly terms and I asked him what was going on, when did we expect to march? He looked furious.

"March, muck!" he answered with an oath. "The bastards all scurried away to swear allegiance to the National Council."

"To the leaders of the rabble?" I asked in a shock. "That's treason!"

The captain was not listening, he was looking toward the city. Finally he burst out.

"You'd think the bastards would find room for another fellow officer. They could always crowd one more in." With that he stuck his spurs savagely into his horse's flanks and galloped away.

The crowd was very near now and we could distinguish the cheers.

"*Viva! Viva!* Long live the National Council! Long live our brave artillery. *Viva* for Hungary! Hooray for the National Council! Hooray for the artillery!"

The artillerymen left the column and advanced to meet the crowd. In no time at all the crowd was all around us, enveloping us, absorbing us. Everyone was cheering and shouting, shaking hands, embracing, clapping shoulders like at a Hungarian village wedding. Then somebody called out in a loud, high voice:

"On to the National Council!" Others took up that cry. Everybody was cheering and the crowd reversed its flow, moving back to the city. I held back and the crowd swirled past me. Soon the last one of them passed, hurrying to catch up. They were singing

30

now and I followed them with my eyes for a distance. Then I turned around and looked back at our column.

There was our proud column stretched back as far as eye could see, field guns, howitzers, ammunition wagons, enough shells to shoot down half the population of Budapest—abandoned, without an officer or man in sight, the riding mounts tethered to the caissons, the draft horses left in harness unattended, deserted. Without giving it conscious thought I foraged through a few ammunition wagons until in one of them I came across some hard sausage and bread someone had hidden there. I took them. I saw an abandoned carbine and I picked that up too, slung it around my shoulder. I did not know what made me take it, for I had my heavy saber hanging at my side. Perhaps I dimly sensed that when things are in ferment a carbine is a handy thing to have. That done, I started my own trek toward the city.

I did not know then that I had just witnessed the final dissolution of the once mighty, centuries-old Austro-Hungarian Empire! Nor could I possibly guess in my ignorance that I was also an eyewitness to something far more fundamental to the organization of human society.

I saw how an armed force could evaporate without firing a single shot in its own defense, how an established government could be cowed into submission merely by the threat of violence.

I was an eyewitness to how state power disintegrates under the hot breath of revolution!

6 THE usual image the word "revolution" evokes is that of violent turbulence: a disturbed wasp's nest buzzing viciously; a vortex of cascading waters that churn furiously; an onrush of drunk-maddened cutthroats with long knives dripping blood—a furious, hysterical, bloodthirsty mob jamming streets and squares, packing them solid with howling flesh that permits no one to escape.

There was no such image in my mind as, munching absently on my sausage and bread, I made my way on foot to the inner city where I expected the National Council to be. That broad, miles-long, cobblestoned principal thoroughfare was completely deserted. Only here and there did I encounter a solitary figure on the sidewalk. I was in no hurry. I recall finding a half-consumed apple on the curb and kicking it forward until it broke into pieces, and then kicking the pieces until there was nothing left to kick.

As I neared the center of the city I saw more and more people, then crowds of them. They were all hurrying in the same direction. An open truck full of people shouting and cheering veered in from one of the side streets. The truck was slowing down for the turn; I held up my arm, the driver stopped, and a dozen eager hands reached down to help me up into the truck. A poorly dressed woman hugged me. Someone yelled:

"Hooray for the armed soldier of the revolution!"

They all cheered and then someone burst into a rousing song in which other voices joined. The song had a quick, thrilling

32

rhythm. I was told it was the Marseillaise, the forbidden anthem of the Social-Democrats.

I felt uncomfortable and out of place. Those around me looked like factory hands and, as a cadet, I did not know how to act in such close proximity to them. But they were very friendly, their arms around each other's shoulders. Someone put his arm around my shoulders and I in turn put my arm around someone else's. Soon I caught myself also humming the Marseillaise. We were in the heart of Budapest now and the streets were getting so thick with people that the truck was barely able to crawl. After a while it became completely immobilized.

I got off and headed in the direction of the National Council. The nearer I approached, the more difficult it became to make headway, but it did not matter. I was not really going anywhere. I was simply moving into the heart of things, drawn by half-formed curiosity and the natural gravitational pull of the crowds.

By the time I reached the building, the crowd was very dense. We stood on the street and waited, for what, none of us really knew. Time was a white-bearded, pleasant old man pausing serenely with us. Every once in a while some civilian wearing a large rosette made of silk ribbon in the Hungarian national colors of red, white, and green, would step out on the balcony and make a short speech. The speaker would invariably be received with rousing cheers although nobody could hear what he was saying. When I would inquire of my neighbors who that speaker might be, nobody would know, nor were they able to tell me what he had said. It did not seem to matter to them. They evidently took it for granted that the speaker had said what they wanted to hear.

The crowd was composed mainly of civilians, men and women, with a small sprinkling of soldiers in uniform, none of whom were armed. After a while I found myself on the sidewalk, near the entrance to the building. The crowd kept a narrow lane open in front and I watched a long procession of officers enter the building.

The officers were of all branches of the service, infantry, artillery, supply, signal corps, transport. They were of diverse ranks, most of them lieutenants and captains, only a few majors. Whenever a high ranking officer, a lieutenant colonel or colonel, entered he was cheered by the crowd. I observed that the military men were not a cohesive group—they did not act under orders, they had come individually and alone. They carried their sabers but no other arms. When I asked what those officers were doing in there I was told they were swearing allegiance to the National Council, that the Council required this of all officers, in fact had issued an order to that effect.

I was only a cadet, the embryo of an officer, neither fish nor fowl, halfway between the officers and men. A cadet outranked all enlisted men and noncoms and was officially a gentleman with the caste privileges of an officer, but not yet one. I could not figure out whether that order applied to me also. (It never occurred to me to question whether such an order had actually been issued, and if so, by what authority the National Council had issued such orders to the Army. Many years later, in Spain, I was to find that in a chaotic situation anybody could issue an order on his own authority and if that order coincided with the general mood, if it expressed and crystallized it, then that order would be repeated by many mouths, transmitted all along the line, and obeyed. When it was contrary to the general feeling, such an order would be listened to with indifference, not repeated, and end up discarded along with similar thousands of others.)

Standing there among the mob became tedious after a while and I decided I might as well go upstairs and present myself, see what was going on. By that time there was a lull, the steady procession of officers had slowed down to a trickle, evidently few officers had been left unsworn. As I elbowed my way to the entrance somebody shouted:

"Hooray for the armed officer of the revolution!"

A loud cheer went up and I blushed. I felt self-conscious and my legs moved clumsily. The shout brought several people to the head of the inside stairs, all of them civilians wearing large cockards made of silk ribbons, also a woman in a light gray houndstooth suit. They were smiling down on me as I climbed the stairs, and the woman applauded.

When I reached the top landing the woman threw her arms around me and kissed me on the cheek. The men shook hands with me.

"Here is one loyal officer the National Council can depend on," one of the men said and slapped me on the shoulder. "He even brought his rifle along to defend us," said another one, beaming in approval. I wanted to correct him but I didn't. Mine was a carbine, not a rifle, but he was a civilian and wouldn't know the difference.

The woman pinned a rosette on me. She picked one of the larger ones out of a wicker basket on the floor, but not nearly as big as the ones they were wearing. Mine was made of narrower ribbons, nor did the ends hang down as low as theirs.

We went into a larger room and they questioned me about my unit. When they learned I was from the Artillery Officers School in Kobanya one of them told me that mine was the unit they had been most apprehensive about, because they did not know how deeply the spirit of the National Council had penetrated our base. Had we not come over, who knows what might have happened.

Another, older man then cut in and told him witheringly that he had erred, that he failed to appraise properly the war-weary spirit and revolutionary ardor which had permeated the army. Here was that young man, he pointed to me, a cadet, the very embodiment of military spirit and indoctrination, yet he had even brought his arms along to defend the National Council. I felt very self-conscious, I never liked to be praised to my face; besides, the way they talked about me was rather unwarranted. I had not taken that carbine to defend anything, I had simply picked it up because I thought it was a good thing to have around. My carbine wasn't even loaded. I had forgotten to check it or take any ammunition along.

The two men fell into arguing, the others joined in and there I was, completely ignored. I walked out and wandered around the corridor, looking into the other rooms. All of them were crowded with civilians and high-ranking officers engaged in excited debates or deep in discussion, and I quickly withdrew trying to appear as inconspicuous as possible. Obviously I did not belong, there was nothing for me to do in that place. I drifted through the building, walked down the steps to the side entrance, and went outside.

By then it was late afternoon and the crowd was considerably thinned out, one could walk around freely. I heard shouts and noticed people running, all in one direction. I ran, too. Soon I was gaining on them and even outdistancing all but a few ahead of me, but no one could tell me what was going on. In order to sprint faster I was carrying my carbine in my right hand, the regulation way of going into attack. I was soon in the lead when I saw another group standing in front of a store, pointing down a side street where a few other people were running and yelling to me excitedly, "Looters, looters!"

It was a jewelry shop with its iron shutter forced halfway up, and the show window smashed. I did not pause but kept on running to catch up with five or six civilians who were chasing three looters. At the next block the looters separated. One ran down a side street and I followed him while the civilians kept after the other two. I was gaining on him rapidly and finally cornered him in a doorway before he had a chance to slip into the building. He was a tough-looking boy of about seventeen; he was all out of breath and he thrust a gold watch out to me. As I took it he suddenly yelled, "Look out!"

I turned around involuntarily and he bolted and ran diagonally across the street. I was about to take after him again, then gave

36

up—after all, I had recovered the looted watch. Breathing hard, I walked back to the jewelry store. By the time I got there the shop was black with people. They were shoving and pushing, all the showcases were smashed, and the floor was crunchy with broken glass. A short fat man and a tall skinny one were tugging at a large silver tray, another was hugging a large silver pitcher to his stomach with his left arm and flailing about him with his right, fighting his way out of the melee. Those who had managed to get hold of something were fighting to get out while others kept pushing and shoving, trying to get in. I had come back to the store to return the watch, but certainly these were not the proper people to take it. Every one of them in there was looting by now. In a few minutes the store was stripped bare and the people were scurrying away. I stood there for a while waiting for a policeman to come around so I could hand him that watch but none showed up. Some other people came who kept asking me what had happened. I got tired of answering them and I walked away also. On my way I examined the watch. It had a golden lid and when I pressed the stem it opened, revealing the Greek letter Omega on its face. My father had an Omega watch and I knew it was expensive. I stuck the watch in the pocket of my tunic and buttoned the flap down; I was wondering what to do with it and did not want to be held responsible for losing it.

As I was walking along slowly considering what to do next, a black limousine drew up to the curb and stopped near me. Four soldiers were riding in it, two of them carrying rifles and two unarmed. A chauffeur in a black private uniform was at the wheel. The two unarmed soldiers got out, shook hands with the other two, and departed. I went over to the car and got into the vacant front seat, next to the chauffeur. No one said anything, but they were watching me. I said nothing either and the chauffeur started the car.

"Where are you going?" I asked the chauffeur. He glanced at

me. "I don't know," he said miserably. "Wherever those two drunks want me to take them." He told me they had commandeered his car that forenoon and that the car was owned by a member of the Upper House of Parliament. He told his name but it did not register with me.

I stretched out luxuriously, for that was the first time in my life I had ever sat in an automobile. Of all the events of that day the realization that I was riding in an automobile was what impressed me the most.

We rode around aimlessly. The two drunks in the back were singing and frequently one or the other would poke his rifle through the window and fire in the air. They offered me a drink out of their bottle and when I refused they taunted me, calling me a baby. I was not a baby. I was a man. I was fully eighteen years and three months old. I had taken drinks before and I would have liked to take one then. But I was obliged to refuse. It was against regulations for cadets to drink with enlisted men.

After a while their bottle was empty and their ammunition spent. By now it was dusk. The soldiers asked to be driven to a certain corner and got out. That left me alone with the chauffeur who eyed me warily.

I pulled out my remaining bread and sausage, for I was hungry again, and offered to share it with him. He was only a chauffeur but being a civilian that was not improper. He accepted eagerly.

"This is the first bite I've had since morning," he told me.

While eating we took counsel together. He told me that his boss had fled to his country estate and he wondered what he was expected to do. He had very little benzine left.

I offered to take care of him and said I would even get him benzine from our base. I had nothing specific in mind, but I wanted to postpone parting with the car as long as possible. The chauffeur was single, tubercular, and hence unfit for the army. He said he was very poorly paid. The chauffeur drove me to Kobanya to my apartment. We reached there late in the evening.

38

Keresztessy and his belongings were gone. He had left a note for me on the table. It was brief.

"Adieu! old pal!" the note read. "I scooted home. Pater will need me there to help him keep an eye on the peasants. I took your pistol and left you the salami, also the jug of rum. You can get another pistol here while I won't need food at home. . . ."

I didn't mind about the pistol. It was army issue. I was glad about the salami. The chauffeur's lips began to twitch when his eyes fell on it. I invited him to eat all he wanted and by the time he had finished I had to stand on tiptoes to reach the salami to cut a slice for myself. I ate, too, but not nearly as much as the chauffeur, and we washed it down with rum. I let the chauffeur sleep in Keresztessy's bed. He liked the bed very much. He told me he did not have a room, all he could afford was to rent a bed in the family of a baker. He had the use of the bed at night while the baker was away working. The baker in turn had the bed during the day, a very common arrangement among the working people in Budapest.

Before we fell asleep I remembered the watch and showed it to him. He was very excited about it; he kept opening and closing it, breathing on it and polishing it. He wanted to know what I intended to do with it.

"Turn it over to the police, of course," I told him. He said the police would steal it, it would never get back to the owner. He said he knew where that jewelry store was and volunteered to keep the watch until he found a chance to return it to the owner of the store personally. I was very glad of the solution. He was really a very accommodating chap, saving me further bother about that watch.

The next morning we rose early and bathed. The chauffeur was grateful and even obsequious. That was the first time he had had a bath in a private tub, he told me. He looked very skinny undressed, all skin and bones, his ribs and his shoulder blades sticking out. He was coughing a great deal.

39

We drove over to the base. It, too, was deserted, not a single officer or cadet around. There were a few artillerymen loafing around the stables but no horses or guns were in sight. I wondered about the horses, I supposed they had been stolen, simply unhitched from the column and led away. I hoped that had happened, that they had not been left standing there in harness thirsty and starving. I talked to some of the men. They had no homes to go to and said that was why they had come back. I found the benzine and we filled the tank.

"Now where to?" asked the chauffeur. I did not know.

"Let's go to the National Council," I said, remembering that woman there, thinking she might have something for us to do.

As we were driving into town many soldiers tried to stop us, attempting to get on. I waved them all off with the carbine. This time it was loaded.

As we were nearing the center of town, a well-dressed civilian waved to us frantically from an empty streetcar stop. The street cars were not running, everybody had to walk. Everybody but me. I had a private automobile and a chauffeur. It was a pleasing thought.

I told the chauffeur to stop. The man ran up to us excitedly.

"Whose car is this?" he asked with a ring of authority in his voice. I resented that from a civilian.

"Mine," I told him curtly.

"Where did you get it?" he asked sharply.

"I commandeered it."

"I think this is the car that was assigned to me by the National Council," he said excitedly. "It was supposed to have picked me up at six o'clock this morning. I have been waiting till past seven and it did not show up. I am the new Undersecretary of the Food Ministry. I was appointed last night by the National Council. In the name of the National Council I now commandeer this car!" He said that last one in a loud and official voice. It sounded like an order.

He was old enough to be a colonel. I was apprehensive, but I did not want to give up the car. Besides, he was only a civilian.

"Let's go," I said to the chauffeur. He put the car into gear.

"Wait, please, wait!" pleaded the civilian, the tone of authority now gone from his voice. "At least, please, take me to the Food Ministry. I am very late and it would take me at least an hour on foot."

I hesitated.

"If you take me there I'll see that you get a piece of imported Swiss milk chocolate, a full pound each."

"Get in," I told him.

On the way he explained to me what the Food Ministry was. The Food Ministry was in charge of rationing all food in the country. It also had a huge warehouse full of imported food-stuff which was heavily guarded. The Commander of the Guard, a lieutenant, had disappeared two nights before and had not come back. He proposed that I take over command of the Guard and assign the chauffeur and car to the Food Ministry.

That sounded all right to me and I turned to the chauffeur inquiringly. He had one question to ask.

"Is there a kitchen for the personnel?"

The civilian laughed.

"The best in the country. Food you never even heard of in all your life. Imported food and delicacies."

It was all settled. The Food Ministry was housed in an enormous building surrounded by a thick brick wall and it had a massive iron gate. Two indifferent looking guards with rifles carelessly hung on their shoulders were at the gate when we rolled up. We tooted the horn but the guards made no attempt to open the gate. The civilian got out of the car and walked over to them.

"I am Doctor . . . (I can't recall his name for I always called him Doctor; he was not a medical doctor but a Doctor of Philosophy), the new Undersecretary of the Food Ministry," he said impressively. "Open the gate."

The guards just stood. One of them finally said:

"Nobody allowed inside without a pass. Those are the orders."

I got out with my carbine in my hand.

"I am the new Commander of the Guard. Open that gate!"

They opened the gate but did not salute me. I decided not to notice that. We drove inside. The Doctor and I went upstairs, the chauffeur stayed in the courtyard with the car.

The Doctor went into a big office and I followed him. The men there greeted the Doctor with deference. He took one of them aside and they went into a private office. Soon the man came out, introduced himself, and then led me to the Guard's quarters. The Commander's room was of fair size, it was furnished with a desk, two chairs, and an iron cot with a spring and mattress on it. I liked it. We then went to see the sergeant.

The sergeant was a fat, jovial man in his late forties, a grandfatherly looking person. He looked me over, neither friendly nor wary, evidently not ready to make up his mind about me. The civilian then left us.

I asked the sergeant for a report. There were 24 men in the guard detail, 25 including the sergeant. Two men on duty at each of the two gates, one man each at the two main doors inside leading to the warehouses. It was an easy detail. The food was good and plentiful, the men were satisfied, but they would have liked an eight hour change-off.

"Most of us are older men, we don't take too much to soldiering," he concluded.

I was satisfied with the report and told him that I had no intention of changing anything, wanted him to run the outfit as before, but that I would work out a change in schedule so everybody would have eight hours off. I sat right down and worked it out. The sergeant liked it and we were friends, perhaps a bit more friendly than military regulations allowed but it seemed

42

all right to me. I was getting used to treating military regulations as less than sacred. Besides, I had no superiors to take me to task.

That night we drove the Doctor home and promised to call for him at eight in the morning. Then we drove out to Kobanya, picked up my gear, and moved it into my new quarters in the Food Ministry.

Days passed and I was getting very bored. The sergeant ran the Guard and I had nothing to do. The most fateful events in the thousand year history of Hungary were then taking place just outside of the gates but I had little awareness of them because I lacked interest in politics. The newspapers were full of political news and changes but I hardly glanced at the headlines; I was more interested in the features. I simply noted the headlines announcing the end of hostilities and demobilization, without giving them any thought.

Nor did the frenetic enthusiasm with which the newspapers greeted the sensational announcement by the newly appointed Defense Minister, General Landry, "I do not want to see any soldiers any more!" create any impression on me. I did not realize that with that single statement he had dismissed the entire army! I was still a soldier.

One morning the sergeant reported that some of the men wanted to go home and asked me to meet with them. I consented. I had the sergeant parade the guard, then made my first public speech. It was short.

"Men," I said, "the sergeant tells me some of you want to go home. The war is over, the army is disbanded, so I read in the newspapers. I see no reason why any man who wants to go home can't do so. Just report it to the sergeant. Dismissed!"

But the men would not dismiss. They all crowded around me. The sergeant was one of those who wanted to go home. Others asked me whether they had to go home. These came from those far parts of Hungary, Croatia, Slovenia, Rumania, where the nationalities were reportedly in revolt, committing atrocities against Hungarians. I told them they could stay on as long as they pleased and they felt relieved. All told, fourteen of them decided to go home, which left me with ten. I gave the departing men permission to take all the rations they could carry and they left with bulging packs. Then I cut the guard down to one man at each gate, abolished the rest of the posts, and that was all there was to it.

The next forenoon I was strolling the main corridor, bored, and debating whether to leave for home myself when the Doctor, whose door was open, noticed me and called me in. We were quite friendly by then. There was another man with him whom he introduced as a medical doctor, the owner of a private sanatorium at Lake Balaton, the largest lake in Hungary and a famous summer resort. That doctor had come to Budapest to seek military assistance.

As he explained it to me, the peasants were rising in the neighboring villages. Several large summer homes and estates of the wealthy had been pillaged and set on fire afterward. Peasants friendly to him had informed him that his sanatorium was also on the list. That sanatorium had been used during the war as a convalescent home for officers and was filled with good linen, silver, and expensive therapeutic equipment, all of which were his personal property. Since his sanatorium had catered only to field grade officers, the peasants entertained a particular hatred for it. He almost cried as he related it.

He needed guards for protection. He had appealed to the Defense Ministry but they had no troops at their disposal, they were barely able to mount a guard of their own. In desperation he came to see his old friend in the Food Ministry to see if the latter could help him.

I told them I had only ten guards left myself. This news left them disconsolate. I was outraged and would have liked to teach those peasants a lesson they would not easily forget. I was also bored. I had an idea.

"If you can get me arms I'll get a guard together and go down with you," I told him.

The doctor looked at me with a sour face. He informed me that he had received an authorization to draw arms but he couldn't induce any soldiers to go although he had been at two army barracks.

"Will you pay them the new army pay?" I asked. The new government, realizing that it had acted too hastily in disbanding the army, had tried to rectify its mistake by publishing a new high rate of pay with which to induce soldiers to stay in service. The new schedule was a uniform 10 kronen a day for enlisted men, 30 kronen for officers.

The doctor's face became more sour. He hesitated, then said he would pay it if he had to; he acted rather bitter about it. I did not take to the man but I would not let that bother me.

"Come with me," I told him and led him to the barracks nearest to us. The doctor, a flabby, jaundiced man, protested that he had been there that morning, but I kept walking ahead and he had to follow. When we reached the barracks I told him to wait for me inside the gate and left him.

The first two barrack rooms I entered were not promising. The soldiers, lying on dirty strawsacks on the floor which served as bedding, did not look good to me. In the third room I found a number of younger men, including a sergeant, a husky fellow in his thirties. He looked tough and a leader. He was sitting on his strawsack talking with three other men. I walked over to them.

"Sergeant, I need a guard." He looked at me without replying. The others also kept silent.

"I am recruiting twelve men to guard a sanatorium on Lake Balaton. The pay is ten kronen a day. The food is good and there is a bed for each man to sleep in. We will only mount guard at night. Who of you wants to come?"

This got them on their feet.

"Will there be any nurses there?" one man asked.

"There sure will be servant maids, you dumb ox," said another, which set everybody grinning. That aspect of the mission had eluded me.

Instantly dozens of men were milling around me, asking questions. All were eager to come but I needed only twelve. I called the sergeant aside and asked him to help me pick out twelve good ones, fighters, for we might have to battle looters, and informed him that he would be second in command. He saluted, the first salute I had received since we marched out of Kobanya.

The sergeant lined the men up. By that time there were about thirty of them, and still others were coming from the other barrack rooms attracted by the news. We picked out twelve and they all looked strong and tough. Among them were the trio who were with the sergeant when I first addressed them. The selection raised a minor uproar. The rest clamored to be included, arguing they had as much right to go as the ones I had picked.

"Clear the room!" the sergeant ordered and he charged into the crowd, the other eleven after him. I stepped aside. I was not supposed to mix in a brawl. After a brief scramble the room was cleared. The sergeant lined the men up and said:

"Sir, we're ready to move. Sir, how are we going to get arms?"

I told them that had been arranged and led them out to the doctor. At sight of them the doctor recoiled. They really looked tough, they were much older than I, thirty or over. We walked over to the armory which was guarded by a strong sentry of armed city police. The doctor showed them his authorization and they called the Officer of the Guard. He was a police lieutenant and he read the document over carefully, asked the doctor for his credentials, then ordered the door unlocked and told my men to line up single file outside. He then called me aside and asked

46

me what I needed. I told him I needed enough small arms and ammunition to hold off an entire village if necessary. He listened to the story I outlined and then asked me rather gently:

"Son, do you think you can handle them?"

I felt certain I could. I doubted the peasants would dare start anything while we were around. The police lieutenant shook his head; he did not mean the peasants, he meant my men. A couple of those men, particularly the sergeant, looked like real bad eggs to his practiced eyes. I agreed the men looked tough, but they were all right; the sergeant was eager to take orders from me.

He shook his head and asked, did it occur to me why it was necessary to assign the police to guard the arsenal with all those soldiers available? Precisely to prevent characters like that sergeant from getting hold of arms and turning loose on the civilian population. "Keep your distance, son," he advised me. He went over to the armorer and told him to let us have what we wanted, and then left.

My men fell to it. By the time they were finished they were armed to the teeth. In addition to rifle and bayonet, they each took an attack dagger, a steel helmet, a couple of potato mashers (hand grenades with handles attached), and all the ammunition they could carry in their musette bags. I took a dagger, a pistol with a holster to be worn over the shoulder, two egg grenades. Then I reconsidered and put them all back except the pistol and holster. Next the men spied a stack of brand-new uniforms in a corner and went for them.

"You are not supposed to take uniforms," shouted the armorer. He was a sergeant major, a lifelong professional, the highest ranking noncommissioned officer in the Hungarian Army. He barred their way.

"Don't argue with me," said the sergeant and rammed his shoulder into him, pushing him aside. The armorer fell silent.

After the men were outfitted, we filed out and I lined them up for inspection. The doctor's eyes bulged. I felt proud and power-ful as we marched through the courtyard in parade step. Soldiers came running out of the barrack rooms and watched. I wished I had picked a bugler also but by then it was too late.

We marched over to the Southern Depot. It was not too far. The station and platforms were packed with people, the ticket window surrounded by a howling, pushing mob. We did not bother to stop for tickets and headed straight for the train.

The platform in front of the third class carriages was bedlam. Women with large bundles, men loaded down with suitcases, parcels, boxes, children with smaller bundles, were all trying to get on the train at once, with the steps hopelessly jammed; a number of hardy souls were making themselves comfortable on the roofs of the coaches. Everybody was toting something that was invariably too heavy for him. I was thinking of a way to board that train with my men but it seemed hopeless. Then the sergeant at my elbow spoke up:

"Shall we clear one of the coaches, sir?"

That was one solution that had not occurred to me. I reviewed the problem. It did not seem difficult. We could cut through that mob on the platform, pull the people off the steps, yank them out of their seats, throw their bundles after them, finish! The opera-tion would take only minutes.

I was about to assent when my eyes fell on a peasant woman who was sobbing loudly. She was sitting on a large bundle with three badly frightened children around her, surrounded by the swirling mob. The children were also crying, tears and mucus blending on their faces. "Please, in the name of the Lord, some-one help me on the train," she wailed. "My husband is sick and we must get back home." There was a helpless desperation in that wail, as of hope abandoned. "It would be people like her whom we would be pitching off the train," the truth dawned on me, and I knew it would be unjust.

"Hold it," I said to the sergeant, "I have another idea. I'll be

48

right back. In the meantime, put that woman and her children on the train if you can." I watched the sergeant talk to his men and in no time they pushed their way to a window. They boosted one of the men through the window into the coach and the others handed the children up to him one by one, then two of them picked up the woman and were squeezing her through the window when I left them. It was a smooth job. Those were capable men.

I made my way to the front of the train. The three second-class carriages there were similarly thronged. There was only one first-class carriage; it looked full, but not jammed. The steps were clear and I saw only a few people at the windows. That meant there was room in the corridor.

Enlisted men and noncoms belonged in the third class. Cadets and junior officers went second class. Only field-grade officers traveled first class. Those were the rules. I was mulling that over in my mind when I saw our doctor enter the first-class carriage. That decided me. I went back to the men.

"Come on. We'll travel first class."

They looked at me and grinned. The sergeant regarded me with approval. I must have passed some test with him.

We boarded the first-class carriage and the men settled themselves in the vestibule. It did not go off without a commotion, other passengers had to move out of their way. The doors of the various compartments opened, well-dressed civilians, men and women, looked out and hurriedly pulled the doors shut behind them. My men behaved in an unusually subdued way. This was the first time they had ever set foot in a first-class carriage. The same held true for me.

I opened the door of one of the compartments in search of a seat for myself. A colonel was sitting at the window. He went into a tantrum when he saw me coming in. I gave him a stiff salute but he ignored it.

"This is an outrage," he attacked me in a shrill, nearly falsetto voice. "How do you dare enter first class! Get off this car at once and get those men off too."

My knees were quaking. There had to be a way out. I recalled the night I led an M.P. patrol for the first time and blandly demanded that all officers, even those I knew, identify themselves. It was a good joke even though I was reprimanded for it later.

"Who are you? What's your name?" screamed the colonel.

I reached out my hand. "Your identification, sir, please!" My voice came out even more falsetto than his.

"What's this? Where are you from?" he spluttered, his voice considerably down. My men, attracted by the scene, were now crowding around the door.

"National Security, Special Guard Duty Detachment, sir!" My voice was now back to normal except for a small quaver in my throat.

"Never heard of that. Let me see your credentials." But there was no command left in his voice any more. It was a request, not an order. I had no more to fear from him.

"Sorry, sir! Your identification, please!" He handed it over and I read it over carefully. This was my first chance to see the credentials of a high-ranking officer, and I was curious. I even read the print in the back. It took time. The colonel began to look apprehensive. I handed it back to him.

"Everything in order, sir. Thank you, sir." I saluted him. He looked greatly relieved and this time he saluted back, rather friendly. I went out and decided to stay in the corridor. I did not want to take any further chances.

We ran into trouble only once more, with the conductor. He insisted we move into a third-class carriage. I settled it by making out a voucher in his book for first-class fare for thirteen military personnel and signed it:

"National Security, Special Guard Duty Detachment." I began to like that name. It sounded impressive even to me. It satisfied the conductor also, only he wanted it stamped.

"Our stamps are being made now. We are a new service," I quieted him. The men watched my transaction with the conductor with great satisfaction. I was definitely beginning to rate with them.

I was learning again, but I did not know it then. I learned that in a time of confusion it is sufficient merely to assume authority to have it respected. That lesson served me well later in Spain.

7   WE left the train at a village before it reached Siofok, the only town of any size on Lake Balaton. The carriage awaiting the doctor had room for only four. The sanatorium was quite a distance from the station so I had all our equipment except the rifles loaded in the carriage and sent the sergeant along with the doctor to make arrangements. The doctor was quite cramped and grumbled that the men should carry more of their equipment, but I made believe I did not hear him. I marched with the men although the natural thing would have been for me to ride with the doctor. But I was apprehensive about the sergeant because he seemed to have more than the usual hold over the men, especially his three pals, and besides, it was setting a good example to have the men see me walk with them. The road was very dusty and made us cough. Setting an example always exacts a price.

The sanatorium was a huge, sprawling building with many outbuildings right on the shore of Lake Balaton. It had three wings, balconies, a few ornamental turrets, and accommodations for about forty convalescents. It had no patients then. They had pulled out when news of the revolution in Budapest had reached them. When we arrived, the sergeant was waiting for me outside; there was trouble about the billeting. The sanatorium had servant quarters for the maids, also separate quarters for the nurses. The doctor wanted the men housed in the stables.

"We will billet with the maids, we will billet with the nurses, or we will billet in the sanatorium," said the sergeant to me, "but

52

we will not billet with the horses and cows. There are no patients here, all hospital beds are empty."

I went back to the doctor to take up the question with him. He was resentful.

"If I'd put them in with the servants they'd have all the maids pregnant in a week, and full of venereal disease. I would have to set up a venereal ward to treat them. If I'd put them in with the nurses, they'd rape them. Those are enlisted men, the stable is good enough for them." He definitely seemed to be less happy about us now that we were here. I reminded him that I had promised the men beds to sleep in.

"But my beautiful linens! Those men are filthy!"

I told him he had bath facilities and the men would enjoy a good bath. The linen could be laundered. The men would have to sleep in the sanatorium.

"This is my hospital. I am in charge here," he shouted. "They will sleep in the stable. I give the orders here."

Here was trouble. I anticipated trouble from the peasants, trouble even from some of the men, but not from him. Apparently there was more to running a detached unit than Captain Sulacek had taught us. It was getting late. We had not eaten since morning and I was becoming irritable.

"It is your hospital but it is now under government protection. You asked for that protection and you now have it." Since I was in charge of the men, I informed him, I was in charge of finding suitable quarters for them according to army regulations and, therefore, they would sleep in the hospital. I also told him we needed provisions, and that he could either feed us from his own kitchens or provide us with supplies, in which case we would set up our own kitchen.

"Oh, the food!" he groaned. "I will now have to provide food for twelve people."

Evidently he had failed to think the problem through before he went to Budapest. He must have acted in panic.

"Thirteen, with me," I said precisely. I was not afraid of him any more.

"They can eat with the servants," he decided, and left to arrange for it. At the door he turned:

"I'll hold you responsible for the conduct of your men," he threatened.

"I am assuming that responsibility," I said, with official formality. It sounded good, but within twenty-four hours I had reason to regret that statement. He really held me responsible and, in all fairness, he had many points on which to bring me to account.

I billeted the men in three rooms which held four beds each. The sergeant and his three friends stayed in one room together. The men ate their supper in the kitchen with the servants. The doctor did not invite me to have supper with him. I felt slighted but underneath I was glad. I had my meals served in my room.

After supper I called the men together and explained the tactical situation to them. Peasants were early risers and went to bed early. If a mass assault was being planned by them, it would develop shortly after dark. Therefore, we should all be in readiness from dark until ten o'clock. After ten we needed two men on patrol until twelve, to chase off marauders. After twelve, a single guard relieved every two hours would be sufficient until six in the morning. The day would be their own except for a daily parade at eleven followed by a one-hour drill period.

They liked it all but the drill. The supper was good, the beds were clean, the mattresses soft, the pay was high, and the hours of duty were a cinch. They presented no objection until the sergeant said that they needed no drilling, they were all experienced combat soldiers, which I obviously was not. They all chorused agreement.

That was no good. Discipline loosens without drill and respect for command diminishes.

"The drill is not for your benefit but to impress the countryside," I told them. "It is a show of strength. The peasants will never dare attack when they see such a body of armed and disciplined soldiers."

That made sense to them and it also made good sense to me as I heard myself voicing it. I had not really thought it through before. There were no objections to the drill after that, not even from the sergeant.

"Let's put out a noisy patrol tonight, two patrols of six men each, and whenever you see anything suspicious, fire. Let everybody hear you for miles around, let the peasants know that we are here," I concluded the instruction.

The men did plenty of shooting that night. They did not hit anyone, nor did anyone even approach the sanatorium. They were shooting at shadows, or just shooting. They must have shaken everybody in that village out of his sleep. Even I emptied the clip in my pistol, right under the doctor's bedroom, shouting loudly:

"Head them off! Get them! They are heading towards the poplars!"

That brought a volley of answering fire from the men. It was fun.

The doctor cautiously opened the shutters on his window upstairs and whispered:

"What happened?"

"Marauders. They were trying to sneak into the pigpen," I whispered back.

"Did you get them?" he whispered.

"Wounded one of them, I believe," I whispered back. I did not know why I was whispering. There were no marauders. We certainly had no reason amid all that shooting to keep our voices low. I could see why the doctor was whispering, he was scared, but I had nothing to be scared of. Whispering, like fear, is contagious.

It was a good night's performance. All the sanatorium's personnel, including the doctor, was pleased. In the morning there was an evident relief from fear and anxiety all around. The maids were casting admiring glances at the soldiers, who in turn told them and each other how they had fought off the attempted night assault. As I heard them rehash the events of the night I wondered whether they really believed the stories they told. Maybe they did, and maybe they didn't. Maybe they only half believed them. They must have known they were exaggerating, yet convinced there was a core of truth in it.

We paraded that morning at eleven. It would have been customary for the sergeant to do the drilling. I changed that. I told him to take over the calisthenics and give them fifteen minutes of that, let them rest for ten minutes, and I would take over the drill after that. I had no conscious reason for wanting to do the drilling myself, perhaps I wished to feel the power of command and to play at soldiering. Whatever the reason, that decision was to save my life later.

I joined the men in calisthenics for I knew I was good at it. I took up position in front and set the lead. After the calisthenics were over and we were resting, one man told me, half smiling, half serious:

"It takes a young limb to have a snap to it." There was laughter.

"Young roosters hop high!" remarked another. There was more laughter. It made me feel good and I laughed with them.

Afterward we had our drill. I did parade formations, evolutions, commanding them with drawn saber. All the servant maids, even the nurses, turned out to watch. The audience made the men strut. They drilled rather well and put a snap into it. They enjoyed it. By the end of the seventh day, when we left the sanatorium, I could have taken them to any parade ground. They were really good.

I wonder why armies do not recruit female audiences. It would speed up basic training considerably.

56

8 THE days passed quietly and so did the nights. Although rumors reached us that this castle or that estate in outlying villages had been looted or set aflame, we were not molested. The men enjoyed themselves, they had a real vacation for the first time in their lives. They had food, women, and very little work to do. For companionship they had each other and the maids. I had neither and I was getting bored, not being accustomed to idleness. In that entire sanatorium there was not a single book to read. Field-grade officers in the Austro-Hungarian Army had no need for a library. They knew everything, for rank was knowledge. I asked the doctor for some of his medical books to read but he would not lend them to me for fear they would get soiled. I would walk out to the frozen lake shore and hunt for wild ducks with a rifle. I knew I wouldn't hit any, yet every time I missed I felt disappointed.

The doctor annoyed me with his daily complaints.

"The men cut up a brand-new sheet for foot covering," he accused me. Soldiers of the Hungarian Army were not supplied with socks. They would use rags to wrap around their feet before putting on their boots.

"It won't happen again," I solemnly assured him, more on hope than knowledge.

"The men are interfering with the work of the maids," he would complain.

"I'll put a stop to that," I would reply, knowing full well I had no intention of interfering. I wouldn't have gotten anywhere with it anyway.

"The men are forcing their attentions on my maids against their will," he came storming to me one time. "I will hold you responsible for their behavior." I promised to investigate that complaint at once and went into the kitchen.

I saw four women working there and I called one of them out. She was a buxom, very pretty young woman with rosy cheeks, about twenty-two, I guessed. She was a bit embarrassed and was twirling her apron.

"Are my men molesting you?" I asked her. She blushed and said nothing. "The doctor is telling me our men are forcing themselves on you." She still didn't answer.

"Come on, don't be afraid. Tell me the truth. If they are bothering you women, I'll put a stop to it quick."

"They are sure no worse than those old officers we used to have around here," she said spiritedly. "Those old goats were really terrible. They were practically ordering us to go to bed with them. And when they pinched it really hurt." She giggled.

"What about my men?"

"Oh, they are sociable. They don't pinch so hard."

I wanted to get to the bottom of it. "What do they do?" I asked her.

She giggled some more. I pressed her for an answer.

"Aw, go on with you!" she said, raising her eyes coquettishly to mine. "You know what men do. Why don't you try it sometime? Or maybe you are too young."

I wasn't too young and I would have liked to try. I thought of it often enough. But I had to set an example, and you have to pay a price for that. Nevertheless, I felt myself blushing. I blushed too damn easily, just like a young boy.

"Are the men forcing you to do things against your own free will?" My voice was playing tricks on me again. I had been having trouble with it lately. I had a good voice for dealing with men but with women it sometimes came out wrong just when I most wanted it to sound firm. I hoped she did not notice, although she was giggling again.

"Aw, go on with you," she said. "They are men and we are having fun. It is nice to have your own kind around after all those high and mighty officers. You are a nice young one, why don't you come down to the kitchen one evening and find out for yourself?" She was laughing at me openly, all her former diffidence gone.

"That will do," I said gruffly and dismissed her. It did not come out gruff, it sounded more like a squeak. She laughed and went inside. I decided against questioning the other three women and walked back. I had to take it slowly and hold my saber at the grip to keep it from getting between my legs from behind, although the normal way to avoid that is by making a kicklike circular motion with your right leg before you put your foot down.

The next day I told the doctor I had found no evidence that the men were forcing themselves on the maids. The doctor scoffed. He claimed to have it on good evidence, several of the nurses had reported it. I decided to visit the nurses after supper. I had known them all by sight but had had no personal contact with them up until then.

I shaved carefully that evening, the second time that day, although there was no necessity for it. I could easily have skipped my daily morning shave as well without anyone noticing it much. I was blondish, and besides being very light in color the hair on my face grew at a distressingly slow rate, considering my age. I had been shaving daily because that was supposed to make the beard grow thicker and faster, although I had not found that true in my case.

The nurses were six in number and occupied three rooms in a separate wing, one of the rooms being used as a sitting room. I knocked on their door, entered, bowed formally, wished them good evening, and addressed them in my most official manner.

"Ladies, I am here on official duty. I came here to investigate." Suddenly I did not know how to continue, their stares disconcerted me. It was hard to put it into the right words. I started all over again.

"I came to investigate the . . ." I still couldn't get any further. That was most unfortunate for they started to smile and this disconcerted me even more. A little red-haired nurse, the youngest of them, was giggling out loud. She did not look much older than I. The others were all much older. The head nurse, a thin woman with a wrinkled face, turned to them disapprovingly.

"Leave the boy alone. He is only a child. What is it you want, young man?"

I was blushing, which made me mad. I was grateful to her and yet angry at her. I was not a boy and certainly was no child. I would show them that I could use strong language if that is the way they wanted it.

"About my men fornicating with the maids," I said in manly fashion.

They burst out laughing.

"Raping them!" I added for emphasis. Now they were really laughing. One of them exclaimed:

"That would be a new experience to those sluts." That set them laughing even louder, the little redhead the loudest of them all. It is easy to say "investigate" but in practice it can be quite difficult.

"I am going to prepare an official report on it and submit it to the higher authorities." This was according to regulations and it went much smoother. "If you have any evidence, you can inform me here, or if that would embarrass you, I am ready to see each of you alone in my room, in private." I should not have added that last because it set them laughing again.

"What evidence would we have?" asked one of the nurses finally.

60

"Eyewitness evidence. The doctor said several of you reported it to him."

"Oh, the doctor. Don't pay any attention to him. He is mean. Sit down and visit with us. Here, have some candy." They were all speaking at once and they were very friendly. I sat down and we had a most enjoyable time. They were teasing me about my youth, about my presumed innocence and lack of experience. "I would like to show you, especially this redhead," I told them, and now she blushed. I was thinking how to isolate her and take her for a walk but there was no chance. Those nurses presented a solid female phalanx. When I left we were good friends and they invited me to visit them again.

The next morning I told the doctor the nurses had no evidence. He gave me another one of his sour looks. He had a bigger complaint now. My men had killed one of his pigs, the largest and fattest one.

I went to investigate that. I found it was pure accident. One of the men had accidentally discharged his rifle and it hit that pig. That pig screamed so loud that it had to be killed to put it out of its misery. There were plenty of witnesses, including the entire kitchen help.

I gave the doctor a full report on the case but it did not satisfy him. He said somebody would have to pay him for that pig but I disregarded that remark. That night we had fresh pork for supper and it was a welcome change in our diet.

The next day two fat geese were killed. Again it was an accident, brought about by a most complicated chain of circumstances. We ate the geese.

Next there were towels missing from the laundry. The doctor wanted me to search the men's packs. I told him I had no reason to suspect my men. The doctor kept insisting on the search. I informed him I was planning to have an inspection soon and then we should see.

"How soon?" the doctor wanted to know.

"Thursday," I told him.

"Today is Thursday," said the doctor. I had lost track of the calendar.

"Next Thursday," I said coolly.

The more contact I had with the man, the less I liked him. He disliked us even more. I was wondering how all this would end when suddenly I heard my name called. Two men came running after me. I was wanted in the office, urgent! Emergency!

I ran to the office. I found two civilians with the doctor and they rose when I entered. One was a portly, older man, with a handle-bar mustache, dressed in black with a heavy golden chain across his vest, the President of the Town Council of Siofok. The other was the Town Clerk of Siofok, in Hungary the highest executive official after the Mayor. He was around forty with a blond English mustache, his hair parted in the middle. His clothes looked very elegant and expensive for the Town Clerk of a small town. He was very pale and very excited. He did most of the talking while the other one just sat, pulling and twirling his thick mustache and nodding in assent.

They needed help at once, desperately. Siofok, only twelve miles away, was in revolt!

9 SIOFOK was the largest town in that Lake Balaton area, a famous summer resort surrounded by a belt of smaller villages inshore, with a permanent population of a few thousand. (Less than a year later, it was this town where Admiral Horthy set up his headquarters to organize his march on Budapest.)

Trouble had been building up in Siofok ever since the revolution broke out in Budapest and was about to reach its culmination that evening. The revolution had raised the pent-up discontent and misery of the war in that town to a point of explosion.

Even before the revolution the people blamed their privations on the Town Clerk and members of the Town Council. They attributed the meagerness of war assistance to the families of the soldiers, the inadequacy of war pensions for war widows and orphans to bribery, graft, and corruption on part of the public officials. The officials, and the Town Clerk in particular, were accused of taking bribes to keep the rich exempt from draft; of favoritism; of forcing wives and daughters of absent soldiers to submit to their lust. When the Town Clerk talked about that, he became even more nervous, patting his hair, clearing his throat, pleading with his eyes the absurdity of those charges. The town officials had also been accused of extortion and other misuse of their official powers. Since all governmental decrees, all measures for the sacrifices demanded by the war, such as tightening of rationing, came down to the Town Council, the Mayor, and the Town Clerk for execution, they became the natural focus of

63

all accumulated hatred, and now, they were the targets for revenge.

The early signs of impending trouble appeared trivial. The grumbling grew louder and became more ominous. Next the peasants and laborers stopped taking their hats off to their betters, they would look away or, worse still, brazenly and defiantly stare straight at them.

The next stage started when a woman waiting in line for her war-assistance payment became disorderly, insulting, and even abusive. When the Town Clerk told her to quiet down or he would hold up her payment, someone in the crowd yelled out: "Wait until my husband gets back from the front, he'll take care of you and the rest of you almighty potentates." That started a demonstration of wild curses and foul abuse. The women tried to crowd into his office and the two town constables had a most difficult time before they could restore order.

Shortly afterward, several large homes and summer residences in the surrounding area were looted. The number of those lootings had increased in the past days, since the first few ex-soldiers had made their way home from the front.

Just two days previously the Clerk of a near-by village had been seized in his office by a bunch of wild women assisted by some returned soldiers and other trouble-makers. They had stripped the Clerk naked, hung the village drum around his neck, and then forced him to parade down the village street, to beat the drum and cry out, in mockery of official announcements:

"I, the Village Clerk, officially announce by order of the higher authorities that I am a crook, a cheat and a no-good whoremaster."

He was jeered, spit upon, and made to repeat that announcement several times before they would let him go. He fled the village that night and was given shelter by the Siofok Town Clerk until he departed for Budapest.

That very night the military storeroom at the railway depot

in Siofok was broken into and stripped bare of all blankets, boots, army uniforms, rations, and other equipment. Luckily no weapons had been stored there. A large mob participated in that looting. Simultaneously, an imposing home of a wealthy Budapest family had been set on fire to divert attention from the looting.

The previous day the Siofok Town Council had sent a delegation to Szekesfehervar, the largest town and military base in the area to ask for emergency aid. But the authorities had been unable to assist them, they themselves lacked sufficient forces to assure their own public safety.

When the delegates had returned empty-handed this morning they were met by a jeering, hooting crowd shouting threats and insults.

"Where are the bayonets, your excellencies?"

"The Red Rooster will fly tonight!"

"Your feet will be dancing in the air after dark."

Someone threw a rock through the Mayor's window, frightening him so badly that he had fled the town. Having heard that a strong military force was stationed in this sanatorium the Town Clerk and the President of the Town Council decided, in desperation, to try their luck here. They needed help at once, they implored.

The Town Clerk was talking in jerky sentences, unable to stand or sit still for a moment, twirling his mustache with twitchy fingers, mopping his brow, pulling at his fawn-colored vest. The doctor had caught his panic and became twitchy too, his face turned ashen, his breath was forced out loud from his open mouth. The President of the Council just sat, fat thighs wide apart, his head bobbing up and down in assent.

I was eager to help. I told the Clerk that although I had a force of only twelve men, they were well armed and disciplined, that I was confident we could handle the situation.

The Town Clerk became despondent; twelve men were nowhere near enough to deal with that mob. I insisted we could do it. I was a soldier and it was my duty to restore order in accordance with the Articles of War concerning Domestic Uprisings. Besides, it sounded thrilling.

The doctor cut in unexpectedly. He vehemently asserted he would not let us go; we had been assigned to him to guard his sanatorium! That amazed me. After all his complaints I expected him to be glad to see us depart. Personally, I was eager to leave and told the doctor that the safety of the town of Siofok was of far greater importance than his sanatorium. The doctor was adamant. He insisted since he was paying us out of his own pocket we were under his orders and would have to stay with him.

The Council President now spoke up for the first time and wanted to know how much the doctor was paying us. I told him the doctor was paying the new army rate, 10 kronen a day per man, 30 kronen for me as an officer.

"The Town of Siofok will triple that," he said, looking at the Town Clerk who eagerly assented.

I thought that exceedingly generous of them. I had no understanding then what had prompted that generosity. They knew what I did not, that the country was then in an actual state of anarchy, and in their eyes we were a group of mercenaries whose allegiance could be bought by the highest bidder. Had I guessed that, I would have walked out right then. I was motivated solely by a blind sense of duty to establish law and order. The sanatorium did not need us. Siofok, a town faced by immediate revolt, did. I told the doctor to pay us off, assured him he could count on our aid any time he needed it, and went out to get the men ready.

The men listened to me in silence. Surprisingly, my indignation failed to communicate itself to them. When I informed them about that challenge to law and order, and when I spoke of our great opportunity to uphold the honor of our arms, they stood impassive, manifesting a singular lack of interest in this new mission. I sensed I would have to find a new approach. While I was thinking about that I casually mentioned the triple pay. This brought an immediate change of attitude.

"Thirty kronen a day!" one of them exulted. "We'll clean that town up with a toothbrush for that!"

It was settled. We got our gear and I paraded the men. Their sufficiency in arms, their erect military bearing, cheered the Town Clerk and the President of the Council visibly. The daily drill had transformed them into a proud force as they stood at stiff attention for inspection. It was agreed that the Town Clerk and the Council President would drive on ahead and we would be following them in three carts borrowed from the doctor.

The doctor paid the men off dourly. When it came to paying me he said he had run out of cash, he would send on my pay to me in Siofok.

I believed him!

10 WHEN we got near Siofok, I told the drivers to take us to the rear of the Town Hall and stop a block away. It was close to seven by then and it was dark. We weren't hungry. The men had scrounged enough bread, hard sausage, smoked Hungarian bacon from the help in the Doctor's kitchen to have our fill on the way over. When we got to within fifty yards of the rear of the Town Hall, we got off, brushed the straw off our uniforms and I had the sergeant line the men up. The street was dark. There seemed to be some light in the square in front of Town Hall and a murmur was rising from that direction.

My plan was to show maximum strength, I explained to the men. We were to march into the square in a double file, but stretched out in length to give us a column twenty yards long. We were to enter in parade step, rifles at ready, bayonets fixed, then deploy into a long skirmish line in front of Town Hall. By the time we had that all straightened out a small crowd had collected, gaping at us in silence, and more people were hurrying toward us. It was time. I drew my saber and commanded in loud parade drill voice:

"Attention! Fix bayonets! Rifles at ready!"

The movements were executed with precision. The daily drills did prove effective.

"Forward, march!"

The cobblestones resounded under the parade steps. We rounded the Town Hall and marched on to the square, the people scampering out of our way to clear space for us. We deployed in front of the Town Hall. The line looked imposing. It reached almost from one corner of the building to the other.

I faced the crowd, mainly women and old men with a sprinkling of soldiers in faded worn uniforms. Our uniforms were new.

I raised my saber, stood at attention, and called out:

"In the name of the law I order you to clear this square at once and disperse to your homes." It was from the manual, except I left "the King" out before "law."

Nobody moved. There was silence.

Suddenly someone shouted:

"Tin Soldiers. Go home! Nobody wants you here." That raised a few other shouts but not so loud and distinguishable.

"Who said that?" I challenged.

A huge man in a torn army blouse stepped forward. There was a loud murmur of approval from the crowd.

"Tell them, Steve," a voice encouraged him.

He walked forward and faced me.

"What if I said it?" he challenged in a loud truculent voice.

"You are under arrest," I snapped.

"On whose orders?" he jeered.

I motioned to the sergeant. He stepped forward, raised his rifle and brought the steel butt down full force on the soldier's head. The man collapsed. Women screamed. The crowd edged back.

"Anyone else care to say anything?" My voice sounded very shrill.

Nobody did. A couple of women started crying.

"I give you one minute to disperse or we'll fire," I warned, my voice pitched very high in excitement. The crowd broke and hurried off, the last ones breaking into a run.

Only then did I take a look at the man on the ground. He was gasping for breath with a snoring sound and blood was running down his face. I was suddenly struck with remorse.

69

That man might die! Everything on the square had come off as I had anticipated, but it had not occurred to me that someone might be killed. The Town Clerk and other civilians now came running out of the Town Hall, all excited, all of them talking to me at once. I did not hear what they were saying, I couldn't tear my eyes off that bleeding man. Finally I told them:

"Get a doctor! That man is hurt! Take him inside and bandage him!"

He was carried inside and I followed him in. They put him in a cell and somebody started to bandage his head. Everybody was crowding around and you couldn't move in that small cell. I sent a civilian to tell the sergeant to send me a guard, told everybody to clear out, instructing the guard to stay with the man in the cell. I left with the civilians who took me to the Council Room.

The Council Room was in a hubbub. I was escorted to a seat next to the Council President and we all sat down. There must have been nearly twenty civilians around the table, all older men, older than my father. They looked rich, they wore thick golden watch chains, heavy rings, dark heavy clothes of expensive material. A big coal stove was burning in the center.

It did not look at all like what I had imagined a council meeting would be. The Councilmen appeared overexcited, talking in overloud tones, practically shouting. They acted scared. Finally the Town Clerk quieted them and made a short speech. He said that for the time being things were safe and described how we had dispersed the mob. When he mentioned me they all clapped their hands and shouted "bravo," which embarrassed me. The Town Clerk then said that they were there to decide what to do next, how to keep the mob in its place, and asked for proposals.

A number of them spoke at once. A big red-faced man kept yelling, "We have to teach them a lesson, a lesson they'll never forget, by God!" They all agreed with that and then one of them asked, "What kind of a lesson? And how?"

The red-faced man, he owned a large livestock farm just outside of Siofok I was told, had the answer.

"We got a prisoner, the leader of the mob. Let's take and hang him. That will teach them the lesson they need, teach them to stay away from people's property and steal their pigs and livestock."

A few people shouted their assent. The others suddenly turned very quiet. That was an altogether new idea. I felt scary.

The Town Clerk then turned to me and asked me directly what my idea was on the subject. The question caught me unawares, I never had thought I had anything to do with that.

They were all staring at me waiting for my answer. I pictured the man lying on the ground with blood all over his face, his breathing so strained, and I became still more scared. I had not meant for the sergeant to club him over the head with a rifle butt. All I had intended was to put him under arrest so that the rest of the crowd would then disperse, and now they wanted to hang him.

The silence was stretching.

"What do you propose to do, Commander?" the Town Clerk prompted me again.

"Military guards can't hang people," I finally managed to bring out. "They can only fire at mobs when they don't obey commands, or offer resistance." I went on to explain the military rules relating to mobs and domestic disorders. As I spoke, my confidence returned. I was citing the manual which I knew by heart and the words came out fluently, allowing me to think ahead while I spoke. They listened intently.

I explained that in order to make those people respect authority we had to demonstrate to them they had to obey and couldn't get away with breaking the law. I proposed that next morning we make a house-to-house search and confiscate all military property looted from the depot. They cheered that. I also proposed that we patrol the streets once in the morning, once in

71

the afternoon, and twice in the evening from dark until ten o'clock. By then most people would be in bed.

They liked all but the last part. They wanted to have the patrol out all night.

That was not practical. I told them I couldn't divide my men. A two-man patrol wouldn't look too formidable. The guard had to stay together because as a unit, even if they were not out on the street, they constituted a strong armed force which was more than the mob could expect to cope with, and the mob would be aware of that. Besides, the men had to have their sleep and rest.

They heard me out but they still insisted on an all-night patrol. That gave me an idea.

"Let's organize a civilian patrol out of you men and I will assign two of my men to lead you. Then the guard will still be kept together as a strong reserve."

They finally agreed. I asked the Town Clerk to call together next afternoon all those who would want to serve on the patrol, bringing whatever weapons were available in town—shotguns, pistols, etc.—and we would organize them.

They assigned a large room right in Town Hall as quarters for my men and agreed to supply them mattresses and three free meals daily, while I was to be the guest of the town and provided with a luxury room and everything else I desired, gratis, in the best hotel in town. By the time the meeting adjourned everybody was cheerful. They came up to me, shook my hands, clapped me on the back just as if I were one of them. I did not feel that way. I was not fully at ease with them.

I went outside and told the men about the arrangements. They liked it. We went to the designated hotel and the men all had a fine meal, each ordering whatever he wanted. They were even served a *spriccer* each, wine with soda. Afterwards they got their mattresses, toted them over to the Town Hall, and settled down.

I told the sergeant to take the patrol through the town later that night and to make plenty of noise so the people would know the town was being patrolled. Since it was late in November and very cold, I decided not to station a guard outside the Town Hall, but to post one inside the door, relieved every two hours. That was most satisfactory with the men and it was a sound arrangement, for there was no danger of attack.

Next I went to see the prisoner. His head had been bandaged and the blood washed off his face but he was still unconscious and breathing very hard. It made me feel uneasy; I was scared that he would die.

My assigned hotel was close by. A couple of the Councilmen were in the restaurant and they invited me over. I did not feel like eating and they treated me to drinks. I soon felt woozy. I excused myself, went to my room, undressed, and went to bed.

I couldn't have been asleep long when a persistent knock at my door woke me. I grabbed my pistol and opened the door. It was the hotel porter with a weeping peasant woman dressed in black, a woolen shawl over her head and shoulders.

"She insisted on seeing you, sir, and she wouldn't stay away," the porter explained apologetically. "I kept chasing her but she would keep coming back and crying so loud I was afraid she would wake the whole street. I thought it would be better for you to talk to her, sir."

The woman, who stood there sniffling during the porter's speech, now burst into a loud wail.

"What's going to happen to my husband? They told me he was dying. What's going to become of our poor orphans?" She was the wife of the prisoner. I felt very guilty. I got dressed in a hurry, told the woman to come with me, and led her to Town Hall. It took a lot of knocking before the guard opened the door. He was groggy with sleep.

"I must have closed my eyes for a second," he apologized sheepishly. I took the woman to the cell with me.

The man was still lying unconscious, his eyes half open but not seeing, his breath whistling through his parted lips.

73

The woman let out a scream and threw herself on her husband, wailing "Stevie, oh Stevie, what did they do to you?" She wasn't directly referring to me, but the accusation struck home. I told the woman she could stay there with him as long as she wished. She paid no attention to me. She squatted down on the floor and gently lifted his injured head into her lap. I left them, walked back to the hotel, and went back to bed.

The next morning I divided my men into four details and we made a house-to-house search in the section where the poor lived. We confiscated four cartloads of boots, blankets, underwear, uniforms, packs, and other army material.

The people whose homes we searched were sullen. Many of them offered me bribes to let them keep the stuff, others muttered that we didn't care if they froze to death. I never anticipated that the job would turn out so distasteful. I did not relish confiscating those blankets and clothes, but of course it was looted stuff, it did not belong to them, it was government property.

During the next three mornings we recovered enough army clothing and other property to nearly fill the box car in which I deposited them for eventual shipment to the Szekesfehervar Army Base. The three-man team I personally supervised recovered more looted material than the other three combined. I was proud of that achievement. I attributed it to the keenness of my eyes in spotting army equipment. It did not occur to me that the eyes of the others might have been just as keen or even keener, but more sympathetic to the poor, or that perhaps the other men were not as unresponsive to the offered bribes as I had been. I saw no need to have the freight car guarded, for the situation was well in hand. I had a stout padlock put on it and took the key with me.

The organization of the civilian patrol did not prove difficult. About fifty men volunteered and they had eighteen shotguns and a few pistols among them. I divided them into three groups, the first one to patrol from six to eight in the evening, the second from eight to ten, the third from ten to twelve. They were older men, the most substantial citizens in town.

I assigned my men to lead them. Since there were not enough firearms to go around, some carried heavy canes.

The patrol worked out fine. I checked every patrol before it went out, and we joked quite a bit. They were rather proud of themselves and talked and laughed loud when making their tours, which I liked. There were no disturbances.

One of the Councilmen who was a processor and exporter of Hungarian paprika, took a particular liking to me. He took me home for dinner and introduced me to his daughter. Her name was Yolan but everybody called her Yolly. She was seventeen, a year younger than I, a very pretty girl with dimples in her cheeks, especially when she laughed. She told me she had a deep admiration for me. We fell in love at sight and I came to spend all my free moments in her house, particularly since her mother and father insisted that I make their house my home. Her mother would cook special dishes for me and bake my favorite cakes. Yolly and I got together every time I was free, and we kissed at every opportunity. That was about all we did; Yolly was not talkative, and I, too, preferred that to conversation.

I also had a personal problem. The hotel where I was living had a blond cashier and she would slip into my room at night when she heard me coming home. I had a few bottles of liqueur in my room, a present from the hotel, and I would find her there half drunk. She smelled heavily of perfume and underarm perspiration. She had a big bust and she was full of smutty re-marks. She would smooth my hair and make other advances. I did not like her and always had a difficult time sending her back into her own room. Once she even sneaked into my bed after I was asleep, but I did not enjoy it. From that night on she would make eyes at me during meals and ask me when would I be nice to her again. It was most annoying; since she was much older, I had to treat her with courtesy.

Within a few days the situation in the town was fully under control. Most of the trains in the country had stopped running because of the coal shortage and the few that occasionally managed to come through had to use wood for fuel, which made them very slow. Because of that, only a few soldiers had succeeded in making their way back to the town from Italy. I spoke with some and they told me hair-raising tales of how the treacherous Slovenes and Croatians, who were part of Austro-Hungary until the time of their revolt, had mistreated them, their former comrades in arms; how they had robbed them of their clothing, even stealing the boots off their feet when they caught them asleep.

The arrested man survived, and I gave his wife permission to take him home. Instead of showing hate, they both thanked me profusely for my kindness. The wife called innumerable blessings on my head, kissed my hand, and her children kissed the hem of my tunic. It was painfully embarrassing and I felt much relieved when they left.

By the eleventh day life had become routine. Then a bit of trouble developed. Payday in the Hungarian Army was every ten days and the men expected to get paid. The Town Clerk informed them that the Council had decided that the President had lacked authority when he had offered them triple pay instead of the official ten kronen a day. The men demanded full pay as promised. The Town Clerk claimed the treasury was short of money. The men became threatening and for the first time disregarded me when I tried to calm them. I never liked to haggle about money, but I had to take the men's part. Finally they got paid in full, 300 kronen each man, which was a great deal of money at that time, more than most of them had ever seen in one lump sum, and they were very satisfied. Since the treasury was short I told the Clerk I was willing to wait for my 900 kronen. He was greatly pleased and thanked me for my co-operation. I was in no need of money, the hotel even supplied my cigarettes free.

That night I had been long asleep when I was suddenly jarred awake by loud knocking and excited voices outside. I jumped out of bed and opened the door. I found three men there, all Councilmen, and they were trembling with fear. There was a riot at the depot. It was then past eleven o'clock.

"Where is the patrol?" was my first question.

They were the patrol, they quaked.

"Where are your arms?" I asked angrily.

Their arms had not been turned over to them that night. When they assembled to relieve the second patrol, the sergeant had sent them home saying his men would take over the third patrol. They all went home except these three, who decided to have a few drinks first. On their way home they had witnessed the riot at the depot and ran right over to see me.

That meant serious trouble. I threw my clothes on in such a hurry that I even left my saber belt off, just snatched up the holster with the pistol, and rushed toward the depot.

It was quite a distance and I was out of breath by the time I reached the depot. The moon was bright and the platform in front of the freight car was dark with people, most of them women.

The door of the freight car was wide open and two of the sergeant's cronies were busy passing blankets, boots, clothing to the people clamoring below. They had improvised an aisle by placing the massive railroad benches from the waiting room parallel to each other and the people had to pass through this to reach the open door of the freight car.

I saw the sergeant standing on the first bench facing his third crony on the opposite bench. Their hands were full of bills, they were collecting money from the upthrust hands of the clamorous women before permitting them to pass through the aisle. The women were shrieking, pushing and pulling each other—it was a riot all right.

I discovered the rest of my men on the fringe of the crowd. They were not party to that organized looting nor did they do anything to interfere; they were just watching. They caught sight of me at the same time I noticed them.

"Follow me." I motioned to them. As I saw them close up behind me, I drew my pistol and went out to the platform. I was boiling mad.

"Stop it," I commanded. "Halt!"

Every face turned toward me. The two soldiers on the freight car froze. The crowd gave way. It was very still.

I walked over to the sergeant.

"You are under arrest!"

The sergeant grabbed for his rifle and cursed. "Get out of here or I'll kill you."

My finger tightened on the trigger. I was ready to shoot him.

"Attention!" I commanded in a fury. The other three men with him snapped to. The sergeant did not.

There was a fraction of hesitation.

"To foot!" I ordered with my pistol extended straight, aimed at his stomach.

The sergeant executed the command. His rifle butt made a loud bang on the wooden bench as he brought it down to position.

"You four men are under arrest." I was still furious. "Take his rifle," I said to the corporal with me. The drilling paid off. The sergeant turned over his rifle and we marched the four of them back to Town Hall. By then the platform was empty, the crowd had scurried off.

We marched them down to a cell and locked them in. I told the corporal that from then on he was in charge and that I wanted a guard over that cell all through the night. Then I returned to the hotel.

On the way back I felt strangely empty. My mind couldn't concentrate. I went to bed, closed my eyes, but I couldn't sleep. I kept seeing that platform, the women milling around, the sergeant with his rifle pointing at me from less than three yards' distance, ready to kill me. That image swirled round and round and suddenly I started to tremble. I wanted to stop shaking but I couldn't. I felt my whole body go rigid and I bounced up and down uncontrollably, setting the bed vibrating. Then I began to shiver again until I climbed out of bed, which stopped it.

Shock has strange effects.

11 THE next morning I went over to the Town Hall early. No one was standing guard and the cell was empty. The sergeant and his three cronies were gone and two more men with them. I discovered that a few cabinets had been broken open and I found chisel marks even on the town safe, but it hadn't been entered.

I walked over to the depot. The freight-car door gaped wide open, the broken lock hanging from it. The car had been stripped bare. That must have been done after I left, later in the night.

I went back to the Town Hall. It was still early but a number of Councilmen were already there busily discussing the events of the night before. I stopped near the door, unnoticed. One of the Councilmen who had called me from my hotel was holding down the center, describing the scene with wide gestures and great detail, embroidering it with touches that were new to me. I came out very well in his story, or so I thought, yet some of the others were saying that I was to blame, I was responsible for the men, I should have had better control over them, the sergeant and his friends were obviously bandits, look how they tried to break even the safe open! How could an officer of judgment have picked such men who were obviously habitual criminals, to guard people's life and property? Well, after all, he is only a young boy! True, yet it was like entrusting wolves to guard a flock of sheep, and so on. I walked away.

I went to my remaining six men, discussed with them what

had happened. They were evasive and I did not press them. I had them clean and oil all rifles including those the sergeant and the others had left behind. I took a rag and, for the first time, helped them with the task; it gave me something to do.

After lunch I went up to my room to sleep. I felt very low, a new mood for me. I slept a few hours and then went to see Yolly. Her father greeted me, but not in his usual hearty "Come in, come in, glad to see you, make yourself at home" manner. He was rather curt, said he had to go back to his office, and left right away.

Yolly was not in the parlor. Her mother told me she was studying in her room. They had news that the schools would be reopening soon, as soon as they could get in a supply of coal. I told her I would wait and sat around playing with the dog. Yolly did not come out of her room so finally I got up and said it was time for me to go. Her mother did not ask me to stay for supper, nor had she offered me some of her cake, as she always used to.

I went out and passing by the window I saw Yolly studying under the kerosene lamp on her table. I rapped on the window and she came over and opened it. We talked but neither of us had anything much to say. She told me she had forgotten all she had learned in school and she had to catch up. She also said that her parents thought we were spending too much time together and it would have to stop, it might lead to talk. That was peculiar, for her parents had been practically pushing us on each other, but I did not mention that to her. She said her room was getting cold with the window open. I said *"Au revoir!"* and helped her close the window.

It was by then nearly six o'clock and dark. I went back to Town Hall. I found a captain there talking with the Town Clerk, the Council President, and a few other people.

When they saw me come in the group broke up, the Councilmen saying loudly to each other, too loudly I thought, that it was time they got home for supper, the wife was raising holy hell about their always being late; then they left, shaking hands with me on their way out.

The captain, who had been standing aside during this time, now came over to me. I saluted him and he returned the salute. He introduced himself, he was the son of one of the Councilmen. He had just returned from the hospital that morning, he had been wounded in the arm by shrapnel on the Isonzo front. He was very friendly and told me from what he had heard I did a splendid job of restoring order, he was personally proud of it. He then casually added that my grave responsibilities were over, that he was taking over Public Safety beginning next morning. He told me to supervise the patrols as usual for that night, next morning he wanted a full report from me, and then we would discuss what would follow.

I left him, checked the patrol which was about to go out, and went back to the hotel for supper. After supper I took the second patrol out myself. The townspeople making up the patrol were overpolite. They made attempts to joke with me but it sounded forced. After we completed the first round, I left them and went back to the hotel.

The cashier was manicuring her nails and she gave me her usual wide smile with her gold teeth flashing. I asked the head-waiter for a bottle of cognac and then went over to her, invited her to come to my room as soon as she was free, we would get drunk and have a real party.

She laughed. She was pleased but she couldn't, not that night. She had a date with the captain.

I went to my room, took a couple of drinks out of the bottle, then a couple more, and went to bed. I felt very much alone.

The next morning I walked over to the depot and found a freight train standing there headed north, the direction of my home town. It was trying to get up steam and the engineer told me they would leave when and if they could load up with enough wood.

I went over to Town Hall to see the Town Clerk. He was busy and for the first time he made me wait. I watched him enter items in a ledger for a while, then touched him on the shoulder and told him I wanted to speak to him officially, I was going home. He was polite, but did not act surprised. He told me the town and the citizens would miss me. He wished me good luck, he did not ask me to stay on.

I asked him for my pay. He said that if the Mayor were in town I would have no difficulty, he could then pay me on the spot, but unfortunately, the Mayor was still absent. He couldn't pay me on his own authority; as commander of the guard I was a sort of town official in charge of public safety; my pay would have to be taken up by the Town Council which would meet formally three weeks later. However, he did not anticipate my having too much difficulty with them.

I told him there was a freight train waiting at the depot, I needed my money at once for I was leaving on that train. He was very sorry, very sorry indeed, he brushed his mustache with a small brush, it was indeed most regrettable, but he personally couldn't do anything about my pay without authorization. He asked me to leave my home address, they would mail my money to me there. I believed him and gave him my father's address. He then offered me a personal loan of twenty kronen as a friend, out of his own pocket. I had 990 kronen coming to me. I declined the loan. We shook hands and I left.

I went to say good-bye to the men. They were sorry to see me go and they showed it. We shook hands all around. I took two blankets off one bed because the weather was very cold and I had no overcoat. I noticed a piece of hard sausage on the table and asked the men if it was all right for me to take that along. It was more than all right with them. They even dug up another piece and two hunks of bread. I took a pack, folded one of the blankets and put it into the pack with the food, and threw the other blanket around my shoulders. That did not look military but I did not care. I made a present of my saber to the corporal and left the pistol and holster on the table with instructions to give them to the captain. That was my demobilization. I was through with the army!

I walked over to the station with the pack hanging from my left arm, on the side where my saber used to be. It felt strange walking without the heavy saber, my right foot would still automatically make that small circular kick that kept the saber from tripping one up. My right hand was clutching the blanket around my neck, for my throat felt sore. My body was hot and I was sneezing, my nose was beginning to get runny. I felt a bad cold coming on. I had an extra pair of trousers and some underwear in the hotel but did not bother to go back for them.

White steam was rising from the funnel of the locomotive. We ought to be able to start soon, said the engineer. The fireman said I could travel with them on the engine, it would be warmer. There was no caboose. I got in the cab with them but there was no room to sit down, I had to stand. The warm fire felt good but my knees began to tremble, I felt weak and wanted to lie down. I got off the cab, went to the first box-car but, strangely, I couldn't make the jump. I had to clamber up slowly, like an old woman, and crawl inside. I was really weak. I struggled with the door for quite a while to close it behind me. I finally managed it by pushing with both my hands and shoulder. I pulled the blanket out of the pack, laid my pack in the corner for a pillow, rolled myself in one blanket and spread the other over me. The boards were hard but it felt very good to be lying down. Never before had I needed to lie down so badly. I was feverish. I did not hear the train start.

When I awoke, it was very dark inside the car and it was also dark through the crack outside. I was very hot and thirsty but I had forgotten to bring along water. I had the sausage and bread but did not feel like eating and went back to sleep. I kept waking and dozing off; my feet were icy cold yet my body was very hot and I kept throwing my blanket off and then pulling

84

it back, over and over again. Sometimes it was light through the crack, sometimes it was dark; when I was awake I kept staring at the crack near the door but I was not thinking of anything, just staring.

A long, long time later I woke again. I was freezing all over, my head was swollen, fiery pains were stabbing through my feet. The train was not moving. I groped for my blankets and my pack, they were gone. Somebody must have stolen them from under me, leaving the door half open. I crawled to the door on all fours and saw we were in a freight yard. I had a difficult time letting myself down from the car. When my feet touched ground, they wouldn't support me and I fell. I raised myself up, but it took time—my legs were numb and very stiff, they did not feel like my own legs at all. The sky was pinkish gray in the early dawn.

Another freight train was getting up steam. I hobbled over and asked the engineer where he was heading. He told me to Gyor, which was my hometown. Resting every few steps, I made my way to one of the cars and after a few starts managed to pull myself up. I was hot and shivering. I did not have the strength to push the door shut so I crawled to the farthest corner and rested. After a while I sat up and leaned against the wall, took my shoes off, and began rubbing my feet. My feet didn't feel the skin of my hands, only the pressure. We traveled for a long, long time and I kept massaging my feet endlessly, over and under, over and under, back and forth. I also had to keep my body rocking forward and back to keep it from freezing, it was that cold. When we reached Gyor, it was evening. I was feverish again, just dimly conscious. I rolled out of the car and dragged myself to a fiacre for the ride home. The family all crowded around and I asked what day it was. It was Wednesday, early in December.

I had been on the road three days.

My folks put me right to bed and it took more than a week before I got some of my strength back. It was the Spanish flu, the Doctor said, marveling that I had survived that trip. My feet were frostbitten, so were my nose and ears, but they were getting better.

When I was able to get up and move around I found I was penniless. I hadn't received my pay in Kobanya, I had forgotten to collect my pay from the Food Ministry, I hadn't received my pay from the Doctor in the sanatorium, I hadn't received my pay from the Town Council in Siofok. I should have had well over 1,200 kronen, big money those days. I sure was an idiot. I had to ask my father for spending money although the family was very hard up because of the inflation. He gave me two kronen, then seeing the disappointed look on my face, he raised it another krone. He couldn't really afford it.

I wrote to the Town Council of Siofok for my money twice. I never received an answer. I did not bother to write to the Doctor, I knew the score there. But a town . . . ? A town council was a sort of government, it shouldn't have acted that way, a government shouldn't cheat a person. . . .

A few nights later I was late coming in, it must have been close to eleven o'clock. I took my shoes off in the vestibule and sneaked in on stocking feet to avoid being detected. My father woke up, he was a light sleeper, and gave me a terrific dressing down. He wanted no son of his to become a vagabond, squandering his father's hard-earned money, staying out that late at night at his age. . . .

I slunk off to bed, feeling very wronged. My father was unjust, totally lacking in understanding. I felt very sorry for myself, my eyes were moist, my throat was choking up. My father was too strict with me, he was too old-fashioned, he wanted me to stay home all evening, my eyes had tears in them by then. I hugged my youngest brother for love and comfort, he was sharing the bed with me. I thought how unfair my father was and I began to cry.

I was back home, again a child.

12   As soon as I got well I went to Budapest and in January, 1919 enrolled in the Medical School of the Royal University of Budapest. I also obtained a job with the Gabor Institute, a private school for the problem children of the wealthy. Some of the pupils were backward, some came from broken homes or were unwanted, others were the unmanageable, the kind no other school in the country would take. I was hired to teach mathematics and physical culture after my classes at the University, in exchange for room and board plus a nominal pay. Since jobs were almost impossible to find, it was a most fortunate arrangement.

I did not relish my job. The children were spoiled and in general looked down on their tutors who, as they well knew, came from poorer families.

One of my colleagues, a brilliant chemistry major just about to receive his degree, advised me to be deferential in my relationship with the boys or I wouldn't last long, because Dr. Gabor, the head of the institute, would invariably side with his wealthy pupils in any dispute.

That attitude, as I very soon found out, presented a grave problem in discipline. The boys acted as they pleased, studied or not, behaved in a loud and disrespectful manner. There was a great deal of masturbation in the dormitories, also some evidence of homosexual practices, and the tutors had to be on the lookout for that.

It was quite an ordeal. Attending classes at the University mornings and part of the afternoons, teaching until seven, supervising the dormitories until ten in the evening, then doing my own studying far into the night, was beginning to tax me. I became irritable and took a firm hand with the boys. This was immediately reported to Dr. Gabor who called me on the carpet. He was a pompous man of very short stature with a grotesquely outsize head on his scrawny neck, the largest head I had seen on a man. He censured me severely, stating that unless I learned how to use more tact and diplomacy I would not last long with his institute.

Since I needed the job badly I gave that problem serious study. Most of the trouble originated with the older boys. They were the leaders and the younger ones simply followed their example or even tried to outdo it. The next day I changed the physical culture routine by instituting wrestling. Wrestling was not an accepted form of exercise; it was considered an undignified activity fit only for street urchins. I even added an extra twist—ending the sessions with a controlled free-for-all. Each day I would choose five or six of the most obnoxious boys whom I wanted to see roughed up and set them on each other.

It worked for a while. The boys took to it and I took good care to prevail upon their manly pride to keep them from complaining. They did a far better job of beating each other up than I would have dared to do, yet my standing with the boys improved. All went well until one of my colleagues reported that I was teaching the children ungentlemanly deportment, and Dr. Gabor called me into his office again. He told me curtly to discontinue wrestling at once, impatiently rejecting my argument that the pupils, by then, actually enjoyed it and that it improved their dormitory and classroom behavior. He told me acidly he was not entering into a pedagogic discussion with me, he was telling me what to do. He added ominously that he was too busy that evening but would see me the next day. This disturbed me.

I liked my classes at the University; losing my job would present a serious problem.

At ten that evening, after the dormitories were finally in silence, I decided to take a walk. It was against the rules of the Gabor Institute for tutors to go out nights without permission, but since I was in trouble anyway, I did not care.

When I reached Erzsébet Boulevard, that broad thoroughfare usually teeming with life seemed quite deserted and this puzzled me. Although I seldom read the newspapers I knew there was a streetcar strike on—I had had to walk to the University that day. I also knew a printers' strike was on, that no newspapers had been published, and that there was some kind of trouble between the Social-Democrats and Communists.

I knew only in a vague way who the Socialists were, they were the workers in the trade unions. Of the Communists I knew even less. I remembered having read some time back that there were thirty-seven of them, all former prisoners of war who had returned from Russia with a man named Béla Kun who was their leader. Ever since then they had been making trouble for the Social-Democrats. Béla Kun and some of his friends had been arrested and beaten by the police. They were still in jail as far as I knew—not that I cared one way or another. Politics did not interest me, I had my own problems.

I was standing in front of a large café trying to puzzle out why there were so few people around when I saw a straggling line advancing in the center of the deserted boulevard carrying crudely lettered placards which read:

"Long Live the Dictatorship of the Proletariat!"

"Long Live Béla Kun."

The marchers were evidently factory hands, poorly dressed, rather scrawny and underfed. I counted them, there were nineteen, five of them women. I was curious. I went over to the nearest man in the line and fell in step with him. He was an undersized fellow wearing a checkered cap. I asked him what they were doing. He looked me over carefully and then said:

"Demonstrating for the proletarian dictatorship." I wanted to know where they were going.

"To the Eastern Railway Depot, to get arms!"

That interested me.

"Why would they give you arms? Have you an authorization?"

"They will have to give them to us, we are in power now. The proletariat in power is armed!" he declaimed.

I became even more interested. I knew what dictatorship was, Sulla in Rome had been a dictator. But I was not quite sure what proletariat meant, although lately I had come across the word frequently in the newspapers, also on some posters. He explained to me. He was a proletarian. He was a factory worker. Proletariat meant all the workers together who had nothing to lose but their chains and the whole world to gain. He said I was not a proletarian, I was a student. When I objected that I was also working, I was tutoring, he said that I was of the intelligentsia. The intelligentsia were not much good, but students were allies. The intelligentsia could be allies, too. I could be a double ally but still no proletarian.

Hearing our conversation a couple of other people moved to my other side so that I was no longer walking on the outside but near the middle of the column. Every time they saw a group of people on the sidewalk they shouted their slogan and so did I—it was fun. They called to the people to join us, but few of them did. Most of them hurried on ahead, some even turned back abruptly.

It was a long march to the Eastern Depot and I got a bit of education. Béla Kun had been released from jail and the Communists and Social Democrats were now the government. Count Mihály Károlyi, President of the Republic, had abdicated and turned the government over to them.

"Who is going to be the president now? Béla Kun?" I asked.

That was a childish question. There was to be no president any more, only the proletarian dictatorship which was much better, and Béla Kun was to be the dictator. Everything would be taken away from the rich, who were capitalist exploiters, their factories, land, castles and everything, and divided among the poor. That sounded fine to me but I did not believe it. I asked many other questions but most of the answers were vague. I concluded they were only guessing, they didn't know themselves. After all, they were only ignorant workers. How could they possibly know?

(It took me more than a decade to realize how incredibly wrong I was to feel so superior to them—in attributing their inability to answer my questions clearly to their lack of formal education. They could not possibly have given me the right answers because nobody knew the right answers then. Even in this nuclear age, when the physical survival of all mankind depends on our finding the right answers, those answers are still shrouded in the mist of the future.)

After we reached the Eastern Depot we milled around for quite a while until a couple of the proletarians finally located the railway official who had the key to the arsenal. They surrounded him, argued with him, but he refused to yield until one of the women snatched the huge key ring out of his hand.

It took time to find the right key to fit the lock and to open it. There were no more than a few dozen rifles inside. I looked around for a carbine but there was none, so I took one of the rifles. There was no ammunition in the room. They looked funny, those proletarian men and women carrying their rifles clumsily, like picks and shovels. I was still wearing my old army uniform but with the insignia removed, for I had no civilian clothes. The rifle looked good on me and it also felt good.

After we got ourselves armed nobody knew what to do next, or had any suggestions, so we decided to disperse and go home.

When I got to the gate of the Gabor Institute it was nearly three A.M. I did not care, I was full of animation and not at all sleepy. I rang the bell, not apologetically and gently as usual but hard and loud, enjoying the clangor. After a while I heard Dr. Gabor inside angrily demanding to stop that noise, and wanting to know what was going on. He flung the door open shouting that he'd "teach . . ."

Dr. Gabor glared at me in his long white nightshirt, shouting angrily, how did I dare come in at that hour of the night, waking up the entire school, who gave me permission to go out, on and on.

I just stood there grinning and then brought my rifle smartly off my shoulder. Dr. Gabor's eyes bulged out in his grotesque head. He started to stutter.

"What . . . What . . . What's the meaning of this?"

"Dictatorship of the Proletariat," I grinned. "It just broke out, a couple of hours ago."

He swayed and I had to grab him or he would have fallen. He was one of the leaders of the moderate Liberal Party and, unlike me, he grasped the real meaning of that change in government instantly. The printers' strike had kept him from knowing the latest developments. He was all shaken up and I supported him to his room.

"Good night," he thanked me in a broken voice.

In all the three months I had been working for him that was the first time he addressed me as "Mister"!

Weeks passed. The Proletarian Dictatorship was developing turbulently yet I was untouched by it. I attended classes, worked in the Institute, studied, rising at six and getting to bed way past midnight, a routine that taxed me to the full leaving me no time or energy to take much interest in the events around me. Occasionally I yearned to share the exciting life some of my colleagues in the University seemed to be leading but no one approached me to draw me in and my time was far too occupied to enable me to seek contacts on my own. I read the newspapers daily but in a superficial way; they were too full of meaningless political jargon and threats against unnamed counterrevolutionary elements to carry much interest for me. I failed to develop sympathy either for or against the Proletarian Dictatorship. Its promises failed to enthuse me; its threats carried no fear for me. The standing slogan displayed on posters everywhere affected me in a reverse way. They showed a steel-helmeted figure with a rifle on his shoulder and a hate-distorted face, pointing a menacing finger at the onlooker and threatening:

"YOU counterrevolutionary slinking in the dark, TREMBLE!"

I would salute the figure, give a mock shudder, wink at him, and depart whistling.

When the Hungarian Soviet Government decreed a general draft of my age group I decided not to obey it and went home to Gyor. This made me a draft evader but I did not care. I was through with the army. My father was worried, however, and asked me to see his friend, Dr. Parányi, a professional army doctor with the rank of major, then automatically serving in the Red Army, to see if he could work out something for me. Dr. Parányi asked me how much medical schooling I had had.

"Four months," I told him sheepishly.

"Splendid!" exclaimed Dr. Parányi. "I'll make you my assistant." The way he said it, service in the Red Army didn't rate high in his esteem, either.

The next morning he gave me a white coat and introduced me to the comrade medical attendants as the "new doctor," his assistant. I escorted him to sick parade and he instructed me to observe him carefully. There were forty or fifty Red Army soldiers in the line, undressed to the waist. They would enter the office one by one, drop their pants, and recite their ailments. Dr. Parányi would have them open their mouths, stick their tongues out; he would look at the tongue, sometimes look into their throats, then hand them a pill.

Every once in a while he would order a man to turn around, bend down and stretch his cheeks. He would then bend closer, take a look and exclaim triumphantly, "Syphilis." He would then call me over, tell me to take a look at the angry red growth in the anus, and remark proudly he could always detect secondary stage syphilis by a man's general appearance.

After attending sick parade with him for three days Dr. Parányi felt I had sufficient practice to be on my own. He turned medical inspection over to me with instructions to refer the seriously ill to him for treatment in the hospital.

We had only four medications at our disposal. A white pill, calomel, which was a purgative; aspirin, a general cure-all; a gray pill, ipecac, an expectorant and emetic; and a yellow powder, quinine, for fever.

I held sick parades daily, distributing the four medicines according to my judgment and sometimes depending on what supplies we had on hand. When we ran out of one pill I substituted another; it worked out the same. I also tried to diagnose secondary syphilis according to Dr. Parányi's method, by picking a man at random and then taking a look. My score was low. I would mistake scabies, hemorrhoids, or even simple scratches for lues, Dr. Parányi would inform me, sending the men back.

From then on I quit that type of detailed examination. It wasn't aesthetic anyway. I would simply ask every man whether he had or had had syphilis and if the answer was affirmative I would send him to the venereal ward. This improved my score greatly. Dr. Parányi was pleased with my progress and told me I had the makings of a good diagnostician. I accepted that praise with modesty.

One morning when I appeared for my customary sick parade I found no one in line waiting for me. I finally located an attendant who told me that Béla Kun had resigned, the Soviet Dictatorship was over, that all the men, including the ward patients, had miraculously recovered and left for home.

I went home, too.

It did not affect me one way or another.

After the fall of the Proletarian Dictatorship a number of workers were arrested. Since I did not know any of them that made little impression on me at first because neither I nor my family or friends were involved in any way. But when Admiral Horthy's White Army entered my town and the White Terror began in earnest my outlook changed completely.

Gangs wearing white armbands roamed the streets dragging people off trains, out of their homes, or off their jobs on the merest suspicion of having been involved in Communistic, Social-Democratic, or trade union activities, then brutally torturing, even murdering them. One young boy whom I knew personally had been taken to a concentration camp merely because he had joined the Cabinet Makers Union, although in that shop it was compulsory for all apprentices to join. When he was released four months later he was a cripple and it was said he had been castrated. I went to see him and he sobbed that it was true. He was then sixteen years old.

The Horthy régime needed a scapegoat and, as usual in history, we Jews became it. We were being called unscrupulous finance capitalist exploiters and also Communists, both at the same time. We were accused of being responsible for the loss of the war; also for all the miseries suffered by the people because of the centuries-old feudal oppression. Anti-Semitism became the official policy of the government and Parliament was debating proposals ranging from the complete extermination of the Jews to the comparatively mild one of barring them from all jobs and professions and expropriating their property.

In Gyor the *Catholic Herald* appeared under the standing banner headline:

WHAT ARE WE WAITING FOR? LET'S SETTLE
WITH THE JEWS!

My father, who had received several offers before the war to go to the United States and another one right after the war, finally decided to pull up roots. The family emigrated to the United States in the fall of 1920. I stayed behind to finish medical school but that proved impossible.

Bands of young hoodlums armed with clubs, brass knuckles, and *bikacsek* (the Hungarian version of a blackjack, made of the carefully desiccated genitals of a bull), would burst into the classrooms of the University, demanding that each student stand up and "identify" himself.

This "identification" was not a request for the showing of documents. It called for each male student to drop his trousers and expose his genitals for inspection, disregarding the presence of girl students. All those circumcised were then identified as Jews even though many had medical proof to the contrary, and they were mercilessly beaten by the thugs, mainly on their heads and genitals, crippling many of them for life.

In my classes a large group of us, including many non-Jewish colleagues, got together and armed ourselves with short lengths of lead pipe and with brass weights appropriated from grocers' scales. When these roving bands would hit our own classroom, we would give battle royal. Desks would be overturned, chairs smashed, precious instruments destroyed, floors and walls splattered with blood. Our example spread to other classrooms, and finally the University had to be closed down and all classes abandoned.

I went back to Gyor and spent my days in corroding idleness, staying in bed all morning and playing cards in the afternoon, until I felt my muscles grow flabby and my mind empty. To hell with becoming a doctor, I concluded, sold the family furniture, and booked passage to America.

96

I arrived in New York on July 1, 1921, and by the next day I had a job in a fur shop as a combination sweep-up man and errand boy. In Hungary I would sooner have starved than take such a humiliating job, akin to that of a stable boy, but here I was happy and proud. This was a republic and a democracy where each man was free and equal. This is where I belonged!

Two days later a startling sound of explosions woke me out of my sleep. I listened intently, the firing seemed to have spread all over the city. I distinguished not only single shots but also a short burst of a machine gun in action. So it had reached even the United States! The revolution had come to New York.

I threw my clothes on hurriedly and rushed out, wondering where could I get hold of a carbine. The streets were deserted, the stores, usually open by that time, were all closed. It was the revolution all right. There was nobody around except children. Naturally, there was no use asking them, they couldn't know. The firing sounded quite close and it was coming closer still.

I was making my way toward the subway station when I saw a man emerging from there. I rushed over to him and asked him what was happening. He looked at me in obvious puzzlement, uneasy over my anxiety. I repeated my question very slowly to make sure he understood my heavily accented English and asked him where the main fighting was, what the revolution was about? He still did not comprehend. Just then there was a loud explosion right behind me and it made me jump.

"Didn't you hear that?" I yelled, exasperated.

He looked at me, then threw his head back and roared, just roared with laughter.

It was the Fourth of July celebration.

13   Working in the fur shop was exciting. It was a sweatshop but I did not know that then. I worked a seventy-two hour, six-day week. My working day started at seven o'clock in the morning. The boss would come in ahead of me and after unhooking the Holmes Burglar Alarm System he would lay out the work. When I came in at seven, I would sweep the place and wet the skins for the cutters. The men started at eight, quit at five. Afterward I finished up after them, did whatever the boss told me to do, and left some time after seven in the evening. The boss would leave with me unless something went wrong with the Holmes system, which happened often. In that event, we would have to stay and wait until the Holmes men came, checked, and mended the break. Often that took until eight or later. On Saturdays the shop would close down at twelve but the boss and I would stay on. He liked to stay late and always found enough for me to do.

My pay was $12 a week. My parents lived in Philadelphia then and I had taken a furnished room in New York with my cousin. He had arrived in America a few months ahead of me and he was also working in a fur shop, making the same money as I did. My uncle was a skin dealer and he had found his job for him also.

We each paid four dollars a week for the room. Sixty cents of our pay went for carfare, $1.05 for cigarettes, $1.00 for laundry. That left us each $5.35 a week for food and all our other expenses. It worked out to 76 cents per day, 79 cents for Sunday, a holiday. It was very little, but we managed.

Breakfast came to ten cents for a cup of coffee and two hard rolls. After a while we discovered a place where the cups were larger and the rolls the size of a fist.

For lunch I would go to Max's Busy Bee on Sixth Avenue, right around the corner from the shop. They served a big fat hamburger on a big roll for five cents, which included the gravy. I did not ask what kind of meat they used. The burgers were big, the gravy was heavy, and I was always very hungry. I would have two of these hamburgers and a sweet roll with a dab of pink jelly on top. That feast set me back thirteen cents each day, but I considered it well worth the price. It was at Max's Busy Bee that I first discovered how inadequate was the conversational English I had taught myself from books before coming to America. I would ask the people standing at the counter alongside of me: "May I bother you for the salt cellar?" and they would just stare, uncomprehending. My cousin who was learning his English here finally told me how to say it in American.

"Gimme de salt," he taught me. He was a good teacher. I had no more such troubles.

For dinner, my cousin and I would usually splurge. We would buy two quarts of milk, two stale loaves of bread, and two full pounds of liverwurst, the cheapest meat by far and most delicious. That dinner would come to 35 cents each, leaving us with a surplus of eighteen cents daily for luxuries such as an occasional banana, for cultural needs such as a newspaper, or to be saved up for emergencies such as buying razor blades or handkerchiefs.

I usually went through my entire pay but my cousin managed to save part of his. By the end of three weeks he had accumulated considerable capital. He wouldn't tell me how much but I suspected he had at least three dollars saved up. I envied him and made bitter reproaches to myself for being a wastrel, too self-indulgent for my own good. I knew I needed self-discipline and made resolve after resolve not to be such a spendthrift but I simply lacked the necessary firmness of character.

Of course, from time to time certain complicated borderline

cases would arise that made it difficult to decide what was the more economical practice to follow in this puzzling land. Take the case of the handkerchiefs.

The air in all fur shops is full of flying hairs, a constant irritant to nostrils unaccustomed to it, as ours were, necessitating the use of an unusually large number of handkerchiefs. Our landlady did not allow us to wash them in our room and the laundry charged four cents apiece. So far, all good and well.

However, peddlers would come around the fur market selling handkerchiefs for five cents each, six for a quarter. This posed a real dilemma. Laundering six soiled handkerchiefs cost twenty-four cents, while here were six brand new handkerchiefs for twenty-five cents, costing only a penny more. What was the economically sounder practice?

My cousin decided to continue to have his laundered. A penny saved was a penny earned, a bird in the hand was worth two in the bush.

To me, the latter analogue rested on a false premise. Birds fly away but handkerchiefs were solid, tangible objects which once bought became personal property, i.e., wealth. I decided on the long-range capital gain, buy new ones, save up the soiled.

Life proved my cousin right. Months later when we decided to move from that place, I found my suitcases filled to overflowing with brand new but soiled handkerchiefs. It was either pack them or my clothes. One or the other had to be left behind, and of course the clothes won out. My capital accumulation was wiped out at one fell swoop—my first painful experience with that economic phenomenon termed "business cycle." My cousin who was secretly worried about my daily rising stock of handkerchiefs, now showed open relief. He was gracious enough to console me, however, by explaining:

"One day you're up, the next day you're down. That's America."

14 THE shop was fun. It was hard work, manual labor, but I enjoyed it. When other new immigrants complained about their "degradation" and cried for their old life in the "old country," I treated them with contempt. My old life was all in the past, buried and forgotten. It was wonderful not to be idle, a pleasure to be working.

Mr. Kourash, my boss, saw to it that this pleasure was prolonged. He kept me busy every minute of the day for the twelve hours I worked. Ours was a nonunion shop and I had to be all over the place helping everyone, cutters, operators, nailers, "working to their hand." Mr. Kourash was smart, said to have been in vaudeville in his youth, a fact which increased my respect for him. He was far above the workers in his shop in brains, also in schooling. Most of the men in the shop could hardly write, some did not even know how to keep their tallies accurate. One thing in particular astonished me. There would be constant arguments between the boss and the cutters as to whether a certain skin was or was not large enough for the given pattern. The boss would usually insist it was, the cutters would argue it was not. To me there was no basis for all that heated dispute, a few quick measurements with the ruler would give the total square inches in both skin and pattern. When I would demonstrate that, the one in the wrong would look at me with mistrust, being ignorant of the most elementary trigonometry. Of course I would be proven right every time by actual results, which made them suspicious of me. After all, I was a greenhorn, certainly no furrier, so how could I foretell with certainty how much one can get out of a skin, when that ability supposedly required years of practical experience.

Within a few weeks I had my own chores sufficiently well systematized to find time to assist the nailers in their work. We really needed another nailer but Mr. Kourash would not hire one, preferring to press for higher production. The nailers produced between forty to fifty collars each. Soon I nailed an additional 15 to 20 collars, which greatly eased the pressure on them.

My cousin had been raised by his boss to $15. Next Saturday I was eagerly awaiting my raise but it failed to materialize. My cousin taunted me about how much better his boss was; besides, that three dollars made a tremendous difference between his new standard of living and mine—he could now afford to eat more. Finally, after another week went by, I mustered up enough fortitude to speak to the boss.

"Mr. Kourash," I approached him with trepidation. "I would like to talk with you." I did not have the chance to continue because he cut right in.

"I want to talk to you, too," he said. "I want to tell you how pleased I am with you. You're intelligent, you're ambitious, you're honest, you're dependable." It was quite a speech and it filled me with gratitude. I *thought* he liked me but now I *knew*.

"Now," he paused dramatically, "I'll show you how great my confidence is in you. Here are the keys. I am entrusting you with them. From now on you'll open and close the shop." I was both elated and touched. I was advancing rapidly, indeed. Here I was, only five weeks in America and already entrusted with the keys to an entire shop. Mr. Kourash did not say anything about the raise and it would have been indelicate to mention that in that uplifting moment.

What if I didn't get the raise! I had the keys. It meant getting up still earlier to have the shop open by 6:30, and leaving later in the evening, but it did not matter. I had the keys! One night something went wrong again with the burglar alarm and I had to wait until ten before the Holmes people fixed it. When I mentioned that to Mr. Kourash the next day, he was most sympathetic and told me that next time that happened it was all right for me to nail up a few more collars while waiting.

My cousin was far less impressed with the significance of the keys and I was wondering whether he wasn't right after all. I was determined to ask for a three-dollar raise the next Saturday. It was just and I had more than earned it. The more experience I gained the more work I had to do, and the harder I worked the hungrier I became. I was already in debt to my cousin for $1.20, all of which I had spent on additional food.

The next Saturday I called the boss aside again. "Mr. Kourash, I would like to talk to you." I started where I had left off the previous Saturday.

"I want to talk to you, too," again he interrupted with a majestic gesture. "I want to tell you how pleased I am with the progress you are making. To show how much I think of you, beginning this week I am going to pay you one dollar more."

He was giving me a raise voluntarily without my even asking for it! He was really a good boss, a fine man to work for. True, I had intended to ask him for a three-dollar raise but I couldn't do that under these circumstances. A man is not a pig.

Thirteen dollars a week still did not allow me to buy all the food I needed. I was always hungry. My cousin had been raised to $18 that week and the week after that to $20, all without his even asking for it. The season was on, the men in the shop were all working overtime and got paid for it, I didn't. My cousin asked me to go to work in his shop, he had talked with his foreman and he was eager to take me on. That Saturday I went to the boss and asked him for $18 a week. In truth I had planned to ask him for $20, but faltered at the last minute.

Mr. Kourash was deeply wounded by my action. Here he was treating me like his own son, entrusting me with the keys, giving me all the opportunity to learn the trade. He had been accustomed to people taking advantage of his trusting confident nature, of his generosity. But never, never did he dream that I, of all people, would show such ingratitude. He became real angry, and gave me a terrific dressing down, accusing me of treachery, of cold-bloodedly stabbing him in the back.

I felt wretched and miserable. Had I known he would take it so personally I would rather have cut my tongue out than bring up the subject. I tried to explain to him that all I wanted was a few dollars more and only because I was always hungry, that the hard work and the long hours, which I did not mind at all, gave me a much bigger appetite, which in turn put me deeper in debt to my cousin. But every time I wanted to interrupt him he waved me aside. By the time he finished it was too late for that explanation, I was too choked with emotion to talk. I took the keys, laid them silently on the table and went to put on my jacket to leave.

"Where are you going?" asked Mr. Kourash, his voice again gentle and kind as it had always been with me.

"Home," I answered miserably, "you don't want me here any more."

Mr. Kourash was amazed. Of course he wanted me, hadn't he told me dozens of times how highly he thought of me, how much above the average, the common run of shopworkers I stood in his esteem? Not only that, he was going to raise me one dollar to fourteen dollars a week.

But my jacket was already on; besides, I was too emotionally disturbed to listen. To prove how unjust he was in his accusation I told him that my cousin had been raised to $20 without ever having asked for it. Mr. Kourash's face turned crimson.

"So that's what it is?" he roared. "It was he who put you up to this!" He knew my cousin, he would often come to the shop and wait for me to have lunch together. My cousin had a full lunch hour while I would get away only when I could. Now that

Mr. Kourash discovered what was back of it all he was no longer angry with me. He told me that he knew from the minute he laid eyes on my cousin that he was a born trouble-maker and predicted that he would come to no good end. He advised me to stay away from him in the future and to inform him that he was not to set foot again in his shop, ever. He realized I had been misled and offered me $15 a week.

By then I was stubborn. I had not mentioned my cousin's pay for the purpose of bargaining but merely to refute his accusations. Now that Mr. Kourash had blamed my cousin, it was important to set the facts straight. "My cousin is getting twenty and I know the trade better, produce more work than he."

Mr. Kourash picked up the keys, handed them to me and said in a soft, gentle, paternal voice, "You will be paid $18 beginning next week." He was so kind about it I felt like embracing him. The raise was to start the next week and it would have been absolutely in bad taste to remind him of that extra dollar for this week he had first offered. That dollar would have bought me an extra hamburger and a double sweet roll at Max's Busy Bee every day that week, for which I greatly hungered, but—a man can't be a pig.

It was a very good season for furs that year and the rush was on. The nailers got hopelessly behind and there was not an unemployed nailer to be found in the entire fur market. Mr. Kourash called me aside one day and asked where my cousin was, he hadn't seen him around for quite a while. When I reminded him that he had forbidden my cousin to set foot in his shop he waved that aside and asked me if I could influence him to quit his job and work for him. That way, since we were close friends, the two of us could be together all day. I told him that my cousin was by then making twenty-five dollars a week. Mr. Kourash said to offer him thirty. My cousin was willing but wanted thirty-five. Mr. Kourash was outraged over that impudence from a greenhorn yet he not only hired him, but also agreed to pay him for overtime, on which my cousin insisted. The entire shop was working overtime until nine every night and my cousin was getting prosperous. He bought himself a new suit, a pair of shoes, three shirts with silk stripes, and even a sapphire tie-pin for thirty dollars.

I was turning out more work than my cousin, I put in fourteen hours a day, and I was still getting only eighteen dollars a week, no overtime. In addition to that I had acquired other responsibilities. I had a system worked out and knew even better than Mr. Kourash where and how to straighten out bottlenecks, what orders had to be rushed out first, and so on. The men would rather turn to me than to Mr. Kourash if they needed anything, preferring to take their instructions from me. It was a gradual change-over and no one knew how it had come about but it definitely improved production. I took stock of the existing situation and then approached Mr. Kourash, boldly asking for an outright raise to thirty-five dollars plus overtime pay, like my cousin was getting.

This time Mr. Kourash did not roar. He took me to his office, invited me to sit down and we had a long talk, a confidential one. He told me, in the strictest confidence, that all the workers in the shop would be laid off as soon as the season was over, all except me. He did not consider me on their level, a worker, but as his assistant, his right-hand man—I was to have a steady job with him as long as he lived. Furthermore, he was getting old. I was making excellent progress, eventually he would turn the entire shop over to me. He had been working hard long enough, he often wanted to take it easier but he had never been able to find anyone sufficiently trustworthy until I came along. It was a serious talk and it opened up a bright future for me. America was really proving to be the land of unlimited opportunity. He also raised me to twenty-five dollars right there and then. As a steady employee, who gets paid whether the shop works or not, of course I was not entitled to overtime pay—a fair and reasonable conclusion.

My cousin and I had been getting along very well except for his occasional cynical attitude which I resented. He jeered again when, in strict confidence, I related my talk with Mr. Kourash to him. Having been less confined to the shop than I, he had broader contacts with other fur workers on the market. He said that all fur workers expected to be laid off after the season, that was why he wanted to make all the money he could to tide him over until next spring when the shops opened up again. He ridiculed me for overvaluing my position, he did not mind from whom he was taking orders, me, Mr. Kourash, or anybody, as long as he was paid for it. My cousin had also been a student in Hungary and I told him I was distressed to see how rapidly he had assumed the attitude of a common shopworker. He laughed and told me I would soon find out that a shop was not an officers' club and the word of a boss in America was not the bond of a gentleman. I saw no sense in arguing against such a prejudiced attitude and so I dropped the subject.

Four weeks later the season was over and all the men in the shop were laid off, including my cousin. My approach to my job had paid dividends. When I pointed that out to my cousin, he merely shrugged his shoulders—he hoped for my sake that I would be proved right.

The next week in the shop was like a dream. I nailed up the few remaining collars and then a small order came in. Since Mr. Kourash was no mechanic that left it all to me and I cut, sewed, nailed, and finished up that order brilliantly all by myself. I was really getting to be an all-around master furrier, the kind that was getting scarce in the trade.

After that order had been filled I set about to clean the shop. I swept and mopped every corner, every inch of the floor, sorted all the patterns, took inventory of the stock, bundled up all loose skins and hung them neatly on the racks. When everything was spick-and-span and a joy to behold, I called Mr. Kourash in and proudly displayed the shop to him. Mr. Kourash examined everything minutely and was greatly pleased. He then pulled out sixteen dollars and told me he wouldn't be needing me any more, I should see him next spring, and to leave the keys on his desk.

He wouldn't even let me finish out the week!

He even shortchanged me thirty-five cents!

15 That winter was tough. I had very little saved and couldn't keep up with my cousin's new high standard of living. He wouldn't eat in any more, he was taking all his meals in lunchrooms and delicatessen stores, sometimes even in a real restaurant; so we separated. I moved to a filthy bug-infested room just off Tenth Avenue, not quite a flophouse but the nearest thing to it. Even though I pulled my rusty iron bed into the center of the room and sprinkled insect powder all around the legs the bedbugs still outmaneuvered me. They crawled around the ceiling above the bed and then just plopped down.

I did not find another job for months. By then I was actually down to starvation level, subsisting on one meager meal a day. I had developed an almost continuous cramp in my stomach and spent hours in front of restaurants just reading the menus. In fact, that was all the reading I did because in that state I couldn't concentrate on anything outside the "Help Wanted Male" ads. Always a voracious reader, I would now sit in the library for hours with a book open in front of me, without turning a page. I was so hungry my eyes would blur and my mind wander, developing delusions.

I had only a few pennies left in my pocket, seventeen to be exact, the day I finally landed a job.

That evening I asked the boss for a dollar loan until payday. The next night I did the same and every night thereafter until the end of the week. I had been hired at twenty-five dollars a week as a nailer. Nailers were then paid thirty-five to forty dollars and

I was a fast one, but I had asked for only twenty-five so as to get the job.

On payday the boss handed me thirteen dollars. I looked at the money and then at the boss. I told him there was a mistake, after deducting the five dollars advanced I still had twenty dollars coming.

The boss said: "No."

"But you hired me for twenty-five a week!"

The boss did not dispute that nor did he claim that my work was unsatisfactory.

"All I am paying is eighteen a week. Take it or leave it."

Borrowing those dollars each day had told him about my desperate situation. He knew I had to take it.

I was learning. I learned that there are variations and degrees in human exploitation. My first boss, Kourash, had exploited my zeal, my naïveté, my ambition; characteristics for which I was personally responsible. Kourash was a rascal; he outwitted me and I could take that without much rancor. But this boss had exploited my desperate need for food, my starving condition, for which I was not responsible, a situation beyond my control. That was inhumanly cruel. I felt like springing at his throat.

I learned that cruel exploitation germinates hate.

Murderous hate!

16 MOST fur shops were small, would run out of work often, and then the men would be laid off. The bigger shops had more work and paid better, but most of them were unionized. In the spring of 1923 I went to the Fur Workers' Union to join up. To my amazement I was curtly informed the union was not accepting any new members, that the union already had more members than there were jobs in union shops.

An intuitive flash illuminated to me the flaw in the logic of that policy, and I was ignorant enough to call that helpfully to the attention of the business agent who had rejected my application. I began to explain to him that if they would let all of us nonunion workers join, there would be more union shops, in fact all shops would be union then.

He wouldn't hear me out. "Are *you* going to tell *me* how to run this union?" he roared. "Gerrare here, you scab, before I break your neck!" He rose from his chair angrily, a big beefy man with a thick bull neck, his hands balled into a menacing fist.

I did not tarry. Although logic was unquestionably on my side he had the more powerful argument. I was puzzled by the union's attitude. I couldn't see how leaders of a trade union organization could miss such an essential point in deductive reasoning. I was too ignorant to know that they were way ahead of me in a higher, more practical form of logic—that they were collecting money from the owners of the nonunion shops to leave their workers unorganized.

I did manage to join that union though, less than a year later. Another fur worker with whom I became friendly "fixed it up" for me, and with that very same business agent, to boot. He took me downtown and told him I was a pal of his, an OK guy, not the kind of a bird who mixed into politics. The business agent was friendly, he even shook hands and promised to take me in, but it would cost me two hundred and fifty bucks "to fix it." That was steep, but I did not protest. I handed him fifty dollars, all I had, and promised him fifty more every other week. It was tough to squeeze that much out of my weekly pay of thirty-five dollars and I had to go back to taking my lunches at Max's Busy Bee. When I made my final payment the business agent took me to another office, had a girl make out my union card, then handed me a receipt.

I had made it—I was finally a union man.

The receipt was for ninety-nine dollars.

Union shops paid better, and we were making more money even though we had to kick some of it back to the business agent; the shop chairman did the collecting.

In some of the shops I met a few so-called "left wingers" who were fighting the existing union leadership, accusing them of corruption. One of them once persuaded me to attend a union meeting in Cooper Union which he claimed would call for a showdown vote with the "right wingers." The leader of the left wingers was Ben Gold, a slender, nice-looking young fellow.

The moment I entered the hall, I sensed a great deal of tension. No sooner did the meeting open than a left winger rose to ask for the floor. A couple of men rushed up the aisles and grabbed him while his supporters jumped up on their seats, shouting and yelling in protest. The speaker, who by then was being dragged toward the exit, was digging his heels in, trying to resist, when my business agent rushed over, hauled off and punched him square in the face. That started a free-for-all on the floor. Others leaped up and started to swing at each other. But amazingly most of the members remained in their seats, watching the fight impassively.

I got excited. I was seated on the balcony and started to yell, "Don't hit him! Leave him alone!" when the two men next to me suddenly pulled me back to my seat, a third one reached over from the back and clapped his hand over my mouth, hard. They warned me to shut up or I'd get it, then demanded to see my union card and asked my name. By then I knew better. I gave them a false name, told them my shop chairman had taken my union card to have the dues stamp put into it, and gave them a wrong shop as my place of work. I also denied knowing any of the men who started the row, which was true, and gave as my reason for yelling that I had become excited. Since none of them had seen me before nor could anyone around me identify me, they let go my arms but watched me suspiciously throughout the meeting. After the left wingers were cleared out one union official made a long speech in English, followed by another official who spoke in Yiddish, but I didn't catch anything of what was being said. That closed the meeting. No vote had been taken.

I attended only one more union meeting after that. By that time the left wingers with Ben Gold were in control of the union and they made attendance at that meeting compulsory under threat of a fine. As it turned out, that meeting was in honor of Benjamin Gitlow, the leader of the Communist Party I was told, who had just been released from jail. I was surprised at that information. I had not known we had Communists in America; I thought Communism was confined to Europe and China alone. Gitlow was greeted by thunderous applause. He made quite a long speech but I was not attuned to politics and it made no impression on me.

Shortly after that meeting I obtained a job as a foreman and since foremen did not have to belong to the union, I quit—I was fed up with being bossed around and was glad to wash my hands of that gang.

17 I DIDN'T do much "roaring" in the early twenties. Those years were spent in groping after knowledge, perfecting my English, taking courses in theater, aspiring to become a playwright.

In those years, my life in America was the isolated existence of the uprooted immigrants who had lost their old environment and were unable to find the right new relationships to substitute for it.

Working during the day, reading, studying, writing by night, gave me no opportunity to meet people with whom I could exchange ideas and discuss the rich manifestations of life around me. I felt very lonely, as if separated by an invisible wall from the teeming population around me. Those were also womanless days. I recall those aching Saturday and Sunday evenings when, having spent my day writing at my desk, I would walk the deserted dark streets downtown desperately longing for companionship, welcoming even the query of an occasional lost passer-by seeking direction. Sometimes entire week ends would pass without my having uttered a single sentence, eating my meals in the Automat, picking up newspapers and cigarettes at the corner stand, tendering my money and receiving my change without a word exchanged. Those bleak anchorite week ends are still etched in my memory. The following Mondays in the shop my vocal cords would feel strangely constricted when forcing out the first words.

Innocent as I was about politics I nevertheless began to observe some ugly cracks in the façade of democracy. The corruption of the Harding administration, the lynchings and floggings by the Ku Klux Klan in the South, the execution of Sacco and Vanzetti, two harmless Italian anarchists clumsily framed for murder, made me realize that everything was not milk and honey in God's own country, either.

As my skill in the trade increased, so did my earning power. By 1927 I was a foreman and making good money. I moved out of my furnished room and rented a four-room railroad flat in an old brownstone house in Greenwich Village, back of Loew's Sheridan Theater. I furnished it comfortably in a Japanese motif —which was the cheapest—with mats, lanterns, Japanese prints, and a huge Japanese paper umbrella hanging from the ceiling for atmosphere; and with two wide beds, for hospitality. Company was no longer a problem, particularly as the news spread in the neighborhood that that well-heeled Hunkie usually had a supply of bootleg liquor on hand. No more lonely Saturday and Sunday nights for me; week ends I always had some kind of a party going on. Gin was seventy-five cents a bottle delivered, five bottles for three dollars. Usually I bought the five bottles where three would more than do, and woke up with a bigger hangover for a dividend.

I met people, a multitude of people, the type of people I had longed to meet—writers, artists, poets, philosophers. I even met the kind I had not wanted to meet.

Life became gay, with company ever present and I enjoyed it to the full, until one night I suddenly looked around and inspected everyone in that crowded apartment. Every nook and corner was filled, people were even perched on the radiators, window sills, on top of the piano, or just sprawling on the floor.

That sight was sobering. Not a single one of those present did any actual creative work to my knowledge. The writers did not write, the artists did not paint, the poets would redeclaim the same few lines they had composed ages ago. I couldn't recall a single instance where I had succeeded in holding a worthwhile discussion with any of them on any serious literary or artistic subject. They were forever talking about their need to express themselves, yet never did a thing about it. Only the girls who were flocking to the Village from all parts of the country managed to approach that goal. Once they discovered what their best medium of expression was—usually a couch—they expressed themselves well, and often.

In all that crowd I was the only one who actually did write, who turned out a play a year. Yet these people were acting patronizingly toward me because I was holding down a job at the same time. They considered me bourgeois! It was a revealing moment. I took my remaining two bottles of gin, poured them into the sink, and declared the party over. That caused quite a fight until the police came and took a wagonload of my guests away. The place was left in shambles and I emerged considerably bruised in flesh but free in spirit. I moved to Lexington Avenue, thus ending that Bohemian phase of my life.

However, life in Greenwich Village did have one positive aspect—it speeded up the process of my Americanization. It had brought me into intimate contact with native Americans from all parts of the country who, outside of an occasional crack at my thick Hungarian accent, never made me feel inferior because of my foreign birth. By accepting me as an equal they helped me to become an American myself, proud of my country, cherishing our traditions.

The "land where my fathers died" has ever since been America to me.

18 By the middle of 1928 I finished my third play. Shubert had taken a five-year option on my first one: with two other plays now going the rounds, a Broadway production did not seem too far off.

Next I turned experimentally to the short story and wrote two. *Vanity Fair* bought them both and invited me to submit more.

I was awed when I saw my name appear in *Vanity Fair* along with such famous writers as Aldous Huxley, Sherwood Anderson, D. H. Lawrence, Ferenc Molnár, and even G. K. Chesterton, not to mention Alexander Woollcott and Deems Taylor. Shopworker or not, I was sure beginning to travel in illustrious company.

There was but one fly in the ointment. I was disappointed in my writing. As a great admirer of Bernard Shaw and Galsworthy, I wanted to write about social problems instead of turning out amusing froth. Now I decided to chance it even though I felt I was treading on unsure ground.

For plot in my new play I drew on my experiences in the Hungarian Revolution. The hero was to be a naive young man suddenly confronted with the problem of whether to uphold law and order which meant protecting the corrupt township officials, or to side with the victims which meant giving in to mob rule.

The play was shaping up well, the characters were coming through sharp and clear, the situation showed rich dramatic promise, when suddenly my foundation began to totter. In trying to delineate the conflicting views of the opposing characters, questions arose in my mind that led to other questions, more and more fundamental ones, such as:

What was law and what was order?

Since those town officials were undeniably guilty of misusing their governmental powers and of cheating those defenseless war widows and orphans out of their allotments, was it still morally justifiable to shield them from mob justice? Is mob justice really justice or vengeance?

Where does justice end and vengeance begin?

In any case was it justice, was it morally justifiable to strip those wretched, freezing peasants of their looted army blankets and clothes when, after all, those were government property?

To whom does government property belong?

Was the Károlyi revolutionary government a legitimate government?

When it comes right down to it, what makes a government legitimate?

Those questions kept breeding like rabbits until I found myself way beyond my depth. I tried to read up on the subject but each source seemed to contradict the others. I felt stymied and when a girl invited me to go with her to visit Norman Thomas, head of the American Socialist Party, I jumped at the chance.

Norman Thomas lived near the Village. His paneled and book-filled study reminded me of a sacristy. I didn't know then that he had actually been a minister. He was tall, handsome, gracious, and cultured, but I found myself tongue-tied and although he invited us to visit him again, I never did. He didn't fit in my play.

That mob leader who challenged the hero in my play was a wild peasant agitator with blood in his eye and Norman Thomas just didn't fit that part. I couldn't imagine him using the words a rabble-rouser was supposed to say.

118

I fretted and fussed, putting my own speeches into the mouth of that mob leader, but they sounded unconvincing. How the hell did I know what those damned peasants really thought or wanted besides looting and stringing up those town officials? Then I recalled the *Uj Elore,* a Hungarian daily published in New York. I had read a few copies of it when I was a new immigrant but it was too radical to interest me. I went out and bought a copy. It was even more radical now; it had gone completely Communist. Those people ought to know all about it if I could only gain entry to them. Then I bethought myself of Emery Balint, a Hungarian writer whose novel I was once asked to translate into English. I knew he was part of that *Uj Elore* crowd, he ought to be able to help me.

I called Balint, outlined my problem, told him I would like him to help me meet some Hungarian radicals so I could acquaint myself with their lingo. Balint was most co-operative and said he would do even better—he would arrange for me to meet some of the men who actually took part in the Hungarian Revolution. As a start he invited me to a public meeting of the Anti-Horthy League scheduled for the following week.

I thanked Balint for his assistance. This was indeed a lucky break. I considered radicals and Communists secretive, clannish people and had never expected that a simple telephone call would get me near them.

That telephone call proved even more potent, could I have divined it. It started me on a journey that made a professional revolutionary out of me and led inevitably to Spain.

19 As I entered the meeting hall of the Anti-Horthy League in the Hungarian section of Yorkville I was rather disappointed in the size of the audience. In my inexperience I had expected to find at least a few hundred people at a meeting supposedly "public" but I counted only fourteen including the three men on the platform, one of whom was Balint. The meeting was already in progress. Balint was speaking but no one seemed to be paying him any attention, the audience was engaged in private conversations of their own. As I made my way to a seat in the rear all eyes regarded me with curiosity and what seemed to me suspicion. I must have been the only "new face" there.

Hugo Gellert, a prominent Hungarian artist widely known for his drawings in the *Sunday World* magazine section, was presiding. He had received considerable publicity a little while back when he was fired by the *World* for refusing to tone down his illustrations for a series of articles dealing with the brutal excesses of Mussolini's Fascist government in Italy. As Gellert related it to me later, the publishers had called him in and told him:

"When we hired you we thought that we were hiring an artist. We find we have hired a radical."

Hugo Gellert's answer was equally to the point:

"When you hired me you thought you were hiring a prostitute. You find you have hired a man."

I do not now recall whether it was Gellert or Balint who gave the main address. The speaker talked about the necessity of fighting the Horthy terror which, translated by him, meant building the League. Later I was to learn that formula well. In left-wing circles to fight for or against any cause is always equated with building the organization.

The discussion was mostly about the long-overdue issue of the Anti-Horthy League magazine. The League had difficulty in raising the required funds and in consequence the monthly had not been coming out monthly at all.

Before the close of the meeting Balint called on me publicly to join the League. This unexpected invitation took me unawares. I replied I had not given it any thought as yet, besides as I understood from that meeting, the Anti-Horthy League was an affiliation of Hungarian societies and not an organization of individual members.

Balint said that was right but I could join the League as an unofficial representative of the Furriers Union. I replied that I had withdrawn from that union, foremen did not have to belong.

Balint still persisted, wanting to know what other organizations I belonged to. At first I thought of the Green Room Club. I had joined that once when it looked as if my first play was about to go into production but resigned shortly afterward, finding it a waste of time. I really wasn't a joiner. Finally I remembered Murphy's Democratic Assembly Club. I had not quit that, I simply never went back again. Perhaps that might do.

"The only organization I belong to is the Democratic Assembly Club," I informed him.

There was a loud gasp. It came from a girl whom I later came to know as Blond Elsie. She was a natural "gasper" which made her presence a valuable addition to all protest meetings. She was a person easily astounded, horrified, made indignant, or filled with sorrow; a veritable human organ who responded instantly to all such calls to emotion with a solitary but powerful gasp. She had a deep bass voice due to a prenatal obstruction in her throat which enabled her to project her gasp to the very last row in the audience—a great political asset in the radical movement.

Balint looked at me incredulously. Could I have been betraying him?

"The Democratic Party, did you say?" he reproached me, sounding shocked.

I was aware I had started something although I wasn't sure what. I explained how I had gone and enrolled immediately after having received my citizenship papers. That was the first time since the start of the meeting that all conversation on the floor had ceased. They listened to the explanation of my motives in attentive silence as if in court.

When I finished Balint looked relieved. He and Gellert went into a hurried consultation with a third person referred to as "Comrade Kovess" who had been sitting alongside of them at the presiding table. (I was introduced to him after the meeting, his full name was Louis Kovess and Balint whispered impressively that he was the "Secretary of the Hungarian Bureau," making it sound important.)

After their consultation Balint announced officially that everything was in order, they would expunge from the minutes that I was a member of the Democratic Assembly Club and the by-laws of the League were hereby amended to allow for individual membership. It was a simple solution. Rules are made by men and can be unmade by them.

I was in and was immediately appointed to the Press and Publicity Committee and also to the Executive Board of the League.

They certainly recognized talent when they saw it. I felt rather flattered.

20   AFTER the meeting Balint, Gellert, Kovess, and I repaired to the Hungarian Workers Club Restaurant in Yorkville and we talked.

There really wasn't any League, except on paper.

The Anti-Horthy League was a disguised attempt by the Hungarian Communist Bureau to extend its influence over the non-Communist Hungarian masses by uniting all Hungarian societies hostile to Horthy into one League secretly controlled by them. The League got off to a promising start when a number of non-Communist organizations responded to the alluring call for unity, only to withdraw hastily when Communist control became evident to them. In consequence, by the time I was elected a member of the Executive Board the League was only an empty shell desperately trying to prolong its existence, although I was not aware of this at the time.

Hugo Gellert, the president, was not a Communist Party member. He was a sincere liberal who hated all Fascists and who was convinced that the Anti-Horthy League could be of great service in curbing the Horthy terror in Hungary.

Balint, the executive official of the League, was a Communist in ideology but not officially a member of the Communist Party, either. I was convinced that he was, because he always referred to himself proudly as a Communist. Only later, when I myself became a member of the Party, did I discover that Balint had never joined. He was too much of an individualist to submit to the authority and discipline of the Communist Party.

Balint, then in his mid-thirties, was a brilliant person, a near genius albeit an erratic one. By profession he was a fresco painter specializing in restoring murals in churches. He was also a musician and composer of sorts, and a powerful writer with the emotional impact of a high-velocity shell. He wrote in Hungarian, Hungarian novels revolutionary in content which made the publication of his books in Horthy Hungary an impossibility.

The third person in the restaurant with us that evening, Louis Kovess, was a shabbily dressed man of thirty-one, of medium height, with a noble forehead and sunken cheeks. He was extremely tense and his eyes glowed with the feverish shine of the tubercular, which he was.

Kovess had been one of the leaders of the Young Communists in Hungary during the Béla Kun dictatorship; it was said he had been arrested by the Horthy police but managed to escape from jail. As the Secretary of the Hungarian Bureau he exercised top leadership over all Hungarian Communists in the United States and Canada.

From that evening on I became one of the most active members in the Anti-Horthy League. Since Hugo was usually too busy with his art, this raised the number of active members in the League to two, Balint and myself. Our own activity was not overtaxing, either. It consisted mainly in the two of us getting together from time to time in my apartment, having a few drinks which Balint called "getting a perspective," and then hatching schemes. The more "perspective" we poured into ourselves the bolder the concepts became and the more feasible they appeared.

As an outcome of those "executive meetings" every once in a while we would "issue a statement," sometimes a MANIFESTO, occasionally even a PROCLAMATION in the name of the Anti-Horthy League which we claimed represented the "might of all the hundreds of organizations united against Horthy," which would then be prominently featured in the *Uj Elore*. In those pronouncements we would invoke dire threats against Horthy and his government, indict them under all counts ranging from castrations to murder and then brand them with our verdict "in the name of the people of Hungary" and, for good measure, in the name of "all mankind and eternal history."

At first I would question how the two of us could take on the responsibility for such sweeping statements. Balint would lecture me, explaining how the two of us, "in the larger historical sense," actually were "the true expression of the muted voices of the millions of Hungarians writhing in oppression." Besides, it was not the two of us, actually, who did the speaking; we were merely articulating "the mighty voice of the powerful Anti-Horthy League which made Horthy tremble"!

Whether we made Horthy actually tremble or not I had no means to ascertain, but we did have one yardstick by which to gauge the effect of our pontifications. When we really hit home we would be vehemently denounced by those American Hungarian newspapers which were subsidized by the Horthy government. Occasionally voices of warning would be raised against us from the various Hungarian pulpits also, thus providing a much wider dissemination of our pronouncements, even if in a negative way. We chalked up all such responses as gains and promptly issued even bolder "manifestoes."

Shortly after I had embarked on this activity our "pipeline" to the Hungarian Consulate in New York (in reality the wife of an artist whom Balint knew and who worked there as a translator) warned us that my name had been put on the Index, charging me with high treason against the Hungarian government, making me subject to immediate arrest and possible execution if I ever set foot in Hungary. It was a disturbing sensation to be so proscribed but I shrugged it off. I was an American. I had no desire whatever to return to my native land. All I was interested in was helping those poor Hungarian masses oppressed by Horthy regain their freedom. Having reasoned that out I became proud of having been placed on the Index. I had long known of Horthy, let him now know of my existence! My being put on the Index seemed to have personalized our relationship and added new zest to my activities. It is far more satisfying to stir up trouble against a dictator for whom one entertains a personal grudge.

One day Balint called me excitedly. Matthias Rakosi (sixteen years later the Communist boss of Hungary) who had been arrested in Hungary and faced a sentence of death, had gone on a hunger strike in jail. Kovess ordered that the League must take the lead to help Rakosi. We were to have an "emergency mass meeting" that night.

Only four people showed up at that emergency mass meeting: Kovess, Balint, Hugo Gellert, and myself. Kovess informed us that Rakosi had been on his hunger strike nearly a week, that protest demonstrations had been planned in Rakosi's behalf in front of the Hungarian Embassies in France and Austria, and that our League must organize a similar demonstration in Washington.

I couldn't see the point. Rakosi was a Communist, while the Anti-Horthy League was a nonpartisan, non-Communist organization. We had nothing to do with the Communists. Let the Communists demonstrate in Washington if they so desired.

Hugo and Balint kept silent. Kovess was most patient with me. The League was anti-Horthy, wasn't it? Of course it was. Rakosi was certainly anti-Horthy, wasn't he? I couldn't dispute that either. Well, didn't that make for a common cause? Besides, neither Horthy nor world opinion would pay any attention to whatever the Communists did. The "whole world" knew that the Anti-Horthy League was a non-Communist organization. I was a non-Communist, a published author. Hugo was a non-Communist, a well-known artist. A demonstration by the League led by the two of us would carry far more weight with the public than any Communist demonstration could. If the two of us were arrested and we then told our story at the trial, that would be news and it would reach American public opinion. His exposition was logical, it definitely made sense, yet the idea of my taking part in a demonstration was repugnant to me. At that time demonstrations were still rare occurrences in the United States and the participants were generally considered to be, even by me, disreputable characters, definitely outside the pale.

The possibility of being arrested appealed to me even less. I was a law-abiding citizen. Arrest to me meant dishonor, disrepute, the antithesis of everything I strove for. In short, I was afraid, very much afraid of the consequences and attempted to hide my fear by raising various objections. The Anti-Horthy League had only three active members. How could the three of us stage a demonstration, and in Washington at that?

I was an innocent. Kovess had anticipated all my excuses and had everything planned. The Hungarian Bureau would send twenty Hungarian Communist Party members along with us from New York. They would be reinforced by thirty other Hungarian party members from Baltimore and from other near-by points in Maryland. In addition, the American Communist Party had also agreed to co-operate and promised to send us another sixty to seventy of their members. All in all we would have more than 100 people participating.

I had nothing more to say. Kovess had confronted me with logic, facts, and figures, a combination I had never been able to resist. A demonstration it was to be, with myself as one of the two leaders. I wanted very much to back out but I couldn't see any honorable way to effect it.

The next night we left for Washington. Only five of the twenty New York Hungarian Communists promised by Kovess showed up. We had about twenty placards with us, one intended for every five demonstrators. We traveled by coach and I tried to sleep but couldn't. I, who from childhood on had intermittently been plagued by two fears, that of going blind or of being confined in an isolated jail cell, was now deliberately traveling on a train to put myself in jail. Why? How come?

I reviewed the salient points in my life. I wanted to be a writer of good plays. I wanted to know life and understand it. I dreamed about fame although not too often. I hoped to be rich but not seriously. What I wanted fundamentally was to be doing the things of which I felt myself capable. I wanted to see injustice done away with, a happy life for everyone. If I could personally help the Hungarian people regain their freedom my life would have a fuller meaning. I recalled with irony my previous trip to Washington, the first and only time I had been there. That had occurred about a year and a half before, when I was spending my vacation as a guest of a distinguished Southern family in Virginia, invited by a lady interested in getting a part in one of my plays. We had been driven to Washington by a uniformed chauffeur in a luxurious Locomobile limousine and my hosts had introduced me to their senators and congressman who greeted me with gracious charm, and who even went so far as to have the recently completed Pan-American Building opened for us when I expressed disappointment that it was closed that day.

Now I was on my way to Washington again, not in sunshine but in cold drizzling rain, not as a promising playwright but as a bum to be arrested. As I contemplated the strong possibility of going to jail I discovered that my former feeling of apprehension was gone, that it had been replaced by a growing sense of exultation. I was being called, I was being chosen. It was a spiritual glow I had never experienced before. It was as if I were floating way up high in the clear sky, supremely confident of the purity of my mission and in perfect communion with the spirit of all mankind. I believe it was a truly religious experience. I saw myself a symbolic knight riding a spirited charger to avenge injustice—and floated off to sleep.

We arrived in Washington shortly after six in the morning,

bleary-eyed and weary. We cleaned ourselves up in the wash-room, smoothed our crumpled collars, straightened our ties, called up the newspapers, and then took the streetcar to the Hungarian Embassy. We saw two women waiting there and soon discovered that those two sleepy-eyed, middle-aged housewives were the sum total of all the revolutionary forces that the American Communist Party and the Hungarian Bureau were jointly able to mobilize from all of Washington, Baltimore, and the State of Maryland. Discouraging as that was, Gellert and I adjusted ourselves to the existing situation.

There we were, nine of us, clustered around the Embassy and not another soul in sight. The gate to the building was shut, the windows closed and dark, the Embassy appeared abandoned.

I was neither nervous nor afraid any more. It was cold and drizzling. I was carrying about a half dozen rolled up placards under my arms bearing slogans such as "DOWN WITH THE MURDEROUS HORTHY GOVERNMENT," "HUNGARY NEEDS BREAD AND FREEDOM—NOT GALLOWS," "FREE MATTHIAS RAKOSI," and so on. There had been one stating "HANDS OFF HAITI," but I couldn't see what Horthy or Rakosi had to do with Haiti and I had left that one in the train.

About an hour passed and the group was getting impatient. We were a sorry, rain-soaked lot, looking more like shivering pedestrians waiting for a streetcar than a determined band of avengers ready to shake to their foundations the pillars of the Horthy government.

We were anxious to get started but Hugo wanted to wait until the newspapermen showed up.

After a while our group attracted the attention of a passing policeman. He continued his walk to the corner and then stopped, watching us from a distance. It was getting close to nine o'clock in the morning and there was some traffic on the street now. Hugo and I agreed we might as well start.

I lined up the people in single file, spaced six feet apart to make the line look longer, rolled one of my placards down in front of me, and told the others to do the same. With each of us displaying a poster the line seemed transformed; stretched out to nearly sixty feet it looked definitely impressive. Hugo and I took position in the lead and then we started marching. I glanced in the direction of the policeman on the corner to see how he reacted in order to formulate my plans accordingly. He was hurrying away.

It was a most awkward line. We were nervous and couldn't keep six feet apart, we would unconsciously bunch up to avoid the sense of isolation around that deserted building.

The few passers-by gave us a quick glance, then hurried away —that was all the notice we attracted. I brought the column to a halt, there seemed to be no sense to it that way. We went into a huddle and decided to shout so as to provoke some reaction from inside the Embassy. Each of us began to yell but the sound seemed to die, absorbed by that big stone building and by the broad empty street.

We changed to shouting in unison, chanting: "Free Rakosi!" "Down with the Horthy government!" That sounded better. A few passers-by stopped. We were drawing a crowd, although not a big one. They watched us from the curb, not too curious, merely to see what might develop, with that half-interested stare accorded to freaks outside the tent of a side show, all right for free, but not worth the price of admission.

A porter from inside the Embassy now came up to the gate and watched us impassively. We continued marching and chanting in a desultory fashion. It was getting to be a bore, also ridiculous. We were all dejected. My throat was getting hoarse, my arms were tired from holding my poster and carrying that additional bundle of placards under my arm. It was an unnatural position. I had to keep my arms glued to my side, I couldn't raise my elbows or the roll would have fallen.

Suddenly the crowd, which had been slowly increasing, showed a quick sign of excitement. All faces turned to the corner. Six policemen with a sergeant in the lead were coming down the street. Our line tensed. The policemen carried big revolvers in open holsters, held their night clubs gripped in their hands with the black straps hanging from their wrists. They were big beefy men. They were not marching, just walking, heading straight toward us. It was a menacing sight, doom about to descend. The police were now only a few steps away and relentlessly closing in. I stiffened and shouted:

"Free Rakosi! Down with the Horthy government!" The sound did not come out as loud as I intended. A few of the demonstrators responded, but not above a mumble.

The sergeant came right up to me, tightening his grip on his night stick. I drew a deep breath and straightened up. We were face to face, his eyes boring into mine. My neck turned rigid in anticipation of the blow.

"What are you doing here, boys?" His voice was gruff but not hostile, he was on official business and he wanted to know. The tenseness in my neck eased but my muscles were still coiled.

"Demonstrating against Horthy," I replied. He seemed to contemplate that for a second, so I followed it up with further explanation. He listened for a few moments then cut in.

"All right, you've demonstrated enough. Now hand me those posters and go home." While he spoke the other policemen went around and confiscated the placards. There was no rough stuff. They simply reached for the posters and took them. They met no opposition. I sensed that psychologically there couldn't be any resistance, yet that was still wrong.

The sergeant reached for my poster and took it from my hands. Then he pointed to the rolled-up bundle under my arm.

"How about those?" he said.

Somebody had to offer resistance.

"I am going to keep them!" I defied him and tightened my hug on the roll.

"O.K., keep them," he shrugged. "Now get going, break it up." By then his men were efficiently separating the demonstrators from each other. The sergeant next turned to the crowd, which was sizeable by now.

"O.K., break it up—get going. It's all over—keep going, keep going." The crowd obediently dissolved into individuals, each proceeding on his own way. Our people were moving singly toward the corner. Hugo and I remained standing where we were. The policemen barely glanced at us. Just then a taxi pulled up spilling three newsmen and we saw another one sauntering up the street. They talked with the sergeant and then came up to Hugo and me, wanting to know what was up. We gave them the information but they did not appear much interested, took only a few notes. The sergeant then told them and us that that was enough, and we all left, the newspapermen going in one direction, we to the corner where our people were waiting. We instructed them to meet us at the railroad station.

On the train back to New York the demonstrators were elated, recalling to each other in detail just what each of them did and said, what a successful demonstration that had been.

I felt weary and grossly deflated. I was no longer the shining knight and appeared ridiculous even in my own eyes. The entire performance was silly and senseless, the demonstration had accomplished nothing.

That judgment proved wrong. The demonstration made the Washington papers. The news had also been transmitted by the wire services; some of the New York papers picked it up. Abroad, that news item was prominently displayed in the Communist and Socialist press and even in some liberal papers; it made the front page of *Pravda* and other Soviet papers. The greatest significance of the story was that the demonstration had taken place in Washington, citadel of the greatest capitalist nation in the world. That story gave spurt to other demonstrations in other parts of the globe, including Latin and South America. Because of that world-wide spotlight, Admiral Horthy did not dare to have Rakosi executed; he commuted his sentence to twenty years' imprisonment.

My judgment had been based on what had actually happened, on our sorry showing in Washington. I had failed to comprehend how well Kovess understood the art of propaganda.

Our demonstration had indeed saved Rakosi's life.

When Rakosi was installed in power by the Soviet Red Army in Hungary some sixteen years later the Socialists and Liberals everywhere were too disunited to organize demonstrations to save the lives of the untold numbers of Liberal and Socialist Hungarians Rakosi had sentenced to the gallows. Not that it would have mattered. Rakosi, as a Communist, understood full well the power of aroused public opinion—he owed his life to it. When he came into power he saw to it, through terror and censorship, that public opinion reflected but one point of view.

His!

21   MENTION the year 1929 to anyone familiar with the history of the twenties and he will immediately think of it as the black year of the stock market crash in October. But this was still summer, one of those beautiful lazy Saturdays which brings songs or at least a gay whistle to the lips. I rose late, made my breakfast, and leafed leisurely through the morning paper. A small news item caught my casual attention. It stated that beginning at midnight, according to an announcement by the Bell Telephone Company, regular transatlantic telephone service would be instituted between France and the United States. The call to France could be made from any regular phone in the United States and the price for a three-minute telephone conversation was given as seventy-five dollars.

For some unaccountable reason this little item pleased me as if I had been handed an unexpected little present. I cast an affectionate glance in the direction of my private phone which I treasured as a mark of personal achievement. To me that private phone signaled the end to those furnished-room days when the landlady would yell up from the bottom of the stairwell, "Hey, there's a phone call for you." It meant the last of those suspenseful moments I had experienced every time the phone rang downstairs, the anxious search for a nickel before I could put a call through. This was my very own private phone; when it rang it was for me! That item made me gaze even more fondly at my phone, practically telling him, fellow, you don't know it, but beginning at midnight anyone can pick up a receiver just like yours and talk straight to Paris.

Over my second cup of coffee I wondered what kind of a man would want to talk to Paris badly enough to throw away seventy-five dollars for that whim. What a thrill it would be to call up someone in Paris out of a clear blue sky. "What's the charge, operator, seventy-five dollars? That's all right, put him on." And then my thoughts wandered off to wherever such fancies fade away.

Further back in the paper I came across another brief item which stated that Count Mihály Károlyi, former and first President of Hungary, his visa difficulties smoothed out with the State Department, would visit the United States to go on a lecture tour for a well-known New York lecture bureau.

I was glad to hear that Károlyi had finally received permission to enter the United States. I made a mental note to attend his lecture and perhaps find a way for a personal visit with him. I wanted to learn more about the 1918 October revolution from him for my play.

I spent the rest of that day in a manner befitting that balmy Saturday. I walked to Central Park, took a ride on top of the Fifth Avenue bus, and decided to top off the evening by having dinner at the Hungarian Workers' Home Restaurant and talk some Hunky for a change.

As I entered the crowded restaurant fragrant with the spicy odor of goulash, stuffed cabbage, and chicken paprikash, I noticed Kovess, Balint, and Hugo Gellert in an excited and what even appeared to be a conspiratorial huddle over a table farthest in back. They were sitting right under one of Hugo's cubistic, violently red and blue-green murals. There was no food on their red-checked tablecloth. They were not dining, they were having a meeting. I waved hello to them and was about to seat myself at another table when they called me over.

It was an emergency meeting. Kovess was very agitated, Hugo

was pale and nervous, and the usually witty Balint looked solemn and serious. Their discussion was about Károlyi's forthcoming visit. They felt themselves betrayed. I didn't know why, so I inquired.

There seemed to be quite a few angles to it.

Count Károlyi, who had been vacationing in France in 1914 at the outbreak of the First World War and who had been subsequently interned by the French, had opposed Hungary's entry into the war from the start. In 1916, when the French finally released him, he came to the United States to rally the Hungarians to his cause. His liberal views, his advocacy of land reform and redistribution of the land—all these coming from a Count, one of the richest members of the old Hungarian aristocracy, made him an idolized figure among the Hungarian immigrants, mostly former peasants now working in the mines and mills of Pennsylvania, West Virginia, Ohio, Indiana, Illinois, etc. Old mustachioed Hungarians openly wept, women kissed his hands and the hem of his garment, and they donated over $100,000 to a Károlyi Fund for land reform. Subsequently, when the United States entered the War against the Central Powers in 1917, this Fund was frozen here by the government.

After Horthy seized power in 1919, Count Károlyi went into exile in Paris where he drifted closer and closer to Communism by maintaining contact with Béla Kun in Moscow and the Hungarian Communist Bureau in Paris. Although he was not an actual Communist Party member, Károlyi had become such a close sympathizer that he had submitted himself to Communist Party discipline.

Kovess, a man of bold imagination, had tried to bring Károlyi over here for another tour to build up the Anti-Horthy League and the Communist Party. Károlyi had been willing, but when he attempted to enter the United States in 1927 he was refused a visa and turned back at Ellis Island. Hence the announcement in that day's *Times* came as a bombshell to Kovess. Károlyi had evidently now received an entry permit and was coming here, not for the Hungarian Bureau but to lecture in English to American audiences, under the auspices of an American lecture bureau! That was an outrage, a betrayal of the Hungarian revolution.

"We will break up every one of his lectures," Kovess vowed. I was amazed at that attitude. Károlyi certainly did not deserve that kind of hostile treatment. Why not let the Count finish his scheduled lecture tour in English and then be asked to go on a Hungarian tour for the Anti-Horthy League, I suggested.

Hugo seemed to agree but Balint dismissed my idea with a wave of his hand, intolerant of my "political ignorance."

"That would be like sending a whore down from the officers' bordello to the enlisted men after the officers got all the juice out of her." Balint was fond of military allusions.

"We can't have him second-hand," Kovess objected. "He wouldn't draw the crowds—the novelty of his presence would be worn off by then."

I persisted. I argued that Károlyi's lectures in English before American audiences would not detract from his appeal to exclusively Hungarian audiences later.

My stand made no impression on Kovess. He kept insisting that Károlyi would have to lecture for us first, or be prevented from lecturing at all. Hugo Gellert now also came to Károlyi's defense. They were personal friends; he had spent considerable time in Károlyi's company on his last visit to France.

"I believe Count Károlyi is not fully aware of the political implications of that lecture tour," Hugo asserted. He suggested we send the Count a letter at once explaining the situation and asking him to lecture for us instead.

"Your observation is sound but your accompanying suggestion is not," Kovess reprimanded Gellert. It would take two weeks or more for a letter to reach Károlyi and another two or three weeks to receive a reply. Besides, it took time to organize a successful Hungarian tour. Taking the matter up with Károlyi by cable was also ruled out by Kovess on the grounds of needed secrecy.

Hugo had another suggestion. He proposed to drop his work and sail to Paris immediately if the fare for his passage could be raised. We looked expectantly at Balint who then proceeded to give us a treasurer's report on the current fiscal status of the Anti-Horthy League. The League had a minus balance of $28 in cash, money paid by Balint out of his own pocket for current expenses, plus a couple of hundred dollars of other negative assets, such as long overdue printers' bills, etc. Kovess next reported that the Hungarian Bureau was equally flat broke, he hadn't collected his $15 a week salary for over a month. He had been living on short rations.

It was a dark, insoluble problem when I suddenly had my inspiration!

"Why not call up Károlyi?" I suggested.

They all looked at me as if I had gone insane.

"Call him up? He is still in Paris!"

"Sure, call him up in Paris." I enjoyed my triumph. "Right one second after midnight." And I explained it to them. That changed the entire aspect. They were greatly excited. The problem then boiled down to one question: Where could we get hold of $75 cash? I had twenty-odd dollars on me, Balint had about ten, Hugo two and Kovess some small change. We next explored the possibilities of borrowing that seventy-five dollars until Monday. They were nil. Then another inspiration hit me. I was sparkling that night.

"Why not make the call from my phone? That would give us time until next month to pay the bill." This idea was accepted with enthusiasm. I may have been politically naive and inexperienced but I certainly proved to be a reservoir of decisive practical proposals. We agreed to split the cost of that phone call among the three of us, Hugo, Balint, and myself, each contributing $25. Kovess also offered to chip in five dollars but we turned him down. He protested, although he knew he couldn't raise that five dollars, and so did we.

We repaired to my apartment in a state of great elation. I was particularly exultant over the juxtaposition of those two small news items. I could never put such an incident into a play, I mused, no such coincidence would be accepted by the critics.

In the apartment we all sat down with pencil and paper, planning. The problem, as outlined by Kovess, was twofold.

First, we had to formulate our plans and proposals so clearly that Károlyi could not possibly misunderstand them; secondly, we had to boil our message down not only to fit into the allotted three minutes but also to allow Károlyi sufficient time for his reply.

It was not easy, although we had a couple of hours for it. According to Hugo, Count Károlyi had a strict, never-varying routine. He would get up at seven, shave, shower, get dressed, bring in the morning papers and sit down to breakfast precisely at the stroke of eight. Consequently, taking the five hours time difference into consideration we decided to make the call at 3:00 A.M. sharp, New York time.

We worked away in deep concentration, discarding draft after draft as being too long. Kovess then announced that we should divide the call into five distinct parts. One minute for our message, forty seconds for Károlyi's answer, thirty seconds for our second argument, twenty seconds for Károlyi's second reply, ten seconds to be held in reserve for emergency, in case Kovess had to invoke party discipline to force Károlyi to conform.

That was precision planning, my first chance to witness the superiority of Communist organization, to observe a Communist Party leader in action. Everything foreseen by the scientific method of dialectical materialism, split-second provision for all possible emergencies! I could now see why the Communists had a valid claim on the future. I was awed.

It was superior organization and with four excellent brains working in brilliant co-ordination we had the problem eventually licked. We cut and cut, formulated and reformulated, evaluated and re-evaluated, phrased and rephrased, until we arrived at the irreducible which was yet crystal clear in meaning and purpose. Kovess then read the text aloud to Hugo. Hugo was to do the actual talking because Károlyi knew him personally and thus he would not doubt the authenticity of our proposal.

We sat in suspense while we timed it.

"Hallo! Count Károlyi? This is Hugo Gellert speaking in the name of the Anti-Horthy League and the Hungarian Bureau. Now that you evidently have your American visa we insist that you cancel your scheduled lecture engagements and go on tour for us. We guarantee a mass audience of over two hundred thousand Hungarians. You will speak in New York, Cleveland, Chicago, etc., etc."

Kovess read it rapidly, but it still took one minute and forty-three seconds—far too long. More cuts were needed and we fell to it at once.

We cut out "Hallo"; this was no time for formal greetings. We cut out "Hugo" for Károlyi knew what Gellert's first name was. We cut out "speaking," it would be evident that Gellert *was* speaking, Károlyi wouldn't hear him otherwise. Out of the phrase "Now that you evidently have your American visa" we cut "now," for Károlyi would know we were referring to the present. Cutting out "now" automatically eliminated "that" because then it would have referred to nothing. We eliminated "American": since we would be calling from New York Károlyi ought to be able to deduce the reference was to America, and so on down the line. It was a severely tasking effort of excision, the editors of the digest magazines would have applauded our determination.

Kovess now read it out loud again. By racing through it, he made it in 58 seconds flat with two precious seconds to spare.

We were jubilant. I turned the script over to Hugo to read it over to himself a few times, and when ready, I would time him.

When Hugo began to read out loud we turned pale. Hugo was slow of speech and as he plodded on in his slow drawl the speech seemed to stretch into eternity. It took him one minute and fifty-five seconds to finish—a catastrophe. It was impossible to cut that message any further without loss of clarity.

In desperation I set myself to coach Hugo in his delivery. Kovess and Balint were hanging on each word, their lips moving silently with Hugo's. All I managed to achieve was to bring him down to one minute forty seconds. It wasn't nearly enough. He had to speed it up more.

I asked Hugo to read it over again, to stress his consonants, which would compensate for slurring his words and thus gain time. He tried it. Kovess and Balint were leaning forward, their eyes glued to Hugo's lips, practically pulling the words out of his mouth. Hugo was laboring under a strain. He became more and more nervous, his face became flushed, beads of perspiration appeared on his brow. Suddenly, without any warning, he went into a stammer.

"The Anti—Ho . . . Ho . . . Hoho . . . Hohoho . . . Horthy Lllllll . . . Ll . . . Lll . . . It was no use—he had the stutters, all right. We had no alternative but to let him rest for a while.

Hugo did not touch liquor so all I could offer him was water. There was nothing we could do but sit it out. After a few minutes' wait Kovess wanted Hugo to try again but I demurred, it might have brought on another attack of stutters. We agreed instead to let Hugo speak in his normal delivery, allowing him all the time he needed, and to omit the rebuttal and re-rebuttal. Let Hugo take his one minute and forty seconds and close with:

"You have one minute and twenty seconds to reply."

Time was passing rapidly. At ten minutes to three I called the operator again to remind her that we wanted the call to Count

Károlyi put through at exactly three in the morning. A few minutes later the operator reported back that the lines were clear and she expected the call to go through as scheduled.

Zero hour, three o'clock, was rapidly approaching. We were sitting in a tight circle, leaning forward to the phone, our eyes glued to the second hand of my watch; the clicking of each second sounded staccato loud in the room. When the phone rang we all jumped and four hands grabbed for the receiver. We recovered in time to let Hugo lift it.

"Ready with your call to Paris, sir?" asked the operator.

Four heads nodded in silent assent.

The operator couldn't see that.

"Ready with your call to Paris, sir?" asked the operator again, with a slight edge in her tone.

"Yes, operator!" we shouted in chorus. It burst forth in a roar, we had each found our voices at the same time.

"Thank you!" said the operator and we heard her converse with the operator in Paris. We were so close to the phone that our noses nearly touched. The phone in Paris rang. Then rang again.

No one seemed to be answering. Our tension mounted. The phone rang twice again and then we heard the receiver lifted.

"Hallo" came over the wire and it was Károlyi, we recognized instantly the characteristic impediment in his speech. Four pent-up breaths escaped whistling into the air.

"Hallo" came Károlyi's voice again over the phone. "Who is there? Who is calling?"

This wasn't on our schedule. We nudged Hugo, who swallowed and then began to read his speech.

"Count Károlyi, this is Gellert speaking in the name of the . . ."

"Just a minute please," interrupted the Count. "Hold on just a minute. I just ran out of the shower when I heard the phone ring. I am dripping all over the floor. Hold the line please while I get a towel." The connection was terrific. We even heard him shuffle off.

This was definitely not according to the schedule. We glared at Hugo. "The Count with his never-varying schedule!" The paper was trembling in Hugo's hands.

My watch was ticking away at 41.5 cents per second. Kovess grabbed the script out of Hugo's hands and made a lightning quick correction. It now read: "You have 52 seconds to answer."

The Count came back to the phone and said, "Who is this calling please?"

Hugo started all over again from the beginning.

"This is Gellert speaking in the name of the . . ."

"Who?" shouted the Count.

"Gellert," Hugo shouted back.

"Gellert?" asked the Count puzzled. "Gellert who?"

"Gellert, Gellert. Hugo Gellert," said Hugo, desperately urging recognition.

"Hugo Gellert!" the Count shouted happily. "Hallo Hugo, when did you arrive in Paris?"

"I am not in Paris," said Hugo. "I am in New York."

"In New York? How can you talk to me then if you are in New York?" The Count was both puzzled and incredulous.

"Over the phone," said Hugo.

"Over the phone? From New York?" the astonished Count repeated.

"Yes," said Hugo.

"Amazing," commented Károlyi. "Imagine, over the phone, from New York! Can you hear me?" It suddenly occurred to him.

"Yes, I can," said Hugo, by now completely befuddled.

"I can hear you, too," verified the Count. "What time is it in New York?"

"Three in the morning," said Hugo.

"It's eight in the morning here in Paris," said the Count. "It's the difference in time, you know," he added for clarification. "Is it raining there too?"

"No, it's not raining here," said Hugo. "Is it raining hard over there?" By now Hugo too had become infected with the Count's delight in light conversation.

This was a rout. We were paralyzed, unable to breathe.

"No, it isn't much of a rain," the Count assured Hugo. "It may let up any minute. Wait, I'll take a look." We heard his footsteps depart and a door being opened.

"The speech, the speech, read him the speech," Kovess hissed to Hugo, pointing to the paper in his hands.

We heard the footsteps returning and the Count picked up the receiver.

"It's still raining outside, but it may soon stop. Again, it may not," he qualified, a statesman unwilling to commit himself.

I glanced at my watch, then held it up for the others to see. Three minutes and eight seconds had already passed. We watched the second hand race on in mute horror.

Finally Gellert managed to get down to business and read the message, including the final part, "You now have 40 seconds to answer." Kovess had had the presence of mind to cut it down again.

"Hmmm . . ." mused Karolyi, "I can't do that, Hugo. I am under signed contract to that lecture bureau, you know. I cannot lecture in America for anyone but them. You know what, they are even paying my passage," he exclaimed with delight.

"Tell him that he must, he must," Kovess urged Hugo frantically, "tell him it is a Party decision that he must."

Hugo tried but he wasn't successful. The Count would hardly let him put in a word, he wanted to do the talking. "Write me a letter," he finally concluded, "and I'll explain it to you more fully in my reply."

Suddenly a last thought occurred to him.

"Hugo, we shouldn't discuss this over the phone," he admonished. "You may not be aware of it but a call to Paris must cost money, you know." He hung up.

We were aware of it. His weather forecast alone concerning that slight rain in Paris, inconclusive as such amateur forecasts usually are, cost over eight dollars and sixty-seven and a half cents. When the phone bill finally came it was for $189.55. Balint paid me his $25. Hugo was broke, so he owed me his. Kovess never reopened his bid to pay the five bucks and that was that.

My curiosity as to what kind of a man would actually want to call Paris and pay $25 a minute for the privilege had been fully satisfied.

Eventually enough money was raised by the Bureau to send Hugo Gellert to Paris to deal with the Count in person. He wasn't altogether successful. The lecture agency had threatened an injunction to prevent the Count from speaking anywhere in the United States except under its auspices. Finally a compromise solution was reached. The Count would finish his lecture tour and then speak in a few selected towns for the Anti-Horthy League. When Károlyi gave his first lecture in Carnegie Hall Kovess had thought fit to teach him a lesson anyway, to warn him and to impress on him the consequences of breaching Party discipline. He had a number of Communists planted in the hall who caused quite a disturbance, embarrassing the Count and frightening the audience.

On his tour for the Anti-Horthy League Károlyi did draw large audiences but nowhere near the crowds Kovess had anticipated. Organizationally the tour was a flop, very few members joined, and the League remained a paper creation. Later it changed its name to "Hungarian Anti-Fascist League" to add its weight of a feather and its nonexistent prestige to another Communist front organization, the League Against War and Fascism.

Kovess did succeed, however, in his secret objective, which at the time of that phone call had been carefully hidden from me, and which was the actual motivating force behind all that effort. With Károlyi here in person the Communist Party was able to set into motion that necessary legal machinery which eventually succeeded in unfreezing the Károlyi Fund which by that time, with interest, had grown to well over $150,000. It was a shady kind of deal involving bribery and whatnot, and there were too many hands in it, including that of the Central Committee of the Party. The fight over the division of that loot was finally settled by Béla Kun and the Comintern in Moscow. Károlyi personally did not take a cent of it, the lion's share went to the Comintern and to the Central Committee of the American Communist Party. After it was all divided up and the expenses deducted, the share of the Hungarian Bureau and *Uj Elore* together was far below the figure Kovess had dreamed about; it came to less than $19,000. Louis Bebrits, editor of the *Uj Elore,* challenged even that figure when I discussed it with him later. I could never verify the actual amount even when I became manager of the *Uj Elore,* for the movement never kept records of such transactions.

Just before Károlyi departed from America I managed to spend an evening with him in his suite in a downtown Fifth Avenue hotel, the Brevoort, I believe. I found him a most charming and gracious patrician, a statesman and a patriot, a leader who automatically commanded loyalty. When we discussed the 1918 October revolution he admitted that even though he had firmly believed that the monarchy was a tottering corpse which would fall apart at the first real challenge, neither he nor his associates ever dreamed that it would disintegrate so rapidly under its own dead weight. They were completely confounded when the October revolution came to pass bloodlessly.

I told him about the Kobanya incident, how we had marched out to shoot down the revolution, and, had we been given that order, we would have fired unhesitatingly and accurately to kill.

Károlyi recalled that incident.

"I am glad you did not have to shoot," he smiled at me.

Twelve years had passed since then. Time brings many changes. I was glad, too, by then. Very glad!

22 Kovess and I came to see much of each other; he would drop in on me whenever he could snatch a free evening from his crowded routine. As the secretary of the Hungarian Bureau he was the leader of all Hungarian Communists in the United States and Canada, directing and supervising all their activities. He was also responsible for setting editorial policy for the *Uj Elore,* the Hungarian Communist daily, and writing editorials for it. In addition, the Central Committee of the Party had charged him with the task of involving the Hungarian Communists in general party work as part of the process of "Americanization" of the Communist Party, the membership of which, at that time in 1929, was overwhelmingly foreign born. His visits to me were his momentary escapes from the constant pressure he was under and I encouraged him to come and relax. This was my first experience with a real flesh and blood Communist leader and I found him the most stimulating intellect I had met until that time. He would challenge my every concept of society with biting comment and pungent observation, approaching every problem from a fresh slant and with startling originality.

The key to this insight, as he explained, was the Marxian dialectical approach. To acquire this slant, reading Marx alone as I had done under his urging, was not enough—it had to become "part of one's blood through participation in the class struggle." Marx had merely developed the basic laws governing society, namely, that all social institutions have grown out of the eternal struggle between the masters and the slaves, between the exploiter and the exploited, and explained the methods by which the ruling classes have successfully managed to mask the depraved character of their activities behind a veil of hypocrisy. To penetrate that mask required a constant probing into the question: "Whose economic interests are being served?" However, a person militantly involved in the class struggle no longer had to grope for this answer, he developed it automatically in the course of fighting the class enemy.

One night the talk turned to the concept of an ideal society. I maintained that Communism was a utopian dream. Kovess challenged that. His Communist society was beautiful in concept and plausible. He painted an enchanting picture.

In a Communist society every person would have an equal right to a full share of the products of that society. With private profit eliminated, the productivity of such a society would grow so plentiful that working time would be cut to four hours a day, possibly even less. Leisure time would be taken up by hobbies, most of them socially useful.

There would be no hoarding of goods for it would make no sense. Where a person was free to go to a warehouse and draw at any time whatever clothes or supplies he needed, he would find it not only silly but also a bother to load himself up with, let's say, a dozen suits and clutter up his home with them, to brush them, clean them and otherwise personally take care of them. He would take what he needed and come back for more at another time. Those who liked to see themselves surrounded by clothes, goods, or foodstuff would be made happy by being permitted to clerk in a store.

Thieves—there wouldn't be any. No one steals a sea shell off the beach. If he wants to bother carrying it home it is there for the taking. If he wanted a particular shell that someone had already picked up, he could be trained as a small infant can, to recognize that certain toys belong to an older brother and sister, and to look for some other shell for himself.

What about rare objects, masterpieces, a unique location on a lakeside, mountain top or seashore? People's tastes vary. Not everyone likes a mountain top; the climbing may be too steep for some. Others find the seashore too monotonous, too humid, the frozen lake too cold and desolate in the winter. Objects in great demand and strongly desired would be placed in the public domain, masterpieces hung in public halls for all people to enjoy.

Criminals, homicidal maniacs, sex perverts are sick people—they would be medically treated.

Money was an artificial incentive, developed as a convenient medium of exchange in a culture based on private ownership. Greed was a by-product of that culture. As Lenin said, come the revolution the public urinals may as well be lined with gold as with any other metal.

Capitalism rested on the incentive of monetary reward and on punishment by starvation. Yet even in a capitalist society it wasn't money which drove men to perform the most valued, most respected, socially most important acts.

Does a mother nurse her child, change his diapers, because she expects pay for her services?

Does a father stay up all night with his sick child because he expects a cash bonus for it?

Does a volunteer rush into a burning building to save his neighbor's life because he expects to tender a bill for it later?

How much cash did the man who did not know how to swim demand in advance before he jumped off the dock to try to save a floundering child and who himself drowned in the attempt?

What is the cash value of a Congressional Medal of Honor?

How much money did the early Christian martyrs demand for refusing to say *"Ave Caesar"* and for letting themselves be mangled to death by the hungry lions?

Does a medical missionary elect to practice among the aborigines in the jungle, instead of among the well-to-do in the suburbs, because he expects to gain a higher annual income?

Men give their best for pride in achievement, for their inner satisfaction and peace of mind; to win the approval, praise, and admiration of their fellow human beings. A Communist society would bestow all those rewards and, consequently, because money would not be needed for a medium of exchange, the abolishment of money would cause not a ripple in the social fabric.

Would people be happier in a Communist society?

Kovess hedged on that. All unhappiness caused by poverty, by inequality and social discrimination, by lack of opportunity, by lack of freedom, would simply disappear when their underlying economic causes had been removed.

I found the chink in the armor and pressed it hard.

What about other causes of unhappiness? What if a man loved a girl who preferred another? What if a man was born ugly? What if a man wanted to be a great painter, writer, composer and he simply did not have it in him? What if some people wanted to sleep at night while others wanted to make music?

Kovess brushed all that aside. There would always be individual problems. That was a matter of education, it belonged to the field of psychological research which would eventually yield the solution.

A Communist society would be a happy society, the only possible happy society. It was an historically most desirable goal, the good society of the future. It was practical, feasible, and therefore historically inevitable.

It was an enchanting vision. There was still more to it. This conception of an ideal society was no longer a dream. It was in the process of realization right then in the Soviet Union, under the leadership of the Communist Party, the elite guard of the proletariat. The Communist Party was destined to lead the downtrodden masses into similar revolts all over the world when the right historical moment arrived. Kovess then urged it was high time I quit my ivory tower and took an active part in remaking society, handed me an application card, and invited me to join the Communist Party.

I was entranced. Although the sweatshop in which I worked could hardly be classified as an ivory tower, the vision held out by Kovess was truly inspiring. This was the purpose in life I had been searching for—to help elevate mankind—and now I was offered a chance to participate in it.

In the light of my subsequent experiences it would be easy to claim, as so many ex-Communists have done, that "I was duped." I hadn't been duped, nor was anyone else who ever joined the Communist Party. This is particularly true of those former Communists who joined the Party in the thirties when the great depression laid bare the glaring injustices, brutality, and fundamental weaknesses of predatory capitalism. Each of them, like me, had been led to the party by the vision of a perfect future society, each was motivated by the wish to become, as Kovess had put it, "one of the architects of the happy society of the future." I know I was. When I took that application card I was merely worried about one thing—whether my character was sufficiently strong to brave the hardships and hazards of the class struggle—whether I was indeed ready to sacrifice my material well-being for such a remote ideal. Well, time would tell, I might as well give it a try, I reasoned, as I signed the application card. Kovess was greatly pleased.

"I knew from the moment I met you that you were the right Party material, only I didn't anticipate it would take you this long to come along."

We then went for a walk and Kovess explained that since I knew English he would turn my application over to the New York District for assignment in general party work. This would put me in the mainstream of the American mass revolutionary movement. I was awed by the prospect.

We were just rounding the corner to Gramercy Park when a policeman passed us. Kovess suddenly grabbed my arm in a nervous clutch and I saw his entire body grow tense. I became worried and asked what was wrong.

Kovess' eyes were distended with hatred and he started to revile that policeman under his breath, the first time I heard him curse.

I was astounded. That patrolman seemed a nice, rather friendly looking young man and I told that to Kovess. His voice in reply was harsh.

"Police are all bastard breeds, born inhuman monsters. No humans, only beasts, could be induced to seize their fellow creatures made of flesh and blood and keep them locked behind bars, to deprive human beings of their freedom which is more precious than life itself."

I was deeply impressed. That view of a policeman's function was rather new to me. Thus spoke a real Communist, a true champion of human freedom. I wondered would I ever develop such a spontaneous recognition of all threats to liberty.

A few months after that incident Kovess was transferred to Moscow to work in the Comintern. About a year later he sent me a card from a sanatorium in the Crimea; he was critically ill and his lung had been collapsed in an attempt to save his life from the further ravages of tuberculosis.

That was the last I heard about him until the late forties, long after I had quit the Party, when by chance I encountered one of my former comrades who had just returned from Hungary. After describing the brilliant careers achieved by those of our comrades who returned to Hungary after the Communists took power, he suddenly asked:

"Of course, you know about Kovess, don't you?"

"Is he still alive?" I exclaimed in astonishment. I had thought him long dead of tuberculosis.

"I should say he is. He is back from Moscow and he holds one of the most responsible jobs in the country. He is in charge of all the concentration camps in Hungary!" he added impressively.

"What?" I exclaimed incredulously.

He repeated it and added that Kovess was doing a terrific job.

I burst out in explosive laughter and I laughed uncontrollably until my breath came in gasps and I realized I wasn't really laughing at all. I was back in Spain at the time of the Civil War, my mind on the overcrowded SIM jail in Albacete in the Guardia Nacional, bent on the hopeless errand of rescuing one of our American volunteers from the clutches of the Communist secret police. I have never forgotten those verminous cells jammed full beyond their capacity, with barely enough space to stretch out on the cold stone floor. The nauseating stench of that human cage in that Communist prison suddenly filled my nostrils again and transported me to Communist Hungary.

. . . Two o'clock in the morning, when body resistance is lowest.

A loud knock at the door. Rough voices demanding: "Open up!" Men in black leather coats with machine pistols drawn ransacking the apartment, ripping open mattresses, tearing down curtains. A wife or mother near hysteria and panic, crying children cowering in fright. A rough shove implemented by a kick with a boot: "Get moving, you filthy imperialist swine." The torture chambers of AVO in every Hungarian town, the crushing of fingertips, the squeezing of genitals, whips savagely slashing the naked buttocks of prisoners: "CONFESS, CONFESS!"

. . . Electrified barbed wire with machine gun towers; armed sentries patrolling with savage police dogs unleashed at their side. Inside the concentration camps half-starved wretches writhing in their sleep in dread of the morrow; toiling from dawn to dark like slaves of old under the lash of well-fed, warmly clad brutal overseers. Lording over them all stands the Chief Warden of all the concentration camps in Hungary, Comrade

154

Kovess, patting the Order of Lenin and the Red Star of Rakosi on his breast that he has just received for doing a "terrific job."

. . . That Chief Warden with the master whip, that Red Simon Legree, is Comrade Louis Kovess who some twenty odd years ago had told me in Gramercy Park that no humans, only beasts, could be induced to seize their fellow creatures made of flesh and blood and keep them locked behind bars, that human freedom is more precious than life itself.

It couldn't be, yet it was. It added up. It was dialectics.

Yet there was more to it.

This was dialectics with a vengeance!

23 WEEKS passed and then in September I received a letter. It came in a cheap white envelope, very poorly typed, with no return address. It instructed me to report to Section Headquarters of the Communist Party at eight o'clock in the evening on Broadway between 27th and 28th Streets where I would be assigned to a party unit.

It was an old building and I found Section Headquarters on the second floor, as I recollect it, in a large unpartitioned open loft. A bewildering hubbub of loud voices filled that hall and I couldn't attract anybody's attention. The entire floor space seemed jammed with people grouped in circles; some sat on folding chairs, some of them stood, others squatted on the dirty, littered floor.

It was a scene of utter confusion. The people in the center of those circles were talking to the people around them who in turn were calling and talking to people in the other circles. The groups seemed to overlap. I stood befuddled trying to orientate myself in that chaos until I managed to get hold of someone to show him my letter. He yelled out "Comrade Shapiro!" a couple of times and after a while a slightly built, red-haired young man came over to me. He had a peculiar gait, half shuffle, half shamble; he was slouched forward and he held his shoulders considerably hunched. He was around twenty-five years of age, with a prominent hooked nose and an incongruously thick lower lip; his pinched, narrow face resembled that of a fox. He was

Shapiro, the Section Organizer. There was an air of vagueness about him; he appeared to be lost in all that confusion.

He glanced at my letter, wrote the unit's number on it, then pointed to a group past the center of the room, close to the rear.

I weaved and bumped my way over and handed my letter to a woman who was sitting on a folding chair with piles of books, magazines, and pamphlets by her feet on the floor. She read my letter and announced in a pleased voice:

"Attention, comrades. We have a new member here," and she smiled at me. The others in that group, there were nine, gave me a casual glance and resumed their conversations.

The lady (she was the chairman and unit organizer) was friendly. She was a chunky, plain-faced woman around thirty; she wore her hair braided and fastened into a ring. She had two flashing gold front teeth and was wearing a darkish unattractive dress. She had no make-up or lipstick on and she looked like most finishers in the shop, women but not females, or maybe females but not women, whichever it is that is not a sex object. She spoke with a heavy Polish-Jewish accent. She told me that as a fur worker I would be assigned to work with the furriers' fraction in the Needle Trade Workers Industrial Union. I informed her I did not belong to the Union.

"So you'll join it." She shrugged, disposing of that objection. "Why, you are very young. You should belong to the Y.C.L. You are a youth, you belong in the Young Communist League."

I did not like that at all. I told her I had been a grown-up man for quite a while, a man twenty-nine years old was no longer a youngster by any standards. She insisted that the Young Communist League had to be built. I did not dispute that, merely stated, not out of youngsters my age. She then dropped that subject and read me a long list of topics they planned to discuss that night.

The term "discussion" was misleading.

She started the meeting by reading a long-winded appeal from the International Workers Relief—I.W.R., she called it. It was about a strike somewhere and the poor strikers and their families were starving and the I.W.R. was feeding them, they needed help urgently. A collection was then taken up. She turned to me first and I gave five dollars. The others gave nickels and dimes.

Then came the International Labor Defense. Some strikers had been arrested, I do not recall whether they were the same starving ones or not. Money was needed for their defense. I now gave only two dollars, the others nickels and dimes.

Next came a collection for some other fund, then still another. I gave one dollar each time, the rest, nickels and dimes.

Then came the main topic. The *Daily Worker* was in a very bad financial situation, it faced suspension unless immediate substantial aid was forthcoming. I felt I had given enough by now so I contributed a dime. The others gave quarters, half dollars, someone even a dollar. Everyone was staring at me. It was most embarrassing, I even blushed. I would gladly have contributed more had I but known. But by now I resisted it; I wouldn't let anyone shame me into anything.

The chairman must have sensed how I felt and said to the group in general, "He is just a new member. He can't tell yet what is important and what is not."

Then they went on to literature. It had to be bought. I bought a copy of everything they had, about two dollars' worth. Each of the others bought only one pamphlet for a nickel. As I recall they made seven collections that night, maybe more.

Next came the distribution of collection cans; there was to be a Tag Day that Saturday. I do not recall whether it was for the *Daily Worker* or some other cause. I was handed a shiny tin can with a slot on top and the chairman assigned me to the uptown stairway of the Lexington Avenue subway station at 28th Street. That was exactly one and a half blocks away from where I lived.

I was appalled. I had always entertained mixed feelings about beggars like most of us do, a mixture of annoyance, pity, disturbed conscience, and strong resentment at being accosted. Now I was assigned to become a beggar, right in my own neighborhood where I was known to all storekeepers, waiters, and clerks as a financially stable citizen. That was a situation I had not anticipated when I had filled out my application card. It was quite disturbing.

Next I was given an armful of leaflets to be distributed on my way home from work and in my shop.

I read the leaflet right there and it made very little sense to me. It was in English but a most peculiar kind; each word taken separately was clear but strung together in long sentences they seemed to have lost their meaning. It affected me like hearing "double-talk" for the first time. I told the chairman I was puzzled, I did not understand the meaning of that leaflet. She smiled at me encouragingly and assured me in her heavily accented dialect: "Never you mind, you shouldn't ought to worry, after you should be in America as long as I been, you'll understand English just as good as me, you gotta be patient."

When we adjourned the chairman flashed one of her warm gold-toothed smiles at me; she was fundamentally a nice person in her squat, shapeless way. As I was walking home I noticed it was past eleven o'clock. I was carrying an armful: leaflets, all the literature I had bought, and the collection can. Twenty-eighth Street was deserted. I passed an ashcan. There was no one around and on an impulse I dumped all the leaflets in the ashcan, except one which I kept to wrap around the can. As I walked away I became conscious of a strong feeling of remorse. I turned around to retrace my steps and retrieve those leaflets when I noticed a group of people turning in from the corner. That settled it. The leaflets really made no sense. Besides, I had been shamed, shaken loose from close to twenty bucks, had

159

been handed a collection can like a beggar. That was enough for the revolution for one evening without turning myself into an ashcan scavenger as well.

Came Saturday and I dressed most carefully. As a final touch I even put on my new 100% camel's hair topcoat, though the weather did not call for it. Much as I loathed the idea of panhandling, as long as I was going begging I might as well do it in style.

Saturday morning traffic on Fourth Avenue was not heavy. I took my place at the subway entrance, my camel's hair coat over my arm, the can covered by the coat. Three youths who were together went down the steps. I let them pass. Two other men came, one following a few paces behind the other. I held out my can to the first one. My hand was hesitant, my timing poor, he never noticed the can as he walked down. I thrust my can out to the second man. He saw it, all right—he looked like a salesman or a clerk—he faced straight ahead pretending not to notice. Two girls came. I held out the collection can to them. They snickered, elbowed each other, and went down the steps giggling and whispering together. I became aware of a deep blush spreading on my face.

More people came, men and women both. My arm motion became more and more automatic, more precise. The reaction of the people continued the same. They either pretended they didn't notice the can, or appeared puzzled, or contemptuous. I decided to be selective, to try to guess who would give, and solicit only them. The same reaction. A man came by whom I knew and I hid the can quickly under my coat. Then traffic became heavier, working people, tieless shopworkers. Some of them gave me a sullen look, some grinned at me derisively, one man contemptuously slapped the can away with his hand. I felt like jumping on him but it was too late by then. My anger was rising, I felt like blocking the entrance and shouting to them: "You poor damned miserable bastards, you'd better put something into that can!

I'm doing this for your own benefit," then knock their heads together to teach them how to respond to kindness, to an effort made for their welfare.

I stood my assigned post past my lunch time without receiving a single contribution. I would have quit long before except that my anger against those passers-by had turned into hatred against mankind in general and made me too stubborn to move. By two o'clock, traffic became so sporadic that I did quit. I walked into the cigar store farther down the block and asked the clerk, whom I knew, if he had $20 in change. He had. I went back home and as I broke open the rolls and dropped the coins one by one into the slot my anger slowly evaporated. At any rate, I had done my share and if the people were too stupid to realize their own interests, it was their own hard luck. At least the Party was not out any money even if it had to come out of my own pocket.

The next week at the unit meeting when it came to handing in the cans I was somewhat apprehensive. I wondered whether my collection would be deemed sufficient, I feared they would guess I had not stayed all day.

The first can was handed in and the chairman rattled it—it sounded empty. The comrade explained he had been too busy, he had been kept too long at a Section meeting, he hadn't found time to go out. The next can was handed back empty also. The third can rattled loudly. It contained 37 cents. The fourth can came back empty. When I handed over my can the chairman exclaimed happily.

"Comrades, this feels real heavy."

She rattled it and the sound came dull and muffled. A couple of comrades helped her count it, they announced it was $20.87. It should have been $21.12, for I had also dropped $1.12 of my other change in it. They evidently miscounted a quarter. I almost corrected them before I realized what I would be doing. Everybody enthused and the chairman made a little speech. She told them how that proved again the importance of recruiting new members to the Party, they had enthusiasm and took their assignments seriously. One of the comrades grudgingly remarked that he also would have done much better had he a chance to go out among the masses, had most of his time not been taken up by inner Party work in the district. He was the one who had collected 37 cents. The other comrades spoke in similar vein, they complained that all their time was being taken up with going to meetings in the Section, they had no time left for outside activity.

The chairman partly agreed with them. She was the unit organizer, she had had to go to four meetings that past week, and yet she had found time to do some collecting because that was the most important task, the party couldn't function without finances. After all the money was in, the total came to a little over $25, the highest sum ever collected by that unit in any Tag Day. It was a big success and everyone was jubilant. Again I was handed one of the cans that had been returned empty. Since I was so good at collecting and had no other party assignments, I might as well continue with that party activity.

The rest of the second meeting was similar to the first; continuous wrangling and mutual recriminations about tasks not carried out. I gathered that the activity of party members consisted mainly in going from one party meeting to another, now in the Section, now in the District, listening to what should be done but with no time left for doing it.

One of the first things I learned was that a party member, in order to retain his good status, had to be dishonest with the Party, he had to know how to think up plausible excuses for not having attended all the meetings at which his attendance was compulsory, although he couldn't possibly have found time to go to all of them.

I also discovered that in the Party nothing was ever carried out the way it had been planned or originally agreed upon. Our unit had two long-standing projects, one of which was the holding of open air meetings at which all comrades were supposed to be present. The first of these meetings I went to was supposed to have been held in an empty lot somewhere in the West 100 block, a slum section near Central Park West. That meeting did not materialize because aside from myself and the Unit Organizer no other comrade showed up. The second open air meeting we went through with, although, including the Speaker who had been sent by the Section, there were only four of us present. Another comrade who also showed up promptly explained to us that he couldn't stay because he had to go to another most important party meeting. The speaker, a heavy-set man with a strong Brooklyn accent, spoke from an orange crate while the three of us stood around loaded with pamphlets and leaflets.

The speaker was very dull, he talked about Lovestone whom he denounced, ridiculed, and damned in turn. I tried to follow what he was saying but couldn't. All I learned from that speech was that Lovestone was a most repellent, physically deformed degenerate, a slimy counterrevolutionary, and a hairy capitalist tool. (Years later, when I met Lovestone personally in Cleveland at a CIO meeting, so strong was the impression that street-corner speaker had made on me that I found it almost impossible to believe my own eyes. This Jay Lovestone, who had been General Secretary of the Communist party but later expelled, turned out to be a handsome, charming, highly cultured individual.)

After mopping the floor with Lovestone, the speaker talked on, and it was pathetic. It was like talking to the wind for we were unable to draw a crowd. A few passers-by would stop, listen for a minute or two and walk on. Some of them would accept the literature handed to them, most of them wouldn't. They would leave as soon as they saw us approach with what they must have thought was "the pitch."

The comrade speaker did his very best to interest them. He would raise his voice successively louder as he saw his audience walk away. Soon his voice was hoarse and scratchy. He kept this hopeless task up for about three quarters of an hour and then he quit.

After he stepped off that orange crate, he and the unit organizer estimated that we had drawn about fifty people. I thought they were joking.

However, at the next unit meeting the chairman, in giving an account of that street meeting again set the figure of the people in the audience around fifty, pronouncing the meeting a very successful one. I had to challenge that, she was deceiving the party.

In contradicting her report I told them what I had observed, that nobody paid any attention, that the few people who stopped did so out of mere curiosity and then immediately moved on. I told them that it was most important for the Party to stick to the truth because Marxian dialectics, like all logical systems, depended on recognition of the true facts for the development of appropriate tactics and policies. The facts were that a meeting of that sort could not draw or hold a crowd.

I can't say I expected to be applauded, but I certainly did not anticipate the reaction that ensued. Comrade after comrade, none of whom had been at that street meeting, rose indignantly to point out my ignorance and even to condemn me. According to them, that street meeting had been a success. The Communist Party had set a brave example by holding that meeting, it had demonstrated to the masses that the streets belonged to them. The Party had exerted leadership, had taught the masses how to use their rights and voice their grievances publicly, had imbued them with courage to stop and listen. What if they had stopped only for a few minutes? That was an excellent beginning, soon they would stay longer for courage grows by being put to test.

As they went on stressing that demonstration of Party leadership, that "exhibition of courage" began to take on heroic proportions. One comrade actually stated that the storming of the Winter Palace of the Czar in St. Petersburg in 1917 by the Bolsheviks would not have succeeded had the masses not been inspired by exactly such courageous Party examples. Then the discussion turned personal. I was criticized for having fallen down on my party work as proven by my poor collections of late. There was some truth to that charge, for having realized what a fool I had been I took to dropping only my loose change in the can.

Finally the Agit-Prop, the comrade in charge of Agitation and Propaganda, summed it all up. He welcomed my misdirected criticism, unfounded and ignorant as it was. The fact that I felt free to voice it was in itself a repudiation of the slanders of those antiparty elements who claimed there was no democratic discussion permitted in the Party. Then he pointed out the false petty bourgeois logic on which I had based my arguments. My arguments, first of all, showed defeatism in wanting the Party to abandon its right to free speech. Then he invoked Marxist-Leninist science which went far deeper than bourgeois science. It had been conclusively established that more than fifty people had stopped. That meant a representation of fifty families, say 250 people. Every one of those people had at least four friends, which brought it up to 1,000. Here we were dealing with one thousand people who had directly or indirectly been exposed to a demonstration of Communist leadership and courage, which in turn must have left an indelible impression on them. Come the right time, the right revolutionary situation, those masses would suddenly recall that meeting, they would receive inspiration from it and would go into action, give impetus to the revolution. In short, the seeds of revolution had been planted deep. He was applauded at this point. Finally he warned me that although the Party encouraged discussion I should refrain in the future from trying to spread defeatism and rotten bourgeois cynicism within the ranks of the Party.

Those people were absolutely cuckoo! I was angry with myself for getting mixed up with them in the first place.

I was through with that bunch.

24 ONE night, weeks later, I received a telephone call; it was the unit organizer. She sounded both plaintive and excited. Where had I been? What had happened? To shake her off, I told her I was being kept busy in the shop. I am a poor liar and my excuse sounded lame even to me.

Her mind wasn't on that. "You must come to a special meeting tomorrow night. You absolutely must be there," she said with a trace of hysteria in her voice, brushing my excuses aside.

"I can't tell you why, over the phone. You're the huskiest man in our unit and we're all depending on you." That made me vaguely uneasy.

"I'm sorry but I can't make it," I told her firmly.

"But you must, comrade, you must. Our entire plan is built around you." She was practically crying. "Maybe you're afraid? You are not really afraid, comrade, are you?" she screeched.

I wasn't, not until then. But when she raised that question I immediately became so, which gave rise to the urge to deny it. I told her I would be there and she hung up in happy relief.

I felt neither happy nor relieved. I had three clues to go on. They considered me husky, they wanted me to do something that required physical display of strength, and there was danger involved. What did they want me to do? Beat up somebody? Throw a bomb? As I pondered over it I became aware of actual fear. My imagination was racing wild.

Had they picked me to shoot it out with prison guards, to

assassinate someone, to lead an attack on Wall Street? I tried to reduce it to absurdity to allay my apprehensions.

I was wretched and miserable when I crawled into bed that night, dreading what the morrow would bring. Paradoxically, the one thought that would have eliminated the problem at a single stroke, that of not appearing at that meeting, did not occur to me. That would have been contrary to my innate sense of honoring an obligation.

Section Party headquarters was packed that night. The crowd was far bigger than usual and since the number of chairs was the same, more people had to stand. I noticed an intermingling of the units that usually met separately, the comrades were agitatedly conversing with each other. As soon as she spied me the unit organizer came over to me, gave me her biggest gold-toothed smile, and said she knew the unit could depend on me, that she had assured the unit I was the most sincere new comrade she had seen in years, and kept generally gushing over me. I resented that fussing and thought I would let her discover soon enough how mistaken she was in her judgment of me.

When the meeting came to order there was but one point on the agenda—a mass demonstration slated for Saturday. The new District Organizer, I. Amter, intent on "bolshevizing the Communist Party" and turning it into "a real fighting arm of the working class," had called for a militant mass demonstration to protest the sending of additional American Marines to Haiti. The demonstration was scheduled to take place in front of the New York Post Office downtown in defiance of a police ban, and a police attack was definitely anticipated. I wasn't much interested; Haiti was merely a geographical location to me.

It soon developed why my unit needed me. My unit had been assigned one of the big placards and I had been selected, as the unanimous choice of the unit, to carry it. We were instructed that the police would concentrate its attack on smashing those

168

placards and we were to defend them. Other, smaller placards would be carried under overcoats or rolled up under the arm to be displayed at the right moment. Amter would lead the demonstration in person.

My first reaction was a definite letdown. Is that why they called me, to march around with a large placard like the bums advertising Max's Busy Bee? Had I been asked to throw a hand grenade at City Hall I would have been more gratified. The demonstration was not exactly devoid of danger, the possibility of being attacked by the police, of being shot at, arrested and jailed was not one to be contemplated with equanimity. But I had faced that threat once before in Washington when demonstrating for Rakosi. I accepted my assignment as a test of my courage which, for my own self-respect, needed reassurance badly.

The demonstration was to be a city-wide one, ours was only one of the sections participating. The *Daily Worker* had headlined that coming event for days, ordering all party members, under threat of expulsion, to turn out for the demonstration, and most of the front page of that day's issue of the *Daily Worker* had been devoted to mobilization for that supreme effort. We were going to have a real army, I thought, and that picture gave me confidence.

Saturday morning dawned gray and cold and drizzly again, just like that time in Washington. I got dressed, paid my rent two months in advance, just in case, so I wouldn't be dispossessed if arrested. At that time I was wholly ignorant of American court procedures, of the legal safeguards protecting the accused in a democratic society, of bail, trial, sentence. I still thought in terms of the administration of justice in Hungary, where once arrested they threw you in jail and kept you there without trial as long as they pleased.

The demonstration was scheduled to start at eleven in the morning. We were to assemble at Section Headquarters at nine-thirty at the latest, pick up our placards, literature and leaflets, and leave by ten o'clock in small groups. At City Hall Square we were to form into units, the units into sections in their given order, and then march in a single mass column on to the Post Office where Amter and other speakers would attempt to address the crowd. It was quite a well-thought-out military operation except for a provision for reserves, and it merited respect.

At nine o'clock sharp I left my home. I knew that would get me there a bit early but I was too keyed up to dally around. I forced myself to take slow steps and to look into shop windows to while away the time. I arrived at headquarters building at 9:25, just the right time. I walked up expecting to find a large crowd. When I reached the top of the stairs the door was open but the hall looked dark. I saw the shadow of a man just inside the doorway, he must have arrived only a minute or two before me. When he switched on the light his face looked somewhat familiar, he must have been the Comrade Janitor in charge of the hall.

That empty hall in that dim illumination looked dismal, and it was filthy with rubbish, cigarette butts on the floor, the chairs facing whichever way in hangoverish disarray. The appearance of that hall made me recoil in disgust. What was I doing there? Why was I getting mixed up with that queer messy bunch?

"Where are the rest of the comrades?" I demanded sharply.

"They'll be here," said the Comrade Janitor with indifference.

"We were all supposed to meet here at 9:30 and it's 9:30 now," I asserted.

He shrugged his shoulders. "They'll be here," he repeated.

"But we're having a big demonstration today!" I exclaimed in exasperation.

He shuffled over to me. He was a shabbily dressed, unshaved person, a worn-out, beaten down, superannuated waiter or cloak-maker operator such as you see all over the slum districts without giving them a second look.

"You're a new comrade, ain't you?" he asked. I couldn't see what that had to do with it.

"You new comrades are always in a hurry. You want to see a revolution ipsky-shmipsky right on the dot. It was the same way in Kiev in 1905 when we did have a revolution. Comrade, this is not Russia, this is America. The revolution will take a long time to come. I won't see it, you won't see it, your children won't see it. It will come, but it won't come on time."

I wasn't asking for philosophical dissertation, I wanted action. "What about the demonstration?" I demanded.

"It will be held, don't worry. If not in the morning, in the afternoon it will be held. The comrades will be there, the Post Office will be there, Haiti will be there, the police will be there, everything will be there. The comrades like to sleep late Saturday. So keep your shirt on."

I left him and went down to Horn & Hardart for another breakfast to give me something to do. I deliberately stayed away until after ten. Let them wait for me now.

It didn't work out that way. There were still merely a dozen or so people in the hall when I returned. My unit organizer was there, she was all dressed up, eager and excited as if going to a party. The other women comrades appeared similarly dressed up and stimulated. My observations later made me conclude that women in general are less apprehensive about being physically harmed. Putting women in the front line of action when violence is anticipated has always been sound revolutionary tactics. First, because women usually exhibit more militancy; secondly, the enemy, usually men, is far more reluctant to employ the same degree of brutality when faced with women that it would use against men alone. As to the morality of exposing women to the danger of physical assault, the revolutionaries make up their own moral code to suit their aims. . . .

At ten-thirty the hall was still quite empty although we were supposed to have left that hall by ten; we were now a half hour late and not even the placards had been delivered. Finally the placards arrived and I was given mine. It was about thirty-six by twenty-four inches, made of heavy cardboard nailed to a crossbar fashioned of one-by-two white pine, designed to be hung from a hook screwed into a four foot pole also made of pine. The pole was roughly planed and the placard read:

H A N D S

O F F

H A I T I

JOIN THE COMMUNIST PARTY!

We decided to wait until eleven for the others to show up. When we finally left at 11:30 we were still only about thirty-five strong, although the party plan called for at least three hundred from our section. Out of my unit of fifteen, outside of the unit organizer, the Agit-Prop and myself, only two other comrades, both women, put in an appearance. The unit organizer expressed the hope that the others would meet us at the square. I laughed cynically. I was rehearsing a speech in my mind which I was planning to deliver to her right after the demonstration. It was to go something like this:

"Listen, sweetheart! I carried your placard, I went to your demonstration, I bought your literature, I gave you money. But that is all your Communist Party will ever get out of me. You write and it makes no sense, you make speeches and they have no meaning, you plan and it is all on paper. You go on, piddle with your Communist Party, but I have other, more important work to do. Now good-bye comrade, give my love to the proletariat."

It was quite a satisfying speech and the longer I waited in that hall for the comrades to arrive the more I embellished it until it became polished like dialogue in a play yet to be written. I was itching to deliver it to her right there and then but to have it sound really effective—that had to wait until after the demonstration.

We took the Broadway subway downtown, traveling in groups of two and three in a conspiratorial fashion, acting as if we did not know each other. We were about as inconspicuous as a flock of sheep on Madison Avenue but it did not matter. The other occupants of the subway car contemplated us with that vacant curiosity New Yorkers would give to anything, including sheep.

When we arrived at City Hall, instead of the thousands I was led to expect I found only a few hundred people who looked like comrades. They loitered around with a furtive air, elaborately avoiding recognition of each other. Some of them carried pine posts similar to mine, hiding the placards under their overcoats.

We stood around until Amter arrived. He was about fifty, tall and lean, smooth-shaven, with a sharply chiseled profile, his jaw twisted slightly to one side. He was surrounded by some of his lieutenants and appeared too nervous to be a good leader, but when I saw his eyes it was all right, it wasn't from fear. I had developed a sort of apprehension over the fate of this demonstration, I feared that it would turn out to be a fizzle, very much like that open air meeting our unit had held. I didn't give a hoot about Haiti but once I had committed myself to that demonstration I wanted to see it through. As soon as I had laid eyes on Amter from a close distance I knew that the demonstration would go through, even if not on schedule, even if only a fraction of the comrades would turn out for it.

Soon the word came down and we formed into an irregular column, four-five-six in a file. I took my place next to the unit organizer. She was a peculiar person, but basically nice; I wanted to protect her.

We marched a short distance to what I guessed was the Post Office, a grimy old stone building, as I recall. A narrow sidewalk ran all around it, at least we circled it, marching around and around in silence without crossing another street.

Policemen were stationed all over the place. They were nervous and apprehensive, fingering their clubs, alternately tightening and releasing their grip. I observed a strong line of them drawn up on the far side of the sidewalk, and a number of mounted police were patrolling the street that separated us from them. The horses were excited, they kept neighing and rearing, the police who rode them were taut and nervous, which made us taut and nervous also. Those sleek, well-fed horses loomed huge and threatening, arousing the primitive dread of the beast. As I watched the horses clawing the pavement with their hoofs, champing at the bit, their beefy, powerfully built riders with clubs and pistols openly exposed holding them in rein with effort, my mind flashed back to the quivering Indians of Mexico when they were first faced by the mounted monsters of Cortez. We shuffled around in tense silence, around and around that Post Office endlessly, when the order came down to shout slogans. I couldn't think of any. Then I remembered the slogan on my placard and started crying:

"Hands off Haiti! Hands off Haiti!"

Everybody was shouting his own slogan and it made quite a noise although the words were indistinguishable. We expected the police to charge us at any moment and were bracing ourselves to meet it but nothing happened, and soon the order came down to raise our placards which until then we had kept hidden under our coats.

I hooked mine up and raised it, so did the others, and in a flash that drab picket line burst ablaze with signs of all description. That spark of action and the splash of all those multicolored signs triggered our pent-up tension. We burst into a wild chant: "Hands off Haiti, Hands off Haiti." Then there was a rush and the police attacked us, the mounties in the lead.

The charge hit us broadside right where I was, a policeman on his horse slamming into us right in front of me, men and women trampled down by the horse, the policeman swinging down at them with his club. I heard a horse snort back of me,

174

charging in, and I whirled. The horse was coming right at me. I was trapped, the sidewalk was too narrow to shift. The horse was going to trample me down! The horse was coming in fast, his snort bursting at my eardrum, the mountie standing in his stirrup, his club raised, two more steps and the charge would pin me right against the building. I raised my pole and thrust it in the face of the horse. The horse reared, jerking its head aside, and I side-stepped, grabbing for his bridle. It was high and I jumped for it when I was jarred by a terrific smash, the mounted policeman clubbed the placard right off its post. The swing carried him ahead of me, he half turned back in his saddle, he raised his club again, then lowered it to control his horse which was now rearing high on its hind legs to avoid smashing into the building. The horse was teetering, it was about to come down on me, and I blindly thrust up my pole to stick it into its flank but the horse avoided it and came down on all fours sideways, carrying the mountie away from me.

I was in a daze, trying to catch my breath, when a blinding pain exploded in my left shoulder. I swung around. It was a policeman on foot raising his club again when a third policeman smashed right into me and I was flying in the air, sailing into the street. I landed on my palms, toes, and one knee. I jumped up and the fight by now had by-passed me, the policemen were running ahead of me tackling what was left of the column which was all broken up. I saw Amter and a few others running toward the Elevated. I thought of following them but they were too far ahead for me to catch up. The large crowd of bystanders who had been held on the opposite sidewalk by the police now came swarming all over the pavement. It took me a few moments to realize I was now safe among them. My palms were sore and dirty black, the knuckles of my right hand were skinned, my spine and my shoulders were throbbing, my left arm felt paralyzed. The pain in my arm was agonizing, it was as if a red-hot iron rod had been rammed into the marrow of my bone. I moved

175

my fingers, they were O.K.; I tested my arm, it could swing back and forth although the motion was excruciating; it could also move in a circle though I couldn't raise it, so it was not fractured.

The pain in my arm was centered in the biceps and it wouldn't let down, it was a stabbing ache and I was growing more and more angry. "The sonofabitches! The sonofabitches! They had no right to do that to me." The street was littered with torn placards. I looked for mine and found an irregularly torn piece of it. I picked it up. It now read:

A N D

F

H A I T I

"And you, too!" I thought. I did not think it funny, I was bitter. I rolled up that torn piece and put it under my good arm, I don't know why, I believe as a sign that I hadn't surrendered.

I was making my way to the subway when I saw my unit organizer. She was still full of tension and I was glad she hadn't been hurt. She was talking a blue streak in her excitement but I wasn't listening, I kept repeating over and over to myself, "The sonofabitches! The sonofabitches!" Then I heard the unit organizer ask me again:

"What is it you said you wanted to tell me after the demonstration, Comrade?"

I looked at her and remembered, and came out with it. But it wasn't the speech I had so carefully rehearsed that morning, not even remotely like it.

"What is our damn unit doing besides attending meetings?" I asked her grimly. "I want to be really doing something, be real active."

She told me about the long-range project the unit had, the organizing of a laundry. They had been working on that on and off for months but she couldn't get the other comrades to help her systematically, they were too busy with their other meetings. We discussed the problem and we agreed right there and then that we would distribute leaflets in front of that laundry next Wednesday immediately we got off work. She would bring the leaflets, she had them at her home. That was just fine with me. "The sonofabitches! I'll show them yet. . . . !"

I spent half of that night nursing my arm, it was painful far beyond anything I had ever experienced. I couldn't call a doctor, he would have had to report me to the police.

I was learning, learning on my skin and bone, that authority could arbitrarily draw a line in utter disregard of constitutional guarantees, in violation of free speech, free assembly, and woe to him who dared challenge that arbitrary action. But I also learned that those unlawful acts can be challenged and must be challenged, otherwise those rights would be lost by default. Personally I was for challenging it; I was in the Party to stay.

I wasn't quite sure what was going on in Haiti, but we had a right to voice our protest. No harm would have been done had they let us demonstrate; they could have let us parade up and down, let us listen to Amter, then have the police disperse us as they had in Washington. We hadn't provoked violence, we hadn't started it. The police had started the violence, they were the ones who had invoked it and used it. We had offered no resistance except in self-defense. I decided that the next time I would want a sharpened pole to take along with me.

Violence is a double-action weapon. Some people may be clubbed away, some people may be clubbed right back. I did not know it then but that bit of unjustified police violence was to make a Communist organizer out of me, a professional revolutionary, as Lenin had advocated way back in 1908.

"The sonofabitches! The sonofabitches! And just when I was quitting the Party for good!"

25 WEDNESDAY afternoon I left the shop early. I didn't tell the boss why and he didn't ask. My arm was still stiff and I had hardly done any work anyway. I had blamed my injury on a fall and nobody in the shop had questioned it. I met the unit organizer at Pennsylvania Station and we took the subway to Times Square, shuttled over to Grand Central, and took the local uptown. The laundry was located in Harlem, near the East River.

On the way uptown I read over one of the leaflets and I was dismayed. It had been crudely mimeographed, a blotchy, messy job, you felt like throwing it away unread. The message it contained was even worse.

Whoever wrote that leaflet was addicted to those long, involved, intricate sentences that impede the flow of the original thought, obscure enough to begin with. The general drift of it was that the workers in that laundry were being exploited and brutally oppressed by the Wall Street imperialists and finance capitalists, who were doing the same thing in China and other parts of the world. In order to better their miserable conditions and wretched existence, the leaflet urged them to build the TUUL, organize the Laundry Workers Industrial Union, and defend the Soviet Union.

It was a general tract utterly divorced from actual life. It could have been equally directed to any group of workers by simply changing the word "laundry" to that of some other industry. It took many years for the inept Communist Party to learn that workers in different industries had to be approached specifically, that one hat did not cover them all. That leaflet was as practical, in a reverse sort of a way, as those articles in the Sunday magazine sections that explained how easy the road to riches actually was; how others have become rich by simply getting hold of a few mines, railroads, banks, then consolidating and merging them—a real practical guide, any American could do it easily if he went about it the right way.

I was questioning in my mind if there was any sense to distributing those leaflets when the train lurched and threw me back against the seat. My arm started to throb again and then I was sure there was good sense to it. "The sonofabitches!" Some seed might take hold, some seed might sprout . . . Had that general party mobilization not been a flop, had we had a few thousand more workers at that demonstration, we could have made hash of those horses, we could have chewed up those policemen!

The laundry loomed huge and grim in the dusk, the big windows shone dull yellow from the electric lights burning inside. It was nearly five, the workers would be coming out soon. We took up positions a half block away from the gate, on the left sidewalk where most of them would be passing. I suggested that we each take one sidewalk but the unit organizer advised that we stay together, and I readily saw her point.

The employees' entrance suddenly opened wide and the workers started coming out. Most of them were women, mainly Negroes, but there were a few whites among them too, mostly men.

The older women walked quickly and usually singly, the younger ones more slowly and in groups of two or more. We thrust our leaflets at them as they passed us. Most of them ignored us and some even pushed our hands away, but a few accepted the leaflets and glanced at them before putting them in their handbags or pockets. The crowd soon began to thin and we were coaxing them loudly: "Here, take it, take it home and read it, it will tell you all about the union," and so on. Some of the workers were definitely hostile, particularly the men, but most of them manifested indifference. A few of those who took the leaflets did so with a smile.

The crowd was now definitely gone, only a few stragglers were coming out of the laundry. We hadn't done too well, we still had most of our leaflets left. Two Negro girls were approaching and I offered them each a leaflet, saying:

"Here, take this, this will do you good."

They stopped in front of me chuckling and looked me over provocatively. They were nearly as tall as I, young looking, full bodied, their laughter was deep and rich. One of them slowly pushed my arm away and said:

"I got somethin' too, that'll do you good, white boy. How'd you like a nice black pussy for a dollar?"

They both laughed and that made me smile too although I was a bit embarrassed. Then the other one spoke up.

"How about it, white boy? How'd you like to change your luck?"

Now they really laughed. I turned away from them and they left, chuckling deep in their throats.

The show was over, it had lasted less than twenty minutes. I felt very low. I had quit my shop early to help these laundry workers to a better life and not only were most of them indifferent but some were downright hostile and insulting. It was a difficult task indeed to elevate the masses!

The unit organizer was in an entirely different mood. She was elated over our success and told me she would report our accomplishment directly to the District. She praised my effort, told me I was quite an extraordinary new member, and invited me to her house for a bite to eat and a glass of tea to warm up. I declined. It was too early for dinner and I wasn't cold, I was wearing my new camel's hair coat.

I went home, changed, went out for dinner, came back, picked up a book to read but was unable to concentrate on it. My mind kept going back to that laundry. I relived that scene, the workers swarming through the gate, their walk, their faces, their gestures, how they ignored or waved aside the leaflets, the look on the faces of those who had accepted them. It was an endless procession of images and it wouldn't come to a halt.

I was listless and restless. I dropped the book and paced up and down in my room. I recalled those two Negro girls with their rich, throaty chuckle; the unit organizer inviting me to warm up with a hot glass of tea.

"Tea . . . !" It suddenly struck me. I knew now what the trouble was. I went to the phone and made a call.

The party did not answer.

I called a second number. She had a date for that evening. If only I had called a half hour sooner . . .

The third girl I called was out.

The fourth expressed herself as thrilled. However, she was indisposed.

"How about next Monday? Or if you're in the mood to spend a quiet evening . . . ?"

I wasn't.

I called a fifth number. She had just left.

The sixth number didn't answer. It was no use. My thoughts went back to the unit organizer. She was chunky and had flashy gold teeth, yet she wasn't so bad. I decided to call her, then realized I did not know her phone number, nor her address. I put on a record but the music sounded flat.

All in all, quite a frustrating evening.

26 A FEW nights later Kovess called. It was most urgent, he couldn't discuss it over the phone, he wanted me to see him the next day, Saturday afternoon, in the editorial offices of the *Uj Elore*.

The editorial offices were on the third floor of a shabby walk-up building at 16 Union Square. When I asked for Kovess he came out to greet me and invited me for a cup of coffee in the co-opera-tive cafeteria downstairs. I wasn't a coffee drinker but went along with him. Instead of taking one cup, Kovess placed two cups of coffee on his tray, both for himself, led me to an empty table, put sugar in both cups and, stirring both simultaneously, he plunged right into the subject.

The *Uj Elore* was in an editorial crisis. It was already down to a staff of five, one of whom was a secret Lovestoneite and had to be kicked out, which left only four. To add to the crisis the Central Committee had decided to move Kovess out of the Hungarian field and promote him to Secretary of all the Lan-guage Bureaus in the United States, which left the *Uj Elore* with a staff of only three who could not cope with the task of bring-ing out a national daily paper.

For a permanent solution they had appealed to Béla Kun in the Comintern to send them a man from among the revolution-ary Hungarian writers living in exile in Moscow. Béla Kun came through, he wrote that a man had been picked and steps were being taken to smuggle him into the United States, but that was expected to take two months. The Hungarian Bureau had decided that I was to fill in for those two months, until the arrival of that comrade from Moscow.

I was flabbergasted. What did I know about Communism? How could I possibly interpret Communist Party policies?

Kovess readily ceded those points. In quality, a Communist paper definitely ranked far above an ordinary capitalist newspaper not only because of its superior Marxist-Leninist editorial approach but also because of the quality of the people on its staff who were carefully chosen from the ranks of the most able leaders of the revolutionary working class. I clearly did not qualify but—this was an emergency. Was I ready to start on Monday?

I wasn't ready to start at any time. For one thing, I had little respect for the *Uj Elore;* it was very poorly written and edited. Secondly, I liked my job and was loyal to my boss. I told Kovess I wasn't interested.

"It is the decision of the Party that you go on the staff of the *Uj Elore!"* Kovess informed me. "A Party decision is binding on all Communists!" he added incisively.

It was now a question of was I really a Communist. I wasn't sure. I felt my arm. It was still sore, but not too bad. I still said automatically, "The sonofabitches," but without any heat.

"What if I won't accept that decision?" I challenged.

"Then you could no longer belong to the Communist Party!"

"So what! I could still be a Communist from the outside."

Kovess' face turned harsh, there was fury in his voice.

"No, comrade. Once you quit the party you're automatically on the other side. Remember that soldier in John Reed's *Ten Days That Shook the World* who kept repeating: 'Those who are not with us are against us'? He was a simple, illiterate muzhik, but even he understood that historical truth. Your attitude reflects the historical weakness of the petty-bourgeois intellectual, the typical vacillation of the liberal fence-sitter who in a crisis usually sides with his own petty-bourgeois class and personal interests."

It was an effective speech. My respect for Kovess went up another notch. Here was a person who would view every problem with historical objectivity. I did not know then that this was "standard operational procedure" to be used against all who wavered in their loyalty to the Communist Party, and that I too, as a party functionary, would be using it in the same way countless times in the years to come.

I told Kovess that I wasn't at all enchanted by what I had seen of the party in action. Their discussions were vapid, their work was ineffective, their discipline was poor. In fact, I considered belonging to the party a waste of my time and was seriously considering quitting it anyway.

Kovess' entire attitude changed and his voice took on a conciliatory tone. Yes, most of what I said was unquestionably true. But didn't I see that was precisely the reason the party was being bolshevized, why the party desperately needed new blood, new leadership material like me. At the *Uj Elore* I would be working with mature, experienced Hungarian revolutionary leaders, unlike those sectarian rank-and-file American comrades in the unit—a rare opportunity for my political development.

"You'll find those two months the most rewarding experience in your life," Kovess tempted me.

Well, it was for two months only, and the prospect of my political development did sound rather attractive.

"Will you start on Monday?" Kovess pressed.

"I couldn't possibly walk out on my boss just like that, I'd have to give him at least two weeks notice to find someone in my place."

"Nonsense," said Kovess. "You're a Communist, you must rise above such petty-bourgeois conceptions. Loyalty to a boss is the loyalty of the slave to the whip."

184

Here was that dazzling insight again. How unerringly these people cut straight to the core of every social relationship. To develop that faculty, one really had to be part of the class struggle. My boss was all right, a good man as far as bosses went, but still a chiseling exploiter. He had only paid me for a one-week vacation that summer although he had promised two.

"You'll get paid twenty-five dollars a week," said Kovess. I was then getting a hundred. Twenty-five dollars a week would barely cover my rent and phone bill. That seventy-five dollars a week difference plus my Christmas bonus of five hundred coming to me for all the overtime I had put in and which I would now be forfeiting, would come to about a thousand dollars—a tremendous dent in my savings. But why on earth should I be thinking about money—that was only incidental. The only pertinent question boiled down to this: "Was I or was I not a real Communist?" At that moment I was and was not. Working for the *Uj Elore* would provide the definite answer.

"It's only for two months, comrade," coaxed Kovess, sensing my indecision. "A chance to turn into a real bolshevik."

I decided to give it a try for another two months.

27 THE *Uj Elore* was a Communist newspaper, which is quite different from the concept generally evoked by the term "newspaper." Its main function was not the dissemination of news but agitation and propaganda. Every item it published had to carry a strong Communist slant. The capitalists had to be portrayed as brutal subhumans and the proletarians as either akin to angels in virtue, or as cruelly wronged victims of the capitalist system.

The editor was Lajos Bebrits, a tall imposing man weighing over two hundred pounds, with a friendly smile and deceptively shy academic manners. He was then just under forty, a former railroad official in Hungary, a revolutionary from his youth, who had fled jail to come to the United States.

Bebrits was a man of encyclopedic knowledge who towered head and shoulders in intellect and character above everyone else in the Hungarian movement. He took an instant liking to me, the only friend I was to have on that staff.

The news editor was John Nagy, his real name Joseph Gyetvay, a former Catholic priest defrocked for his revolutionary activities in Hungary. He was around forty; somewhat hunched from the habit of carrying one shoulder higher than the other with his neck held to one side, as if fearful of a blow. He was a secretive, humorless, uncommunicative man with a narrow sectarian outlook and rather limited mentality. To my surprise he was a writer of penny proletarian novels in which idealized but sterile housemaids were relentlessly pursued and cruelly forced to submit to the lust of depraved, sex-fiend aristocrats whose diet, be-

186

cause of their wealth, consisted exclusively of caviar, roast pheasant and champagne, nutritionally a rather poor fare. (The last I heard, Gyetvay was in Ankara, the Hungarian ambassador to Turkey.)

The third man on the staff was Emery Lustig, a young, broad-shouldered soccer-football player who was esteemed an excellent organizer because of the effective way he was dealing with the Hungarian followers of Lovestone who refused to embrace the new Foster line. There was nothing subtle about his methods; he would invade a Lovestoneite meeting with his gang and break it up physically. (The last I heard he was district leader of an electrical workers' union allegedly still under Communist control somewhere in New York State.)

The fourth man was John Santo, a member of the illegal Young Communist movement in Rumania before he came to the United States on a student visa. He had been working as a barber in Chicago before Nagy brought him to the *Uj Elore* staff. (He was to rise to a high position in the government Meat Trust in Communist Hungary after having been deported from here.)

The *Uj Elore* was a national daily with a circulation of 50,000 from New York to California. Most of our copies went by mail to subscribers who would receive them anywhere from one to five days after publication. Under those circumstances it mattered very little whether the news in the *Uj Elore* was printed one or even three days after the event occurred.

Our favorite news source was the New York *Times*. The news we clipped had to have class interest and we would rewrite it to suit the policy of our paper. Of course all newspapers, capitalist or Communist, reflect the policy of the publisher. However, when it came to slanting the news we had no peers—even *Time* magazine was a novice by comparison. The *Time* staff had greater finesse because of the higher cultural level of their subscribers yet we had the edge on them because we were not handicapped by a feeling of delicacy among our readers. Where *Time* magazine had to resort to some such mild adjective as "unkempt" to create a subtle prejudice against a labor organizer, we could bluntly call a capitalist "bloated," and if we wanted to please our readers even more, we would add "with the blood of workers."

The two examples cited below should suffice to illustrate how we treated our news stories. Both items were clipped from the inside pages of the New York *Times,* recorded there in a few brief lines.

The first reported an explosion in a coal mine in West Virginia in which two miners with garbled but unmistakably Hungarian names were killed, and three injured; it said that an investigation had been started to determine the cause of the accident. I was handed that news item to rewrite and did so carefully, correcting the spelling of the names of the victims, and then handed it to Nagy. After Nagy read it he snorted, gave me a withering glance, and retired with it to his desk. A short while later when reading proof on his version of that item, I had no doubt left in me about my "lack of political development."

The story carried a five-column headline.

BLOOD FEEDS COAL BARONS' GREED

It was subheaded:

Coal Profits Demand New Human Victims

A lower subhead proclaimed:

Fresh Orphans and Widows for Wall Street Molochs

Wheeling, W. Va. The grinning death skulls of the Coal Barons, those blood brothers of the Wall Street imperialist finance capitalists, are again licking their greasy chops in glee. They have just fed anew on miners' flesh, on miners' steaming blood to satisfy their blood-bloated bellies. Those vampires chose for their latest victims two unfortunate Hungarian workers who had fled the brutal, torturing, Fascist hyenas of Horthy Hungary only to die in agony on the profit-slippery altars of American plutocracy.

The story then gave a bloodcurdling description of the explosion, of the scorching flames and choking fumes, gave precise details of how the two miners were mangled by the collapsing walls of the tunnels, and how the blast seared and injured many other miners who at that writing were on the verge of death, writhing in pain.

Next it went into a denunciation of Wall Street, the coal barons, the Horthy government, charging them all with special responsibility for that disaster. The news story ended with a ringing appeal to all Hungarian miners to join the National Miners Union, under the leadership of the Communist Party, and subscribe to the *Uj Elore* which could never be bought, nor intimidated, which alone told the truth!

I congratulated Nagy on that story, praising his insight. He wasn't gracious in accepting my compliments. He implied that I could read Marx until doomsday and still fail to become a good Communist reporter; to write a good Communist news story one had to be part of the class struggle.

The second story, that impressed me even more, had also been written by Nagy. It was based on a brief dispatch in the New York *Times* stating that the Budapest police had arrested three cabinetmakers for distributing Communist propaganda leaflets in their shop. Without giving any further details, the dispatch concluded by saying that the police were investigating the source of those leaflets.

The next day the *Uj Elore* carried this eight-column headline:

THE HORTHY GOVERNMENT IS QUAKING!

It was subheaded:

SAVAGE REPRISALS, BLOODY POLICE TERROR FAIL TO PREVENT BOLD COMMUNIST ACTION.

The lead went something like this:

Terror struck today in the heart of the murderous, degenerate, bloodsucking ruling class of Hungary. Panicked by fear, they again hid behind the shutters of their castles built with the blood of the destitute Hungarian workers and peasants. Once more they shriveled under the hot breath of revolt, heard the crowing of the red rooster setting flame to their rooftops. The proletariat of Hungary received new hope and courage from this fearless and bold action of the underground Communist Party which raised its red banner high to show that the time of the final reckoning is rapidly approaching.

It was a three column long story, all based on that six-line news item in the New York *Times*. That was dialectical materialism in practice, a science that not only foretells the future but also divines the past. That couldn't be learned from books either, you had to live it to master it.

Once I nearly came close to it. We were short of a filler for our Sunday supplement and I was handed a large glossy of a French movie actress on the Riviera wearing a fabulous half-million-dollar pearl necklace. I was asked to write an appropriate caption for it.

It was quite a photo. Posed by a French photographer, the lady had laid bare practically all but her soul—the pearls were the least of her physical attractions. I sat gazing at that enticing figure for a long time trying to class-angle it. Finally I gave up, oblivious of my political inadequacy. Just for fun, to spoof that solemn Nagy, I wrote:

X-Y, celebrated actress, favorite playmate of the parasitic scions of the ruthless oppressors of the French toilers, displaying her fabulous pearls worth $500,000, the cost of which has been squeezed out of the hide of the starving French masses.

I was grinning when I handed it to Nagy. He didn't notice that. He read the caption carefully, reached for his pencil and made a few corrections.

He changed *playmate* to *concubine, celebrated* to *notorious, displaying* to *brazenly flaunting,* raised the $500,000 to a million, and stuck the adjective *feudal* in front of the noun *oppressors.* Otherwise it had passed the test.

Evidently I had acquired the secret yet I made little use of it. Every time I caught myself straying into that kind of Communist journalism I simply recalled those pearls, grinned, and stopped in time.

Our fiction was clipped mostly from the German Communist newspapers—this was before Hitler. Once, tired of translating those dull and repetitive stories, I protested to Bebrits. In those German Communist epics the capitalists were invariably inhuman, cunning and cowardly monsters while the workers were all outspoken and self-sacrificing heroic demigods.

I told Bebrits those conceptions were childish, that the true picture was quite the opposite. Most workers were far from being outspoken; in my personal experience they were a most easily intimidated lot. I proposed that I rewrite those stories, adding a touch of reality, thus making them more believable to the workers who could then see a closer resemblance to themselves.

This was in the evening, after the paper had been put to bed and the two of us were left alone in the office.

Bebrits sighed, stuck his pen wearily into his inkpot, stretched, and then leaned back in his chair.

"You are an intelligent person," he addressed me mildly, "a man of culture, which is rare among our young Hungarian comrades. Yet you don't know about workers at all."

I protested that immediately. I knew workers, I had worked in shops with them for eight years, I had eaten with them, stood in the fur market with them, I was on familiar terms with more workers than the rest of the *Uj Elore* staff put together. In fact, I was the only genuine manual worker on the entire staff.

Bebrits heard me out and then replied.

"You know individual workers, but not the working class. The average worker is a piece of turd, a cowardly, cunning, selfish, double-crossing, often moronic son of a bitch. He is deformed in body by toil and warped in mind, willing to betray his own grandmother. He is servile and fawns on his boss, ready to tuck in his wagging tail and run at the first harsh word from his master."

I looked at Bebrits in astonishment. I would never have gone that far in my indictment. Bebrits continued, his eyes lost in contemplation.

"I know what workers are like from way back when I was assistant railroad station master in Transylvania. Of course not all workers fit that description. I know workers from that famous railroad strike in Hungary during World War I that set Germany's Rumanian offensive back an entire week by stopping all troop movements.

"What good would it do to the working class or to the Communist Party to depict the workers as they are, to hold a mirror up to them and say, 'Take a look at yourself and see what miserable crud you are!' The worker knows that better than we do, he would crawl back deeper into his dank crevice, even more hopeless, even more dejected and defeated.

"What do we do? We paint him a picture which shows him a giant with the features of Apollo and the muscles of Hercules, brave as Mars and towering like Jupiter.

"We keep presenting him with this picture and drumming into him: This is your portrait, this is the true mirror. All other mirrors are deceptive, they have always been deceptive, they were purposely so invented by the capitalists to reflect a distorted image in order to keep you humble and ignorant, to hide your real strength and character from you.

"We keep drilling that into his head, we play up examples, we portray situations where the hero—and the hero is always the worker—performs the most prodigious feats of daring, until the worker starts rubbing his eyes, begins flexing his muscles and vaguely wonders if he isn't actually the kind of worker we insist he is, instead of the miserable wretch he knows himself to be.

"We give him self-confidence and some day, somewhere, the

occasion arises where he is put to test. He will inevitably be provoked by some exceptionally revolting act of capitalist injustice, some stupid act of suppression, some extremely cruel act of exploitation which capitalism by its very nature must historically invoke. He will then remember the countless examples we have cited him and, as likely as not, he will rise to the occasion. He will then discover that there is truth in what we have said, that by virtue of his overwhelming numerical superiority he is far stronger, more capable of revolutionary action than he has ever believed himself to be.

"Even though he still has his own doubts about himself, he believes that the other workers with him are more of that heroic mold. Thus he gains strength from the presumed courage of his fellow workers and finds that mass courage really is superior, that ultimately it can sweep all resistance away.

"This is why, comrade, you just go back and keep translating those fictional stories as they are published in those German magazines. The German Communist Party is the largest party outside of the Soviet Union. The German comrades know best how to transform that miserable wretch of a worker into a fighting revolutionary hero. In a few years you will see how that transformed German revolutionary worker will sweep the Krupps, the Junkers into the ash heap of history, how those German workers will plant the red banner of the successful proletarian revolution firmly in Europe for the rest of the nations to follow."

I had no grounds to dispute the correctness of that theoretical foundation of Communist propaganda although I was of the opinion that Bebrits was far more contemptuous of the individual worker than the facts warranted. That conversation took place in the fall of 1929 and subsequent developments in Germany tended to bear out Bebrits' words concerning the psychology of the worker. However, actual events proved different in one basic essential from Bebrits' prophecy. Hitler and Goebbels, who took that line over from the Communists, proved greater masters in its application—they were the ones who convinced the German masses that they were the *Herrenvolk* whose superiority destined them to rule over all other nations—and it is now a matter of historical record that they nearly succeeded. But that was still in the future that evening. As our talk became more intimate I pressed Bebrits for the details of that railroad strike in Transylvania. He was at first reluctant but he yielded finally. As he went deeper into his story, he became more and more animated and I found myself transported back to the years of the First World War in Hungary.

The Germans under Field Marshal von Mackensen were then concentrating for an all-out assault on Rumania to knock that country completely out of the war. The hub of all railroads from Germany to Rumania was Temesvár, where Bebrits held a comparatively high post for a young man then in his twenties, that of Assistant to the Station Master. The railroad workers in that town had chosen that moment to demonstrate their antiwar sentiments and went on strike, bringing all rail traffic to a halt. The German High Command responded by arresting hundreds of railway workers, threatening to shoot all of them unless they resumed work. The railway workers held out. Mass executions were about to begin when suddenly Bebrits volunteered to take a hand. He was well liked and respected by all ranks and when he approached the higher railroad officials with his plan they were happy to recommend him to the German High Command.

Bebrits offered to persuade the men to go back to work and start traffic moving under two conditions: that all death sentences be revoked and all other retaliatory measures be canceled. He also wanted permission to speak privately with the arrested men. Those requests were granted. The men returned to work and Bebrits took over.

To the delight of the military, the most feverish activity in railroading history developed instantaneously right under their own eyes. Locomotives were getting up pressure, black smoke and white steam poured from the long-dormant funnels. Engines started puffing and snorting all along the tracks. Jets of hot white steam hissed round the elbow-shaped, shiny steel driving-shafts, punctuated by short penetrating toots of railroad whistles. Trains shunted back and forth, cars were coupled and uncoupled. Bumpers clashed, transmitting a shivery impact from car to car along the length of the trains—each car came alive with a shock when it received the rude jolt and passed along the momentum, snake-like, to the next car, to the delight of the military.

The German Army Command was fascinated, that was railroading at its peak of perfection, the Christmas dream of a child come true. Semaphores flashed red, green, and yellow, their arms went up and down or halfway; brakemen signaled with their red flags by day, with the arclike movement of red lanterns by night. Every railroad man was at work, every car was in motion, the rails were hot with friction, the flashing wheels glimmered silvery by the light of the stars.

It took days before the German Military Command discovered that with all that day-and-night feverish activity not a single train got through, that every southbound train was now facing north, that military units had been broken up and separated, that guns had been divorced from their ammunition and, worse still, every crossing, every switch was blocked by a long string of cars. It was the traffic jam of the century. The harder Bebrits worked the worse the tangle became.

They called Bebrits on the carpet but they couldn't prove their suspicions. Bebrits had been working day and night without sleep, his eyes were bloodshot and circled, he was near the point of exhaustion. He had shouted himself hoarse and he could barely whisper his rebuttal that that was the way of railroading, that all the trains were in motion, that the men had kept their pledge and were carrying out all orders faithfully. Not having any tangible proof, the military had to let Bebrits go.

It took four more days before the first train finally left for the Rumanian border. The news of that exploit spread like wildfire throughout the land, it sparked further antimilitary resistance. Bebrits was eventually jailed for sabotage but he wouldn't tell me about that part and I did not want to press him.

That was the kind of revolutionary inspiration I had been looking for, it deepened my respect for the old-time revolutionary leaders. We discussed many topics that evening, points about Communism that bothered me, particularly dialectics and historical materialism. I questioned the accuracy of that supposedly scientific guide to the foretelling of the future development of history. My question was, what would happen to that theory after the establishment of Communism when the opposing class forces presumably disappeared?

Bebrits' eyes took on a dreamy look. He pondered the question and then replied that there would always be opposing forces. The struggle in society would then move on to a higher plane. A society then might clash over the kind of music to play, over the kind of poetry to write, whether to increase the population or to apply compulsory birth control, and so on. No society would ever be in full equilibrium, there would always be forces that clashed. But that was all in the future, something for our grandchildren to face. . . .

From that evening on, Bebrits and I became rather close, but our relationship was soon to be interrupted. Summoned to an inquiry into Communism by the Hamilton Fish Congressional Committee in 1930, Bebrits did not evoke the Fifth Amendment but attested his faith in Communism and was subsequently ordered deported. He went to the Soviet Union where he became a trouble-shooter in the reorganization of the Soviet railways. He wrote a few times at first; then I lost track of him.

In the late fifties I came across a short feature story in an American magazine or newspaper describing a fully operating small-scale railroad with miles of tracks built by the Ministry of

Transport in Communist Hungary for the amusement of children near Budapest. The children had full rights to run the locomotives, to man the switches and signals by themselves and thus become educated in the ways of railroading. Even though that article did not identify the Minister of Transport by name until the very end I guessed who he was right from the start.

It was my friend Bebrits all right.

28 SHORTLY after I went on the *Uj Elore,* Comrade Lustig disappeared. My query as to what happened to him met with a shrug of the shoulder meaning it was none of my business. It wasn't and I soon forgot about him although from then on I had to carry most of his work load also.

My eight weeks were about up when Gus Mayer, Kovess' successor, called me in. He was a former blacksmith from Indiana, built like a bear; he gave the impression of massive strength and unshakable proletarian conviction and sincerity behind his rough manners. He asked, rather told me, that I was an American citizen, wasn't I? When I affirmed that, he growled:

"Go and get packed. You're leaving for Canada."

Before I had a chance to recover, Mayer outlined the situation. The Canadian Hungarian revolutionary movement had been organized three years previously by the American Hungarian Bureau. Within that short period of time the Canadian movement had grown to the point where it had started a weekly paper of its own. However, the Canadian Hungarians were mostly semiliterate peasants and they depended for top leadership and for editing their paper on comrades sent from United States. That's where Lustig was now. He was due to be relieved but the comrade sent to replace him, not being a citizen, had been turned back at the Canadian border, as was the second man sent after him. Lustig, who was a family man and eager to return, reported that he had reorganized the Canadian movement and it now had a firm leadership of its own. He proposed that I be sent to replace him; I was sufficiently qualified to edit their paper and that was all that was expected of me; the newly reorganized Canadian Bureau was strong enough to provide me with political leadership.

I protested immediately. All I had promised Kovess was that I'd help out the *Uj Elore* for two months and my time was up. I was quitting that Saturday.

"No, you won't!" Mayer banged on the table. "It is a party decision. You'll go to Canada or we'll expel you from the party and publicly expose you!"

"Go ahead!" I was mad. "You can start right now!" I headed for the door.

Mayer's attitude changed abruptly. He told me about those poor peasants lost in Canada without leadership, the prey of any Hungarian reactionary who might happen along. He accused me of being one of those bleeding hearts who cry over the plight of the ignorant, exploited masses but who wouldn't lift a finger to better their lot. He reminded me of some of the lectures I gave on evolution and on the origin of Christianity before Hungarian clubs and how well they were received—what right did I have to deny those peasants in Canada, so eager for the knowledge withheld from them by the feudal landlords of Hungary, to understand the world in which they live. Besides, it would be for two months only. That was my opportunity to live among the masses, among the proletarians, the real dispossessed, to learn from them and become a seasoned revolutionary.

I was tempted.

"For two months, did you say?"

"Yes, two months. This is a promise," he added solemnly. "I won't let you down. Any time you need any kind of assistance, money, just write me. I want you to take the train tonight."

I did not take the train that night, I left the day after. Mayer gave me twenty dollars for my fare and expenses, which incidentally came to more than one hundred dollars. I had to buy a trunk and other travel gear; the Pullman ticket alone cost more than the twenty I had received from Mayer.

I turned my apartment over to Kovess who had asked for the use of it, promising he would take good care of it in my absence.

By the time I was relieved by the Bureau and returned from Canada, nine months later, my apartment was long gone—furnishings, books, and all.

I learned many things in that nine-month interval. The most important lesson, however, still eluded me.

A Communist promise binds only those to whom it is given, but it is *never* binding on the Communist leaders themselves.

29 Taking a Pullman to Canada instead of a coach as was expected from a Party functionary, was my own idea. It proved to have been a sound one even though the difference came out of my own pocketbook. I had no difficulty at the border. When the Canadian immigration officials woke me before dawn, the winter sky—gray and streaked with smoke from the engine—appeared grim, inhospitable and forbidding. I was sleepy and yawned—they asked very few questions. All they were interested in was how long I intended to stay, was I an American citizen, and how much money I had.

I replied I intended to stay a few months, was a naturalized citizen, and had enough money for my needs. They did not ask me to show them my citizenship papers but they wanted to see my money. It was then December, 1929. Unemployment was steadily increasing and although no one as yet suspected that unemployment would soon rise to crisis proportions, officialdom was already worrying. Before my departure I had closed out my checking account and had a thousand dollars in travelers checks and a few hundred dollars in cash on me. I showed them that, which ended the inspection.

I entered legally, had answered all questions truthfully, violated no law.

When a few months later the drive to deport alien Communists from Canada panicked quite a few comrades, the consciousness that I hadn't violated any law enabled me to stand my post calmly without the furtiveness which draws suspicion and leads to denunciation. Nor was I molested.

I reached my destination, Hamilton in Ontario, early Friday morning. No one met me at the station. I left my trunk in the baggage room and took a taxi to the editorial offices of the *Kanadai Magyar Munkas* (Hungarian Canadian Worker). The taxi took me to a side street in the working class section and stopped in front of a residential building. I was apprehensive that the driver had stopped at the wrong address but I did not want to arouse his suspicions and got out. There seemed to be no life in the house, even the street looked deserted. I was about to walk up the stoop when I discovered an open concrete stairway leading to the basement. I walked down to inquire from the janitor, or whoever would be there. The steps led to a door with a glass panel over which a window shade had been drawn. Tacked on the door was a printed news strip yellowed with exposure, the masthead of the *Kanadai Magyar Munkas* (from here on to be referred to as *Worker* to make it easier for the reader).

I tried the door, it was locked. I somehow sensed there was life behind and knocked. The door was soon opened by a sleepy-eyed man in his shirtsleeves who had evidently been sleeping on the leather couch under the window. He was rubbing his eyes and for some reason looked embarrassed. I asked him where Comrade Lustig lived—I cannot now recall the party name he used in Canada.

The man didn't know but said Lustig usually came in around ten. He then asked me whether I was the new comrade they were expecting. When I told him I was he started to apologize for sleeping in the office; he had been dispossessed and he hoped to be taken in soon by some of his buddies.

The editorial office of the *Worker,* for that's what that basement was, had only one window the top of which was level with the sidewalk, affording no other view than an occasional dog or the legs of the passers-by. It was lighted by two large unshaded electric bulbs; whitewash on the damp walls was flaky and green in patches. The center of the room was taken up by a crudely nailed, twelve foot table with two benches made of unpainted, roughly planed fir. That, with the leather couch, some crude shelving made of discarded orange crates, and a number of folding chairs, comprised all the furniture. There was no desk, typewriter, filing cabinet—there was nothing in that room to indicate even remotely that it was an editorial office except perhaps the disarranged pile of *Workers* stacked in one corner.

I tucked a copy of the *Worker* in my pocket and told the comrade I was going out for a walk and breakfast; if Lustig arrived before I returned let him wait for me.

Hamilton was the second-largest city after Toronto in the province of Ontario, with a population of a little over 150,000 in 1929, a drab industrial town. As I walked down one dreary street after another shivering under the icy blasts of the arctic Canadian winter winds, my spirit sank. This was proletarian life all right, the life I had chosen, but now that I was face to face with it, I felt myself shrinking inside. I was both angry with me and feeling sorry for myself. I thought of Lee and Swannee, of Helen and Ruth, of my snug apartment with my collection of records and the oversize bed. What the hell was I doing here in a basement in Canada, messing around with the proletariat! I cursed myself for a romantic fool as I walked into a lunchroom, glowering over the *Worker* as I waited for my order.

The *Worker* was a lousy sheet, full of typographical errors; it consisted entirely of reprints clipped from the *Uj Elore* and from Hungarian publications in Moscow and Paris. The only items identifying it as a Canadian publication were a few puffs about bazaars and affairs for the benefit of the *Worker*. Comrade Lustig hadn't exerted himself in editing that paper, that was sure.

The lunchroom was agreeably warm, the hotcakes were fluffy, the bacon crisp, and the coffee strong—emotion was receding before reason. The life of a pioneer was always one of hardship, the fathers of the American Revolution did not whore away their time in bed. History was not made by weak sybarites. What the hell was I bitching about? I had to be ready to make sacrifices. The sun was also coming out; feebly as it shone, it still radiated light and heat. As I retraced my steps to the *Worker* I was definitely in a confident mood.

I entered without knocking this time. The room was crowded and the air was hazy with tobacco smoke. My nose was assailed by a heavy sourish smell, a mixture of dried sweat from unwashed bodies, seldom changed underwear and dirty socks, the reek of old boots and the only suit that is being lived in, the penetrating odor of garlic mingled with cheap hair oil—the "peasant smell" they called it in Hungary. It was the universal smell of the poor that always hits you when you enter the cramped quarters of the underprivileged—whether in a Mission House or a tenement—the smell of humans who are overcrowded, who have neither the sanitary facilities nor the necessary change of clothes to keep themselves fresh and clean. Poverty stinks everywhere, and so do the poor.

I paused inside the door to get my bearings. I saw Lustig there surrounded by a crowd of men with typical Hungarian faces. Lustig greeted me with a handshake and with what almost passed for a smile of welcome—that was about the friendliest he had ever acted toward me. He then introduced me to the comrades as Kalman Lakatos, my party name in Canada. He did not introduce them to me individually and I felt like a man visiting distant relatives for the first time, who is being slyly appraised by all, and who in turn is trying to puzzle out what his relationship to each may be.

The comrades were deferential in a friendly way, they asked me questions, primarily about the *Uj Elore,* but also about the Hungarian movement in America in general. I was able to answer the first but had to parry the second because I was fairly

204

ignorant about the movement outside New York. Luckily, as their questions showed, they weren't much better informed either and I passed the test.

About a half hour later Lustig pulled out his watch and announced he had to leave at once if he were to catch the train back to New York.

This was contrary to what I had been told to expect. Lustig was supposed to stay with me for at least two weeks until I became familiar with my duties. More important still, he was to take me to the Central Committee of the Canadian Communist Party and ask them to provide me with close guidance and (this is what Mayer emphasized most) with a subsidy for the *Worker* from the secret press funds of the Comintern. Now Lustig was pulling out, leaving me stranded like a blind owl in a strange belfry.

"Just a minute, Comrade Lustig. You haven't told me a thing about the paper, you haven't taken me to the print shop, I am not even acquainted with these comrades here. There are many problems we will have to discuss before you leave." I kept my voice low and tried to keep the edge out of it, but we were in an open room, all present had heard me, and now they faced us in silence. It looked like the beginning of a row and they were all aware of it, Lustig particularly so. He did not reply to me directly, he addressed us at large.

"Comrade Lakatos does not know the great organizational progress we have achieved during my short stay here. I am proud of the Canadian Hungarian movement!" He said that with a flourish and flashed us a wide oratorical smile which, I noticed, met with feeble response. Then turning to me, he related how he had reorganized the entire movement, how well the Canadian Hungarian Bureau was now functioning, how he had appointed Comrade Kovacs, a slender young man of about twenty-four, a tool and die maker apprentice, business manager of the *Worker*. He further informed me that there was more than enough copy

205

in the hands of the printer for the next issue, leaving me a full week to get acquainted.

Next he turned to Kovacs and asked him how much money the *Worker* had. Kovacs emptied his pockets, counted the contents including the small change, and announced it was twenty-nine dollars and some pennies. Lustig then took twenty-five dollars out of that pile to pay for his room and his fare back to New York, shook hands with everyone there, including me, and left. Dismayed as I was, I couldn't help noticing that there was a singular lack of warmth in those handshakes, that not a single comrade bothered to see him to the door.

The next afternoon, I stopped at the print shop and found Lustig had misinformed me. Far from having an abundance of copy, the next issue of the *Worker* was two full pages short.

A Bureau meeting had been scheduled for that night in the *Worker's* office. Twelve comrades were present and while I was waiting for them to open the meeting I occupied myself writing copy, all-Canadian news for a change, clipped from the Toronto papers. Finally I asked them why they delayed calling the meeting to order. A short discussion made it clear they expected me to do that, the comrade sent in from the States had always been the Secretary of the Bureau and the leader of the Canadian Hungarian movement.

The following night I attended a meeting of the Workers Singing Society; I wanted to see how one of our mass organizations functioned. Out of the fourteen singers in that chorus, eleven were familiar to me—they were the members of the Bureau.

The next night I went to the meeting of the Workers Dramatic Club. I found nine actors there, all of them members of the Bureau.

I was also asked to attend the meeting of the International Labor Defense but by then I was suspicious enough to ask who the members were. My hunch proved correct. They also had a

Hungarian branch of the Workers International Relief organized —all Bureau members. The comrades were also talking about organizing a Workers Soccer Football Club—they had just the right number of prospects for it—eleven members of the Bureau for the team and the twelfth member for a substitute. Those comrades were certainly well organized.

At that time I blamed Lustig for the situation. It did not take me long to learn that this was typical Communist organizational practice. Many Communist organizations existed only on paper, their active membership consisted of the same pitifully small number of party members. This explains why the same names keep turning up on dozens of membership rolls on the list of designated subversive organizations.

In less than two weeks I had to face up to the truth—there was no Hungarian workers movement in Canada except in a very loose sense. The movement was actually in its infancy and it fell on me to chart its course, although I myself lacked previous organizational experience. As it happened, this ignorance proved more of an asset than a handicap; it enabled me to develop my own methods along pragmatic lines and they worked out far better than those of Lustig's mechanical party procedures.

30 INFLUENCED by the utterances of the late Senator McCarthy and similar professional patriots, most Americans—especially the younger generation brought up on lurid television programs and the fanciful accounts of self-confessed Communist spies—have been conditioned to think of the Communist Party as a wickedly cunning and devilishly efficient organization disposing of an inexhaustible war chest and commanding a vast army of fanatic professionals trained to a razor-sharp edge in every trickery to ensnare the ignorant masses. That was not my experience in Canada. Before my first week was up I found myself enmeshed in problems stemming from the utter poverty and ineptness of the Communist movement. Worse still, as I discovered to my dismay, the comrades around me not only blithely assumed that, as the editor of the *Worker* and therefore the leader of the Hungarian movement, it was my responsibility to solve those problems, they also took it for granted that I had the training and the experience to cope with them.

The first problem I had to face was that the *Worker* had no funds and the print shop refused to extend credit unless we settled the old bills piled up by Lustig. I solved that by paying them out of my own pocket.

Next there was the problem of the party fractions—where they were, what they were doing, just how many Hungarian party members there actually were in Canada. It soon transpired that there were less than a dozen, not even the members of the Bureau were all members of the party. The people hanging around the *Worker*—usually more than a dozen, they came and went with new faces showing up all the time—called each other comrades, considered themselves Communists, but were not actually members of the party. Outside of a few men like Kovacs they had no contact with the Canadian party whatever.

I decided to change all that. Whoever came to see me from then on was asked to sign up. Most of the Hungarians in Canada then were migratory workers, riding the freight trains from one end of the provinces to another in that vast country in search of jobs—digging coal for a few months in Alberta, working on some farm in Saskatchewan, turning up afterward in New Brunswick or Nova Scotia to cut pulpwood for the paper mills. They would make the *Worker* their headquarters between jumps, and in a few weeks I not only made friends with a sizeable number of them but also signed them up in the party, assigned them responsibilities within the limits of their abilities such as recruiting other party members in their camps, and to support the *Worker* in an organized manner. From the reports they sent me it soon became clear that no matter in what remote logging camp these men happened to land, the Red Flag soon became a topic of most intense discussion.

But it wasn't at all easy; it took immense effort that kept me on the go all the time with barely time to sleep. I needed help and advice badly and wrote to Mayer repeatedly about it; he didn't even reply. Finally I decided to contact the Canadian party leadership and call on them for help and political guidance.

31 COMRADE Resnick, the local party leader, was a cheerful little man in his late forties; he ran an alteration tailor shop. When I introduced myself he greeted me most effusively. He was happy to welcome me, the Local Executive Committee of the party was having a meeting in his shop that evening, would I care to attend? That was a greater stroke of luck than I had anticipated. Now I could lay my problems before a high body of seasoned revolutionary leaders and the very name "Local Executive Committee of the Communist Party of Hamilton, Ontario, Canada" awed me. A customer came in just then with a pair of pants to be pressed and I left, promising to return that night.

There were six people in the rear of Comrade Resnick's shop when I arrived. Comrade Resnick introduced me proudly as "a leading comrade from the States, the Editor of the *Worker,* and the leader of the Canadian Hungarian Movement." The comrades greeted me with a deference which I found disturbing.

My uneasiness increased when Comrade Resnick announced that the L.E.C. (Local Executive Committee) was grateful for the presence of such a leading comrade in Hamilton who could greatly help them in doing more effective party work. He moved that I be drafted to become a member of the Local Executive Committee and before I had a chance to protest, I found myself duly elected.

As the meeting progressed, I was asked my opinion on every point on the agenda. I did not know the City of Hamilton, I wasn't much interested in *their* problems, my mind was on my *own*. I did not participate in the discussion for I was only half listening and when pressed for my opinion I gave it only after all of them had had their say. I did not know then that that was the formula employed by all party leaders; as a result all my opinions were approved.

As the meeting progressed it became clear I couldn't expect any guidance from that group, they were taking their leadership from me, an utter tyro.

The main topic of the meeting was an unemployed demonstration, the first to be held in Hamilton. Unemployment was growing rapidly in Canada and industrial centers like Hamilton were the hardest hit. They had been promised a speaker from the Central Committee in Toronto, now the problem was, how to reach the unemployed and induce them to turn out. They were planning to mimeograph five thousand leaflets, a ridiculously small number, I thought. Further discussion established that they had a problem distributing even that number because of the 36 comrades on the membership roll less than half were "active."

I proposed to print 5,000 additional leaflets and to distribute them with the aid of my Hungarians. I also suggested that we notify the local newspapers about the demonstration, thus giving it added publicity, and I volunteered for that task. Both proposals were met by admiring comments. They must have thought me a wizard of an organizer. . . .

The demonstration fell on a very cold winter day. The unemployed were shabby and poorly clad, they were miserable and shivered in the icy wind. Ten o'clock passed, then ten-fifteen, the speaker from Toronto still hadn't arrived. The crowd was growing impatient, even I was beginning to feel the cold. After a while I told Comrade Resnick to forget about the Toronto speaker and start or the crowd would disintegrate. To my utter amazement he then proposed that I speak, taking for granted that I was an experienced speaker. Before I half knew what was happening, they boosted me to an empty steel drum amidst stormy applause.

I was utterly confused. The barrel had a sprung bottom, it teetered precariously under my weight, and my mind was concentrating more on how to keep from falling off than on what I was supposed to say. The applause ended, hundreds of pairs of eyes were fixed on me expectantly, the crowd moved closer and so did the Canadian bobbies. I had no choice, I had to speak. But say what? I remembered the text of our leaflet and started off with that, trying to think ahead while I was talking. The crowd received it well, applauding the slogans calling for relief measures and unemployment insurance. That was good as far as it went, but it was over too fast—I had to keep talking. I remembered my early days of unemployment and hunger and went into a description of that episode, reliving it as I talked, embellishing it as I went along. It went over well. Finally I noticed a commotion around the members of the L.E.C. and saw a stranger talking with them, he must be the Toronto speaker we were expecting. I cut my speech short and breathed a sigh of great relief as I dismounted and felt solid ground under my feet again. I had spoken in public, in English, to a strange audience, in a foreign country from a bobbing barrel, starting off a demonstration. There was nothing to it.

Of the many comments I received on that maiden speech of mine, two stand out in my mind. One comrade wanted to know why I had been facing only one part of the audience; why hadn't I rotated from left to right taking in all the audience like other speakers, instead of merely rocking back and forth, and facing but a single segment of the listeners. Frankly, that had never occurred to me. Evidently there were techniques to public speaking other than merely bellowing words at the top of one's lungs.

The other remark was intended as a high compliment but I fail to consider it as such even to the present day. It was uttered by one of the Hungarian comrades in the group who came up to me proudly to congratulate me.

"You know, comrade," he said, "we have listened to speeches in English before, but we couldn't understand them. But when *you* spoke we understood every single word you said."

The others chimed in enthusiastically and one of them added:

"I never knew I understood English so well until I heard you speak this morning!" I was sorely troubled in consequence, wondering how many non-Hungarians in that crowd, if any, had understood my heavily accented English.

Be that as it may, we succeeded in organizing an Unemployment Council as a result of that demonstration. Later on we held other demonstrations and additional Councils were organized.

It was all started by that Local Executive Committee of six members, by a total membership of 36 Communists in that town of 150,000. In other towns throughout Canada other inept Communists of similarly insignificant numbers did likewise and the influence of the party grew rapidly among the unemployed.

32 My life in Canada soon settled into the routine of a party organizer in a more or less virgin field—differing from that of a missionary mainly in that the faith we preached was redemption through joining one of our organizations and salvation through revolution, through the overthrow of the capitalist system right here on earth. I tended my flock, made new converts, brought them to a closer understanding of life and society by lecturing on such subjects as evolution and the class structure of society, all strictly according to the gospel of Marx and Lenin. My congregation consisted mostly of peasants who had broken with their old church and came to look upon Communism as a new religion, on the editor of the *Worker* as not only their spiritual but their lay leader as well, bringing to him their personal problems as well as their disputes, and abiding by his authority. I was even called upon to deliver funeral orations in which I was expected to console the bereaved by extolling the virtues of the departed not only as a good family man but also as an outstanding example of a class conscious workingman. I was invited to name the newly born and I still take credit for naming none of them Vladimir after Lenin or Krupskaya after his widow.

The one incident that was anything but routine occurred at our May Day demonstration in Hamilton in 1930 and the memory of the part I played in it still makes me uneasy.

It all began when the party selected me chairman of the United May Day Committee which was formed to organize the demon-

214

stration. By that time I had become accustomed to leadership.

At our first meeting all went well and in harmony until a nonparty delegate raised the question of applying for a police permit. The delegates seemed in general agreement on the advisability of that—I alone stood in opposition. I reasoned that the police had shown increased apprehension of late over our growing activities, particularly among the unemployed, and by risking the denial of a permit we would be playing right into their hands. That would give them a pretext for smashing our demonstration and on top of this, to charge us with provoking a riot by willful violation of the police ban.

Leadership is a heady wine. One gets used to power just as easily as to having money enough to burn, without giving it a thought. Since the majority opinion seemed to be definitely against me I used the chair's prerogative. I asked for someone to move that we should not apply for a police permit. Some comrade mumbled something to that effect; I called for seconding, some other comrade did so. I then immediately called for a voice vote and when a few comrades said "aye," pronounced the motion carried.

At our next meeting one of the delegates made a peculiar report. He claimed that he had been approached by a police captain who objected to our announced route. Our plan called for marching up one main avenue and then turning right on the most important thoroughfare in the city. The police wanted us to turn left at that crossing to avoid traffic being paralyzed.

His report caused considerable agitation but I quickly ruled out all discussion of it. The way I interpreted it, that was merely a request to make things more convenient for the police. After all, we did want to tie up traffic; the worse the traffic jam, the greater the impression we'd make on the bourgeoisie.

At our final meeting a few days before May first, another delegate, this time the President of the Veterans' Unemployment Council, came in with a still graver report. He had been called in by the Police Chief himself and warned that under no condition would the police allow us to turn right on the main avenue. If we turned left, they would leave us alone. But if we turned right they would await us with machine guns and we would then be held responsible for whatever ensued.

This threat couldn't be ignored. A number of delegates asked for the floor at once, including two members of the Local Executive Committee of the Party. To be democratic I recognized a delegate of one of the Unemployment Councils first—besides, I wanted to know how he felt. He spoke for changing the route, arguing that what we were primarily interested in was a demonstration, not a bloody clash with the police. He spoke with heat and it made good sense to me. The majority seemed to agree with him.

After a few other delegates spoke in a similar vein, I finally recognized one of the official Communist Party delegates, one of the members of our Local Executive Committee.

He was vehement. May Day was a day for "militant" demonstration. The workers themselves would decide where and how they wanted to demonstrate. The route of the demonstration had already been publicized, binding us to our plan. If the police interfered, the responsibility would rest squarely on them, and on the capitalist government!

After he spoke the other party members became silent. They did not approve of his stand, but the party had spoken and that settled it for them. It settled it for me too, although I did not like it either. That police threat might well have been a bluff, to scare us out of tying up traffic at that key corner. On the other hand, the threat of machine guns might not be an idle one in view of the growing nervousness of the city authorities. But the party had spoken, I was the chairman, it was my task to put its decision into execution. After the motion to leave our route of march unchanged had been carried, although with a notable lack of enthusiasm, I decided I might as well put the best face on it.

"If the Police Chief approaches any one of you delegates again, simply tell him we'll march as announced, that we'll turn to the right even if they face us with cannons. The streets belong to the people. The working class of Hamilton will assert its right to demonstrate peacefully even though that may inconvenience the bourgeoisie."

That speech was met by great applause and it restored the confidence of all delegates except mine. Inwardly I felt that our stand was wrong. The real issue was not whether the police were provoking us or we were provoking the police, but that a good number of people might be gravely hurt. The party had egged me on, I egged the party on! They had committed me, I had committed them. Leadership meant responsibility—come what may, I would have to face it.

May Day broke sunny and beautiful. The profusion of red flags and banners put the crowd at the assembly point in a festive mood. Both sidewalks were jammed with onlookers—those prudent comrades who were one with us in spirit but who nevertheless considered it wiser to separate their bodies from the common cause.

It took quite a while to line up the column in the most colorful and yet, if attacked, the most effective position for defense. There were a considerable number of women and children among the marchers and to protect them we concentrated the huskiest men on the flanks so that from there they could rush quickly into the fighting. The plan called for me to march in the lead with one member of the United May Day Committee on my right and another on my left.

We started our march on schedule, singing the *Internationale*, and shouting slogans at intervals. The crowds on the sidewalks kept step with our progress, people waved to us from the windows, the sun shone bright and warm—it was an exhilarating demonstration.

As we neared the contested intersection I subconsciously slowed down which must have affected the spirit of the crowd. The singing died down and this in turn reacted on me. I felt my feet dragging and when we reached the crossing the column came to a slow halt.

The street left of the intersection lay clear of all traffic. The crossing to the right was blocked curb to curb by a line of motorcycles. Two policemen in full battle dress manned each motorcycle, the driver leaning forward, one foot on the pedal in readiness. The other in the gondola slouched low in the unmistakable posture of a machine gunner ready for instant action. A police captain, feet planted apart, was facing us in the center of the road.

The marchers were moving up closer. There was a momentum to that column—it was physically pressing me on. I felt the eyes of the comrades boring into my back. The Communist Party was leading that demonstration. I was the picked leader of the party.

To the left the street stretched open and enticing. It beckoned: "This way to joy and peace!"

To the right the police line was tensing. That way lay fire, flame, and bullets—the road to destruction.

It was my responsibility to the party, it was my decision to make. I made it.

I raised my right arm and shouted loud and clear: *"Lo-o-ng li-i-ive the soli-i-da-a-a-arity of the interna-a-ational working cla-a-a-ss!"*

"Long live the solidarity of the international working class," the shout thundered back from the crowd.

"Long live May Day!" I shouted, and brought my arm down decisively, pointing firm and straight to the right, to the police line ahead. I executed a sharp right turn and marched resolutely ahead, the column following in my wake.

I was marching on stiffly. One . . . two . . . three . . . I drew my shoulders back . . . Four . . . five . . . six . . . A few more steps and the police would open fire! The Police Captain raised his arm in a signal and shouted a command. Here it comes! I marched grimly on. One . . . two . . . three . . . The motorcycles came alive with a roar . . . Four . . . five . . . They are heading into us . . . Six . . . They are going to ride us down . . . Seven . . . I threw my chest out. Shoot, you bastards, shoot! Yes . . . ! No . . . ! Yes . . . ! The motorcycles parted into two, the road was no longer blocked, the motorcycles were pulling over to the curb to let our column pass.

An immense cheer rose and the column broke into the *Internationale,* we marched victoriously on, shouting and singing, and I changed my stride from parade step to route. I looked back—everyone was happy and triumphant. I was not elated, I felt remote and detached as I kept marching on.

That evening, at the May Day dance and celebration, I was listless. I shook hands, accepted congratulations, answered the small talk, but my attention was not there, my mind was hovering over a vast empty space with no landmarks on which to alight. I excused myself early, went home and to bed. I was curiously exhausted, but I couldn't sleep and couldn't read—the page blurred in front of my eyes. I turned off the light and closed my eyes. Sleep wouldn't come. Suddenly the sky lit up and there was that police motorcycle line right in front of my eyes, the column in back of me pressing me on, and I was out in front, the decision resting with me.

I watched the motorcycles roar to life and suddenly I saw those machine guns spitting fire, heard the screaming of the comrades, saw men, women, and children crumpled up on the pavement, moaning in pain. I was responsible for all that; it had not happened that way, yet my action could very well have resulted in such a massacre!

I tried to twist and turn out of it, I argued with that phantasmagoria but it wouldn't dissolve. That was not leadership, that was not responsibility to the masses, that was an out-and-out provocation. I, the party leader, had deliberately disregarded the possible consequences, had led the workers to be massacred—to uphold what? A party decision and my position of leadership. But for the mercy of that police captain, many of those workers would now be lying in blood, screaming in agony, those women and children, too—all for the glory of the Communist Party!

I shook and shivered until sleep brought oblivion.

33 WHEN I returned from Canada after an absence of nearly nine months, early in September 1930, I found a vast change. I had expected a change—I had kept in touch with events at home by reading both party and nonparty American newspapers, magazines, other publications. Visual contact now reinforced the mental image I had formed in Canada and charged it with emotional content—we, the party, were being proved right! Capitalism was on the downgrade and was sliding rapidly into an abyss.

The appearance of the City of New York seemed to have altered. Not only the city had changed but also the eyes with which I was viewing it. My experiences in Canada had made me more perceptive; my eyes had learned to pick out highlights; my mind had become trained in the "political approach"—to consider most manifestations of life from the point of view of the "class struggle."

Physically New York looked shabby, dirtier, run-down. The former infectious gayety, the determined rush, the purposeful hurry was missing from the stride of the pedestrians—the spirit of the people seemed to be running down.

I still detected the pushing and the shoving, the rudeness of manners, that stone-cold indifference and self-centered concentration of the New Yorker which seems to say, "I'll have to look out for myself, no one else will." Yet there was an evidence of mellowing manifested in the warmer sympathy afforded to the unemployed apple sellers, to the long lines of dispossesed queuing up in front of the many soup kitchens. The eyes of the passers-by had lost their former self-assured look—they reflected the same uncertainty, the self-doubt—the haunting feel of insecurity I had come to recognize so well in Canada.

When I left New York, the visible trouble had been mainly at the top. The big capitalists, the big exploiters were then the ones who had been reeling under the shock of the Stock Exchange crash. They were the ones who were losing their shirts, jumping out of office windows, putting guns to their temples, taking an overdose of sleeping pills. The causes and consequences of that stock market crash were now affecting the masses. Mills, mines, factories were shutting down one after another and bleak unemployment was spreading its paralyzing grip deep and wide all over the land.

The party had shrilly predicted the coming collapse months before the market crash. Now as our dogma began to prove itself we were convinced that we were the true prophets chosen to carry the sword of Red Islam, even though our muscles were thin and our ranks were sparse. We felt it was our destiny to face up to a task imposed on us by history, and if we were found lacking we would fail history.

The battle for the streets of New York was on. The police were brutal and savage. The official policy was, "Suppress the symptoms of distress; choke the cry for relief back into the throats of the hungry; banish the bastards from the streets; prevent the starving from exhibiting their sores in public—and this crisis will pass, we hope it will pass, Christ, it's gotta pass, we gotta show those bums who is the boss!"

In retrospect, at this writing when our national income is running at more than 500 billion annually, when we enjoy a standard of living unprecedented in history and any criticism of the free enterprise system is considered subversive, it seems ironic to record in how cowardly a fashion capitalism behaved less than three decades ago, how little faith the capitalists themselves had in the survival of their own system, in the validity of their own thinking. Instead of asserting faith and leadership, they squirmed, twisted and turned; instead of thinking and planning they struck out blindly. Unable to fathom the mysteries of their own economic system, the capitalists resorted to incantation and black magic; they invoked suppression, praying that the lid would stay clamped down.

The seat of the tumor was in the United States and the malignant growth was spreading all over the globe—except for one sixth of the earth.

The eyes of the world—except for those whose gaze was fixed on the rising star in the East—were fastened on the United States where the High Priests of Capitalism reigned. The world turned to them in supplication but the eyes of those High Priests were glazed.

The High Priests were basically little men. They had not been trained to think in terms of human society. They had been encouraged to grab; to stake out claims; to gather in and to hoard; to ride roughshod over everyone who stood in their way to the glimmering harvest. They had been brought up in a one-way street ruled by "heads I win and tails you lose." Now they found the one-way road had become a dead-end street where the once reliable coin wouldn't perform and even the "heads" lost, and they sat down in confusion.

The High Priests had their Supreme Priest presiding over the nation, the symbol of human genius at its apex, begotten out of the political wedlock of engineering and big business. But they knew his feet were also made of clay and heeded not his admonitions.

The Supreme Priest invoked the old magic chant.

"Prosperity is right around the corner!" he intoned.

Prosperity failed to respond to blandishments. It regressed further.

The Supreme Priest called a conclave in Washington.

223

The High Priests all responded and officiated in the rituals of exorcising the Devil. They solemnly pledged to cease being frightened, to stop further layoffs, to start rehiring, and to resume normal production. No sooner had they left the White House than the High Priests rushed to their long-distance phones and called their plant managers. As long as the other fellow was hiring that was a good time to sneak in a rabbit punch, to take a bit of advantage. The workers lining up in front of the hiring gates with the folded newspapers in their hip pockets headlining the happy news were met by a flood of men streaming back, those who had been freshly fired that morning.

The Supreme Priest preached the return to the good life, to thrift and austerity.

To set the example he cut the government budget. The haves responded promptly by grimly clutching their belongings and by hoarding even tighter.

"Waste not, want not," they chanted, and cut back their buying, sending production into a further tailspin.

The have-nots clenched their empty palms into fists, yet stood by in dazed helplessness.

The Supreme Priest invoked moral suasion.

"The American people are too proud to accept the dole," he proclaimed from the depth of his Quaker soul.

"Those bums are starving because they are lazy. They don't want to work. Anybody who wants to work can find a job," recited the righteous haves, turning a stone heart to charity as being a violation of moral precepts. For has it not been written that the wastrels are committing an offense against God?

With sermons on their lips and clubs in their hands, the High Priests of capitalism staggered around, preaching they did not know what, laying about in blind fury, in the faint hope that if they succeeded in stifling the screams the epidemic itself would pass. Yet their very own lips trembled, the hands that gripped the clubs shook with palsy. They feared those forces around them which they had once proudly claimed to have mastered. Their ships unaccountably foundered, the Captains of Destiny now found themselves bouncing about in fragile walnut shells. They were no longer steaming toward a goal, but merely bailing in blind desperation, praying for survival.

It is appalling to contemplate how quickly these High Priests of Capitalism, these Captains of Industry, began to doubt the basic soundness of their own productive system, how little they understood the economic laws that govern production and distribution, and determine the prosperity of a highly industrialized capitalist society.

To me the most outstanding fact, the most amazing social phenomenon in that dark early era of depression is that deep in their hearts the capitalist leaders themselves had lost faith in their own system. They found themselves on a toboggan and could picture themselves only as going down. They lacked the imagination to find new ways of getting off the slide and they gave up hope of coming up. They concentrated their energies on digging in their heels to slow down their rapid descent.

Single out one capitalist leader, one important captain of industry, cite one outstanding capitalist economist, if you can, who dared proclaim:

"These are not symptoms of decay, these are growing pains of the capitalist system. Once we overcome them it will be capitalism that will usher in the era of plenty. Capitalism can and will build a land of plenty for our people in our country long before Socialism can rise to that in the East."

Capitalism had apologists, defenders, upholders, whip-wielders, palm readers, soothsayers, and fortunetellers aplenty. Yet in those days of the depression it was unable to produce one single proponent with faith sufficient to stand up in the market place and prophesy:

"Within twenty-five years in these very same United States employment will rise to more than 60 million; nearly two in every three families will own their own homes; our people will be better fed, better clothed, better sheltered than any nation in history—all under a capitalist system!"

The faith of the capitalists was shaken.

The faith of the middle classes, merchants, professionals was shaken.

The faith of the workers and farmers was shaken.

Our faith alone was strengthened. There was no unemployment in the Soviet Union!

The men of good will, the humanitarians and the kind in heart, the sentimentalists brought forth their healing salves. "Man is good in heart," they prayed. "We'll have to reach the hearts of the employers with kindness."

"Give a job," pleaded, urged, cajoled Heywood Broun from the depth of his heart in his newspaper column and over the radio. He received four offers of jobs and 400 applicants stood in line for them.

Men of charity set up bread lines and soup kitchens. "How long have you been waiting in this line, Bud?" I asked one of the men in front of Bernarr Macfadden's soup kitchen.

"I got here a little after five in the morning," the man told me. He expected to get his soup "pretty soon," in about two or three hours. That was at 2:30 in the afternoon.

Nutrition experts gave advice and the papers printed it. There was nutrition in grass, they proved, that could sustain human life if cooked long enough, say six to eight hours, and eaten in sufficiently large quantities, say six to eight pounds. There was still the matter of the bitter taste, but one can't have everything. They did not say how to reopen shut-off gas meters. We Communists had to teach the unemployed that trick.

Other nutrition experts were more realistic. They offered menus for the less destitute. A given minimum quantity of barley and oats mixed with some kind of cheap seed germ, they promised, would provide a nutritionally balanced diet for a person for only one and three quarter cents a day, or seven cents for a family of four. This discoverey, too, was hailed in some papers.

The only people in America who had professed to understand the true causes of the Depression were the Marxists. It was all down there in black and white, in the first volume of Karl Marx's *Das Kapital,* also in the red-inked pages of the *Communist Manifesto.*

The Socialists of Norman Thomas, the Musteites, the Socialist Labor Party, the IWW, all loudly asserted that the depression was the long-predicted breakdown of the capitalist production system which only social reforms could remedy.

But we were not only Marxists, we were Marxist-Leninists. We were certain that we knew even better. At the 6th Congress of the Communist International in 1928, fully one year before the stock market crash, at the height of the boom, Bukharin had warned that we were entering a new period in post First World War capitalist development.

"The Third Period—A period of capitalist crisis, of wars and revolutions," the thesis had asserted.

We Communists far outdistanced in boldness the other Marxists whom we denounced as "social-fascists." We had the brassier lungs, the brasher manner, we had our party discipline, and the fanaticism of martyrdom. We also had something else—we had a star of our own to guide us—the five-pointed Red Star rising with ever-brighter flame in the firmament in the East, while the tired constellation of capitalism was sinking in the West.

We were certain that we alone knew the score and we yelled it from the roof tops at the top of our lungs.

"This is no cyclical depression that reforms can cure."

"Capitalism is in crisis! Times are bound to get much worse!"

The lines outside the factory gates were growing larger by the day. "No help wanted" signs blossomed all over the land, nailed down permanently over the windows of employment offices. The men waiting helplessly outside the gates cast envious glances at the men employed within. The men working inside the plants stole baleful and apprehensive glances at the long line of job applicants outside—the capitalist's dream of the ideal setup for wage cuts.

"Capitalism will utilize the crisis to cut wages—to speed you up!" we trumpeted.

We were vociferously bearish in a declining economy, and we guessed right. Every calamity we predicted quickly came true with a vengeance, and brought in its wake greater human suffering than even we had anticipated.

We exulted in our wisdom! Leninism, dialectical materialism provided us with the key to the secret of the future. We prophesied even more dire events, and capitalism co-operated with us. The more frantically capitalism tried to stop the decline, the more blunders it committed. Instead of expanding the economy, it kept cutting back, bringing more unemployment as a result.

Capitalism was thinking in reverse, it wanted to fit production to declining consumption to eliminate "surplus." As a consequence, the more people were laid off the less they were able to buy. That brought further layoffs which curtailed consumption still more—and the circle thus widened; the more people lost their jobs, the greater the surpluses grew. The national income was shrinking by the day—now was the time for the government to act.

The government did act. President Herbert H. Hoover, the production wizard and economic genius—for had he not by his own efforts in his youth amassed a fortune running into millions—was a hardheaded realist who wouldn't let his Quaker heart enter the calculations of his brains. He pecked away at his adding machine trying to get the ledger to balance. As an engineer he knew that the machinery was jammed yet he bore down harder on the keys in the blind hope that somehow the machinery would right itself and come up automatically with the right answer.

"The budget has to be balanced!" he stated the new formula.

Consequently the currency was even more deflated, making money still tighter to borrow, thus further inhibiting production. Government revenues were shrinking so he fired more government employees, heaping more humans on the castoff pile.

We knew what the remedy was. We shouted for reforms, for government relief, for social insurance.

"Tax the rich to feed the poor!"

We roused the people, we drummed it into their heads:

"Don't starve in silence! Raise your mighty voice! Cry out until your distress is heard, until no ear can be plugged against it in whatever high places!"

We issued leaflets and we distributed them—a handful of us, 3,000 party members in the United States in 1930 out of a population of some 130 million souls.

We worked day and night. We were inept; we were rent by factions. Many of us hardly knew English and those of us who did spoke a strange jargon half of which we ourselves did not comprehend. Our voices were shrill, we spoke with accents guttural and harsh to which American ears had not heretofore been attuned.

We were full of compassion for the sufferings of mankind, we lived in hopes of a better world to come. We were dedicated men, ready to sacrifice ourselves to bring about that better world for all mankind. The masses needed help. They were ready to act if someone would only lead them, if someone would only show them how.

We were eager for that mission! We had initiative—and we had guts. We were ready to learn from the people and also to teach them a trick or two.

A party of 3,000 members of whom not even half were active boldly issued calls for mass demonstrations. Millions responded.

We spoke at street corners and crossroads, in squares and county seats, in towns and villages where we had never set foot before. We talked and the inhabitants listened to that strange talk, the like of which had not been heard even during the presidency of Andrew Jackson, part of which they didn't even understand, much less agree with. But they approved the parts they wanted to hear, the parts they understood because they had already spoken them silently in their hearts and which we now made vocal for them.

"What kind of a father are you? Will you let your hungry children cry because you are too proud to accept the dole?"

"Are we too proud to accept the dole? No! No! A thousand times no!" we thundered raising our fists.

Tens of thousands of other fists rose in unison with ours, hundreds of thousands of other throats shouted with us in defiance.

We not only spoke, we also organized. A young comrade hitchhiked to Allentown, Pennsylvania with five cents in his pocket, to a town where he did not know a soul. He had arrived at the square at two in the afternoon, he told me, sat down on a bench, and started to ask the others sitting there where he could get a job in Allentown.

"You can't get a job in this town," he was told bitterly. "They are not hiring anybody. The mills are still laying off."

By four o'clock he was standing on a park bench making a speech, by five he was chased by the police. By six he had been invited for dinner and had a place to sleep. By seven men were coming to the home of his host for a meeting. By nine that evening the first Unemployed Council in the history of Allentown was formed.

A group of mountaineers in the Ozarks lifted their hunting rifles off the hook and walked down the hill to the country store. "We don't aim to do you any harm," they said to the storekeeper, as reported in the papers, "all we aim is to take some supplies for we are out of groceries and ain't got the money to pay for it." They loaded up with flour, sugar, tobacco, fatback, lard, and cornmeal but did not touch the cash in the till. They were not robbers, only men out of jobs, and they were getting hungry.

230

We sent Comrade Emil Gardos (the last I heard he was one of the heads of the State Chemical Trust in Hungary) to track them down and to recruit them into the party. Gardos succeeded in making contact with them, he told me, and they averred, reckoned, and were mighty proud—neither of us had any ear for dialect—to join such a fine organization as that "Communistical Party" they had heard about. They joined up, about seventeen of them, and then sheepishly said that the Hoskins brothers had a powerful hankering to join, too, but they didn't see how they could be admitted to that "Communistical Party" seeing as the brothers just didn't have any rifles.

"They were a wonderful group to work with," said Gardos with wistful eyes, "but we finally had to drop them. They insisted on bringing their rifles to the party meetings and we couldn't have that. It could have brought disaster on the entire party."

We agitated. We propagandized. We exploited every opportunity to organize.

The Schrafft restaurant chain in New York advertised for busboys—several of them: "Ten dollars a week, college graduates only." Two hundred some odd young college men had been hopefully milling around for hours since dawn by the time the personnel manager arrived. He surveyed that horde of applicants then superciliously called out:

"Graduates of Harvard and Yale, step forward."

In less than a minute that place was a shambles, the besieged manager frantically calling for police from behind his barricaded door. Not a single one of those young college men had until then been a member of the Communist Party, but subsequently quite a number of them joined.

Violence? What would you have done if all you had was a diploma from Princeton, Columbia—or horrors! from the City College of New York?

We organized Unemployed Councils. We organized delegations to call on councilmen, congressmen, mayors, other officials, even in the privacy of their own homes.

At one unit meeting I attended in Cleveland, a comparatively new member of the party, Comrade Lombardi, was listening with ever-diminishing patience to a discussion of whether the unit should lead the proposed unemployed delegation to a certain councilman's home or his office. A desperate relief situation was developing in that district and that councilman was hostile to the demands of the unemployed, dodging their delegations. Comparative merits of either step were discussed at length until finally Comrade Lombardi lost his temper. He banged on the table.

"We go to da house. If he not home we go to da office. We breaka da window, breaka da furniture, breaka da desk and set 'em on afire! Next point on da agend' is da *Daily Worka*. Comrades, da *Daily Worka* is in a very bad *condidution*. . . ."

I lectured that unit, especially Comrade Lombardi, that the party neither approved of such tactics nor condoned them. Comrade Lombardi was amiable.

"O.K., we no breaka da window, no smasha da furniture, no set 'em on afire. We only tear up da papers."

We unofficially compromised on tearing up only a few papers, and those only when nothing else availed. As it turned out, even that wasn't necessary. The unemployed crowded into that office until there wasn't an inch of space left, until that councilman was pushed against a corner, nose to nose with Comrade Lombardi. Lombardi talked and the councilman agreed. From then on he also became a co-operative councilman.

Violence? Maybe. But those unemployed had the right to be heard, to address their grievances to their elected representatives.

When thousands of families had their gas meters shut off and their electricity disconnected we organized emergency flying squads of experts to connect up gas pipes, restore the cut-off current.

Violation of private property rights? Maybe. Have you ever seen a mother with four hungry young children sobbing in the kitchen slumped over a dead gas range, unable to heat even water? I have. And we did something about it. We would also pick up the furniture of evicted families dumped on the sidewalk and carry it piece by piece, two, three, six flights up back to the old apartment.

Interference with enforcement of the law? Maybe. In Cleveland silver-haired Sheriff Sulzman, four times elected sheriff by a great popular majority in the County of Cuyahoga, most heavily populated county in the sovereign state of Ohio, called us aside one time, when he found himself way behind in carrying out the hundreds of writs of eviction issued by the local courts. We had interfered too often, with too many street fights and minor riots, and the arms of his deputies were getting weary with both fighting and lugging furniture down.

"Listen, boys," he said, "why can't we get together on this? Let's be sensible. Why fight? Why not make it easier for both of us? I have to carry out the orders of the courts. Let's have a system. We'll carry a few sticks of furniture out to satisfy the judgment of the court and you won't interfere. You will then only have to carry a few pieces back. Everybody is happy and nobody gets hurt."

It worked out fine. Who said the Communists wouldn't co-operate with law-enforcement agencies?

We organized hunger marches to dramatize the plight of the unemployed. The "marchers" traveled by trucks and they were showered with so much food at every stop by local citizens who gathered around them in sympathy that many of those "marchers" had gained a few pounds by the time they returned. One truck broke down—it had not only been fixed free but came back with two new tires as a gift from some garage man on the road.

In some places bloody fights took place. We didn't start them,

233

it was the police that attacked us, particularly in company-owned towns. We were met with threats, with denunciations, with arrests, with deportations. Firehoses bowled us off our feet with torrents of icy water in subzero weather. We were met with police clubs, blackjacks, riot guns, machine guns, even with tanks, led in person by bemedaled General Douglas MacArthur in a steel helmet, on the flats of Anacostia in Washington.

Scores of us were killed, hundreds of us were wounded and jailed, thousands of us were beaten, had our skulls cracked.

But we couldn't be silenced. Hundreds of thousands of the unemployed followed us, millions of the starving prayed for our success.

We developed lungs of leather and we demanded!

Mayor Davis of Cleveland once told a group of newspapermen—I was one of them—"Those people are too arrogant. Maybe if they were to ask politely we'd let them have something, but I won't give in to demands."

It wasn't arrogance. It was sound tactics.

Those who ask are timid. A supplicant puts himself in a subservient position, he accepts his inferior position as preordained. He submits his fate to the whim of his patron; he proclaims in advance he has no rightful claim and that he would be grateful for whatever favors are shown—please! He begs for charity.

By demanding relief we asserted our claim that all men willing to work in an organized society are entitled to a job, that the government has a responsibility for the welfare of all the governed. That it is the responsibility of governments to keep their economic systems balanced, that a government has to interfere when one third of a nation is ill-fed or nonfed, ill-clothed or nonclothed, ill-sheltered or nonsheltered.

President Herbert Hoover was a man of brains, but his mind did not comprehend that. He had brought the land to near chaos and ruin.

President Franklin D. Roosevelt was a man of heart—his heart comprehended that, and he saved our American form of government.

We demanded, and that was rude. We demanded, and we wouldn't be sent to the backdoor for a handout. When one demands, you have to lick him or negotiate with him—one or the other. When they couldn't lick us, rather they licked us often, but when they found we wouldn't stay licked, they had to negotiate.

It was a fight. What a fight! In the end we won the major part of our immediate demands, thus helping to restore the stability of the capitalist system—although Marx, Engels, Lenin, and Stalin, who inspired us, had exactly the opposite in mind.

We got the dole.

We got relief baskets.

We got Home Relief—in cash.

We got W.P.A., P.W.A., H.O.L.C., F.H.A, and the other F.H.A. (Farms and Homes Administration).

We got Unemployment Insurance and Social Security.

We got the philosophy embodied in the first article in our Constitution re-established, that our government is responsible for the general welfare of the people and must interfere in the economic life of the nation to secure this.

Say what you please! Deny if you wish! Distort our role, or minimize it; give credit for the above achievement to whomever you wish!

One fact is outstanding—it cannot be denied. The Communists were the only organized force during the early part of the depression that relentlessly, with never-ceasing energy, generated the constant pressure compelling those New Deal reforms.

The other day I saw a woman in front of me at the supermarket cash her unemployment insurance check. It was for $35. She had bought a basketful of groceries, butter, and half a smoked ham. She carefully counted her change, then, as an after-thought, she asked for a carton of cigarettes. She paid over the money for that too, tucking the change in her wallet.

I smiled and remarked, "It's quite a load you have." She smiled back and replied, "I prefer to do my shopping all in one, then I'm through for the week." We both agreed that was a good idea and I watched her wheel the wire basket out to her car because her purchases were too heavy to carry by hand.

She was a young woman around twenty-four and she saw nothing unusual in that transaction. I was happy and reflected that was as it should be.

I recalled the riot at Kroger's in Cleveland just about the time that young woman was born, not over a full carton but only a single pack of cigarettes. One of the unemployed, when presenting his relief voucher, had asked that a package of cigarettes be included. The manager refused; by orders of the City Council those relief vouchers should only be honored for food, and he righteously added that the unemployed should be thankful to get something to eat, the nerve of some of them asking even for cigarettes. Some comrades happened to be present and that store was nearly wrecked by the time the manager tremblingly offered to turn over that pack of cigarettes. That news traveled fast, stores outside of the Kroger chain took note of it also. The clerks were speedily instructed to disregard that order of the City Council. From that day on no storekeeper again raised the question whether the unemployed had the right to a smoke or not.

Violence? Persuasion maybe, with a singular lack of tact on both sides.

I also recall a sequel to that incident. The Communists organized a march on City Hall demanding that relief be paid in cash instead of food vouchers. A councilman with a big cigar in his mouth smiled ironically!

"So they could spend it on joy rides, or even cigars, I presume?" he baited the delegates.

236

That cigar was rammed down his throat and a full-scale riot ensued. The police rushed in and blood splattered the floor of the Cleveland Council Chambers. Heads were cracked and demonstrators were jailed. But we got the cash relief.

Violence? Yes. But be it remembered—we bore the brunt of it.

Deplorable? Maybe.

Un-American? Like a hungry stomach.

Subversive? Ask Andrew Jackson.

The ways of the Lord are inscrutable. God in His wisdom may choose whatever instrumentality to impose His will upon selfish men with hearts of stone—even card-carrying Communists.

Aye, that He may.

Come the Day of Judgment, my plea for redemption shall rest on that.

34 SHORTLY after my return from Canada the *Uj Elore* moved to Ohio and I with it. The six years I spent there as a full-time party functionary in various capacities, including that of heading the Ohio Bureau of the *Daily Worker,* the official organ of the party, were years of the greatest social unrest in the history of the United States since the early days of the American Revolution. There was a widely felt popular recognition of the need for a drastic change in government which was manifested most clearly in the rapid radicalization of the intellectuals—the opinion molders of society. A substantial number of writers, artists, teachers, musicians, performing artists, and even preachers not only joined the chorus of discontent but even led it by their voices. For famine stalked the land, not because of flood, drought, or other ravages of the elements, a famine caused by a failure not of crops but of men in high places in government, in legislature, in banking, and industry.

The fields of the small farmer lay prostrate.

"All the peaches you can pick, 25 cents. Bring your own baskets," read the home-scrawled signs in orchard after orchard in the fertile fields of Ohio. One farmer once proved to me with both bills and vouchers that after having sent two truckloads of peaches to market the check he received from his commission produce-broker was twelve dollars less than he had to spend for baskets alone.

Desperate as the situation of the farmer was, pressed as he was by debts, he was still better off, at least temporarily, than his urban brother. He could raise at least part of his food and barter for the rest. He couldn't be evicted overnight for nonpayment of rent; at least until foreclosure, which usually takes time, he was sure of a roof over his head.

The real pariah was the unemployed and there were more than 15 million of him in the land. Daily he had to face the anguished tears of his wife who was struggling to put some kind of a meal together out of scraps for her hungry children. He with his family had to go about with toes sticking out of distintegrating shoes, in tatters that would no longer hold a patch.

But this was not all. He was also turned into a moral leper. In newsprint, in pronouncements from high places, and in conversation he was constantly reproached and damned in tones that only the well-fed self-righteous can command. He was told that he, and he alone, was responsible for his sorry state. He was accused of lacking the habit of industry; that he was a wastrel; that he was deficient in those qualities of thrift and sobriety that elevate the worthy in the eyes of God and make him the rightful recipient of His bountiful blessings. After all is said and done, one has to face up to reality. Not all men are created equal, some are created weaklings. Some men are born with the crazy idea that the world owes them a living. These men are no good, they are too lazy to labor because one truth is self-evident in this here country: *"Nobody needs to starve, anybody who wants to work can always get a job."*

The unemployed worker himself soon began to feel a sense of guilt about being out of a job. He developed a feeling of inferiority; he became mentally unstable, alternating between fits of rage and dumb submission, between outbursts of rebelliousness and hopeless lethargy. Those experiences, which some fifteen years later were given the collective label "the scars of the depression," were to leave indelible marks on an entire generation.

Those who still had a job lived in constant dread of the day when they too might end up on the scrap heap of the unemployed.

Unorganized and thus unable to put up collective resistance, the employed worker fell easy victim to the iron law of unregulated capitalism which, as defined by Marx, was forever driving to extract from him the maximum production while attempting to reduce his share in the products of his labor to the minimum. He was speeded up relentlessly and, far from being given a share in his increased productivity, he was subjected to periodic cuts in his wages. He now lived under the whip:

"If you won't do it, there are plenty men outside who will, and for less money, too!"

The self-employed—the small storekeepers, the white collar men, the professionals, the lower middle class—all feared for their survival. Empty stores lined the business streets; their show windows gaped dark at night like missing teeth in the shriveled gums of shabby old men. Lawyers, real estate men, insurance agents, accountants paced up and down fretfully in their deserted offices. Only the collection agencies hummed with increased activity. Engineers, chemists, technicians had to watch their skills rust away from nonuse. It takes many long years to train a physician—there were eight of them on Home Relief at one time in the city of Cleveland alone, I was told in confidence by a disheartened social worker.

However, not all was shade for everyone.

> Maid for general housework,
> experienced cook. White. Must
> be neat, and good with children.
> Sleep in. Every other Sunday
> afternoon off. $15 a month.
> Good references required!

read the "Help Wanted, Female" ads in the daily papers. There were less jobs than takers.

Colleges of the highest academic standing graduated their yearly quota only to add them to the swelling army of the idle. Countless young men and women, holders of coveted academic degrees, had to go back home after graduation and live off their parents. I had met many of these, some of them couldn't even pay for a cup of coffee; bright, educated, ambitious young persons in their mid-twenties who had not been given the chance to know what it felt like to have a dollar bill in their pocket which was neither begged nor borrowed, but earned by their own talent. A father of one such young man, a mixer in a chemical plant whose wages had been cut to $30 a week, once complained to me about the unreasonableness of the young generation. His son, a graduate of Western Reserve out of college for two years but still without a job, insisted on going steady with a girl. He kept pressing his father for a quarter spending money every time he took his girl out, as often as three and even four times a week. His girl, incidentally, was a qualified high school teacher who also never had a chance of finding employment.

Young daughters, mainly from foreign born families in which there were usually too many younger brothers and sisters to feed and who discovered they still had one commodity to market, took to hanging around lunchrooms and cafeterias. Their demand was modest and geared to the times—it was a meal, whether breakfast, lunch, or dinner.

"I don't eat much," most of them would add with serious entreaty.

Capitalism seemed to be coming apart at the seams, all according to the book. The objective preconditions of a coming revolution, as outlined by Lenin, were beginning to ripen right here in America.

1. *There was a widespread feeling of contempt for the ruling classes in and out of government.* The bankers, the "Captains of Industry," and not only those in Wall Street, became objects of scorn and hatred throughout the land. President Hoover's name was mud. A man in St. Louis or maybe it was New Orleans—I do not remember which, I recall reading it in the Miscellany column in *Time*—had been arrested for committing assault and battery in a movie house on a man sitting peacefully a few rows ahead of him. The accused had suddenly left his seat, walked over to that other man, who was a stranger to him, and punched

him repeatedly in the nose. When asked in court what his motive was for this unprovoked assault, his only defense was: "He looked like Hoover!"

2. *There was a breakdown of the capitalist system of production, choked in its own surpluses.* The most efficient mass-production system in the world, equipped with the most up-to-date machinery, was grinding to a standstill. Fully one third of the greatest army of technically skilled workers the world could boast was reduced to spending its days in enforced idleness. Men highly skilled in weaving textiles, garment workers expert in tailoring clothes, were walking around in tatters; carpenters, masons, building trade workers were huddling in run-down hovels.

3. *There was the demoralization of the ruling class, an abdication of their responsibilities.* The White House conference called by Hoover in February 1932 of the nation's most outstanding capitalists, the leaders in business, industry, and finance, revealed their bankruptcy in ideas. Not one of them professed to understand what caused the economic crisis, not a man among them stated it was their responsibility to come up with a constructive remedy. The most they would hazard was hope and prayer. To quote W. W. Atterbury, President of the Pennsylvania Railroad: "The depression is bound to hit a bottom sooner or later and then things would be slowly building up." That was his contribution—the only one of even dubious cheer at that conference.

4. *Law enforcement was breaking down.* Plants and mills were laying in firearms, tear gas, and machine guns, recruiting their own private armies of hired thugs to stave off the anticipated debacle. Agencies like Berghoff's who dealt in supplying professional strikebreakers and *agents provocateur* did not share in the general business decline, they were thriving and expanding.

Hunger riots, spontaneous flare-ups of violence challenged the authorities of every state.

Near Bowling Green, Ohio, at a Sheriff's Sale to satisfy a foreclosed mortgage on the land and chattels of a farmer with small children the farmers themselves came into the act, carrying firearms. When the Sheriff, the auctioneer, the agent of the mortgage holder, an Eastern insurance company, arrived on the scene they found themselves confronted with a thick noose of shiny rope hanging from a stout limb of the oak tree beneath which were arrayed the Harvester tractor, the battered family Ford, and the rest of the farm implements scheduled to go under the hammer.

When the Sheriff wanted to postpone the sale he was informed by the men who called him by first name that they had dropped their work to attend this auction and they felt sure he wouldn't want to inconvenience them. The frightened agent who looked deathly pale was assured in friendly tones that they had nothing against strangers who knew enough to keep their mouths shut and not to butt their noses into other folks' affairs.

The auction went on as scheduled—no item up for sale brought more than one single bid. The farm, barn, outbuildings were knocked down for $10, the tractor brought $1.40, the car even less, a team of fine horses went for 22 cents. The total came to a little under twenty dollars, all paid in cash and in full by the neighbors, then presented free and clear to the original owner.

Home owners, the traditional upholders of the private ownership system, the embodiment of conservatism, turned out in howling mobs in Cleveland (also in other cities) battling the combined forces of police and firemen to prevent the dispossession of other home owners on whom the banks had foreclosed, until they succeeded in bringing that banking practice to a halt. Most of them were churchgoers and deeply religious, yet they were denounced as Communists which they were definitely not —at least not until the Communists organized them into a Small Home and Land Owners Federation, when many of them did join up.

In Barberton, Ohio, a spontaneous mass strike in a match company flared into armed violence when under a police escort a group of strikebreakers were brought into the plant. I still have in my possession that "Proclamation of Riot" which I rescued

MAYOR'S PROCLAMATION

By the authority vested in me as Mayor of the City of Barberton, Ohio,

I COMMAND

in the name of the State of Ohio, all persons unlawfully or riotously assembled to disperse and depart to their homes or lawful employment

(Signed)
EARL L. DAVIS, Mayor

(The law as contained in the General Code of Ohio provides that: Whoever continues together after Proclamation is made is guilty of riot and shall be fined not more than $500.00 or imprisoned not more than 30 days.)

after it was torn down contemptuously and trampled in the mud, ordering the strikers to disperse, an order the police were unable to enforce.

In nearby Kent, a few weeks later, when the workers refused to accept another wage cut, the management locked them out and brought in a force of armed professional strikebreakers to intimidate the workers and force them to submit. The sight of those armed thugs sauntering provokingly up and down behind the steel-link fence surrounding the plant produced an effect totally different from that planned by the management. Many of those locked out workers happened to be mountaineers from Kentucky. They rushed home for their long-barreled squirrel guns and laid armed siege to the plant.

By the time I reached the scene the strikebreakers had all been driven inside one wing. I squatted down next to one of the mountaineers and watched him draw a bead on the water tower in the yard. The bullet hit near the bottom but drew no squirt of water from that riddled reservoir. He grunted with satisfaction and told me he only wanted to make sure, those yellow-bellied skunks must be pretty parched by now, they must be asweating aplenty. He filled his pipe, then took a shot at a window from which someone had just fired a gun.

"They are whupped!" he apprised me of the situation, reckoning that the ammunition of the strikebreakers must be nearly spent; they had been so "scairt" when they found themselves besieged that they shot most of their ammunition away at the start. He proved right, for in less than a half hour a white towel was hoisted from the window. The sheriff and his deputies, who had been disarmed at gun point when attempting to aid the strikebreakers, were now ordered to go fetch the men and escort them out of town. The professional strikebreakers came out thoroughly subdued, some of them wearing makeshift blood-soaked bandages; they followed the sheriff with dragging feet. My companion, a bony man with a stubble beard, spat, but it might have been the tobacco. In talking with those workers one singular fact struck me. Not one of them was conscious of having committed a rebellious offense by launching a concerted armed assault against governmental authority as represented by the sheriff.

In Toledo, striking Auto Lite workers, women mostly, rushed the strikebreakers, ripped off their clothes leaving only their ties on, then paraded them stark naked down the street in broad daylight, hooting in derision.

That was the mood, the temper, the spirit of the people as I witnessed it in that great state of Ohio, the "Buckeye State," endowed by bountiful nature with fertile valleys and rich mineral deposits; a state boasting of industrial plants and mills among the most modern in the world, and populated by six million industrious, God-fearing citizens.

The conditions prevailing in Ohio reflected the situation throughout the country. Even the dullest sensed that a change had to come. History ceased to be a recital of events long past; it became the living present pulsating with dynamic energy.

People suddenly became aware that the making of history need not necessarily be left to Washington alone. They learned that history can also be shaped by the unemployed on the streets; by strikers on the picket lines; by street brawls and organized assaults on defenseless minorities; by crude but determined men in shabby union halls organizing the unorganized; by intellectuals beating the drums.

The battle lines were shaping up; Red and Black on the two extreme wings, the undecided and the cautious in the middle— the New Deal a bit left of center trying its best to establish a new equilibrium, to restore and preserve the dream that was America.

The land was split into those who hoped for a revolutionary change and those who feared it. There were few indeed who dared maintain with genuinely felt assurance:

"It can't happen here!"

246

35 "WE, the Communists, the leaders of the American proletariat, the vanguard of the oppressed everywhere . . ."

"Led by the Communist Party, the vanguard of the American working class, the toilers of America are uniting to . . ."

While we, the self-styled vanguard, shouted ourselves hoarse on street corners to catch the ears of the casual passers-by, the Fascists who were much better financed took to the air. Father Coughlin, the "Radio Priest," the most influential of all native would-be Fascist leaders, had an estimated audience of thirty million glued to their radio receivers on Sunday afternoons. It need be said that not all those spellbound by his oratory were aware that his social gospel was Fascist in its basic content and that his "Sixteen Points of Social Justice" so temptingly expounded in his golden voice were modeled on the Nuremberg program of Hitler's National Socialist Party in Germany.

By 1936 Father Coughlin thought the time ripe for assuming personal command over his followers and to enter the field of national politics by sponsoring a Frazer-Lemke Third Party ticket in the 1936 presidential election. To give his candidates a flying start he decided to address their national nominating convention in Cleveland in person, making this his first political appearance in public.

To get the "feel" of that meeting it may be of help to know that the ideals of democracy, Socialism, Communism—no matter what opposite courses they may take in reality—are all based on the recognition of the fundamental humanity of man, on the

247

striving for some sort of universal brotherhood in which all men are assured of enjoying certain inalienable rights including that of being permitted to live in peace and harmony with their fellow human beings. Democracy, Socialism, Communism share with true Christianity the concept of love thy neighbor—the early Christians actually lived in a form of primitive Communism. The cruel excesses perpetrated by the Communist rulers wherever they came to power no more negate the basic idealistic content of true Communism than the tortures of the Inquisition negate the teachings of Christ.

The motivating force of Fascism, in contrast, is that of hate. Fascism is based on the atavistic urge to kill every other being who dwells in a different cave, whose manners, customs, bodily appearance mark him as different from one's own clan. Fascism is built on the pagan myth that through sharing some mystic quality in their blood one group of men are constituted a Master Race while the rest of mankind are nothing but subhumans to be exterminated at will, or at best, fit only to serve as slaves to their masters.

I planned to get to that meeting early to have a better chance to observe the behavior of the crowd, and I did.

Yet by the time I arrived both halls of the Public Auditorium, with a combined seating capacity of 14,000, were already packed. A private army of frozen-faced young men in semimilitary uniforms, identical shirts, breeches, and puttees, lined the walls, the aisles, and the wings of the common stage serving both auditoriums, keeping the audience under steady scrutiny. Their baleful eyes were alert for trouble and they made quite a show of resting their hands ominously on the blackjacks protruding from their hip pockets.

The audience was predominantly lower middle class, somberly dressed despite the summer heat; it sat uncommunicative and unsmiling.

It was a creepy sensation—a mass of humanity 14,000 strong,

248

larger than the entire population of many a small town, waiting a full hour before the scheduled start of the meeting in a tense silence which was rarely interrupted by even a whispered sentence. That was Cleveland, Ohio, U.S.A. They were Americans but their behavior was not that of a normal American audience of squirming and gaily chattering people waiting for the main event. This was an almost motionless group with jaws grimly set, upper lips partially pulled back from the gums by taut facial muscles, gripped by some mystic anticipation. Physically they were one crowd yet spiritually they were not—each of them seemed to be alone with himself, his eyes glued to the empty stage but focused inwardly. They were waiting with muscles coiled like felines before the pounce, like epileptics on the verge of a seizure.

Walking down that long aisle to the press table in front under those unblinking, suspicious eyes was like running a gauntlet. I had a sudden urge to break into a run and it took great effort to saunter down slowly, jaunty and casual, to repeat with the right amount of bored indifference "Reporter" whenever challenged by those uniformed thugs, praying that I be allowed to pass without being asked for my press card which would identify me as the correspondent for the Communist *Daily Worker*.

All at once it came, as startling as the onrush of a sudden gust of storm—the sharp hiss of a gasp, the sucking intake of breath by thousands of open mouths.

"Father Coughlin is coming!" the whisper rose into a shout and the chamber erupted in a hoarse elemental roar. That roar was totally unlike those heard at National Party Conventions; it was not the cheer of the baseball park, nor the jeer of the picket line. That was the savage howl of the human pack, unarticulated and pulsating, a release of emotions so elemental and brutal that they had been long relegated into the unconscious by thousands of years of civilization for the self-preservation of mankind; an animal howl so primitive that no single individual when alone is capable of sounding it except in moments of stark insanity. That was the cry of humans gone berserk, an emotional explosion that needs to find an outlet in violence, or be sustained until total exhaustion sets in.

The entrance of a corps of drummers marching with military precision now raised the already deafening frenzy to a pitch near agony and suddenly Father Coughlin materialized—a broad-shouldered, muscular man moving with the bounce of an athlete under the cassock of the Roman Catholic priest; flinging away his skirt with an impatient sweep when mounting the platform. He stood there with his feet planted wide apart, a triumphant smile on his face, listening to the howl of the mob as his rightful due. His stance radiated supreme self-confidence; he was the leader surveying his frenzied troops before unleashing them; only his tightly clenched fists belied his outward calm.

I can't recall a single sentence of what Father Coughlin said that night and I doubt there was a single individual in that audience who could have accurately retained any part of his address. That speech was not meant to be rooted in the memory of the audience—it was intended to sear the emotions of the listeners and to sensitize them to the point where they would react with similar violence at the slightest stimulus in the future.

Father Coughlin was unlike any other speaker in my memory. He was a spellbinder like Hitler, he could carry an audience, rub their emotions raw and juggle them at will. His voice was clear tenor with an operatic ring, there was a pent-up savagery in each of his sentences which he punctuated with his arm like the downward thrust of a stiletto. Unlike Hitler, he did not threaten, cajole, or thunder that he was the Fuehrer whom they had to follow. To me he was the reincarnation of Arnold, the Abbot of Citeaux, standing before the gates of the besieged city of Béziers, replying to his followers when asked how to distinguish true believers from the heretics in the heat of the assault on that town:

"Kill them all; God will know his own!" As he spoke on I

heard Abbot Arnold reporting back to Pope Gregory the Great with pride in his accomplishment.

"Nearly twenty thousand human beings perished by the sword. And after the massacre of the heretics the town was plundered and burnt, and the revenge of God seemed to rage over it in a wonderful manner."

Who were the heretics in America in the thirties thus to be put to the sword?

For answer let me quote from another would-be Fascist leader who is still around, the Reverend Gerald L. K. Smith, who at the time I met him was an itinerant preacher and part-time evangelist talking folksy and preaching politics under the guise of religion. He was the convivial sort, walking around with a small, black-leather-bound Bible protruding from his hip pocket. That was not a preaching Bible but merely an oratorical device. Every time he wanted to make a point, he would pull that Bible out of his pocket, hold it high in his left hand, then give it a hard punch with his right fist. That Bible must have had a special acoustic binding for it responded with a resounding "C sharp" crack.

I talked with Smith twice. He was proud of his start with the Louisiana Kingfish, that incipient Fascist Huey Long; he did not hide from me that he was out for fame, power, and the easy fast buck. He did not relish being seen in public conversing with the correspondent of the Communist *Daily Worker* and was somewhat guarded with me, but not so with Gerold Frank, then a reporter on the Cleveland *News,* and I am now quoting from the interview Frank had with him:

"I am a reactionary.

"Reaction will produce a ruthless, intolerant, dynamic nationalistic movement which will capture the imagination of the American people. I shall lead that movement. . . .

"I shall attack, and ruthlessly attack a Jew, or an Italian, or a Negro, or any other man because he is a Communist. And he doesn't have to be a member of the Communist Party to be a

Communist. If he's imbued with Communistic philosophy he's a Communist. They're all one to me.

"I shall not attack any minorities because they are minorities. Some of my best friends are Jews. But I shall attack with all my strength any minority if it's Communistic.

"I shall call for a fusion movement of all patriotic organizations in the country to wipe out with intolerant zeal the last vestiges of Communism and other atheistic destruction. Here and now I announce myself the leader of that movement, a cold blooded, intolerant, frontal attack on the subtle machination of the Communists."

We, the Communists, thus served as a target to divert the rebellious mood of the masses from those responsible for their economic plight. In consequence millions of Americans were living under the dread of an impending Communist revolution. In all America there was but one group absolutely convinced of the impossibility of a Communist revolution in America—the members of the Communist Party.

I had not met a single responsible member of the Party—and I probed hundreds of them—who sincerely believed that we could have Communism in the United States in our lifetime—our grandchildren, maybe yes, if they were going to be lucky.

There was a good reason for our lack of faith in revolution. While our enemies were frightened by the demonstrated vulnerability and weaknesses of their own existing capitalist system we knew full well how inherently strong that system was—we had batted our heads against it innumerable times and had little but bloody bumps to show for it.

While those on the outside were quaking in contemplation of our imagined strength, we were fully aware of our weaknesses, the gravest of which was our inability to grow.

When I arrived in Ohio in the spring of 1931, the total Party membership in the Ohio Party District numbered about 2,200. Six years later when I left to join the International Brigades in Spain the maximum membership we were able to register still fell short of 2,900—a total net growth of less than seven hundred in six years, despite all the frantic work we did among the unemployed, with all the heartbreaking work we did to help organize the unorganized in the mass production industries of steel, rubber, etc., in Ohio.

Not that we had failed to gain new recruits. I had not bothered to keep accurate count, nor is this said in any sense of boasting, but I can safely record that the number of people I alone had personally recruited into the party both here and in Canada must run well into the hundreds. I am equally safe in asserting that most of those recruits quit the Party shortly after they joined.

The unemployed would march with us: "On to City Hall!" The employed would learn from us how to organize, go out on strike, and set up picket lines to safeguard their rights—and then turn their backs on us afterward because of our party line. All that talk about imperialism, about defending the Soviet Union, was no skin off their noses. What they were interested in was improving their conditions right here and now. If they wanted to hear about Kingdom Come they went to church and not to some Red yapping about a Communist paradise.

"Revolution? You bet; that's what many of them foreign countries need, like we had ours in 1776. You're right about Washington; that sure is a mess that needs cleaning out bad. There is a bunch of no good bastards there who ought to be kicked out on their ass; but people are learning to vote for the man who is their friend and that's a fact. Just watch the next election!"

These were the proletarians who made up the American working class—although most of them would have resented being called any such thing, considering themselves a "better class o' people." They were American citizens; yet the party was attempting to force them into a straitjacket cut for a Russian muzhik.

That straitjacket was THE PARTY LINE.

36   ALL Communist activities are governed by the "Party Line"; all Communists are held to the sacred rule:

"The Party Line is always right."

Any challenge to this concept is heresy. Heretics in Communist countries—those not tortured to death or executed outright—usually end their days in jail or forced labor camps. In capitalist countries, as for instance in America, these heretics were usually branded Trotskyists or counterrevolutionary Fascists, and denounced in the *Daily Worker* as paid stool pigeons of the imperialists and embezzlers of Party funds, their pictures prominently displayed in the *Daily Worker* under the standing head:

WORKERS' ENEMIES EXPOSED

Yet the Party Line was an elusive guide. Besides being always right it had a number of other peculiar characteristics. Infallible as it was proclaimed to be, nevertheless it was subject to diametrical changes overnight without conceding in any way that the old line might have been wrong after all.

Another peculiarity of the Party Line was that a comrade's ability to "interpret it correctly" had nothing to do with his intellectual accomplishments or his thorough familiarity with the writings of Marx, Engels, Lenin, but depended solely on his standing in the Party hierarchy. The higher up he stood in leadership—no matter how great his ignorance—the more "correct" his understanding of the Line automatically became.

The genesis of that party line was usually a speech made by Stalin, but sometimes it was Molotov, or some other high ranking official of the Soviet Union or the Comintern who was given the task of sounding off. The sacred text then was immediately broadcast by the *Inprecor,* published and republished in pamphlets, articles, editorials, re-echoed in speeches first by Browder, then the others in the exalted Central Committee, and so on down. It was the same speech, the same clichés "adapted to the special conditions." Such adaptation usually consisted of an added phrase or two by the respective official and it concluded with the stern but somewhat redundant admonition:

"We must bend our utmost effort to carry out these decisions in line with the new party line and adapt them to the special prevailing conditions."

The "line" thus handed down from above could be freely discussed at each step and the membership was encouraged to participate in it, provided this discussion was in the affirmative and not only ended but also started with:

"I agree with the correctness of the new Party Line."

Certain democratic variations were permitted. A party member, in fact, any party member was free to say instead:

"I laud the new Party Line."

The ambitious and eager would usually combine both and declaim:

"I laud the new Party Line and agree with the correctness of it."

That testimonial cinched it good.

One day the comrade in charge of the Cleveland Bookshop called to tell me of a puzzling experience. The night before a man came into the bookstore, asked for a book that would tell him what the party line was. The comrade had tried to explain to him that there was no such book but the man would not accept his explanation. The man insisted that with all the talk about the party line there had to be a book about it, how else could anybody know what it really was, and he accused the comrade of sabotage, of trying to keep people from learning

255

about the party line. To the comrade it was clear he was dealing with a crackpot and to avoid trouble he decided to humor him. He proceeded to sell him a copy of every party pamphlet, every magazine in the store, some of which had long turned yellow with age, and he topped it off with the jackpot—by unloading on him a complete set of Lenin's works, which was really dead stock as far as the average member was concerned. The purchase came to around fifty dollars, the highest single transaction and cash sale in the history of that bookshop. The comrade, although pleased with his salesmanship and greatly amused by the stupidity of that man, was worried that he might have been dealing with a stool pigeon.

I shared his amusement but not his worry—from the description he gave me that man looked like Hall (this is not his true name)—he certainly sounded like him. Hall was one of our new comrades, a newspaperman and one of the original founders of the Newspaper Guild. He was an ardent Guild man and a member of its National Board. He was one of those union men who first became party sympathizers because of the help they received from us when trying to form a union, and who later joined the party when they saw how effective a party cell could be in promoting the growth of a union. I checked with Hall and found my guess was correct. He had just come back from a meeting of the National Board in New York where the party fraction kept rebuffing his ideas with: "You don't know the party line, you don't understand it." Hall was a thorough newspaperman, one of the best in Cleveland; he determined to make up for that deficiency. Hence his visit to the bookstore.

A few weeks later Hall called—he wanted me to meet him urgently and in secret. We agreed on an out-of-the-way bar where neither of us was known and where we would be most unlikely to be discovered.

Hall came in carrying a bulging brief case. He unzipped it and said:

"Voros, I want to tip you off to something. There is graft and corruption in the party and it reaches right into the Central Committee. I have here the evidence to prove it." With that he reached into the brief case and laid pamphlet after pamphlet on the table, all of them carefully marked as to pages with entire passages and chapters underlined in ink.

"Look at these sons of bitches," Hall proceeded to demonstrate, pointing to pamphlet after pamphlet. "They've taken Molotov's speech and plagiarized it. See for yourself, page after page of verbatim quotes from Molotov. This is Browder's pamphlet. But then take Stachel on trade union work, James W. Ford on the Negro question, Gil Green on youth work, and the rest of them. They not only plagiarized Molotov but they also plagiarized Browder, taking entire pages over from his pamphlet. They are making suckers out of the party members, making them buy those pamphlets and rake in the shekels. I have all the proof here. Now, what do you think we ought to do to expose those racketeers and clean them out of the party?"

I was shaking with laughter and Hall got angry. He told me he had always thought me clean and sincere, he hoped I wasn't mixed up in that racket. It took quite a time to satisfy him that there was no graft involved, that that was the way the party line was handed down to membership and "adapted to the special conditions."

From there we went to discussing the "party line" which I explained to Hall as "the proper interpretation of communist policy, strategy, and tactics by the dialectical analysis of any given situation based on the teachings of Marx, Engels, Lenin, and also Stalin."

"That's no line at all," snorted Hall. "To me that's merely a trick to make the membership toe the mark and to enable the leadership to wriggle off the hook when its policy backfires."

That was the trouble with new members, especially with those in the Newspaper Guild. Those "prostitutes of the venal capitalist press" as we used to call them became so corrupted in their thinking by their years of servitude to the Press Lords that even joining the Party was not enough to purify them completely. To them nothing was sacred, not even the Party Line; they looked with cynical eyes even on the party leadership.

But not only new members like Hall had difficulty with the Party Line. Even an old-timer like Phil Bart, former District Organizer of Ohio, a man who always fanatically insisted that the party line must be followed to the letter, admitted to me at one of our intimate parties restricted to the select few in the innermost leadership that once—even though that one time alone —he also found himself stymied by it.

When Bart was in his twenties he had received an assignment to join the National Guard "to bore from within" and to carry on antimilitaristic agitation within its ranks. That was years before World War II. He was frail and undernourished and had a difficult time getting himself accepted. Finally they took pity on him and permitted him to sign up in time to leave with the Guard for their annual three weeks training.

The National Guard Summer Camp was located in the mountains where the air was clear and vigorous, the scenery enchanting. That was the first time in Bart's life that he was away in the country, out of the dirt, filth, noise, and overcrowding of the tenement district where he was born; the first chance he had to enjoy the beauty of nature. The food was rich and plentiful, another marvel he had never experienced. Pancakes, platters heaped with creamy butter and syrup by the pitcher, sausage, ham, or bacon and eggs for breakfast; steaks, chops, poultry, pastry, salad, and vegetables for lunch and dinner, and no limitation on portions! Bart ate and ate and ate—he gained six pounds the first week.

Late Saturday night at the end of his first week Bart sneaked out to a prearranged meeting with his comrades in the far end of the camp. After the exchange of a few furtive words he was handed a package of antimilitarist leaflets for surreptitious distribution in the camp.

When Bart got back safely and undetected he withdrew to the latrine to read those leaflets. They were antimilitary all right, following faithfully the Russian precept—they called upon the guardsmen to protest the foul, maggot-ridden starvation rations on which they were forced to subsist while their officers were gorging themselves. Bart did not know whether to cry or laugh. That night they had had steak for supper, juicy tenderloin steak garnished with mushrooms, asparagus, and French fried potatoes. Bart put away two of the steaks and had a good start on a third which even he was unable to finish. Dessert was strawberry short-cake with whipped cream plus all the ice cream they wanted, and those who didn't like strawberries had two different kinds of pie to choose from.

Bart knew he couldn't distribute those leaflets without causing a Homeric laugh in camp. Yet it was a party task—the purpose behind his assignment to join the National Guard. Finally he came to a decision. He took a shovel and buried those leaflets deep, covered by the night sky, working fast to avoid detection. He slept fitfully during that night, haunted by the guilt of having been untrue to the Party.

The following Saturday night when Bart stole out again, his comrades were eager to learn what impression those leaflets had made in camp. When Bart related what he had done with them a vehement argument ensued. He was chastised, censured, and then handed a new batch of leaflets under strict orders that he distribute them without fail. Before agreeing to that Bart now took the precaution of reading them by flashlight first. It was an appeal calling upon the guardsmen to demonstrate in protest against the arrogant brutality of their officers, and to demand the immediate abolishment of corporal punishment in the camp.

It was a good leaflet in a sense. No different from the kind Bart would have written himself had he not joined the Guard; based on the line that the National Guard was bossed by the Wall Street imperialists and that conditions in all imperialist armies were the same as had prevailed under the Czar in Russia. Now Bart found himself admitting reluctantly to his comrades that his officers in the National Guard were decent young fellows. Worse still, he was even forced to defend those imperialist hirelings, those minions of Wall Street who, when not on duty, acted just like the rest of the men, participating in the games and even in some of the bull sessions. Bart adamantly refused to distribute the leaflets.

The comrades persisted. The party's antimilitarist line was right. There had to be something the men did not like, some grievance that could be exploited. Under relentless questioning Bart finally offered the observation that some of the fellows did seem to grumble while drilling. The comrades pounced upon that. Since there was no time to prepare another leaflet, they ordered Bart to start agitation for the abolition of the drill. To this Bart agreed.

That was the last week of camp, the end of the three-week jaunt. It was a wonderful vacation for all, particularly for Bart to whom it was a happy interval of carefree existence under the open sky, his first experience of luxuriating in opulence. But party decisions had to be carried out. By then Bart, as expected of a good Communist, had managed to build around himself a small group of men who were more or less influenced by him. Most of the men seemed eager to come back to camp next year and Bart thought that was the right cue to introduce the subject.

"You know, men," he told them, "what we ought to do next year is ask them to cut out the drill."

The men looked at him in puzzlement. Then one of them spoke up incredulously.

"Are you crazy? You mean you don't like drilling?"

"If you don't like to drill then what the hell you want to come back here for?" said another.

"What's the sense in coming back here if they'd cut out the drill?" asked the others. Drilling was fun, that was what they liked most about the National Guard.

Bart gave up—the only time he had failed to obey a party decision or admitted the Party Line could be wrong.

In 1935, the Party Line was suddenly subjected to a startling change. Frightened by the successes of the Japanese attack on China, Mussolini's conquest of Ethiopia, and the growing military might of Hitler, Stalin suddenly discovered virtues in the bourgeois democracies. Wishing to make allies of them, the Comintern now called for a United Front of all elements in every nation to oppose Fascism regardless of what ideological differences they might have with Communism. This United Front policy as announced by Dimitroff in his address to the Seventh Congress of the Communist International espoused patriotism as an antidote to Fascism, and the new Party Line now proclaimed:

"Communism is 20th Century Americanism!"

The Declaration of Independence was suddenly given a new hasty reading. Up until then it had been held in contempt, for according to the Party Line it was a hypocritical bourgeois document, a mere instrument in the hands of the rising bourgeoisie of the orginal thirteen colonies with which to fight the rival capitalist class of England. The party now solemnly proclaimed it a sacred document which incontestably proved that revolution was entirely in the American tradition.

The party next set out to prove that the Communists, and they alone, were the only real guardians of American traditions. The intellectuals under Communist influence sat right down to compose folk ballads, to revive and popularize folk customs, and had there been such a thing in the United States as a native garb, the wearing of it would undoubtedly have been made obligatory for all party members.

That sudden conversion to American traditions served me well when I was appointed chairman of the Ohio State Election Campaign Committee in 1935. Up until that time the party had not really been interested in American electoral procedures and it usually entered elections only *pro forma* by putting up a few candidates haphazardly. I now went to work to induce the party membership in Ohio to participate in the elections in earnest. The comrades were hesitant at first. Most of them had never bothered to register or seen the inside of a polling booth.

I exhorted and lectured them on the importance of elections, raised their morale by the publicity I managed to plant in the capitalist press (here my contacts with the members of the Newspaper Guild paid off), and topped it off by obtaining official credentials for Communist Party watchers and challengers—something the party had never thought of doing before—and by stationing twice as many Communist electioneers outside the booths as the other parties in the districts where we had Unemployed Councils functioning. That was easy for me. I didn't have to pay my workers, while the Republicans and Democrats did. Since the ribbons supplied to the Republican and Democratic electioneers were narrow and only lapel size, I ordered for my workers ribbons a yard long reaching from the buttonhole almost to the ankles. My ribbons were flaming red, four inches wide, with the word COMMUNIST printed in the biggest block letters I could find. They made those election polling stations look like kiosks in Moscow.

I added an extra touch. I once saw a historical print depicting an American torchlight parade and had longed to witness one in real life ever since. But torchlight parades were passé, they belonged to another historical period. Now I saw my chance to stage one, and I did.

That torchlight parade was a big success, Cleveland hadn't seen one in ages.

When the results were all in we found that I. O. Ford, Communist candidate for governor, was officially credited with over 55,000 votes, a gain of more than one thousand percent over the highest vote ever registered by the Communist Party in Ohio. For the first time we even polled votes from that bastion of capitalism, the exclusive residential section of Bratenahl on

Lake Erie. Small as was the Communist vote cast there—as I recall it, around 25—it was sufficient to cause consternation among the ultrarich. Old butlers and maids in family service for a generation were now being eyed with suspicion, and many old Union Leaguers took to sleeping with loaded pistols under their pillows. I received news of this with undisguised glee. Little did those patricians dream that those Communist votes had been cast by their own offspring, infected by the red virus on Ivy League campuses. Those snobbish butlers and maids wouldn't touch us with a ten-foot pole.

Our vote in Ohio was second only to that in New York, where the Communist Party polled seventy-odd thousand votes, about 20,000 more than we did. But that was no comparison. In proportion to their membership they would have had to poll three quarters of a million votes to equal our showing.

Speaking of elections, we once succeeded in electing a Communist mayor in Yorktown, in the Ohio panhandle. He wasn't much of a mayor and Yorktown wasn't much of a town, subsisting mainly on mining. Still, he was a real mayor, the only Communist mayor ever elected in the United States. He lost out in the next election because no mayor in America could possibly have fulfilled the campaign promises he had made.

We were campaigning on a revolutionary program:

"Paid unemployed compensation, to all those out of work, of $15 a week. A minimum wage of 50 cents an hour."

To these revolutionary demands—for that's what they were at that time—he added two of his own:

"The abolishment of all debts and mortgages;" and the key one that really got him elected:
"No taxes on liquor—ever!"

37   In the spring, 1936, Comrade Roberts, the Comintern's American representative, fresh from a trip to Moscow, came to attend our District Plenary meeting in Ohio. He greeted me cordially, which surprised me—he usually kept aloof and distant from us. I was late coming in, the meeting had already started. He was sitting alone, as usual, in a far corner and he beckoned me over—quite a distinction to be so recognized by a Comintern leader. He whispered he would see me later in private and that he had some good news for me.

The "good news" that Roberts had for me was totally unexpected. He told me that the election campaign I had carried on the previous fall had greatly pleased Moscow. It demonstrated to them that I really understood the "new party line," how to put into action the new slogan, "Communism is 20th Century Americanism." I was amazed. That election campaign was fun but it had not occurred to me that it would be noted in the Kremlin. The greatest surprise was yet to come. Roberts informed me that he had chosen me to manage the 1936 national campaign of Earl Browder for president and told me to draw up a plan for it. I was astonished, which must have shown in my face, for Roberts laughed, patted me on the shoulder, and asked smilingly did I think we would be able to poll three million votes for Browder.

"At least that!" I answered unhesitatingly. "Maybe even more than La Follette polled in 1924. With our new party line we can really go places!"

Whether my plan would have worked out or not I have no

264

means of ascertaining. By the time I was ready to present it, the party line had changed again. The new line called for concentrating on the defeat of the Republican candidate without endorsing Roosevelt, under the Communist campaign slogan:

DEFEAT LANDON AT ALL COST—VOTE FOR EARL BROWDER.

I opposed that slogan at the National Convention, arguing that it was idiotic—that it made no sense—that it would only confuse our membership. But I was alone in my stand. As long as that was the party line, it made good sense to all other delegates since the party line was *always right.*

I still couldn't see any sense in it and of course that was the end of my appointment as the national campaign manager, although I still had to continue as State Chairman of the Ohio Election Campaign Committee, over my protests.

As the election campaign developed, that slogan created utter confusion in the party. The more the Party Central Committee tried to clarify it, the more it compounded the confusion. When the comrades asked me how they should put into practice the slogan "Defeat Landon at all cost—Vote for Earl Browder," I answered with a straight face, according to the Party line "By defeating Landon at all cost and by voting for Earl Browder."

That enigmatic reply satisfied no one. The comrades tried time and again to make me tell them to vote and campaign for Roosevelt or to vote for Browder, which clearly would not contribute to the defeat of Landon. I stood pat and referred them to our printed party platform.

The result was as could be expected. The total vote for Browder in the entire country came to a little over 100,000, about the same or a few votes less than Foster had received in 1932.

Reporting to the monthly meeting of the Ohio District Committee in January 1937 on the election campaign in Ohio, I pointed to the more than 50,000 votes polled by our candidate for congressman at large as proof that our work had been successful again.

"We still lead every other Party District in the number of Communist votes polled in proportion to our membership. As for the small vote of five thousand some odd for Browder, that must have come from the lunatic fringe for almost every comrade I have questioned admitted to me in confidence that he voted for Roosevelt, which bore out my prediction that the party line was wrong on Browder. Personally, I believe in the secrecy of the ballot and therefore I will not reveal to the meeting how I voted. However I want the record to show that Landon was defeated and as a good Communist I want to be given credit for that accomplishment."

Everybody was laughing. John Williamson, the District Organizer and therefore the leader of the Ohio party, routinely moved that my report be accepted. He rebuked me, however, for my statement that the party line was wrong on Browder. The party line was right, it was always right. He recommended that I study Marx and Lenin again and asked me to admit my error.

That would have been easy to do. I was among friends. All they really expected me to say for the record:

"Comrades, I realize my error and I accept the correctness of the party line."

They would even have been satisfied with the statement:

"Comrades, of course the party line is always right. My mistake was that I failed to comprehend it fully."

We would all have known that to be a mere ritual which in no way would have altered the results of that election campaign; that campaign was behind us, water over the dam, let's put a period to it and go on to new and pressing business.

That was all there was to it. Yet I couldn't get myself to comply. That party line was wrong. Previous party lines had been wrong also. I rose.

"If we are really serious about winning over the masses to our program, the right to criticize a party program has to be established. A precedent has to be made and this is the time to do it, when the facts are incontrovertible, when this party line has proved as disastrously wrong as I predicted it would be at the National Convention."

At the conclusion of my speech I took the deep plunge. I reminded the comrades that although I had been repeatedly promised time off to do some studying and writing, I had always been put off with the excuse, "but not at this critical moment of class struggle." I had been doing full-time party work for the past seven years without a rest and I felt entitled to take a year off for writing and study. I asked for a full year's leave of absence.

"As of now," I said, "unless you can assure me that by postponing my leave for another month or so the class struggle will become less critical."

That took the edge off. My request was granted amid considerable good-natured ribbing.

I felt as if a heavy stone had been lifted from my shoulders. I would now have a full year to do the kind of writing I had always wanted to do.

I forgot to consider one thing—that officially I was still part of the Ohio leadership of the Party, and even if that were not so —at heart I was still a Communist.

38 It took quite a while to get used to my new state of freedom—to have time of my own with no meetings to go to, no responsibilities, no constant emergencies. I took inventory. I owned my car, a 1929 Model A Ford which I had bought for $50 and which was in good condition. I had a considerable library, my own typewriter, enough furniture and almost $500 in cash, the last of my savings from my foreman days, which should be enough to see me through at least a year, living on the scale to which I had become accustomed in the Party.

When I sat down to write I found myself confronted by a totally unanticipated obstacle. Every theme I examined, every plot I outlined ran into a stone wall—it either conflicted with existing party policy or with the party line itself. When in desperation I turned to fantasy, the same problem arose—my elves and nymphs either spoke and behaved in a manner contrary to permissible party custom, or talked in a stilted party jargon. The fact was—although I was not clearly aware of it then—that a thoroughgoing Marxist-Leninist outlook, an approach steeped in dialectical materialism which by then was part of me, exerted a stifling brake on the imagination. Creative imagination in flight is soon brought lamely to earth when it collides with materialistic tenets, and it appears frivolous when contrasted with the graveness of the class struggle. Nor can a Communist writer turn to realism. Any truthful realistic treatment soon runs afoul of the party line which demands that the writer portray persons and events not as they are, but as the party officially declares them

268

to be, which is usually a distortion of the truth. A Communist writer then must choose either to conform to the party line and thus sacrifice his artistic integrity, or clash with the party. When a Communist writer tries to avoid either course and compromises between the two, he will either find himself glorifying the party line at the expense of artistic truth or end up in confused sterility.

I was still wrestling with the problem of how to write literature that was truthful and still conformed to the new united front line, how to show the Communists not as they were but as watered down anti-Fascists as they wanted to appear, when I received an urgent call from Williamson. He wanted to see me at once, he couldn't discuss it over the phone. I was apprehensive that they wanted me to fill some emergency post again and resolved not to yield.

When I entered party headquarters Williamson greeted me with a friendly handclasp although he seemed somewhat embarrassed. He asked how I was progressing with my writing and then, without any preliminary, he blurted out:

"The party wants you to go to Spain."

I blinked. That was totally unexpected. True, eight months back, right after the outbreak of the Spanish Civil War in the summer of 1936, I had asked for party permission to go to Spain to volunteer my services to the Loyalist government, but that permission was refused because at that time the party as well as the Comintern had completely misjudged the character of the Spanish Civil War, declaring it merely a fight between two capitalist factions and therefore of no concern to Communists.

Later, in the fall of 1936, when the Soviet Union belatedly discovered its error and decided to form the International Brigades I volunteered again, along with many other party functionaries who were also eager to take up arms against the Fascists. To our disappointment the Central Committee ruled that the party had too few leading, experienced comrades to spare any of us, that

269

we were all needed here. Since there was no appeal from that decision, I soon put the idea out of mind.

Now Williamson had not said that I had been "granted permission to go to Spain." What he said was that the party *wanted* me to go. That was not volunteering, that was an order. There had to be a reason behind this unanticipated reversal, and I asked Williamson to explain it.

Williamson informed me that Comrade Mills from the Central Committee was awaiting me in the other office, that I knew Mills well and he would give me the details.

Saul Mills greeted me effusively. This was strange. Although we had known each other for years we weren't on particularly intimate terms. He was a short, stout fellow with padded broad shoulders, widely spaced eyes and with an odd, perpetual leer on his thick lips. He was in his early thirties, yet he moved with the ponderous slowness of an old, fat man—a deliberately cultivated habit to create the impression of massive strength behind his grotesque appearance.

He started out by saying that as I well knew the party had been recruiting volunteers for the International Brigades for months. I nodded, that was no longer kept secret. The *Daily Worker* had been publishing stories for weeks about the heroic exploits of the Abraham Lincoln Battalion which, practically unaided, had stopped the Fascists at the Jarama River and saved Madrid from Franco. I knew some of them personally, younger comrades like Joe Dallet, our Youngstown Section Organizer, Johnny Gates, our Akron Y.C.L. Organizer, who were on the lower level of leadership and thus permitted to volunteer.

Mills who was usually very loud in speech now dropped his voice to a whisper.

"The party is in trouble, Voros. All that stuff you've read about the heroic Lincoln Brigade in the *Daily Worker* is crap. If the truth comes out and the enemies of the party pick it up we're going to have a tremendous scandal. The truth is that the Lincoln Brigade mutinied the first day it was sent into action, and had to be driven at pistol point into attack. The comrades in Spain are completely demoralized. They want to come home and many of them are deserting."

That was startling news. Published accounts of the Lincoln Brigade's heroic fight against the Fascists had generated an immense pride even in circles normally hostile to Communists. Mass meetings "To Aid Spanish Democracy and Fight Fascism" were successful beyond anything ever experienced by the party, and great sums were being collected throughout the country. Were the truth to come out it would indeed result in a mass scandal. I asked Mills for an explanation. The reason he gave was shocking.

The American party had recruited and already sent to Spain more than 2,000 young, courageous but totally inexperienced volunteers without bothering to investigate the conditions awaiting them there. Worse still, the party had been too niggardly with its leading cadres to send with those two thousand young men even a few older comrades of established prestige and proved organizational experience, to set them an example and keep up their morale.

To rectify that monstrous blunder the party had now decided to send a minimum of twelve leading comrades to Spain at once. As the Ohio District was one of the strongest in leading cadres, it was ordered to release two. Williamson had picked me as one. When would I be ready to leave?

"Tomorrow!" I said without hesitation.

Mills was highly pleased. He told me I had a few days, I had to apply for a passport first. They had a reservation for me on the first ship leaving New York, the *Queen Mary*. I was to travel alone, without waiting for a transport to be assembled, to get to Spain as fast as possible. The recruiting was going well, he expected a few thousand more volunteers to leave within the next few months.

We then went to see Williamson. I asked him whom he had picked for the other man and when he told me it was Frank Rogers, I laughed. Frank Rogers, a member of the District Bureau, was a highly capable Section Organizer in Cleveland who had lately been critical of Williamson.

Williamson blushed and asked why I was laughing.

"You're all right, Johnny." I smiled. "Since you had to part with two of your cadre you chose the two you would miss the least under the circumstances."

Williamson tried to deny this, but when he saw that I bore no rancor he also smiled.

I told him that the party was free to help itself to my possessions, furniture, books, prints, etc. All I needed from that moment on was a suitcaseful of clothes. After 15 years I was leaving the U.S. with no more worldly goods than I had brought with me, and the chances of my return looked rather slim.

By that evening my apartment was picked clean, the comrades left nothing. Three days later my passport was at hand. In less than a week I was on the *Queen Mary* en route to Spain.

While waiting for my "silk ribbon," the secret identification carried by party leaders on special missions abroad, to be prepared on the "Ninth Floor" in New York and saying good-bye to the comrades on the Central Committee, Alpi, the Language Director of the Central Committee and one of the Comintern's trusted men (then going under the name of Fred Brown), called me into his office. He was a giant of a man with a small goatee trimmed in the urban, cosmopolitan style; his bearing, his suave manners, his quizzical expression, his broad forehead and open countenance presented a vivid contrast to the nondescript appearance of the rest of the top party leaders. A one-time cadet himself, he considered me a kindred soul and we were on somewhat intimate personal terms.

Alpi was born in Austria near the Italian border of Italian parents and had served as an officer in the Austrian Army in

272

the First World War. He had been an Irredentist trying to wrest independence for the Italians living under Austrian rule, and when the Austrian monarchy lost the war Alpi rose quickly in the Italian revolutionary movement. He was one of the principal leaders of the series of uprisings in Italy which were finally quelled by Mussolini's blackshirt Fascists after his March on Rome.

Alpi escaped and wound up in Moscow where his abilities were sufficiently recognized by Lenin to include him in the first Lenin School. That school was organized and taught by Lenin himself, its attendance was limited to leaders of unsuccessful Communist uprisings; it had only seven pupils. Other students in the school with him were Kuiisinen, leader of the Finnish revolution; Béla Kun, leader of the defeated Hungarian Communist dictatorship. Alpi had told me the names of the others also but I cannot recall them.

Alpi said he had called me in not only to say farewell but to discuss the military aspects of the Spanish Civil War. He complained that the military information coming out of Spain was biased and distorted by propaganda on both sides, which made it difficult to assess the true situation there. It was his judgment that by the time I arrived in Spain I would find most military posts of any importance filled by men who had risen from the ranks and that in all likelihood party politics would determine most future appointments. It was his opinion the Spanish Civil War was only a curtain raiser to a general Fascist war offensive in Europe and therefore the lessons of that Spanish war might prove of inestimable value to the future armed struggles against the Fascists. It was of the utmost importance to the party to know how the men both in the ranks and in positions of command reacted in given situations; to review the battle plans, the orders that were issued and the way they were executed, etc. Diaries were the best sources for such information, also unbiased and confidential personal interviews. He had been thinking about that for a long time and my going to Spain now gave him the chance to do something about it.

He had decided to authorize me to do just what we discussed, to collect diaries, to interview personnel, assuring them that their stories would be kept in utmost confidence and used only as a lesson for future struggles. Alpi saw I liked that and he added with a smile:

"That's what I would like to do myself if I could go to Spain. I would want to know what was really going on. This authorization might help you to learn more than the average soldier could, might give you more freedom of movement."

I realized immediately the importance of what he was saying. He, in fact, had authorized me to invoke his name if I found myself stagnating in a piddling party post, to give me a chance to move around. I thanked him for his trust in me and we parted, Italian style, with a warm embrace. When I was at the door, he added wistfully:

"I envy you, Voros. I hope they will find good use for you. That authorization I gave you, I hope you come back alive and bring the true picture with you."

Alpi and I understood each other. He was the only man in the top leadership who tacitly admitted there could be a truth other than what the party proclaimed it to be.

The day my ship was ready to sail I developed an overpowering urge to say farewell to my parents. I had not seen them for years, we had become estranged when I joined the party.

I dropped in on them unannounced. I found them sitting in the living room, they both appeared aged and ailing. It was a sad homecoming. The joy that lit up their faces at the sight of me lasted but an instant—it was replaced by sorrow as I made my way awkwardly to embrace them. After a halting exchange of a few remarks all three of us lapsed into silence, gripped by an emotional web too snarled to unwind by words. Finally my father broke the silence, remarking with sadness, "I see that you are still a bum, still tied up with the Communists."

"The Communists are not bums," I corrected him mildly. I did not want to get into another political argument with him, such as had sent me out of that house, storming, eight years ago, vowing never to return.

"They are bums. They are fighting on the streets," he said.

"You know that I am not a bum. I am fighting for everything that is good, that is decent." It was a plea, not an argument. I did not want to have a fight with him, probably the last time in my life I was to see him.

The old man must have sensed that. He did not want to fight either. But he was firm in his opinions and he shook his head in disapproval.

"You cannot fight for decency with bums. Bums do not know what decency is. To fight for decency you must be with those who are decent themselves. When you are with bums you become one yourself."

"The Communists are the only ones who fight Fascism."

"Bums fighting bums!" exploded my father. "Roosevelt is the one who is fighting Fascism. When bums fight each other you never know when they'll join hands to gang up against the decent people. The Communists are killing each other now in Russia. That gangster Stalin is no better than Hitler."

"You can't mention Stalin in the same breath with Hitler." I was beginning to be aroused.

"*You* can't," said my father cuttingly, "because as long as you are tied up with those bums you have to think as they do. But I can because I am not a Communist. I can smell a bum from a mile. Hitler and Stalin are cast of the same mold, they both smell the same to me. They know it but you don't. Some day you will find out and you will be sorry for having got mixed up with them."

275

It was no use. He hadn't changed, he hadn't learned a thing. He was the same stubborn, shortsighted petit bourgeois clinging to his outworn middle class morality and prejudices. History couldn't teach him anything. No wonder that class was doomed. There was nothing more to say. I rose, kissed my mother, and went for my coat.

My mother was weeping silently. She did not ask where I was going, all she wondered was would she ever see me again. "Of course," I murmured, but didn't promise when. My father's eyes were also moist and so were mine, we each made believe we did not notice it.

My father walked to the door with me and said with a hopeless plea, in a voice choking back his tears:

"You are my oldest son! Stay away from those bums, Communists and Fascists alike. You're disgracing the family."

Christ, what a send-off!

I shouldn't have gone to see them.

That was a fine way to part with a son who, with the thin silk ribbon of the Comintern sewn into a hidden seam inside the lining of his jacket, was to sail within two hours to fight Fascism in Spain.

I wished I had not gone to visit them.

Yet—it was crazy—I was damn happy I had!

PART II

39

THE *Queen Mary* was a new ship, the largest passenger ship then afloat. I traveled with Dr. Julius Hene, a young physician around 28, a recent graduate of a Viennese medical school, who was joining the medical staff of the International Brigades. Our cover story was that we were both going to the coronation in London. Dr. Hene was an intensely serious young man, a native American of German descent. He had become converted to Communism in Austria and had occasionally, by virtue of possessing a genuine American passport, served as a Comintern courier in Europe. He was a sincere idealist and humanitarian—that led him to take up medicine and also to embrace Communism. We were both in a hurry to get to Spain, we had both been made to understand that we were urgently needed. The fact that we were being sent on ahead instead of waiting for a transport of volunteers to assemble emphasized the urgency of our mission.

Going off to war is a profound experience that calls for the mustering of all spiritual resources within a man. When one's nation is at war this ordeal is eased by an overpowering appeal to every man's patriotic duty to protect his country, his family, his traditions and way of life from the enemy. When bugles blow, drums roll, and the adoring population cheers one on, the wavering spirit becomes fortified; one's fears are soothed by the knowledge that whatever sacrifices he may be called upon to render will earn him the gratitude of his nation.

This was not the case with me. I was going off to war surreptitiously. Instead of being cheered on by flags and flowers I had to sneak into Spain. If there was to be any comfort for me I had to find it in the strength of my convictions. It was chilly on deck, the wake of the *Queen Mary* was barely discernible in the foggy mist. It was high time to take stock. I was going to Spain at the request of the party in the full knowledge that I might never come back. Was my faith in the party, in the Communist movement, really justified?

The realist in me said no. Then what was I doing on this ship?

No, I must not look at this problem individualistically, I must consider it dialectically, from a historical point of view. Let's take a look at the American Communist Party, what was wrong with it?

Plenty. When I first joined, it was a queer, ludicrously ineffectual, small sect. In fact, I was ready to quit when that damn policeman clubbed me. After my anger simmered down I would have quit anyway had not Kovess induced me to take a temporary assignment with the *Uj Elore,* to learn the real spirit of Communism from the Hungarian revolutionary leaders there. That Hungarian movement sure turned out to be a cesspool of factional rivalry by the most unscrupulous means for leadership.

Working in the general party was more rewarding, although it was soon evident that the general party was just as dominated by personal jealousies and a scramble for higher posts as the Hungarian movement.

The changes that had taken place in the party in the past few years could in no way be condoned. Inner party democracy had been increasingly suppressed by the top leadership. Hypocrisy was creeping into the party, an un-Marxian practice of withholding the truth even from the membership. I recalled an interview for the *Daily Worker* I had had with Harold H. Burton (later Justice of the U.S. Supreme Court), shortly after his election as Mayor of Cleveland. Burton had received me courteously and answered all my questions fully and sincerely. He denied the accusation that he was beholden to the Chamber of Commerce. He firmly maintained that he intended to be a mayor representing the interests of the entire population of Cleveland regardless of race, color, or political affiliations; that he respected the constitutional rights of all citizens including Communists. Finally he expressed his willingness to meet with us as with all other groups of citizens to consider our program for the welfare of the people.

That interview was really a scoop, a demonstration of the effectiveness of our new united front policy. It was the first time a high elected official had ever consented to sit down openly with a Communist and afford him the same right and courtesy as to any other citizen. At the end of the interview, Burton politely expressed his opinion that the interview would most likely be distorted in publication and he only smiled at my protestations. I sent that story by wire and a few hours later I received a congratulatory wire from James, managing editor of the *Daily Worker,* who had quit the New York *Times* to improve the quality of the *Daily Worker.* He complimented me that I had done it again, this was the type of story the *Daily Worker* needed to transform it into a real newspaper giving information to the working class, another example for the others on the staff to emulate.

That telegram had been addressed to party headquarters and delivered to Williamson by mistake. Williamson asked to see a copy of the article, eager to see what Mayor Burton had said to me, particularly since he had ridiculed my assumption that I could persuade Mayor Burton to consent to be interviewed by the *Daily Worker.*

As he read on, Williamson became more and more agitated and finally exclaimed in consternation:

"The *Daily Worker* can't print that. It contradicts everything we said about Burton before his election!"

I protested at once. I argued that the interview had opened the door for the party to place our local relief program officially before the mayor. This would certainly react to the benefit of the unemployed.

Williamson was adamant. He claimed that publishing that article would create illusions about Mayor Burton among our membership, would make him appear less reactionary than he was. I told Williamson that Burton's opinions as expressed to me were not reactionary—Burton was definitely a constitutionalist, he was a conservative yet not without some progressive leanings. Labeling Burton an out-and-out reactionary would be contrary to the facts and therefore un-Marxian, it would prevent us from developing the right tactical approach to the Burton administration. It was no use. Williamson called up Browder and the story was killed over my and James's protests. What better example was there of deliberate suppression of the truth, of keeping the membership ignorant of the actual situation?

All right, that certainly was no news to me. I knew that all along. Then why did I ask for a year's leave of absence instead of quitting the party?

Because the ideals of a better society, of a Communist society, far transcended the sorry showing of the American Communist Party. The party itself was sound, the rank and file membership sincere, self-sacrificing. Where else could I expect to find such unselfish comradeship, such satisfying human relationships with which I had been greeted in every town, every hamlet, on my organizational and fund-raising tours for the party? Besides, there was this aspect, the party had brought me maturity. I received as much as I gave. The party had provided me the chance to take an active part in shaping history, to play an active part in organizing the unorganized, to act as one of the unofficial midwives at the birth of the Rubber Workers Industrial Union, to cite just one example.

Granted, the American party was infantile, bureaucratic, even dictatorial. The Hungarian party leaders were dwarfs, the American party leaders midgets.

But I was now going to Spain to fight under the leadership of the Comintern, the giants of the revolution; to fight and die, yes, die if necessary on the side of the legendary Communist leaders who had defied prison, torture, consumed by but one ambition—to free the masses from oppression.

My doubts and anxieties were gone, I felt certain I would resolutely measure up to whatever I might be called upon to face. I was startled to hear a voice addressing me.

"You sure look happy, Voros. I heard you whistling even from the far side of the deck. What are you so cheerful about?"

It was Dr. Hene.

"About going to Spain, Julius!" I told him.

"I'm going, too," said Dr. Hene looking at me curiously. "But that's our duty, nothing to whistle about." He was always incongruously solemn.

"That's the German in you, Julius. Duty can be a pleasure if you have the right slant."

I did have the right slant. I was "the hard-tempered steel blade of the class struggle, a Communist." I was "the expression of international solidarity forged into the armed fist of the revolutionary working class by the Comintern." I was "the . . ."

"Take it easy," said a small voice within me. "You're not back home turning out party editorials. You're not a romantic—you're a Marxist, remember? What about the dialectical contradictions . . . ?"

I did not feel like whistling any more.

40 JULIUS and I had no trouble crossing from England into France. In Paris we went to the address supplied to us in New York—the headquarters of a Communist controlled French trade union. After much cautious questioning in our halting French we finally managed to contact the right person. He was a shabbily dressed Frenchman who cursed and swore and wanted to know why in hell we couldn't have got there in the morning when another group of volunteers had arrived. We pleaded that we took a taxi immediately after our train had arrived from Cherbourg. That did not mollify him, he fumed and walked away, leaving us to sit on the filthy cobblestones for well over an hour. When he came back he cursed us again, and then said to follow him. He walked ahead not heeding us, letting us follow as best we could, struggling with our heavy suitcases. After about twenty minutes of going through side streets and back alleys he pointed to a building and turned back without a further glance, obviously relieved to have gotten rid of us. This unanticipated manifestation of international solidarity was a rude jolt, a foretaste of things to come.

The building he pointed out was the French headquarters of the American volunteers.

The man in charge was Parker—a sincere, hard-working comrade in his late twenties. His job was to arrange for lodging and transportation of the American and Canadian volunteers with the French party, which was in over-all control of the International Brigades. The French party gave him grudgingly

284

little co-operation. There were about six hundred American and Canadian volunteers then in France, waiting for weeks to cross into Spain, and more were expected to land with every ship. The Spanish border had been shut tight by the French by order of the Non-Intervention Committee, which accounted for that bottleneck. A number of volunteers were languishing in French jails, arrested by the French while trying to cross the Pyrenees into Spain.

Both Dr. Hene and I had been told in New York that special steps would be taken in Paris to get us to Spain in a hurry through special channels. Parker knew nothing about this. There were only two special ways to get people into Spain; one was by submarine and the other by a solitary small plane—our importance definitely did not rate that. There was nothing for us to do but await developments. Parker told me he was very much pinched for funds, which was rather strange considering all the money that had been collected in the U.S. for Spanish aid, plus what Mills had told me about money received by the party from abroad for the sending of volunteers. The food allowance of the volunteers waiting in Paris had been cut repeatedly and some of the shabby lodgings harboring them had even threatened to evict them for falling behind in their rent. Parker was glad when in view of the situation Dr. Hene and I offered to find our own quarters and pay our own board.

The next transport scheduled to leave was to go by boat directly to Barcelona but there was the danger that the French authorities would prevent her departure and arrest the passengers. A way was found for Dr. Hene to go openly to Spain, by train, as a member of a medical team. An attempt was also to be made to explore a new approach into Spain via the Republic of Andorra. It was a much longer and more perilous climb over the Pyrenees than the previous 12-hour route to Spain, but the Andorra border was far less heavily guarded and the chance of detection was smaller. Because that route was

285

untried and considered hazardous, only a small initial group was to be sent as an experiment. I persuaded Parker to let me join that group—altogether there were to be fifteen of us, of all nationalities. Before we left for Toulouse in Southern France, Parker assigned two other Americans, both seamen, to that group putting me in their charge. One was an American second mate of Dutch origin who told me to call him Van. I forget the name of the other one. (He was later killed in Spain.)

Van was in his forties, a stolid man of few words. The other was a tall, broad-shouldered young man from somewhere in the Middle West. Van was a Communist but the other seaman knew very little about the movement. He was attached to Van and when he saw Van volunteer he joined up also. There was little communication between them and me—they stuck close to each other and regarded me as a stranger.

Before we left for Toulouse a young volunteer who had been helping around headquarters in Paris came to wish me luck. He was a strikingly handsome young man with an ingratiating smile, a winning personality, and erect military bearing. His name was Alfred Wallach, he claimed to have been an officer in the National Guard. He asked me to take him with my group. I had no objection, he was a likable chap, he would have made a good companion. Parker vetoed the request. He wanted Wallach to go by boat, he had recently undergone an operation and Parker thought him too weak for that arduous trip. Wallach accepted the refusal quietly; I showed more disappointment than he. I came to rather like him, little dreaming he would eventually be executed by the S.I.M. in Spain.

Before we left for Toulouse I invited Wallach out for a drink. He took me to a place where he said they liked Americans. It was an ordinary working class saloon on an ordinary street with an ordinary swinging door. The long bar on the left was surrounded by a number of Frenchmen in working clothes. The tile floor was covered with sawdust and girls in pairs were sitting

286

around the small tables covered with cheap checkered cloths placed against the wall. The printed signs above the tables, translated from the French, read:

"15 francs, everything included."

"Soldiers on leave from Algiers, 12 francs."

The girls obviously did like Americans for we had hardly sat down when they surrounded us, one on each side of me, a third perching on my lap. That café was evidently not designed for American fashion buyers in search of the latest in French styles. Those girls wouldn't have been of much help to them— they wore absolutely nothing. It was rather confusing to have a naked girl on one's lap and two others hanging closely on each side—that was not the kind of mass action I had been trained for. As I was unobtrusively trying to free myself from those foreign entanglements another woman appeared at our table. She was as black as black could be, the most enormous woman I ever saw in my life. She must have been the original "five-by-five," as broad as she was tall, with underinflated huge breasts supported by a purple sash to keep them from bumping her knees. She stopped in front of me, winked, and then turned around. Now I understood that wink; it was meant for us as Americans. Her enormous buttocks sported a friendly greeting in white ink, in English.

"Hallo," said the one on her left buttock. "God-bye," said the other. I frowned.

Wallach asked me what was wrong. He blinked when I told him: "She only has one *o* in 'good.'"

41 We didn't see much of Toulouse. The Popular Front government of France had issued new orders for the strict enforcement of the Non-Intervention Policy and reinforced the border guards and patrols. We were warned to stay under cover lest our presence be betrayed by informers, and we spent almost a week cooped up, confined to our little room in a shabby house in the workers' district.

Late afternoon on the sixth day we were suddenly alerted, we would leave by taxi as soon as it turned dark. The cab picked us up around seven that evening; I do not recall the date, it was late in May.

We drove for nearly two hours, out into the country. We were following three other cabs and another was following us—five cabs in all. Van, the sailor and I were riding in one cab with two other men we had picked up. They did not speak English. I judged them to be Poles but they wouldn't respond to my questions. They talked in whispers and acted furtively, as if the police were right after them. Later I learned they were indeed Poles who had come from the Soviet Union. Suspicion had been practically bred into them, they didn't seem to trust even each other.

The ground was beginning to rise, and by the second hour of our ride we were high up in the mountains. Our driver had lost his earlier tenseness, he was relaxed and whistling, he told us the *Salats* had long been left behind and that the first danger zone had been passed. The car was steadily ascending, we noted with satisfaction—the higher the cab took us the less climbing we would have to do.

Finally the cars came to a halt and we debarked. The stars were out but no moon, the night was dark, cold, and damp. Two Frenchmen from the lead car distributed two paper bags to each of us. One contained a loaf of French bread split in the middle for a sandwich, smeared with some sort of a paté as a filler. The other held two bottles of wine—our ration for the trip. A guide materialized from the darkness. He had been waiting on the mountain just above the road; he now descended and joined us. He carried a homemade peasant pack on his back the shape of a small lamb. He held a staff in his hand, his legs were encased in rolled wool puttees. There were no ceremonies and no farewells. We were told by one of the Frenchmen that this was our guide; the cabs then turned and left.

We stood huddled close, watching the lights of the cars until they disappeared around a curve. There was little attempt at conversation; everyone was wrapped in his own thoughts. The mountainside loomed dark and steep, the air was cold and windy, more like February than May, which made us shiver; we weren't dressed for it. I was dressed warmer than most, I had a stout pair of walking shoes, double-soled and waterproofed, that I'd had the foresight to buy at Abercrombie and Fitch in New York. I told them I was going to Africa and wanted shoes that would not look like hunting or military boots yet gave the same service, and they came through handsomely. I was to have numerous occasions to bless both Mr. Abercrombie and Mr. Fitch for those shoes—I doubt I would have come out alive without them.

I had been told in Paris and also in Toulouse to abandon those shoes because they might arouse suspicion, they looked far too stout for ordinary street wear. But I was adamant. I had also been told to leave behind my heavy hand-knit camel's hair sweater which a girl in London had presented to me and which looked incongruous in France at that time of year. I hung on to that sweater, too, but I took to wearing it under my shirt. My socks were also hand-knit of heavy camel's hair. Those socks and sweater and shoes saw me through the whole civil war. I wore them summer and winter until the socks stood up by themselves stiff as boots, and the sweater became part of my skin. A pair of woolen trousers and a tweed jacket completed my apparel, topped off by a gabardine raincoat I had bought in New York which soon turned out to be neither waterproof nor wool. I counted seventeen men in the group aside from the guide, all shivering in their light spring clothes. The guide suddenly disappeared in the dark and we stood there feeling abandoned among the rocks and scrub a million miles from civilization. That was the first taste of the future that lay ahead of us and it was foreboding.

The guide reappeared as suddenly as he had vanished. He counted us with his fingers, hitched up his pack with a fling of his shoulders, and uttered just one word:

"Vamos!"

With that he turned and began walking up the mountainside. The pace he set was very brisk. The mountain was steep, there was no trail, and we soon found ourselves panting. We pleaded with the guide to slow down. He was a Basque and spoke very little French. He shook his head and made us understand that we had to get above the patrol zone before midnight to avoid detection and capture.

We kept on climbing grimly in single file, stumbling and breathing hard. I fell behind from the center and had to walk ever faster to keep up with the column; the man behind me was already half trotting. I summoned up all my energy and with the blood pounding in my temples managed to make my way near the head of the column. My lungs were about to burst but I knew I had to do it—the closer to the guide, the more even the pace would be. The mountain was getting very steep and it was becoming more difficult to walk upright. I watched the guide's step. He was walking with his feet pointed sideways like a man climbing a tree. I tried it and it helped to give me a better footing but I was still stumbling from time to time.

My breath was beginning to come in soblike gasps, my knees were beginning to tremble. I threw away my two bottles of wine to leave my hands free, which helped. We were way past the timber line but low scrub still grew here and there. I grabbed at it whenever I could and pulled myself on. My hands were getting scratched and bruised but I paid no heed. I was no longer a reasoning human being, I had turned into a hulk fighting for air with seared lungs and throbbing temples, with a blind stubborn will to lift a leg, to reach out a hand and grab and pull and put another leg forward.

The guide stopped abruptly and held up his staff. We all halted. I was dazed, my mind was numb, it took me seconds to realize we weren't moving and that my lungs did not ache so much. Lights were bobbing hundreds of feet below us in the dark—the border patrol!

We pulled into the shadow of a protruding rock and waited. We couldn't sit down, we were on the edge of the snow line and the ground was wet with melting snow. We leaned against the damp rock and rested. It was a few minutes past eleven, high time to eat. I pulled the sandwich out of my pocket. It tasted sour. The paté smelled bad and tasted spoiled. I scraped it off and ate the bread. It would have been nice to wash it off with wine for I was very thirsty but I had thrown the wine away. I soon found that all of us had done likewise except the guide. He had not only held on to his own bottles but also managed to pick up a few additional ones which we had thrown away. He now passed those bottles around in obvious disgust at our softness. It wasn't much of a wine, water would have been more appreciated.

After about twenty minutes we moved on. The guide was

obviously frightened. He warned us not to make any noise and then he struck out, setting a stiffer pace than before. The ground was now sodden and streaked with rivulets from the melting snow. I stuck close to the guide. He avoided those freshets nimbly but I found that too exhausting and waded right through them. They were shallow and barely came up to my ankles. My boots were waterproof and my feet felt warm. I was lucky indeed in that—a number of the others complained that their shoes were getting soaked and their feet were freezing.

We labored on and soon I was out of breath again. We pleaded with the guide to slacken the tempo but he shook his head and climbed relentlessly on. Inside my chest a fiery iron band was crushing my lungs and the pressure tightened with every breath I drew. My eyes were beginning to swell and an artery behind my ear started throbbing with the roar of a subway train. I walked and stumbled and scrambled and crawled on and on, ever on, clutching for a root, a branch, a tuft of sod, then another, then another, seeing nothing but the feet of the guide rising, then falling, then rising again. I was stumbling and falling behind, there was a different foot rising ahead of me now, then still a different one, then nothing! All I saw was something to grab onto and pull, crawl and pull.

I was stumbling on in an eternal pitch-black void, crawling through an endless tunnel in a semiconscious state. Existence had narrowed down to sucking in air that wouldn't draw, to a numb pull of the arms, to diving forward into space. There was no aim, no purpose, no thought, no will, only the instinct to drag on and on.

The guide stopped, turned around, motioned us to halt, and sat down. I sank to the ground where I was and lay there in torpor. Slowly, very slowly, conscious thought returned. I found myself stretched on my back with my eyes fixed on the Little Dipper. It was very bright and so close I was sure I could reach up and touch the handle had I the energy. Little by little I became aware that water was trickling by my ears and that my head and shoulders were half submerged in a freshet. The water was icy cold and I was getting soaked to the skin. That might lead to pneumonia, I noted with detachment. The seat of my pants felt damp but not wet and I saw that my legs were on higher ground: I ought to move the rest of my body up there! It was a simple problem in locomotion, so simple I saw it in diagram, my body sketched in heavy black lines where it actually lay, with pointed dots showing where it ought to be. The pointed dots showed my torso lifted from the waist up and then turned to the right, a most elementary procedure. I studied the problem abstractly yet I made no move. The fear of catching pneumonia was nudging me, yet I had no inclination to budge. I wondered what time it was but the image of lifting my wrist and consulting my watch remained in dotted outline. All I had to do was to will it, I knew, but there was no will to my body, only dulled sensations and vague thoughts remotely detached. Here I was, I observed idly, an inert hulk of flesh, reduced by extreme physical exertion in a short span of two hours, more or less, to the point of utter indifference to my fate. I wondered would I move if someone were trying to stab me. I proceeded to conjure up the sight—even the dagger descending—and concluded that not even that would stir me. (That picture of utter exhaustion comes to my mind every time I read accounts of Fascist torture or of Communist brainwashing. A man's body can be so broken by physical exhaustion that it becomes utterly separated from his will.)

We continued climbing all through the night, and daybreak found us up in the snow belt. We halted then for a long rest. We were beyond danger from the French border guards. We were in a land where few feet ever trod, a land of crags and snow-covered peaks that bore no sign of vegetation, birds, or animals. We were in a zone where creation had stopped and frozen in the process, where silence was so deep that it blared and made the ears ring.

Suddenly the guide sprang to his feet in great alarm. He asked us to stand up and took a rapid count. There were only sixteen of us. One comrade was missing, a German. No one knew when and how he had disappeared and we were agitated and concerned. The guide told us to wait for him and started down in search. He was gone for more than an hour. When he returned he was tired and weary. He had found no trace of the missing man. The guide said we must push on, that further search was useless. Waiting for him was futile, the German could never make his way up here and find us, waiting would endanger our own safety. We stirred uneasily. That comrade must be lying somewhere with broken bones, perhaps in pain, alone with his God whom he had disowned, his faith pinned on the international solidarity of the revolutionary working class, trusting us to come to his rescue. If we moved on and abandoned him we would be betraying everything he had worked for, everything be believed in, everything that had led him this far to join the fight against Fascism in Spain. It was worse than that. It would be a betrayal of everything we ourselves believed in, everything that had brought us here.

The guide urged us impatiently to start moving. Now one of those two Poles who had ridden with us in our cab spoke up. He was the shorter and older of the two and addressed us in poor German. He spoke incisively, he was used to making decisions.

"That comrade came to fight Fascism. He is lost to us now, one comrade less to fight Hitler and Mussolini. If we stay on and look for him we will all be lost. None of us will be left to fight Fascism. This is war. In war there is no room for sentimentalism. We must move on."

Those were frank words and brutal. All of us were of the same mind but none of us had wanted to voice it. When that

294

Pole (obviously a high party official, judging by the deference with which the other Pole treated him) had put into words what we were hesitant to advance, not because of sympathy for that lost comrade but out of petty-bourgeois sentimental squeamishness, we felt ashamed. None of us had known the lost comrade long enough to feel sorry for him as a person. Ours was an abstract sympathy, a vestige of our upbringing, a product of a civilization shaped by religious concepts, a call of conscience that made it a duty to help other humans in distress. In all truth we were angry at him for putting us into such an embarrassing position, this made us feel guilty, and we hated him so much the more for it. That Polish comrade had taken the responsibility for resolving the issue for us the way we wished it to be resolved, he took the initiative to rationalize it for us and thereby soothe our conscience.

This was war. We were no longer civilians. In war there will be casualties! We moved on with one accord.

The light of day made climbing somewhat easier; we could at least see where to put our feet down. We were climbing over a snow field now, conquering peak after peak with bursts of desperate exertion only to find that we must descend to climb even higher ones ahead.

Van and I were the oldest in that group. I was one month short of 37, Van was somewhat older. His seafaring life had kept him in condition while my sedentary life had softened me. He and the sailor seemed to have shown the least exhaustion during that grueling climb. By midmorning I recovered my second wind and my knees were no longer rubbery. I was still laboring for breath and my heart was still pounding hard but there was a regularity to both. As we pushed on my physical condition continued to improve and I was no longer among those who kept clamoring for a rest. We had no food and we were gripped by hunger; we ate snow which helped a bit, but only momentarily, yet we kept trudging on without a single voice of complaint. The majestic beauty of those snow-capped, crazy-angled, fantastically odd-shaped peaks which had awed us when revealed by the first rosy rays of the rising sun, were long wasted on us. As the day wore on we reverted to apathy, plodding on endlessly with no sensation other than the painful contractions of our empty stomachs, the agonizing pain of each searing breath, the stabbing glare of white snow on our in-flamed eyeballs.

Late that afternoon we came to a small clearing on a snow-free level patch enclosed on three sides by a waist-high, crumbling adobe wall. That wall had been built by human hands for the protection of sheep and, primitive as it was, it raised our morale—it represented civilization. We saw firewood around and the guide decided to spend the night there. He said we were now only about six hours' climb from our destination but the route was too hazardous to risk at night.

We built a big fire—our first chance to warm up. There was no joking or conversation around that campfire, each of us was too worn out to be concerned about the others. I felt utterly weary, my mind empty of coherent thought. My eyes idly followed the flickering flames struggling to get a bite on that wet and smoky wood, feeling their way tentatively along the damp bark for some choice and tempting morsel, retreating when rebuffed in a puff of smoke only to charge in with a rush and take a big bite, crackling with savage glee when closing down their jaws. Then I smiled because I recognized I was seeing symbols of eating and food in those flames. I stood up to survey the group.

A number of the comrades seemed to be in acute distress. Most of them had trouble with their feet. The foot of the older Pole was a mass of raw blisters, his breath came in sobs as his friend carefully attempted to pull his tattered rayon hose off the bleeding raw skin. His shoes were tramped out of shape and soaked through from wading in the snow all day. Most of the others were also plagued by blisters and swollen feet. I took off my shoes, they were dry inside. I pulled off my socks, my feet were fine and warm—not a sign of a blister, only a reddish sensitive area around my big toes and joints where I had been frost-bitten during my long ride home in an unheated boxcar from Siofok, after the Károlyi revolution.

I was about to doze off when I heard a commotion. We had a visitor, an Andorran shepherd who mysteriously appeared in our midst. The guide and he held an agitated conversation and then we were told the bad news. We had to go on at once. The French border patrol which had a treaty right to enter the Republic of Andorra had received news of us—they were pushing up in force to capture us.

We moved on with difficulty. Many in the group had to struggle painfully to get their shoes on again over their raw and swollen feet and we had to wait for them.

That night's climb was a repetition of the first. I was soon in a daze, following in the footsteps of the man ahead of me, keeping my head down.

Before dawn a loud scream followed by hoarse shouts jarred us out of our lethargy. One of the Poles, the one who was the leader, had missed his footing and disappeared. We halted in our tracks on the narrow ledge, fearful to make a move, until daybreak, when there was enough light for the guide to risk the descent into the steep abyss. The other Pole wanted to go with him but the guide refused, he went alone. The Pole tried to follow him, then he also fell in peril of skidding down. He lay there a while and then climbed back painfully, sideways, on his stomach.

The guide was gone for about two hours. When he appeared he shook his head and wouldn't say anything no matter how hard we pumped him. The remaining Pole was a statue of grief. I went over to him and put my hands on his shoulder, murmuring a few sympathetic words, but he wouldn't be consoled;

he wrenched his shoulder away and spat a few angry Polish words at me.

When the guide rose to his feet we needed no one to make a speech. We all rose silently and started off. This was war and we were getting used to it.

Early afternoon of that second day we made a long descent into a valley, then came across a dirt road leading upward. It was a narrow road, just wide enough for a cart, but it was a road and our spirits rose as we trudged along, our fatigue compensated by the sensation of walking upright again without caring where we placed our feet. Presently we came to a few adobe huts. They were low, the size of a small garage, windowless, with a roughly hewn wooden door for entrance. The guide went inside one of them and soon came out followed by a man in peasant garb. He wore close-fitting black pants with his legs wrapped in cloth to his knees, rope-soled shoes, a faded green woolen blouse with a wide blue sash wound tight around his midriff, and a black beret. He was short, built like a boy, his face was tanned by weather into deep wrinkles.

Soon about eight or ten others came out of their huts, undersized men and women, but curiously only one child. They looked at us silently. The guide was talking with them, asking for food. They shook their heads, they did not have any. Finally they brought forth a small flat round cheese and two flat, hard breads, all they could spare. They were Andorrans living in the highest inhabited place in their republic. We were the first foreigners they had seen in their lives—they had no conception of America, Germany, or the other countries we came from. They spoke a patois of mixed Spanish and Catalan, with a few distorted French words thrown in. The guide asked them to search for the people we had lost, they listened solemnly, and I couldn't tell from their impassive faces whether they really would. I doubted it, they showed no reaction when the guide explained what had happened and described with much waving of his arms the whereabouts of those accidents.

We thought we were near the end of our trail, but that proved an illusion. To avoid the border patrol that was hunting us we had skirted clear across the border into Andorra; in consequence we now had to cross into Spain at a different point than originally planned. By the time we had that all clear it added up to the sad news that we had crossed the Pyrenees all the way into Andorra and now we had to scale them again from Andorra to Spain. That was a deep blow, climbing the Pyrenees twice and at their most difficult points. The usual route traveled by the volunteers took only ten to twelve hours. We had been climbing two nights and two days, now we had to go on for another night and day, equipped more for an afternoon stroll than for climbing over wild, snow-covered mountains without any conditioning, without even food. But this was war and war meant hardships.

We shuffled on, a worn-out, bedraggled lot yet without a murmur of complaint. Many in the group limped wearily in their sodden, disintegrating street shoes. I was numb. I no longer felt separate pains only one all-pervading ache pressing on me with the relentless crush of a boa constrictor. I walked bent way forward, eyes vacantly to the ground. My thought processes were dulled—whenever some stray phrase entered my mind it stuck there revolving in slow repetition, over and over. It was an involuntary suspension of conscious thought, an automatic exercise of life function, of motion and locomotion. I remember little of that night nor of the hours of daybreak that followed; I staggered on in a trance, keeping as close to the guide as I could.

We had to cross a very steep mountainside just below the crest, but the snow was so crumbly and slippery that when we got halfway through we hesitated to continue. The guide coaxed us, he said we had only a few hundred yards more of that and there was absolutely no other way to get around it, and when we still hesitated he walked on ahead making tracks in the snow, then returned making another parallel track. He told us to step carefully in his tracks and we finally followed—every step an excruciating balancing act as if walking a tightrope. Then it happened!

We were almost clear across when I lost my balance. I stumbled and fell and skidded down; down, down, farther down, ever farther down, fast, faster, then still faster and faster and faster. I was thrashing wildly to stop my slide but the skid was out of control, I was sliding feet first, torso at an angle. I glimpsed a brush of dwarf pine sticking out the snow way below and tried to steer myself toward it but missed by a hair and went down and down, although at a lesser speed—the tip of the branch I had managed to get hold of before it was stripped out of my hands by my momentum had slowed me down somewhat. There was another scrub below, I managed to grab that, the impact swirled me around and I landed with my knees against a rock, dazed.

I was conscious of anger, of a deep burning fury that such an outrage should happen to *me*. My knees, particularly the right one, were swelling with pain. I rubbed them and rubbed them until my anger disappeared, and only then did I turn around to take stock of my surroundings. I was lying a few hundred yards from the bottom; I looked up and there was my group way far above, tiny two-dimensional figures with feet wide apart, as if drawn by some cartoonist in black ink against the snowy background of that mountain. I stood up and waved to them, they waved back but without a sound. They must have shouted but I did not hear a sound; I shouted also but my cry sounded feeble in the wind even to me—I was positive my voice hadn't reached them.

The guide started down, then retraced his steps and rejoined the group. There was a small huddle and then the column

300

started. They went on, the bastards had abandoned me! Not a one looked back in my direction, not a one even waved to me again.

"The bastards deserted me," I kept repeating over and over—not in anger nor in fear—my mind was simply stuck in a groove as I watched them disappear one by one after crossing that snowbank. Only then did my mind revert to reality. My right knee was badly swollen but not broken. My situation was desperate . . . No, it was serious, but not desperate. The thing to do was rest until the pain in my knee abated, then work my way down to the valley and continue down and down until I hit something. We were only four hours away from our destination, the guide had informed us, we were heading west, and that was what I would do, that was an easy direction to keep.

"What if . . . ?" There were to be no "what ifs." Panic would be fatal. I was bound to make my way out if I took it easy and conserved my strength. Conserve my strength, that was the key.

"Conserve my strength." I kept that rolling around in my mind as I stretched out to catch a short nap. "Conserve my strength . . . conserve my strength . . ."

I do not know how long I had slumbered when I heard faint shouts.

"Voros, where are you? Where are you?"

"Here . . . Here . . . This way . . ." I shouted back still groggy with sleep. Then I recognized the voices of Van and the sailor. They soon came into sight and I tried to walk toward them but my right knee buckled under and wouldn't support me.

"That was a dumb trick to pull," said Van and he was angry. "We should've left you here," said the sailor and he meant it, he was definitely hostile.

My joy at seeing them turned to anger.

"I didn't ask you to come after me," I snapped back at them. "I saw you go on and leave me. What changed your minds?"

"I am responsible to the party for the three of us," said Van. "I had to come back for you. We'll make it together, the three of us, or we won't make it at all."

Nothing more needed to be said, he was fulfilling his duty. There was no comradeship involved, only the carrying out of a party assignment. I had difficulty in walking and the sailor was half carrying me for a while until my knee was well enough to enable me to rest my weight on my feet, gingerly.

Following a westward course we struck out down the mountainside until we hit the floor of the valley. It was a perilous trip. When we came across rocks that blocked our way they had to pull and boost me up. We waded across wild mountain streams waist-deep in icy water, carrying our shoes tied by the laces around our necks, grabbing hold of rocks in the stream bed to keep from being carried away by the rushing torrent. We struggled on without compass or map, following the direction of the setting sun, two men risking their lives to help a third, not out of compassion, not because he was a fellow human being, but because it was a party assignment. Unlike other working class movements, the Communist Party is singularly destitute of human comradeship. Membership in the Communist Party does not exclude individual friendship, nor is friendship encouraged. Van and the sailor had known each other and were friends. I was a comrade but a stranger. There was no common tie between them and me outside of our membership in the Communist Party. They had risked their lives for me and they knew I would risk my life for them. But they knew and I knew that were I to be killed or they, we would not mourn one another.

Just before nightfall we stumbled on a road. We followed it down about a mile and we came to a few huts. It was dusk and dozens of people rushed out to meet us. We were in Spain. With much shouting, handclasps, and friendly gestures they led us to a house farther down. We found our group there. They had reached it four hours ahead of us and were asleep until the

302

noise of our arrival woke them. There was no joyous reunion. They merely nodded, a few words were said mainly to acknowledge our presence, then they went back to sleep.

"International solidarity . . . !"

I was beginning to wonder.

42 THE home where we were quartered was more primitive than anything I had seen in the poorest villages in Hungary. It was more of a stable than a dwelling, with a rickety wooden stairway leading upstairs to three cubicles opening on a narrow wooden balcony, containing no other furniture than a few straw pallets that served as beds. They were open to the stable, screened only by a bead curtain in the entranceway. The stable floor was ankle deep with sticky manure; a dirt floor room downstairs, also open to the stable, served as the kitchen and family room. The stable housed three burros which bespoke a well-to-do family. The air was hazy and dense with steamy urine and the smell of the fermenting manure on the stable floor. Flies were commuting in swarms from the manure to the food in the kitchen, alighting insolently on our faces, feasting on the sore eyes of the children, crawling in and out of their runny noses. The stable also served as a toilet. There was no outdoor privy—human excrement was valued as the best fertilizer for that rocky soil and had to be conserved—members of the family relieved themselves openly on the stable floor under the eyes of the burros and whoever else happened to be around. That presented an embarrassing problem at first but this was war, there was no other place to go, one had to make do.

The villagers who came to visit us were friendly. No volunteers had come through this way before, this was their first contact with *extranjeros*. They were little aware of events outside their valley. They knew there was a war going on and that

Franco was *muy malo* but had no conception of the real significance of the struggle being waged so far away from them. Later
I was to find that ignorance typical in provinces far removed
from the war zone. Illiteracy was one of the main reasons for
that; preoccupation with eking out a miserable existence, and
lethargy caused by malnutrition were some of the others.

The next day we managed to make contact with a *milicia* post
in another village. The *milicia* men were at first incredulous
that anyone could have crossed those mountains, secondly that
extranjeros coming to help Spain would actually pass through
their village. They belonged to the F.A.I. (Federation of Iberian
Anarchists). They had no arms outside a few antiquated rifles,
single-bolters that must have predated the Franco-Prussian War
of 1869-1870. They got hold of a truck somehow and transported
us to another *milicia* post in another town. Four of them came
with us as escort. One of them proudly displayed an enormous
revolver which was not loaded. I asked him about the shells,
he had seven of them which he carried loose in his pocket. They
did not fit his gun which somewhat marred his pleasure, still he
was proud of his weapon and his munificent store of ammunition.

I took to these Spaniards at once, with a warmth I had not
experienced in years. They were trusting and childlike, and I
was glad I had come. It was apparent at a glance they needed
guidance, direction, expert organization—things I was trained
to supply. The truck bounced up and down that incredibly bad
road jarring my bones to the marrow but I did not mind. I was
lost in reverie, thankful for being a Communist, grateful to the
Communist Party for providing me the opportunity to come to
grips personally with the arch enemy of civilization, Fascism. I
was an organizer and I was confident that I was a good one.
Here in Spain, where the anti-Fascist front was much too broad
to be stifled by Communist sectarianism, I would really be in
my element. Freed of the phrase-parroting, bureaucratic control

of the party leadership in America, we would really be in a position to base our tactics on reality instead of some cockeyed "party line."

It was a happy feeling to be a Communist now that I was in Spain. I was glad of having overcome my waverings, of not having quit the party. This was the fulfillment of life's ultimate purpose for a genuine humanitarian—to serve the downtrodden of the earth. I felt noble and uplifted and I did not awake until many hours later the truck dumped us at the railroad depot in Valencia.

The station was in a turmoil. A train full of volunteers had just pulled in from Barcelona including the survivors of the Spanish boat *Ciudad de Barcelona* that had been torpedoed by a Fascist submarine a mile and a half offshore from the Spanish fishing village of Malgrat, about 22 miles north of Barcelona, the boat's final destination. That was the boat I would have sailed on had Parker not agreed to let me cross through Andorra.

I recognized a number of Americans, Wallach among them. They crowded around me, some still in a state of shock, all of them greatly excited, each trying to impress on me his own version of the catastrophe, the miraculous way he had managed to escape with his life. They thought I was still with the *Daily Worker*. That was their first brush with death, the grim reality of war. Death had descended upon them suddenly, without any warning, and they were not prepared for the experience. In telling me their story some of them had difficulty holding back their tears. After all, they were young, still in their early twenties. They had volunteered in boyish enthusiasm to fight Fascism in Spain. They had not thought through to the fact that Fascism would fight back; that the game was for keeps; that the chip they risked was their life. I was doing my best to calm them. They indignantly demanded that something be done about that barbaric and brutal Fascist attack which, they vehemently insisted, was a direct violation of the Non-Intervention Pact. I couldn't help smiling as I explained to them that the precise reason all of us had come to Spain was to do something about such Fascist acts personally; and as it happened, our own presence at that railroad station was also a direct violation of that same Non-Intervention Pact. They insisted this was entirely different, that the Fascists had no right to do that to *them*. They had intuitively grasped what it took me years to learn, that for Communists there could be but one side to any story, theirs.

Finally I was able to reconstruct fairly closely what had actually happened. There were over 500 volunteers on that boat out of whom nearly half had perished: those trapped in the hold when the torpedo struck, and those who couldn't swim or stay afloat until rescue arrived. None of them knew how many Americans had actually boarded that boat; checking their stories one against another my best estimate came to between 130–135 volunteers of whom only forty-six had escaped. Once I learned those casualty figures I also lost my penchant for objectivity and retired into a corner with my fistful of notes to cable the story to the *Daily Worker*. Although I had not intended to continue to write for it, this story was too hot, the details too sensational; the party could make real political capital out of it. After working on it for about fifteen minutes at top speed I became aware that the volunteers were all rushing in one direction, forming a tight ring around somebody. I followed them and to my delight found that he was Robert Minor, the representative of the American Central Committee to the Communist Party in Spain. Minor was also a member of the *Daily Worker* editorial staff; we had known each other for years.

Bob Minor was a tall, imposing figure, with a heavy frame and silvery white hair framing his massive, bald head. He was a famous cartoonist before he turned Communist and he carried himself with dignity and poise. I had a few messages of a confidential nature for him from the Central Committee, to be delivered orally, concerning individuals some of whom were on their way to Spain and some of whom were to report back immediately to the States. I had been given only the first names; I did not know who the people were, nor was it any of my business.

I noted an indefinable change in Minor's face since the last time I had seen him in New York, about a half-year earlier, and I was puzzled about it. Minor stood impassively in the center, listening to the American volunteers crowding about him without saying a word; but to my eyes he only appeared to be listening, I had the feeling he was not paying attention. I knew he was somewhat deaf but not sufficiently so not to have heard that clamor.

I stood aside and waited until the excitement subsided, then went up to him and greeted him. He regarded me as if he had never seen me before, cold and disinterested. Realizing that my haggard face and tattered clothes after those rugged days of climbing the Pyrenees must have changed my appearance considerably, I told him my name and who I was. He cut me short abruptly; he knew very well who I was and why was I bothering him, didn't I see he was busy? I was quite taken aback by that unexpected response. I told him I had a few messages for him from the Ninth Floor and took him aside to deliver them. He cocked his ear close to my mouth and I realized he was even more hard of hearing than I suspected. I had to repeat my message twice and louder before he nodded his head that he had understood. I then told him I already had all the facts about the sinking of the *Ciudad de Barcelona,* the names of the American survivors, their home towns, etc., that my story was already organized, all I needed from him was a typewriter so I could knock it out in a hurry for the *Daily Worker.*

Minor became livid with anger.

"Give me those notes," he shouted at me and grabbed them out of my hand.

"Not a word of this must be permitted to leak out in America, do you hear? What are you trying to do, demoralize the people back home?"

Something was wrong with that man.

"Bob, this is news, sensational news, the best propaganda we could wish for to arouse the American people," I expostulated. "With the details I have, this story will be picked up by the wire services. Every home town newspaper where a local boy was involved will feature it as: Local boy killed or escapes with life from boat torpedoed by Fascists!"

"Not a word of this must leak out, you understand?" Minor roared at me.

"See here, Comrade Minor, this torpedoing has already been reported in the Valencia papers. It must have been cabled to the United States and published there already. This story will be the follow-up, it will fill in the missing details and shake up those people back home who still do not believe what Fascism really is. This is the propaganda we want, where the facts speak for themselves: Americans torpedoed and drowned on the open seas by Fascists!"

"You're not to mention a word about this to anyone, do you hear! This is an order!" With that he stalked away from me, called the Americans together, and made a speech.

He told us that we were all anti-Fascists who had come to Spain to fight Fascism. He told us Fascism was the last desperate attempt of capitalist imperialism in its death throes to drown in blood the inevitable rise of the working class and that Fascism would meet its tomb in Spain.

He rambled on and on like a *Daily Worker* editorial on the glory of the Soviet Union and finally told us that we had already met the baptism of fire heroically and come out victorious. He then admonished us on our honor as anti-Fascists, as the bravest flowers of the revolutionary working class, not to let a word of that torpedoing leak out, we mustn't even discuss it among ourselves any further because that would only lend aid

309

and comfort to the Fascists who had ears all over, who were listening everywhere, and it would also demoralize our comrades, the other volunteers in Spain.

"That is an order!" he added for emphasis, then walked briskly away.

That speech had its effect. The comrades immediately fell to discussing how they mustn't talk about the torpedoing any more, first in hushed tones, later arguing with each other loudly, citing and inventing gory incidents to prove how easily such news could demoralize comrades less firm in their anti-Fascists beliefs than they.

I was to meet Minor again a few months later, on my way back from the Cordoba front. By then I had heard enough stories about him to make me even more cynical about our top leadership. Minor had been assigned by the American Central Committee to co-ordinate the propaganda efforts of the American and Spanish Communist Parties and, incidentally, also to represent before the Comintern the interests of the American volunteers in Spain. However, Minor had also caught the bug—like other leading Communists, he became convinced that he was a master strategist and a military genius. He spent his time in Spain devising military campaigns and giving unsolicited military advice to the Spanish Communist Party. At that second meeting, after listening for a whole evening to his military theories, I realized he was oblivious of the political and military developments around him and that he was becoming senile. It was this Minor who reported on Spain to the American Party from his hotel in Valencia, and when we read his analyses in the *Daily Worker* we wondered how such naive concepts could be advanced by anyone who had ever set foot in Spain, much less a high-ranking Party leader with access to inside information.

Minor was only one in that host of propagandists who spread a blanket of misleading optimism about the course of the Spanish Civil War. That propaganda was so all-embracing that it brought even the most objective foreign correspondents in Spain under its spell. Ultimately this proved to be a disservice to the Spanish Loyalist Government—in fact, it can be argued that it actually contributed to her defeat by creating false illusions about her chances for victory. Had the actual truth about the precarious position of Loyalist Spain been revealed in time, the democratic nations of the world might have been induced to intervene and find an effective solution to forestall her ultimate tragedy.

As I just now discovered, hindsight is not difficult to develop—anyone can do it if he lives long enough.

43 WE arrived in Albacete in the early morning after another sleepless, overcrowded night's ride. We were marched to an enormous army building, the *Guardia Nacionale*. We must have been around six hundred, close to a hundred of us Americans. We were told to form up by nationalities, and have our pictures taken for our *livret militaire,* our military book. I still have mine. That photo shows a haggard, deeply lined face drugged by going five nights with only snatches of sleep, the eyelids heavy with the effort of staying open.

A snatch of Hungarian conversation aroused me from my stupor. A smartly uniformed man was talking in Hungarian to another soldier who was obviously his subordinate—his uniform was shapeless and faded.

"Are you comrades Hungarians?" I went to them, eager to strike up acquaintance with veterans who were from the old country.

They turned and looked me over. The smartly uniformed one seemed undersized and wore an officer's cap with two short golden bars in two parallel rows above the black visor. His tunic was tailor-made and padded, it made him appear far broader in chest than his scrawny neck and pinched face warranted. He was around twenty-eight or thirty, his mouth set in the stern lines of authority Hungarians seem to thrive on—an expression I hadn't seen since I had left Hungary. The other man seemed to be some kind of an army clerk whose obsequious attitude struck a wrong chord in me.

The officer regarded me with baleful eyes.

312

"Didn't you hear me call that all Hungarians should step over there?" He pointed to a corner where three men, obviously new arrivals, were standing. "Or do you think I ought to extend a special invitation to you, engraved perhaps?"

The good old Hungarian cock of the walk! I remembered his type but had not expected to meet up with it here in Spain.

"Just who are you, comrade?" I asked, a bit uneasy.

"I am First Lieutenant Szasz, the base commander of the Hungarians," he informed me curtly. "Now get over there with the other Hungarians, double step!" he commanded.

I did not expect that development. It took me years of inner party struggle to get out of the Hungarian movement in America and now I was being ordered right back. Joining the Hungarians, to serve under such bastards, was the least of my intentions.

"I am an American, comrade," I explained.

"Don't talk back to me!" he snapped. "You speak Hungarian, you are a Hungarian. We don't care where you come from, all Hungarians belong to us."

I became uneasy, also resentful. What was I, a chattel? By what right does he think he owns me?

"You have the wrong man, comrade. I am an American citizen, my place is with the Americans."

"We have jurisdiction over all Hungarians."

"Not over me."

"Keep your mouth shut! I'll teach you to show respect. Get over there with the other Hungarians at once!" he shouted, purple with anger.

I must still have had some Hungarian left in me at that, for I automatically responded with a string of choice Hungarian oaths mostly about his mother, then turned and walked away.

He ran after me and grabbed me by the arm.

"I'll make you pay for this! You're under arrest! *Guardia! Guardia!*" he yelled.

I wrenched my arm free. By that time we were attracting considerable attention. Other Americans came over, asking worriedly what was up, what did that monkey want of me? A French guard with rifle on his shoulder sauntered over and Szasz ordered him in French to call the commander of the guard.

Szasz was threatening me in the meantime, swearing he would teach me what anti-Fascist discipline was, that he'd show me that the International Brigades were no haven for scum and lumpen-proletarians until the commander of the guard finally arrived. He was also French, the golden stripes on his crushed cap set awry on his head indicating that he was an officer, for no one would have guessed it otherwise. He was sloppy. His faded blue shirt was unbuttoned exposing his hairy chest; the fly of his unpressed, wrinkled pants was open; the belt girdling his bulging fat stomach hung loosely buckled. He was unshaven and unwashed, he was picking his teeth and belching. I realized I had to play it carefully and listened intently as Szasz spoke to him in rapid French pointing to that group of three newly arrived Hungarians waiting at the side and then back to me. Finally the commander turned to me, scratching his stomach.

"What do you say?" he said in French, without too much interest. From the tone of his voice he wasn't too impressed with Szasz.

"*Merde! Je suis un Americaine,*" I said with a show of outrage. "Non-Hongroise," I added, showing him my passport, cursing loud in English.

The commander of the guard took my passport, glanced at it and gave it back to me. He then shrugged his shoulders and threw up his hands to Szasz in the inimitable French gesture, belched, and moved away. I told the beet-red Szasz he made me ashamed to have been born a Hungarian and walked away myself.

Well, I had just come through my first battle in Spain. I wasn't happy over it. Evidently the Fascists I had come to fight were not all on the other side.

314

44 In Albacete we were given personnel forms printed part in French, part in Spanish to fill out, listing name, age, origin, occupation, etc. To the question asking party affiliation I put down "Communist." That was corrected to "Anti-Fascist." I did not know any such party but it was O.K. with me. We were next lined up at the rather depleted supply depot for uniforms. All I could find to fit me were a used pair of flimsy khaki pants and a khaki shirt, an overcoat, one thin blanket. No underwear, socks, or tunic were issued.

Next we formed up and the base commissar made a speech to us in French, which was translated simultaneously into a number of tongues. It was the usual party speech on imperialism, Fascism, defense of the Soviet Union, and concluded with a paean to that idol of the French working class, the beloved leader of the heroic International Brigades—Comrade André Marty! Tired as we were we cheered and clapped at the right places. Then we were told we would not be required to swear loyalty to the Spanish government because that might jeopardize the citizenship of many volunteers. I had been worried about that, and now I felt relieved. We sang the *Internationale* and raised our clenched fists, shouting slogans such as:

Viva la Republica Española!

Muerte al Fascismo!

No Pasarán!

We also *"Viva"*-d Stalin, General Miaja, the International Brigades, Stalin, the Glorious Spanish Army, Stalin, André

Marty, and a number of others until we got tired and hoarse. That made us all officially Internationals and we were quite elated.

That ceremony over, all volunteers with previous military training were ordered to step forward. I was surprised that out of close to a hundred Americans only eight of us stepped forward, including myself; while in the other groups those with previous military training formed the majority. They had come from countries where military training was compulsory.

Next, those with previous artillery experience were ordered to step forward. Of the Americans, I alone stepped forward and then, when the order was repeated, another American about my age joined me. He was from Oklahoma and he was gloriously drunk. I wondered where he got his liquor, I had seen no *cantina* anywhere.

There were only twenty-two of us with previous artillery training. We were to be transported to Almansa, the International Brigades (I.B.) artillery base. Before leaving I took the comrade from the American base commissariat aside, told him who I was, and asked him to tell Bill Laurence, the American Base Commissar in Albacete about my arrival. I would have preferred to see Bill Laurence in person but since I was being shipped out, there was no opportunity for that.

Almansa was about 80 kilometers from Albacete. We traveled in a one and a half ton open Soviet truck built on the Ford model. The truck was sturdy and designed for the poor Russian roads. Since the Spanish roads were just as bad they stood up very well in Spain. The trip took over three hours. We started out at dusk and we were soon traveling in the dark, seeing little of the countryside. All we had been fed that day was some coffee and bread in the morning and we were hungry, yet our spirit was high. We were singing revolutionary songs, the same tunes but different words, in a half-dozen languages. Oklahoma was still gloriously drunk, he was sitting next to me

316

in the truck and I wondered how he was able to keep that glow from dying out.

Oklahoma had attached himself to me from the start but spoke very little, almost in monosyllables. All I could get out of him was that he was half Indian, had worked mostly in the oil fields, had served in the artillery in the U.S. Army at the tail-end of the First World War.

He was not a Communist, in fact knew very little about politics and cared less. He had been in a bar in Seattle, heard some seamen talking about going to Spain to fight the Fascists, thought that was a good idea. He left with them, joined up, was transported to Paris where he became drunk and got lost. Finally he had made contact just before a transport left for Marseilles, was drunk on the boat until he had found himself in the water, clung to something until he was rescued. When I asked him where he got the money to get drunk on, he said "shooting craps." He pulled out a fistful of francs and wanted to give me some but I refused. Now he was sitting next to me, not asleep nor joining in the singing, just drunk and content. He was of medium height, with the most peculiar face I had ever seen on a man. His head seemed flattened as if in infancy someone had put his skull between two palms and squeezed hard. Anthropologists speak of long heads and round heads. Well, his was a squashed head, twice as broad as long, with an extremely wide mouth and a broad flattened nose, a broad forehead no higher than an inch—take a rubber doll, pull her cheeks apart as far as they will go and you will get the effect.

He squatted hunched over his knees for quite a while when suddenly he spoke up in a flat drawl.

"Comra–aa–de, is this the International Bri–ig–a–ade?"

I assured him it was. He contemplated it for a while then asked,

"How come there is only two of us Americans and the rest all Greeks?"

317

"They are not Greeks," I replied in surprise. "They are Czechs, and Poles, Serbs, Germans, Jews, and Austrians."

"Then why the hell do they all speak Greek?" he said truculently. I explained how they all spoke in their native tongues but Oklahoma only shook his head.

"They all sound Greek to me." Then he added an afterthought. "Tell them to speak English, it will be easier on them." I made an effort to enlighten him but he only shook his head, he couldn't see why anyone wanted to speak any other language but English. Suddenly he pulled a bottle from under his shirt and said, "It ain't whiskey, and it ain't gin, they say it's rhon but it tastes like rum. It's better than nothing. Let's drink to those poor bastards who don't know better than speak Greek."

The rum tasted good. "Where on earth did you manage to get hold of it?" I asked in amazement.

"I gave one of them Spanish in the barracks some francs while we were just doing nothing, told him 'whiskey' and he got it for me."

Oklahoma was quite a man, cut from a different cloth than the average American volunteer who was generally either a Communist or a close Communist sympathizer. He was to have quite a lot of trouble later with the I.B., or to be precise, the I.B. leadership was to have trouble with him. He liked to drink and he liked to gamble, both of which were considered to be vices by the fanatics in the party who, like all fanatics, had a strong puritanical streak in them. In addition, when Oklahoma drank he would usually get drunk; when he gambled he would usually win and clean out the rest of the volunteers. He would then generously stand drinks to all losers who, although normally nondrinkers, would want to make the most of the opportunity to recoup their losses even if in liquid form and would drink themselves into insensibility. He was considered quite a problem by his commissars, fretting about the "morale" of their men. Oklahoma went from arrest to arrest and he would have been turned over to the SIM and shot, except that he was totally "nonpolitical" and a willing soldier who never grumbled and who accepted whatever hardships stoically.

I interceded a number of times in his behalf, pointing out in solemn Communist phraseology that he was representative of that vast stratum of the masses whom we wanted to win over, typifying that common denominator of the united front we wanted to establish all over the world; that he was the embodiment of those toilers kept in shameful ignorance by the capitalists of whom we demanded but one thing—to be against Fascism. Since no one could possibly maintain that Oklahoma was pro-Fascist, since the very fact that he had come to Spain proved that his sentiments were definitely anti-Fascist, I argued that we simply had to accept him as the product of his capitalist environment and the victim of our vicious colonial treatment of our Indians; that it was the job of the politically more advanced comrades to tutor him in Communism, to elevate his class consciousness. Expressed in those long-winded and stilted Marxist terms it always worked, no matter how vexed those party zealots were with him.

Oklahoma was always willing to co-operate in the elevation of his class consciousness. He could sit through, and would, without twitching a muscle, hours of the most tedious political harangue which was compulsory and went under the heading of political education. Those sessions were deadly, they consisted of an exasperating rehashing of all the inane party propaganda in an irritating Communist rah-rah fashion, extolling the virtues of the leadership until everyone rebelled against it. Oklahoma didn't mind it a bit. They made him swear off liquor which he did cheerfully. The next time he would get drunk and be charged with breaking his anti-Fascist oath, he would cheerfully volunteer to take another oath, to swear on the spot that he would never touch another drop again.

He was transferred from unit to unit and the last time I

came across him somewhere at the front he was company cook, and a conscientious one. It was during the retreat when everything was in chaotic disorder and I had not eaten anything but scraps for days. He fed me from his secret stores until I could hardly move and when I was ready to leave he said he had something for me. He went to a potato sack and pulled out a bottle of cognac, an incredibly scarce item in those god-forsaken mountains. I demurred, but he pressed it on me, assuring me he had four more bottles left.

"Them muckin' commissars who were after me for drinking are now coming around scared shitless, sucking for a drink," he told me with quiet contempt. "I tell 'em I swore off drinking as they wanted me to. They don't believe me and they sniff but I won't let 'em catch me drinking. I do my drinking at night in the dark, enough to last me through the day."

I still wonder whether he came through alive. I know his kitchen was hit twice, the second time completely demolished. Occasionally I still dream of coming across him unexpectedly in a dim bar in some out-of-the-way joint; ordering up two full pints for him but only single shots for me; the two of us just sitting there with nary a word but in blissful understanding until one of us rolls off his stool—Oklahoma, not me.

45 ALMANSA was a Spanish town with a population of about 15,000, serving as the training base for the artillery units of the I.B. The American battery to which I had been attached did not possess a single gun, not even for training. It had no instruments, no artillery tables, nothing but its name to signify it as an artillery unit. A tall Minnesota-born Swede going under the name of Anderson, who had received elementary military training while attending the Lenin School in Moscow, was acting as our instructor. He had been taught in Moscow how to handle a 75-mm. Russian gun and he was trying to transmit that learning to the battery, quite a task without a gun or any other material to work with.

I found the men in the battery in a state of demoralization. The battery, named after John Brown the abolitionist for its propaganda value in America, had been organized in April, 1937. When I joined it in the first week of June it had grown to approximately seventy to eighty men, nearly half of them Americans of foreign birth who had had some previous artillery training in the conscript armies of their countries of origin.

The battery had no officers, the acting military leader was Anderson. The unit was too small to rate a commissar—political commissars were not assigned to combat units smaller than a company, and the political "responsible" assigned to that battery was a reddish young man, alternately called Slim or Red; he hailed from somewhere in Maryland, I believe. Anderson was around twenty-nine, Slim around twenty-two. Most people in the battery were older men. About twelve of them were seamen whose uninhibited behavior gave Slim, Anderson, and their prissy clique of YCLers considerable concern.

Most men in the battery were an unhappy lot. They had come to Spain to fight and found themselves cooped up within the walls of a small former school building, spending their time in meaningless small tasks, forced to listen daily to long, boring, repetitious political lectures on Fascism delivered with deadly monotony by Slim, a schoolboy rehash of the propaganda material poured out by the ton by the Communist Party in the shape of leaflets, pamphlets, articles, bulletins, etc., to which the men had the same access as he. The food was devoid of all variety, it was usually *garbanzo* (dried chick peas) cooked in water together with some mule or burro meat. The *garbanzo* was hard and the meat was so tough it defied chewing, it was elastic like an old auto tire and snapped back when one tried to take a big bite out of it. It had to be swallowed and left for the digestive juices to do the rest.

The party leadership which consisted of Slim, Anderson, and a solemn, self-important young YCLer from New York called Walsh, were constantly exhorting the men not to frequent the Spanish taverns and to stay away from the bordello; to conduct themselves with dignified austerity as befits Communists. The seamen who liked their vino and their women rebelled against that sanctimonious attitude. This led to constant clashes with the leadership who considered the seamen a blot on the working class.

The greatest sources of irritation to the men were the glowing accounts that appeared in the *Daily Worker* and other party publications describing the heroic deeds performed daily by the Americans in the International Brigades, and the letters they were receiving from home which were inspired by those articles. Those letters were full of hero-worship, expressing the admiration of their comrades and sweethearts who humbly apologized for staying back home while the subject of their admiration was heroically killing Fascists wholesale, braving mortal peril every minute of the day.

The writers of those letters invariably begged for details about their heroes' personal exploits, chiding them about their modesty, imploring them to let them share in the thrill of combat if only by mail. Some comrades in the battery rose nobly to that call and sent back long gory accounts about dead Fascists piled up like cordwood in front of their battery. Then the recipients of the letters would write back relating proudly how they had read those thrilling accounts of victory aloud in their party units and how the letters had inspired and spurred them on to re-double their efforts in collecting money for Spanish aid; how it had helped them in recruiting new members for the party.

Those letters from home accentuated the frustrations of the men in the battery and made them cynical about party propaganda.

Then one day six of those field guns actually arrived. They were destined for the other two batteries, composed mostly of Czechs and Slovaks that had been formed months before ours, but they let us borrow one gun for the time being.

Having a gun with which to train perked up the morale of the battery considerably, so much so that the exuberant Party leadership of the I.B. in Almansa decided to go a step further and induce the Spaniards in the town to abandon their siestas as an inadmissible waste of productive time. To prove to the Spaniards that it is not injurious to health to work during siesta hours we were ordered to start our afternoon training at one instead of the customary four.

Accordingly we would march singing through the town, with bugles blowing, to set a commendable example, until the alcalde of the town felt compelled to send us an official protest about our noisy marching and loud singing that interfered with the siesta of the populace. He coupled this with the formal request that we abstain from such barbarian practices forthwith.

A second attempt to introduce Soviet methods into Spain met with similar results. The party had declared a *subotnik* (voluntary work-party on the Soviet model) to help the Spanish people, and the Internationals were ordered to a near-by village on a Sunday to assist the peasants with the harvest.

We arrived at the village about three hundred strong and were met by a delegation of peasants who escorted us to the wheat-field. The wheat was pitifully stunted, the stalks hardly reached the knee and barely yielded more than a few kernels of grain. The field was full of rocks, the wheat growing sparsely among the outcropping. I had expected we would be furnished scythes but all they had were blunt sickles of cheap-grade steel that neither had nor could hold any kind of an edge. To cut the wheat we had to bend double, grab hold of three or four stalks—all we could reach at one time—and saw the blade back and forth to sever the tough stalks.

The peasants stood by glumly as they saw us trample down the wheat, leave more stalks than we cut, work for five minutes and rest for ten, make them run endlessly for water. And after about an hour of grunting exertion, they watched us stretch out on the ground to rest. After about three hours of that we halted altogether and began clamoring for food. Finally they had no choice but to take us back to the village and empty their meager larders to provide us with bread, cheese, and a small bit of sausage, all the food they had. We were supposed to return the next week but the peasants wouldn't have us again—we had eaten them out of ten times the amount of food that the wheat we had harvested was worth. That expedition certainly failed to cement good will between us and the population; if anything, it increased the average Spaniard's distrust of the *"extranjeros."*

Two days later Sandor Cseresznyes, a young Hungarian from Transylvania who was with the Czech battery and who claimed to have been a journalist back home, came to call on me. He spoke English and showed me a copy of an article he had written about that *subotnik* which he had sent to the *Daily Worker* in New York. He expected to get paid for it and he thought I might advance him some money until he received his check. I laughed at that naïveté, and when I read the copy of his article my eyes opened wide in disbelief. It was a paean to international solidarity, presenting a glowing but wholly imaginary account of the prosperity of the "Spanish village Kolkhozes" which the Spanish peasants, having become the owners of the land formerly belonging to the nobility, were now cultivating with the most modern machinery and farm equipment. It described the mowing of the wheat by huge tractor combines and it ended up with a vivid description of the banquet the villagers had tendered us in gratitude for our help.

Cseresznyes was standing by hopefully as I read on and became completely flabbergasted when instead of praise I told him angrily I was going to write at once to the *Daily Worker* refuting that article and denouncing it as an out-and-out lie.

"But it's propaganda, real good propaganda!" he wailed, and when I told him that I considered those barefaced lies very bad propaganda and harmful to our cause he vehemently disagreed. The bigger the lie, the better the propaganda, that was the way he understood it.

I do not know whether my letter ever reached the *Daily Worker* or not. I do know that about a month or six weeks later I saw that article in the *Daily Worker* and it was given quite a display. It was published under Cseresznyes' by-line and the introduction gave a glowing write-up to Cseresznyes, that fighting young anti-Fascist hero and volunteer. The article was illustrated by a composite photograph showing a huge combine in a lush wheatfield with the close-up of a peasant, who looked more Russian than Spanish, riding a shiny new tractor. The captions explained that those combines were a common sight in the new Spanish co-operatives. (The last time I came across the name of that anti-Fascist hero was during the trial of Vogeler, the American Vice President of the International Telephone Company in Budapest, who was charged with espionage by the Communist government of Hungary. The main witness against Vogeler was this very same Sandor Cseresznyes who had been planted in his cell as an alleged spy himself to gain his confidence and who subsequently gave sworn evidence against Vogeler which the latter denounced as pure fabrication.)

A few days later our solitary gun was taken away from us and reassigned to the Czech battery which was being equipped for the front. It did not look as though our battery would ever get near the front and it was time to make my move if I wanted to see some fighting. Not having heard from Bill Laurence, the American base commissar, I wrote to Joe Dallet who was Commissar of the Mackenzie-Papineau Battalion then in training in Tarazona, and informed him that I was buried in Almansa, that I wanted to transfer to the infantry and join his battalion.

I received a reply from Joe the next Sunday. He regretted that his table of organization was full and complained about the enormous amount of work and immense responsibility resting on his shoulders. He invited me to visit him the first chance I had. I asked Slim for a leave but it was not granted. I was stewing and simmering by the time Bill Laurence came to visit the battery.

Bill Laurence was a man around forty with thick, almost white, gray hair which he wore parted in the middle. He was the Party's District Organizer in New York and had been sent to Spain after the Lincoln mutiny to give the Americans some standing with the base command of the I.B. He told me that at the request of the General Staff of the Red Army in Moscow the Comintern had decided to form an historical commission in

326

the International Brigades. It was to be a small, confidential commission and knowing that Alpi had asked me to do some work along those lines for the Party back home, Laurence had recommended me for its Anglo-American section.

My appointment came through a few days later. I was transferred to the Political Section of the International Brigades, the Party apparatus of the Comintern, assigned to the Historical Commission. When I saw my title, I laughed. I was a *Jefe*—a Chief. In Spanish it really sounded grandiose. I had been appointed:

Jefe de la Sección Ingles y Americano de la Comisión Histórica de las Brigadas Internacionales.

It was still not combat duty. Yet it was better than being an assistant loader of nonexistent shells to an imaginary field gun in a paper battery in a small sleepy town in a remote corner of Spain.

THE ALBACETE GENERALS

On the front of Albacete
Meet the generals of the rear.
Oh! They fight the grandest battles
Though the shells they never hear,
For the wind is in their make-up.
You can hear the generals say:
"Yes, we're going to Jarama
Mañana or next day."
. . . See them strolling in the evening
To the grogshops for their wine,
For they are the brave defenders
Of the Albacete line.
　　　　　—Anonymous British I.B. Volunteer

46 REPORTING from the isolation of Almansa to the buzzing beehive of Albacete, the base of the International Brigades, was like the awakening of Rip van Winkle—it took time to adjust.

Albacete, peacetime population 40,000, capital of the province of the same name in southeastern Spain, had been swollen by war refugees and the Internationals to more than three times its normal size. The Internationals dominated the town. The best public buildings and private residences had been taken over by I.B. Headquarters for their offices—its hotels, restaurants, cafés, two movies, streets and thoroughfares, whorehouses, vinoshops were thronged by volunteers from all corners of the world.

328

I reported to Comrade Fiala, Chief of the Historical Commission—a tall, broad-shouldered, close-mouthed Pole.

A few minutes' discussion carried on in halting German which we both spoke with an equally heavy accent, his Polish, mine Hungarian, soon made it clear to me that Fiala had only a vague conception of how to get the Historical Commission started. Nor did he indicate any marked inclination to stick his political neck out by taking the initiative.

All he had done was to ask the Base Command to send out a letter to all commands in the International Brigades asking them to forward to our commission all documents, including the plans and orders pertaining to their past battles. Fiala's idea was that once those documents came in, and we had to allow time for that, we'd go over them and analyze them. He was rather hazy about what we were to look for in those documents and on what basis we were to evaluate them.

Fiala was a highly intelligent person, a member of the Polish Bureau of the Comintern, in civilian life a Communist professor of history. He was a bureaucrat of the Soviet mold, insulated by layers of suspicion and mistrust he had acquired in the illegal Polish underground Communist movement and more particularly during the years he had lived under the shadow of the purges in Moscow. It took quite an effort to get through to him. I was the first American he had encountered with whom he had a chance to speak at length and he asked me many questions about the way the Party operated in America. My candid replies both fascinated and shocked him; they evidently strengthened his conviction that we were just amateurs blithely unconcerned about the most elementary rules of conspiratorial technique, a bunch of overgrown kids playing at revolution and bragging about it.

I showed him my memos on my interviews with the few early Lincoln members who had been transferred to Almansa, also the few diaries I had collected from them. That bit of news interested him greatly, now at least we had some "documents" to put into the files of the Historical Commission. Then I startled him with the proposal that instead of waiting for those "documents" to be forwarded to us I be authorized to go after them to the Brigades in the field, and asked him to get me a *Salvo Conducto* (literally "Safe Conduct," a military pass) for the front.

I spent the time waiting for that pass circulating around Albacete, striking up conversations and becoming friendly with volunteers of all ranks and nationalities. It was amazing how eager they were to open up after I convinced them their confidences would be respected. I was shocked by my findings. Instead of international solidarity, dog eat dog seemed to be the rule governing the relationships of the various Communist Parties with one another; their leaderships were in cutthroat rivalry for the favor of Moscow.

Moreover, a great schism existed between the "Albacete generals," the recipients of political and military plums, the members of the I.B. command, and the rank and file volunteers, particularly those among the rank and file who were officially pronounced "bad elements."

These "bad elements" were the crippled, the amputees, the men with half-healed wounds, the ill, the shell-shocked, the broken in spirit—the wrecks of those early volunteers who had stopped Franco at the gates of Madrid with little other equipment than small arms and their willingness to offer up their ill-fed bodies for sacrifice. They were of all nationalities, French, Belgian, German, Irish, Scottish, Jewish, British, Slovak, Yugoslav, Czech, Polish, Hungarian, including quite a few Americans. They were swarming all over Albacete tramping from office to office in search of prosthesis, repatriation, postoperative care, back pay, clothing, food, sleeping accommodations, political advice, or merely a friendly word.

The "bad elements" were the rank and file survivors of those early desperately fought battles that had filled with glory the party press of every country. They were the first volunteers on the scene whose sacrifices formed the base for all the Communist financial appeals, whose heroism raised the prestige of the Communist Parties with the intellectuals, liberals, and anti-Fascists. However, the names publicized by the Communist Parties were seldom those of the rank and file who had suffered the most, but of those comrades whom the party wanted to build up. They became the "heroes" while these unfortunates, the debris of those battles, became the "bad elements."

These "bad elements" overflowed the streets, sitting on the curbs and park benches in their tattered uniforms, or simply leaning against the wall outside the offices, feeding each other's discontent by loud descriptions of their hardships, of the cowardice of many of their superior officers and commissars. These were the multitudes found in every society since the dawn of history who were born to the dry teat and predestined for the bottom of the heap; whose misery gave birth to Moses, to Christ, to Marx, to the Utopians.

It was easy to see why these "bad elements" felt themselves betrayed by the party. They had been made to believe that they were volunteering to join a "People's Army" where all would share the vicissitudes of war equally. Then came the shock of reality; they found themselves under a military rule paralleling that of the Soviet Union where caste differentiation and the privileges enjoyed by officers and commissars were incomparably greater than those existing in the armies of the capitalist countries.

The Americans, having been brought up in the easy democratic way of America, particularly resented this unexpected class differentiation between the comrades who were made officers and commissars and the comrades who remained in the ranks. A number of American volunteers who were loudest in their complaints against the party leadership were ultimately made to pay for it with their lives in the jails of SIM.

At that time I merely noted those stories, suspending judgment until they could be authenticated by filling in that six-month gap in the history of the American volunteers that elapsed between their arrival and mine. That was difficult, for no official records were kept of that early period. Luck finally led me to George Brodsky who had been denounced to me by most of those early arrivals as the worst example of the behavior of Party leaders and commissars in Spain.

When I located him George Brodsky was being kept in seclusion by the party awaiting repatriation. I found him a broken old man although barely in his thirties. He wouldn't talk to me at first, he had been pledged to secrecy. When I finally induced him to confide in me, he not only talked, he spilled over.

His account was not quite coherent—he was still unnerved by his experiences, his eyes would dissolve in tears from time to time as he pleaded for my understanding.

The first group of volunteers, 96 in number, left New York on December 25, 1936, followed within days by other, more numerous groups. Except for five or six men with previous military training in the peace-time regular army or the National Guard, none of those volunteers had a real conception of army life, nor had they been prepared for what they might encounter in Spain. Worse still, the party had sent them overseas without assigning to them even a single leading party member with sufficient organizational experience who would have commanded their respect. In short, they were leaderless, which gave rise to immediate factional groupings. Thus the unity of the group was destroyed from the start. Officially, Brodsky had been placed in charge of the group in New York but he lacked the necessary qualities of leadership and experience to enforce his authority.

They arrived in Spain on January 6, 1937, and were taken to the old Spanish fort Figueras near the French border, the assembly center for the Internationals. The camp was run by the French who proceeded to give the Americans their first taste of international solidarity in practice. The French comrades received the Americans with hostility, unwilling to share their rations with them, and bivouacked them in the worst barrack rooms, the floors of which were littered with human excrement. Many of the volunteers wanted to turn back immediately, others openly talked of desertion.

Brodsky had found himself right in the middle; the Americans were blaming him for their treatment by the French, while the French command held him responsible for the rebellious behavior of the Americans. As ranking party member Brodsky next was appointed Albacete Base Commissar for all Americans who were now arriving daily in Spain. The French command in Albacete showed themselves equally discriminatory against Americans, keeping them on short rations, which demoralized the Americans even more.

Brodsky again was in the middle. The Americans raised demands and insisted on conditions which they expected Brodsky to enforce with the I.B. Command, with whom he carried no weight. The I.B. Command in turn, disgusted and contemptuous of those "spoiled cry-babies," those "arrogant Americans," held Brodsky responsible for their conduct. Considering them of little worth, they decided to disperse the Americans, to use them as replacements for other units, the British and Irish particularly; thus denying them the opportunity to serve in units of their own under their own command. (It was the story of General Pershing versus Field Marshal Foch all over again, but Brodsky was no Pershing nor did he have Old Black Jack's political backing.)

333

Had Brodsky been an experienced party leader, had he been entrusted with authority to represent the Central Committee of the United States, had he been given a "silk ribbon," he could have taken a tougher stand, because ultimately all those matters were decided by the party. As it was, the existing situation was permitted to worsen and a number of Americans had actually been detached and sent to other units.

The story culminated in the Americans being sent to the Jarama front without training, under a makeshift and inexperienced command, which resulted in the death of a disproportionately high number of them right at the outset of the battle. The surviving volunteers again blamed Brodsky for that and cried for his head.

Brodsky was eventually removed and a few days after our talk whisked back by the party to the United States in ignominious secrecy. He was still absolutely loyal to the party when we had our talk—he was not sufficiently astute politically to comprehend that the enormous weight of guilt for the needless death of those comrades which had brought about his breakdown was not his but rested with the Central Committee of the American party for entrusting the fate of hundreds into such inexperienced hands.

Incidentally, other early American contingents had similarly sorry experiences with their political leaders, as will be seen subsequently in Major Merriman's account. This explains why the political leaders of the I.B., the "Albacete Generals" from André Marty down, were held in such contempt by the average volunteer.

All hosannas in the *Daily Worker* and other party publications to the contrary notwithstanding—most volunteers hated the guts of those party leaders.

47 FIALA and I soon established a satisfactory working relationship. Although he and my other colleagues on the Historical Commission were content to wait docilely until the "documents" from the combat units of the I.B. arrived he had no objection, in principle, against my going after them in person provided I promised to keep him out of trouble and accepted the responsibility for my individual action. That suited me fine. There was but one drawback. Fiala either couldn't or wouldn't get a *Salvo Conducto* for me from the Base Military Command and was horrified at the suggestion that as *Jefe* of the I.B. Historical Commission he should issue me one on his own authority.

If he was worried about acting as a *Jefe,* I wasn't. I was a *Jefe* too, "Chief of the Anglo-American Section," so I decided to have some official letterheads printed, talked a worried engraver into making a rubber stamp for the Historical Commission without official authorization, and issued my own *Salvo Conducto.* I signed it myself, then stamped it—that's all there was to it. Fiala was jittery over this unprecedented act but I mollified him by presenting that stamp to him for the use of the Historical Commission. He was certain that pass wouldn't be honored but he proved wrong. I traveled with that *Salvo Conducto* all over Spain, into every war zone where the International Brigades fought, without having it challenged once and it gave me entry into all headquarters I cared to visit.

335

The pass I drew up was simple. It was typed on a letterhead which bore in print the heading:

HISTORICAL COMMISSION OF THE INTERNATIONAL BRIGADES

Salvo Conducto

Permission is hereby granted to Comrade Sandor Voros, Chief of the Anglo-American Section of the Historical Commission of the International Brigades, to visit all units of the International Brigades. Comrade Voros is on an important and confidential mission for the Historical Commission of the International Brigades.

The commanders of all army units are requested to facilitate his travel and to give him their utmost co-operation for the successful fulfillment of his mission.

(Stamped)
Historical Commission
of the International Brigades

*(Stamped again
for good measure)*

(Signed) Sandor Voros
Chief of the Anglo-American Section of
the Historical Commission of
the International Brigades

I had that translated into Spanish by our interpreter who added a few *muchisimos* and a couple of flowery phrases of his own volition, and I was in business.

My first trip was to Tarazona to visit Joe Dallet; I was eager to see him for old friendship's sake. I was also disturbed about the rumors circulating about him in Albacete which I found difficult to credit and I wanted to see for myself.

The first complaint I heard about Dallet was voiced by Jack Delehenty who had delivered Joe's note to me in Almansa. Delehenty pleaded with me to have him transferred out of Dallet's unit to the artillery (eventually I managed to arrange that) because of Dallet's intolerable dictatorial behavior. Delehenty claimed that Dallet was universally hated by all men in

336

the training camp. Jack was a young boy about twenty and I did not take his opinion seriously, but later in Albacete I met up with many other volunteers from Tarazona who were unanimous in their condemnation of Dallet, which made me wonder.

I had known Joe Dallet for years. The last time I saw him in Youngstown he was still the hard-working, somewhat naive, solemn young organizer rather on the shy side who had often been criticized by the District for his lack of aggressive leadership.

I couldn't make that picture of Joe jibe with the ones presented of him by those men.

I did not know then how quickly and easily power can corrupt—especially Communists who are conditioned to it.

48 TARAZONA was another small Spanish town not far from Albacete. As I walked into the camp I was hailed right and left by comrades who knew me from the States. Their morale in general was low. Many of them wished that they had never volunteered, others were wishing to be sent to the front in a hurry, partly because they were eager to come to grips with the Fascists and partly to escape that camp. The military commander of the camp, Captain (later Major) Merriman was universally liked and respected, so was Lieutenant Bob Thompson, second in command, although to a lesser degree. The discontent of the volunteers, amounting to near hatred, was directed against Joe, the Battalion Commissar. They considered him a pompous and overriding autocrat who gloried in his power over them; they even accused him of appropriating the cigarettes, tobacco, and other supplies sent from America for his own use to lead a life of luxury. Only Lieutenant Jack Cooper, a leading comrade of the Y.C.L. in Cleveland, commander of the battalion's machine gun section, had a good word to say for Dallet; he thought Joe was doing a good job trying to instill discipline in the battalion but perhaps he was somewhat highhanded and bureaucratic about it.

Joe Dallet welcomed me in friendly fashion. However, there was an unwonted reserve in his behavior which I couldn't help noting. His first words after the usual exchange of personal remarks were mocking.

"I bet you found Spain different than you thought!" he

338

gloated. "A man stands on his own merit here and has a chance to show what he can really do."

This must have been a reference to our Ohio Bureau which had consistently criticized him about the haphazard quality of his work. I changed that subject quickly, congratulated him on his position, the highest then held by any American, equivalent to the rank of major, and asked him to tell me about his job.

He paced up and down, a tall, gaunt young man not yet thirty with a big mop of unruly dark hair, sucking on a vile-smelling Sherlock Holmes type pipe, giving me a lecture on the duties of a commissar taken verbatim from the same pamphlet I was then carrying in my pocket to brief myself on the subject. I let him talk on for a while then interrupted him, saying I wanted to know how he was translating those principles into practice.

His answer was revealing, far more revealing than I was in a position to judge then. Although he had been in his post less than three months he had become fully impregnated with that exalted feeling of self-importance which, as I had occasion to learn later, characterized most of those comrades in Spain who had suddenly found themselves elevated from obscure party posts into positions of great authority. Trained in the dictatorial practices prevailing in all Communist Parties these comrades became drunk with power and gloried in the knowledge that here in Spain at last they were in a position to enforce their dictates by jail sentences and even the firing squad.

I cannot think of a more shocking illustration of the above point than the remark made by Dave Doran, then newly appointed commissar of the XV Brigade, at a banquet honoring a visiting delegation of the American League Against War and Fascism. Those delegates, mostly well-meaning, liberal American women of the middle classes, were particularly intrigued by Dave's youth, he was twenty-eight, and the important position he held. They plied him with questions about the power he, as

339

Brigade Commissar, wielded. Dave, who was visibly expanding under their adoration, straightened up in his chair and, surveying that huge table where, besides the delegates, most of the brigade staff were seated, asserted with pride:

"Well, I can have anyone seated at this table shot!"

The visiting delegates received this information with rapture, that was really something to take back home, to impress their friends with the importance of an American commissar they had encountered in person in Spain. It did not occur to any of them to inquire what could possibly have distorted the mind of a man that young to think of his position in those terms; to entertain the idea that it was within his power to order anyone in his sight, civilians and military personnel alike, placed before a firing squad and executed at his whim. The terrifying fact was that although Doran had no such authority, he had the actual power to do so and he could easily have excused such an action by charging his victims with, let's say, "counterrevolutionary Trotskyism," and even earned a further promotion thereby.

But that was still in the future. Joe Dallet had never reached that mental state although the path he was following in Tarazona was leading in that direction. In his talk with me he kept harping on two words, "morale" and "discipline." He was determined to raise the morale of his battalion by the strictest measures against the "bad elements" whose conduct was a "disgrace to the Communist Party." His ideas on discipline were monastic: the men had to be regimented all their waking hours, denied leaves, prohibited from playing cards, from visiting the vino shops or, horrors, the bordellos. Those violating any of these regulations were severely punished. In addition, after drill the men were subjected to hours of daily "political education." I remembered those deadly monotonous political lectures we had been forced to attend in Almansa, telling us why Fascism and capitalism were bad and the Soviet Union and Communism were good, why we had to fight Fascism when our very presence in Spain was proof how well aware we were of that. I tried to point that out to Joe but he brushed that aside, he even questioned me, did I "actually oppose political education?" I had sense enough to deny that heresy promptly.

I asked Joe whether the disparateness between the living standards of a battalion commissar and his men had anything to do with the discontent. The pay of a commissar was 600 pesetas every ten days, in contrast to the 60 pesetas the men were receiving; also, he lived luxuriously compared to their monotonous fare. Wasn't that situation a factor? He rejected that, saying that it was not he who had set that large differential pay rate for officers and commissars; besides, it was more than just that officers who had all the responsibility should have preferential treatment. In fact, the one other thing he was going to root out in his battalion was the perverted idea held by the volunteers that the I.B. was supposed to be a people's army where both commanders and men received the same pay and rations on the basis of democratic equality. Such notions undermined discipline and an army had to be run by discipline. He was out to set an example, and speaking of example, he had assured his men time and time again that they could depend on his setting an example in battle and come the time, he would be the first man out of the trenches to lead the attack in person.

He was to keep that promise. The last time I met him was in early October 1937, just before the Mackenzie-Papineau Battalion was scheduled to meet its baptism of fire by going into an attack at Fuentes del Ebro. It was around ten o'clock at night by the time I located him. I found him sitting alone in a small hut by the dim light of an oilwick. He was very lonely; he greeted me with genuine warmth this time, grateful for my presence. I had come to learn his immediate orders and plans pertaining to

341

the impending battle but Joe was more interested in recalling the past, our personal exploits in Ohio, confiding that he felt completely isolated from everyone. Although I assured him that in my observation his battalion was in far superior battle shape than any of our other battalions on the eve of their first battle, which could be attributed mainly to his unflagging efforts, he knew that his men were not appreciative and that he was unpopular with them.

He kept repeating he would now prove to them by his personal example that he had had only their welfare in mind in driving them hard to become good soldiers; he would be the first over the parapet to demonstrate he was not one of those "safe behind the line Albacete generals," but a leader who fully shared the dangers to which he exposed his men.

I tried to reason him out of that obsession. I remonstrated that it was a poor way to provide leadership for an entire battalion, that by jumping off with the first wave he would lose control of directing the battle, which was his main responsibility. But Joe was adamant. He insisted on proving himself to his men and I left him with a heavy heart.

He saw me shivering in the cold outdoors and presented me with his own poncho, a charcoal black, warm woolen one, far superior to those issued by the Loyalist Army, also with a pistol. Pistols sold at a high price and I couldn't afford one. Despite my position I ranked as a private and my pay was only six pesetas a day. Before we parted, Joe indulged in a, for him, unusual gesture. He put his arm around me and told me to remember him.

Joe Dallet remained true to his promise. He was the first one out of the trenches after giving the signal for the attack and was cut down immediately after advancing but a few yards toward the Fascist lines. He was hit in the groin and suffered agonies, yet he waved back the First-Aid men, refusing to let them risk sure death in an attempt to reach him. He was try-

342

ing to crawl back unaided when a fresh burst from a machine gun blasted life out of him.

Joe knew he had to die to redeem the prestige of a commissar, to justify in his own eyes the path he had followed in Spain— a victim of his own Communist training.

Requiescat . . .

49 I SPENT three days visiting with the men in Tarazona, seeking out those early volunteers who might help me to piece together a record of the Americans from their first arrival in Spain. Captain Merriman, then Commander of the Mac-Pap Battalion, was one of those first arrivals, in fact he had been the Commander of the Lincoln Battalion when it was first thrown into action at Jarama.

Captain Merriman was one of those rare men who radiate strength and inspire confidence by their very appearance. He was tall and broad-shouldered with a ruddy bronze complexion overlaying his originally pink skin; thin flax-colored hair framed his bald pink scalp. The physical strength of the athlete combined with the reserved manners of the scholar and the introspective expression in his eyes bespoke great inner power.

Robert Hale Merriman was born in 1908 near the West Coast of Scotch-English parents. His father was a lumberjack, his mother a writer—a combination that left its marks on his subsequent career.

Because of poverty he left home at an early age and worked his way through high school—as a janitor in a bank, as a part-time grocery clerk, and occasionally a window trimmer. After finishing high school he considered he had enough of an education and began traveling around the country, working now in a logging camp felling trees, sometimes as a millwright and pulp feeder, and once, for a stretch, as Number Three Man in a paper mill.

In one of those logging camps he met an extraordinary Irishman who was to exert a great influence on his future life. That Irishman would work hard for six months, then quit, spending the other six months of the year in public libraries, studying whatever happened to engage his interest. This way of life attracted Merriman. If studying was that much fun he too would take it up again, and as long as he was to do that, he might as well go to college.

Merriman had very little money saved but he knew that a young man six feet two weighing 190 pounds who had played football in high school ought not to find it difficult to get a scholarship. He applied to the University of Nevada and was immediately accepted; he played end on the varsity football team and even joined a fraternity until he suddenly found himself in the middle of a Nevada winter with gaping holes in his soles and an empty pocket trying to major in economics.

The leaking shoes presented no real problem—he stuck cardboard inside them. But money presented a twin problem, how to make it and how to save it. He tackled the second one first. As an economy move he resigned from Sigma Mu, which caused a great scandal on campus. That was the first time anyone had voluntarily resigned his valued membership in that great fraternity.

As an immediate solution to the problem of making money he joined the R.O.T.C. which paid $7.50 a month, an income which he eked out by trying his hand again at window decorating. The highest point of financial affluence he ever reached in that period came when he succeeded in obtaining a job in a marathon dance contest as a janitor to keep the floor waxed between the feet of the dancing couples and to sweep away the chewing gum wrappers, orange peels, and other waste products of that great contribution to the culture of the thirties. His summer vacations were spent working alternately as a cement mixer at a naval ammunition depot and as a ditch digger for a water company and, when nothing better was to be found, as a hay hand on a ranch.

Upon graduation he became Assistant Instructor of Economics at the University of California where in his second year he advanced to Head Assistant Instructor. At about this time, when examining the contrast between the theories of classical economics he was teaching and the actual facts of life around him in the depression, he was led to conclude that Marx was right about capitalism. That conclusion in turn led to the deduction that to be true to his conscience it behooved him to do something about the existing state of affairs.

The least he thought he could do was help to improve the sorry lot of the migratory workers who were then cruelly exploited by the great growers of California. He was not ready to go all the way and join the Communist Party because he considered the routine of the party much too confining. Instead he joined one of the convenient auxiliary organizations set up by the party for precisely that purpose, the International Labor Defense. Soon he became most active in the I.L.D. East Bay Committee. He organized I.L.D. branches at the University and took an active part in the defense of the Imperial Valley strikers in 1933 whose demands for a living wage and more tolerable sanitary conditions were met by court injunctions and brutal physical assaults, arrests, and vicious jail sentences. His activities in the I.L.D. also involved him in other bitter strikes in that area in which the shedding of blood and crippling beatings by vigilantes and professional strikebreakers were everyday occurrence.

The next phase in Merriman's life started with his winning the Newton Booth Traveling Fellowship in Economics for a field trip in Europe. Money again became a pressing problem, for he needed more funds for the study he wanted to undertake than the Fellowship provided. In addition, he was saddled with the responsibility of partially supporting the family of his girl friend, later his wife, Marion. (She herself would merit a separate

346

study—a brave, wholesome American girl—because of her admirable behavior in Spain where she joined her husband in Tarazona.)

Robert Hale Merriman, holder of the Newton Booth Fellowship, Head Instructor of Economics at the great University of California, knew of only one way to make more money than his academic salary which barely provided a minimum subsistence —manual labor. In consequence he quit teaching at the University and went to work as a body-polisher in the Ford assembly plant in Richmond. The speed-up and unhealthy working conditions in that plant proved too much even for his sturdy frame. When a few brave souls in the plant whispered about organization, Merriman joined with them and helped to get out an illegal shop paper, the first one to make its surreptitious appearance in that plant. Merriman wrote the editorial for it, his first, "What's the Meaning of Industrial Democracy?"

He quit his job with Ford to go to work on an economic research project for F.E.R.A. on "Current Changes Survey: Seasonal Variations." Later he became supervisor of a medical survey in San Francisco; still later, State Supervisor of "Current Changes Study" in California. He made use of his position to hire as many radicals as the payroll would hold who, because of their views, had difficulty in getting placements. During the San Francisco general strike in 1934 he took charge of publicity, rather counterpublicity, to keep football players from signing up with Coach "Navy Bill" Ingram who was then recruiting a special contingent of football players for strikebreaking.

By 1935, Merriman had saved up enough to make use of his scholarship for European travel. He went to the Soviet Union to study on the spot the application of Marxian economics. He studied at the Institute of Economics in Moscow and afterward spent eight months living on various collective farms, making notes of their operation and compiling statistics. His experiences with collective farming in the U.S.S.R. made him curious to know what farming was like in Eastern Europe. He went on an extended trip to Greece, the Balkans, Hungary, and then returned to Moscow to write a book about his findings. He was in the midst of his book when the Spanish Civil War broke out. At first the Soviet Union kept hands off. But when it decided to help the Loyalists strong pressure was brought on all non-Russians in Moscow to join the International Brigades in Spain. Merriman was made to feel ashamed that not a single American was at that time fighting in the International Brigades; he was reproached at every turn for being engaged in the frivolous pastime of writing a book while Fascism was nakedly endeavoring to strangle all humanity. So Merriman left Moscow and landed in Spain on January 11, 1937.

The account that follows is my memo of that interview, typed out hastily for the raw files of the Historical Commission, incorporating data he permitted me to copy from his diary:

ADD HISTORY LINCOLN

INTERVIEW WITH CAPT. ROBERT HALE MERRIMAN,
FIRST COMMANDER LINCOLN BATT'N.

July 11-12, 1937

Merriman arrived in Spain from the Soviet Union where he was studying economics and agriculture on a scholarship, on January 11, 1937.

He came here without any knowledge about the existence of other American volunteers. He contacted representatives of International Brigades in Valencia. They sent him to Villa Nueva de la Jara to join the Americans who had landed a few days before—about a hundred men.

Arriving at Villa Nueva he found the Americans in turmoil. It seemed the command wanted to put the Americans in with the Irish, and the Americans refused. There was strong friction between the two groups—the Americans allegedly sober, earnest, enthusiastic, and idealistic, the Irish drunken and fighting.

348

The Americans lacked both political and military leadership. The first volunteers were almost religiously anti-Fascist, the overwhelming majority of them party members.

When he arrived, Merriman found a grievance committee already established consisting of Royce, Morris, and Bernie Walsh. [Walsh later transferred to the artillery in Almansa—S.V.] Stern acted as political commissar. James Harris was their military leader (at present with Dombrowsky battalion). The day Merriman arrived Hagilow, Acting Sergeant, had arrested and brought in as a prisoner, Comrade Ferrari who was second in command, charging him with being a Fascist.

Met Stamber for the first time who was supposed to be their political leader; Stamber complained he was slighted by the comrades under him because he was not a member of the Central Committee.

There wasn't even a semblance of military organization. The military commander arrested the political commissar. The political commissar in turn arrested the military commander. The grievance committee of three took on the function of both military and political commands as well as that of a tribunal. Party fraction meetings were held with arbitrary invitations. Those party members not invited went into a funk, protested decisions; wouldn't accept decisions.

Stamber and Merriman were called to Albacete to see Marty. Marty was very angry with the Americans, called them spoiled children, and threatened to send them back home unless they snapped out of it. He gave them a party leaflet dealing, strangely, with the agrarian question, and told them to study it carefully because that represented the official position of the party on the Spanish question. Col. Vidal, commander of the Albacete I.B. base, was also present at the conference.

Following the conference Vidal, Stamber, and Merriman went out to Villa Nueva and held a meeting with the men. Col. Vidal told them the Loyalist Army was not a Communist Army and explained the function of the military commander and the political commissar.

The men were greatly surprised at the news. They had thought they were to function the way a party unit does at home, under the leadership of their own party fraction. The comrades were mostly party members approximately on the same level of development, many middle party functionaries among them, none of them recognized as an outstanding leader. Every meeting ended in a fight because each comrade considered his own individual interpretation of the situation to be the right party line and that of the others wrong. The situation was made even more acute by the practice of holding secret caucuses: those not invited felt slighted and organized fractions of their own.

Following the meeting with Vidal, organization began to emerge. Stamber was made political commissar, Harris military commander, and Merriman staff officer.

Harris claimed wide military experience gained with the U.S. Army in China. A former seaman—supposedly a good field leader—he lacked experience in giving lectures. His favorite method was to pose a problem and suddenly ask somebody, without previous explanation: "What would you do in that case?" No matter what the answer was he would invariably reply in front of all the others, "You'd kill off all your men that way."

This answer had the effect of discouraging all who were selected for company and section commanders. They would resign time and time again—especially since the men they were supposed to lead had also heard that answer and therefore wouldn't place much confidence in their leadership. This constant changing and shifting of officers largely accounted for the fact that when the battalion had moved up to the front there were no officers and noncoms to step into the breach and take command when the need for it arose.

Merriman as staff officer received instructions from Col. Vidal to build up Harris. In order to do so Harris had to be isolated

350

from the men so they couldn't observe him closely. He was stopped from lecturing. All orders were drawn up by Merriman for Harris to sign because Harris was incompetent to draft a clean-cut order. The building up of Harris succeeded to an even greater degree than anticipated and had rather disastrous effects later on.

The men at Villa Nueva were entirely isolated from the base in Albacete. They had no trucks, received no supplies—they had to buy their food and supplies with their own money. The men became almost rebellious. They received no news even about the fighting in Spain, didn't know what was going on in the world.

Suspicion attached itself to Harris about money matters also. Harris spent money freely claiming it was his own, that he had received it from the Central Commitee of the party in New York, while there were grounds to believe he had received the money from the base for the men. [This angle of it has not yet been investigated—S.V.]

In the meantime more and more men kept on arriving. The training was at first conducted along American military lines. Later it was suggested to use a combination of French and American formations.

The plan was to train one company, send it to the front, and later build a battalion around it as more men arrived and received training.

At about this time Steve Daduk joined the outfit. Daduk had been in Spain for months, had fought on three or four fronts, and been wounded a few times.

Daduk was appointed Commander of Company I, with John Scott second in command.

The relationship with the population became very good. They had much opposition and distrust to overcome. The French before them had not behaved in a manner that was expected of them. They went on drunken sprees, brawled, they even insulted women and kept their quarters very dirty. Things had come to such a pass that when the Americans first arrived in town the populace didn't even want to show them where the barracks were located.

The Americans went about things in a systematic manner to improve this relation. They donated 6,000 pesetas to the local *Socorro Rojo*. They showed films for the children in the morning, for the townspeople in the afternoon and for the soldiers in the evening. The battalion doctor held daily clinics treating the townspeople without fee, and the population worshiped him. They organized a *fiesta* for the Red Cross and raffled off an American pie that brought in 200 pesetas. Before long they succeeded in winning the affection of the townspeople to such a degree that they were offered the finest buildings in town for their use. The Cuban comrades played a very important role in improving the situation.

Commissar Stamber did a good job in winning over the townspeople. But this didn't hold true when it came to the battalion. He failed to develop political leaders in the battalion—the purpose for which he had been originally assigned. He was supposed to stay with the battalion only ten days but since he failed to develop leadership he had to stay on.

Around this time they decided to hold a military maneuver to demonstrate to Marty and other generals the degree of training they had reached. Just before the maneuver a row developed between the commanders of Company I and II, they both threatened to arrest each other.

Despite the personal friction and other obstacles the maneuver was a success. Marty and the generals were pleased and as a reward they awarded the Americans the honor to be the first unit to occupy the model camp of the International Brigades which was to be completed in Pozo Rubio around February 10 or 12.

By this time Harris had been well built up. The men who

saw little of him thought him a good military commander. Col. Vidal had the idea that Harris had been picked directly by the C.C. of C.P.U.S.A. to command the Americans.

The battalion had grown to 400 men by this time. Merriman suddenly took ill. Harris rushed to his sickbed, all excited, and told him an incoherent tale of how he had overheard a fantastic plot against himself. Allegedly Royce, Morris, and other leading comrades had held a secret meeting at which they were plotting to remove Harris from command.

On February 12 the battalion received orders to move to Pozo Rubio. The same day the British division was moved to the front.

Later in the same day an order came from Vidal in Albacete requesting "Captain Harris and Captain Merriman" to report to Albacete. Since at this time neither Harris nor Merriman held any rank and the usual custom was to appoint the commanders only when they were about to go to the front, Merriman and Harris immediately guessed the situation, especially since the order stated that the battalion was to move to Albacete instead of Pozo Rubio.

Merriman and Harris went to Albacete, the battalion following them. In Albacete they were informed they were going to the front. At Vidal's office Merriman and Harris were given revolvers, field glasses.

The battalion was marched to the bull ring and there equipped. The equipment was issued haphazardly. Bayonets did not fit the rifles; many pieces of vital equipment were missing altogether.

According to instructions, Harris was to act as commander and Merriman as his adjutant. Harris became extremely unnerved and excited. He told Merriman he was equally responsible with him for leading the battalion.

Marty and Col. Vidal made an inspection of the battalion in the bull ring. Harris became more and more unnerved—he grabbed rifles out of the men's hands saying he was a rifle inspector. It was obvious something was wrong with him and the men began to murmur that Harris was drunk. Battalion Commissar Stamber in consequence ordered Harris to bed. Harris went away but came back after a while and fired his pistol off in the *Guardia Nacional,* then disappeared again.

When the convoy pulled out at midnight February 15 Harris was nowhere to be found. Informed about it, Col. Vidal placed Merriman officially in command of the battalion.

The convoy was very poorly organized, the trucks broke down quite often. When they arrived at Chinchon, their destination, they couldn't find Brigade H.Q. Merriman went on to Morata where he was told by General Gall to bring up his men immediately.

Following this order, Merriman ordered his men to take off their shirts and use them to wipe off the heavy grease on the new rifles just issued to them. Since most of the volunteers had never held a rifle in their hands before, he ordered each to fire five rounds into the bushes on the mountainside so as to have some idea about handling a rifle before going into battle.

Merriman, who had been advanced from adjutant to battalion commander, now needed an adjutant himself. He couldn't appoint one of the company commanders because that would have disturbed the leadership of the companies. Against his better judgment he had to appoint Daduk.

When they reached Morata they witnessed their first aerial fight. Our planes chased the Fascists off and brought down two planes. The men stood up well under the bombardment.

On February 17, they moved into the second line of reserve to a position on a hill later known as "Suicide Hill." It was a very steep hill encircled by a railroad on three sides, overlooking both our lines and those of the Fascists, offering a clear view of the Teguna Valley.

The nights were wet, soaking the blankets—the men were drugged by lack of sleep.

354

On February 18, the Fascist planes came over and bombed the battalion again. From then on they were subjected to heavy artillery shelling and at least one aerial bombardment daily. While in this position they witnessed the biggest air battle in Spain to that date, taking place directly above them with about 85 planes participating.

The Lincoln Battalion lost its first man here. Charles Edwards was killed while making observations from an outpost trench. Edwards kept shouting to the men around him: "You got to keep your head down! There is a sniper shooting at us here."

When he, too, in turn was warned to take cover, he retorted: "I am sent here to observe. F . . . you!" The next moment he was drilled through the head by a bullet.

The total strength of the battalion at that time was about 377 men. Their pay was three pesetas a day.

The men dug in on Suicide Hill, although very short of implements. They had only 35 picks and shovels in the entire battalion. Later they received 35 more.

As it turned out, the Americans played an important role by the mere fact of being positioned on Suicide Hill. The Lincoln Battalion acted as a reserve for the entire XV Division. At that time the situation was rather precarious. The improvised Spanish *milicia* units had simply quit the front and the battle-weary Thaelmann and Franco-Belge brigades were becoming discouraged because they had not seen any reserves. As a matter of fact, they no longer believed in the existence of reserves—they thought that was another empty promise.

Now suddenly they beheld an entire new battalion, fresh American troops at that, decked out on the mountainside in plain view of friend and foe alike serving as reserves and they took heart anew.

The presence and example of the Americans also had a good effect on the Spanish troops. The Spanish had an aversion to digging in and they said it couldn't be done there anyway because the ground was too rocky. Now they saw the Americans digging in on even rockier ground.

Whenever the Fascists would bomb the front line trenches the Spanish troops would usually break and run leaving the Fascists free to occupy their positions and would suffer far greater casualties while fleeing than if they had remained in their trenches.

The Spaniards now saw the Americans stay in their trenches despite air raids, bombings, and shelling and thereby avoiding casualties. This gave them more confidence in the protection offered by entrenchment.

The presence of the Americans on Suicide Hill had its effect on the Fascists, too. They saw they couldn't attempt to break through without running into fire from both flanks.

In the six days spent on Suicide Hill the American casualties were low—two men killed and a few wounded.

On February 21, the battalion moved into the old Dimitrov position. The order was given by Lieutenant Wattis, an Englishman on the Brigade Staff, who told them to move in without their packs and blankets. The packs and blankets accordingly were left behind, most of them never recovered. This caused additional hardship in that wintry weather, leaving the men shivering in the cold, night and day.

The battalion was very poorly equipped. It lacked telephones and other necessary equipment. The battalion officers were seldom called to meet with the brigade—most of the time they were ignorant of what the battalion was expected to do. This was one of the reasons why Lieutenant Wattis, who talked big and claimed he was doing all the planning on the XV Brigade Staff, was in a position to give orders.

On February 23, the Americans were ordered to move into the gap that existed between the lines held by the Dimitrov and the 24th Spanish battalions. According to the plan the Americans were then to go into attack, with the Dimitrov and the Spanish moving up simultaneously.

The Americans moved into the gap and according to orders went into an attack, getting fairly close to the Fascist trenches. Had the other two battalions moved up also, they could have broken through the Fascist lines at Jarama. Since they failed to do so the Americans had to withdraw, losing about sixty men —twenty dead and about forty wounded.

[Previous to the Feb. 23 attack Col. Klauss, Chief of Staff of the Brigade, called in Merriman to order the Lincoln battalion to assist the German Thaelmann battalion. Just then Harris reappeared on the scene from nowhere and, taking advantage of Merriman's absence, told the comrades he had been sent to reorganize the battalion and he was taking over command. He gave orders to the battalion to move into a new position. He took the second company out personally and they wandered around in great confusion under heavy machine-gun fire. As the night progressed Harris became delirious. He told the men he saw "50,000 Fascists ready to attack" and wanted to lead the battalion into action until Merriman learned of the situation and had him removed in an ambulance.

This incident happened around February 21 or 22 and is often referred to by the Lincoln boys as the "Moonlight Walk." Despite the heavy fire, that whole evening resulted in only one casualty.—Voros]

Daduk, Merriman's adjutant, also cracked and had to be sent to the hospital. Seacord, commander of the machine gun company, was then made adjutant.

On February 24, the Lincoln moved into the position formerly held by the Dimitrov. They were without food. The same day they received reinforcements—about 65 new American volunteers without any training whatsoever. These men had never handled rifles before, they had no helmets or other necessary equipment—

357

most of them had arrived only a few days before in Albacete. They were rushed to the front with orders that they be given two days' training behind the lines. These reinforcements brought the total of the battalion up to its original strength, around 400 men.

The morale of Franco-Belge and English troops was very low by that time—they had to be taken out of the lines for a day's rest.

On February 26, a Fascist prisoner revealed that the Fascist forces opposing them were very weak. The XV Brigade in consequence decided on an attack.

The objective was to push the Fascists back behind the Jarama River. According to the plan, the 24th Spanish Battalion was to form the spearhead of the attack with the Lincoln to support their left flank in active defense position. After the Spanish reached the road the entire brigade was to move up. The attack was set for the 27th. The plan of operations was as follows:

9:50 A.M.: Artillery barrage lasting 10 minutes.
10:00 A.M.: 24th Battalion to move up supported by tanks on the right flank.

Armored cars to be brought up behind the old Dimitrov position to annihilate the Fascist machine-gun nests. The cavalry to be brought in play to evacuate the wounded and exploit the gains of the attack. Twenty airplanes to participate in the attack, bombing and strafing the Fascist trenches.

Lieutenant Colonel Copic, Brigade Commander, was very proud of the plan and issued instructions that it be explained in detail to every man so they could see all services co-ordinated for one attack.

The Americans had not been equipped with telephone or maps. Telephone and maps were now promised to them for the attack, also new machine guns because the ones they had were so old they could seldom keep more than three in working condition at the same time.

Daybreak found the battalion still without phone connection with the brigade. Maps arrived, but were not worth much. At 8:50 A.M. the Brigade telephone men reported they hadn't enough wire to make connections.

The artillery opened up as per schedule but their shells fell in front of the English reserve positions instead of the Spanish or Lincoln battalions where the attack was scheduled.

Lieutenant Colonel Klauss sent orders to the Lincoln not to leave the trenches till the Spanish battalion advanced at least 50 meters.

No airplanes were in sight. Two armored cars showed up in the rear but refused to participate in the attack.

The Spanish went over the top on schedule, advanced about 15 meters under very heavy fire, then withdrew to the trenches, refusing to advance further without artillery or tank support.

Klauss then gave orders for the Americans to attack to encourage the Spanish to advance again.

The first American company on the right flank went over the top. The second company was also ordered over by Klauss.

In the middle of the attack the Brigade informed the battalion that the reason the planes did not come was that the battalion had failed to put out an airplane signal. The battalion had never heard of an airplane signal until then nor did it know what it was. Once that was explained, the men hurriedly made a T signal out of their shirts and put it out with the leg of the T pointing to the enemy. Comrade Streysand was killed while laying out this signal.

When the phone connection was finally established Brigade Commander Copic claimed that the Spanish had already advanced 700 meters and they were being killed off because the

Lincoln battalion had failed to support them. When Merriman informed him about the true state of affairs Copic angrily interrupted him.

"Don't contradict me," he yelled, and added that the Americans had disgraced the Brigade, they had spoiled the advance by their failure to attack. Although informed of the high concentration of machine gun fire on the Lincoln he gave Merriman ten minutes to make up that 700 meter advance.

Following that conversation three planes arrived out of 20 promised. The planes flew over the Fascists and left after a single sortie.

Signaling with his arm to the men to go over the top, Merriman was hit in the left shoulder by a bullet that broke the bone in five places. Seacord, the battalion adjutant, having been killed, Merriman turned over command to Phil Cooperman, the Battalion Clerk, and though wounded, talked personally with the Franco-Belge and English to take over the trench before permitting himself to be carried off. He ordered his reluctant stretcher-bearers to take him to Brigade Headquarters to speak with Copic. When he arrived Copic stated Merriman was too weak to be allowed to speak and refused to hear him.

On February 27 a number of mistakes were made. Usually an attack is called off when certain key conditions don't materialize. The services did not participate in the attack in the co-ordinated manner as planned. It was also a mistake to inform the men in detail what support to expect in the attack because when the promised support failed to materialize they became reluctant to advance.

The Americans were insufficiently trained. They either went over the top in groups, not singly in face of the heavy machine gun fire, or refused to go over at all and had to be forced to do so at pistol point by Lieutenant Wattis, Brigade Staff Officer, who even tried to force the machine gunners to go over the top. [This is when the Lincoln "mutinied."—S. V.]

360

Stamber, Political Commissar, was nowhere to be seen during the attack. After the attack on the 23rd, Stamber suddenly discovered that there were a lot of improvements to be made in the cookhouse behind the lines and accordingly stayed there.

The Fascists showed their weakness in not counterattacking after the February 23 attack. Our attack on the 27th was the first counterattack against the Fascist drive to cut the Madrid-Valencia road.

The attack on the 27th had a strong positive feature. When the Fascists saw so many new troops advance on such a narrow front they became scared of the unexpectedly strong forces opposing them. They eased their pressure and stopped their advance. The Madrid-Valencia road was saved.

S. V.

50 MERRIMAN, who was wounded early on February 27, did not know the real extent of the casualties suffered by his battalion. As I was able to piece it together later, out of a total number of 377 effectives on the battalion list, 153 had been killed on that day alone. That was the day the Lincoln mutinied and demanded to be withdrawn. About the casualties, if I err it is on the conservative side. For the appalling fact is that no one in the Communist Party in the United States or in Spain bothered to keep a record of the names of the first volunteers sent to Spain. The Party was paid by the head, it received its cut from the World Tourists travel agency on the transportation of every volunteer shipped; its interest was in the amount of that total take. The identity of the individuals was a matter of total indifference to the party.

The volunteers who arrived daily in small groups did not know each other well, couldn't tell who was missing in battle outside of those in their own narrow circle. My effort to compile the actual list was made even more difficult by the fact that more than one out of every two American volunteers who participated in the Jarama battles had been killed right in those early days, and many of the remaining survivors lost their lives in the battles of Brunete before I was able to reach them. Thus the list will never be accurately completed.

There is more to this story. If failing to keep a list of the volunteers sent overseas were not bad enough, the Party, instead of notifying the wives, parents, or other close relatives of men

362

killed in battle, actually prohibited news of their death from being sent out to them from Spain. The party preferred to prolong their agony in order to squeeze the last ounce of energy and monetary assistance out of them, lest their grief make them unwilling to contribute further support. Let me quote here at random from one of the hundreds of letters from home marked "Dead," that I found moldering in a trash can in the American Base Commissariat. One of the comrades who worked as a censor tipped me off to their existence, first swearing me to absolute secrecy. It was dated March 18, 1937, and addressed to Walt Durham, *Socorro Rojo,* Room 17-1, Albacete, Spain. (I have changed the name—why break open old wounds?)

Darling—

Today is a month since I heard from you, a month of watching the mail box. The only thing that cheers me up a little is when I read in our paper—of the many victories of the Loyalists. Then I forget myself and my own heartache and consider the wonderful thing you are doing, and all the fighters of democracy, to ease the heartache of the whole world and make it a better place. Sweetness, although I get no mail from you I will continue to write every Thursday and Sunday as I have been doing. I know you are writing if you are able and I have the utmost faith that through all these hard times and lonely days you will someday soon come back to me and we will take up our life together, but it will be a thousand times sweeter than before.

Darling, tonight at our meeting the comrades all asked that I convey to you their love and good wishes. Charlie, who had stayed away all this time came tonight and promised to come to the next meeting. We are right on the job with leaflets every week and good leaflets too. Our unit is also collecting a lot of money for Spain, also food and clothing.

Darling, otherwise there is no news . . . On the outside my life is the same as before except that I feel more responsibility toward my party work. I am trying to take your place as much as I can. But sweetheart in my heart there is a steady longing that does not leave me for a minute. That longing for you, for your sweetness. Darling,

I hold on to your few letters and read them over and over, also all the old letters. I carry them with me to work every day and darling your presence has never left my mind. Darling I will close now with my best and sincerest wishes to all your brave comrades and to you the same plus all my love and a million kisses. Darling I wait hopefully for a letter. . . .

Your comrade and wife
Olga.

P.S. Love from your two sons.

Comrade Durham had been dead for a month by then but his grieving wife and comrade was calculatingly kept in ignorance by her comrades in leadership of the party. They did not want her to know that she was a widow and her two sons half-orphaned. They let her continue to pen tear-soaked letters twice a week in despondent hope, without even affording her the consolation of the certainty which, heartrending as it may be, affords an anchor for the distraught mind and permits the healing process to begin. Let her be tormented by gnawing uncertainty and despair, the facts that really counted were that Charlie was coming back to the meetings and that the unit was raising even more money for "Spanish Aid," which, of course, went into the party kitty.

Less than a cent out of every dollar, not a full one per cent of the monies collected for Spanish Aid, had been turned over by the party for that purpose.

Pressed hard at a subsequent congressional investigation to account for the expenditure of these funds, the party, with its usual lying ingenuity, first denied having received anything but a small, insignificant sum, then claimed that it had actually devoted seventeen per cent to the purpose for which it was raised. Then came the joker. The party did not dare to assert that even this small percentage had been expended in cash. This seventeen per cent had been computed as the alleged value of the used clothing sent to Spain—an allegation which in no way explained what

364

the party did with the cash contributions amounting to millions of dollars.

The extent of this infamy is best illuminated by another incident. During the time of the Aragon Fascist offensive in the spring of 1938, when newspapers in the United States were full of the debacle of the Spanish Loyalist Army, in the period when Herbert Matthews, known for his sympathies for the Loyalists, reported in the New York *Times* that the International Brigades had been cut to ribbons and only about 150 Americans had managed to escape with their lives, all through those agonizing weeks and for nearly two months thereafter the letters sent by the surviving volunteers in Spain had failed to reach their families in the United States. The letters the comrades were receiving from home were frantic with fear and despair, begging for at least a line of assurance that their beloved son, husband, or father was alive, even if crippled and in the hospital. We were so disturbed by the avalanche of those tearful letters that we organized a "write a letter home" campaign in the XV Brigade, assigning not only my staff but demanding of all commissars to see to it that every surviving volunteer actually wrote at least one letter home. Yet the pleas from back home kept arriving, ever more desperate, ever more frantic. I went up to Barcelona to investigate. All those letters had left Spain for France as usual.

Finally the truth came out—those letters had been left piling up for months in the Paris office of the American Communist Party, instead of being mailed to America by affixing French postage stamps on them. The explanation? Some comrade in the office had absconded with the stamp money. When I raised hell, why hadn't the party immediately provided other money, I was told the party was short of funds! Collections in the U.S. were at their peak then and were even further stimulated by the news of the debacle—yet the party at home found better use for that money than to lay out another hundred dollars or so for stamps for the surviving volunteers in Spain.

I had made many excuses for the party before that incident and also later. After all, I and the rest of the comrades put together constituted the party. Some of us would occasionally try to separate ourselves from certain acts and policies by blaming it on the "party leadership." Yet we were all part of that leadership even though the higher-ups had all the say and the lower-downs none.

This is why I don't know yet whom to blame for letting those frantically awaited letters from the battlefields lie there for months because of those niggardly few dollars. I only know what I said when the comrade from Paris tried to justify that act, protesting and proving to me he wasn't responsible for it.

"I believe you, comrade, individually you are not responsible. But collectively, every single son of a bitch of us is."

51 By late fall I had gathered much information on the early history of American participation in the Spanish Civil War. I had been to every front, tracked down every detached unit, made a survey of every American medical installation, and it was time I saw some action, too—no longer as a visiting observer but as an active participant. I put in for a transfer to the XV Brigade, having discussed it with Major Merriman, Chief of Staff of the XV Brigade, and Dave Doran, Brigade Commissar, both of whom favored the idea.

Fiala, however, claimed that the Historical Commission needed me and refused to release me. I finally won his consent by appointing Paul Wendorff, on my own authority, as my assistant in Albacete, and by agreeing to remain fully responsible politically for my post on the Historical Commission even while with the Brigade. Paul Wendorff was a history major from New York who had served with distinction as a machine gunner with the Lincoln battalion. He was an excellent man for the position and being somewhat battle-fatigued was grateful for the appointment.

As soon as I reported to the Brigade, Doran sent me to Madrid to assist Captain Frank Ryan with a souvenir book of the history of the XV Brigade which had been promised to the men in time to be sent home for Christmas presents and which was long overdue. My job was to complete that book and expedite its publication.

Captain Ryan's office and living quarters were at the political headquarters of André Marty which occupied the palatial home of the Duke of Velasquez, and I moved right in with him. I mention this because it afforded me the opportunity to meet informally many of the highest figures in the international Communist movement who usually stopped there on their way to or from Moscow. They seemed to be a rather special breed, or perhaps products of the same mold patterned in Moscow, highly intelligent and razor-sharp in discussion, yet very vain and strikingly egotistic even when in their cups. Their professed concern for the downtrodden masses definitely excluded any sympathy or responsibility for the fate of the individual—they all made fun of my "vestiges of bourgeois American sentimentality clearly reflecting the political immaturity of the infantile American Party."

Frank Ryan was unmistakably Irish in the proud way he carried his bushy gray-haired head, from his ruddy face and large hooked nose, and his six-foot-and-some robust figure. He had been a member of the Irish Republican Army, had served a jail sentence in Ireland for terrorist activities, had participated in the early fighting in defense of Madrid, and he was more than half deaf from concussion in a shell explosion. He gave me a rousing welcome and took me out "to wet our gills" before we got to work.

What kept him bogged down was the long list of American officers and commissars he had received from Doran and whom he was to "play up" in the book. That list was broken down into categories I, II, and III, indicating the prominence each man on the list was to receive. In addition, he had been given a similar list by the British, and naturally he had a preferred list of his own on the Irish. His problem was how to glorify all those selected elite and still find space for some sort of history of the Brigade that would include at least some reference to the run-of-the-mill volunteers without whom the Brigade would have had no history at all. I had no stomach for that sort of work but luckily it was not my baby and that harassed wonderful Irish fighter had my sympathy.

I sat down and contributed the missing chapters on the actual history of the Brigade and also worked out a sort of running narrative to tie all the "press agent stuff" together, which completed the book. (On the whole it was a sorry job but the comrades in the Brigade—particularly those whose name or picture or both appeared in it, liked it.) After checking arrangements with the printer, I convinced Ryan that he had seen enough action already and it was my turn now; he was to stay in Madrid and see the book through the printshop while I was to return to the Brigade, which was then fighting around Teruel.

I never saw Frank Ryan again. He was captured by the Fascists during the Aragon retreat while trying to rejoin the Brigade and had been sentenced to death. He languished in Franco's jail for years, because the Irish Republic for whose independence he had fought, would not lift a finger to free him. It was the hated imperialist British government which finally interfered to save the life of this Irish rebel and ultimately secured his release.

52

Have you ever been alone?

Alone for nearly three weeks, in midwinter, groping from one desolate mountain to another in heavy snow until your very thoughts seemed to have congealed; sleeping in abandoned stone huts, chewing on rock-hard chunks of granite-gray Spanish bread with aching jaws blue with cold? That's what it took to catch up with the brigade which was on the move from Teruel.

The commissariat was quartered in a couple of huts near the brigade command post but Doran was away at a meeting with the XXXV Division to which our brigade belonged. Comrade Robert Cooney, chief of the commissariat, was a ruddy, round-faced young Scotsman—he did not know what assignment Doran had in mind for me but told me I could spend the night there and report to Doran next morning. I threw my musette into a corner and went outside. That musette contained all my chattels and worldly goods—an extra pair of wool hose, a number of notebooks, a few packs of cigarettes, a battered old can that served both as soup bowl and drinking cup, an aluminum spoon, a canteen, and two clips of ammunition for my pistol. Not much of a fortune for a man past thirty-seven but enough for my kind of party functionary—we were the 20th century red monks who had renounced wealth for the Hammer and Sickle, to spread the gospel of Marx and Lenin and the glory and the kingdom of the proletariat.

Outside I bumped into Dave Gordon, a former leading member of the Ohio Bureau whom I had known for years. I greeted him enthusiastically but his response was considerably more restrained. He was a prematurely bald, undersized man in his late twenties who had practically been raised in the party. He had held leading positions since his teens but his political future in the party was already behind him. He was highly intelligent but self-indulgent and vindictive, known for his intrigues and readiness to stick his political knife in the back of any of his associates at the opportune moment.

I knew from Laurence that Gordon had got himself in the doghouse here in Spain also, first because of his intrigues against the leadership in the training camp, secondly by having asked to be sent home because of an alleged chronic stomach ailment which the doctors could neither localize nor discover.

As we exchanged information about the Ohio comrades I detected a bitter streak of jealousy in his comments. Frank Rogers was commissar of the Mac-Pap battalion, John Gates was then acting base commissar in Albacete in place of Laurence who had gone back home, Jack Cooper was a captain and commander of the brigade machine gun company—excellent backgrounds for all of them for a future career in the party back home, while Gordon's accomplishments were, if anything, on the negative side. I sensed he was somewhat jealous even of me although it was well known in Ohio and in the movement in general that I had no political ambitions whatever and was not in rivalry with anyone. While we talked Gordon belched continuously which I found disconcerting. He blamed it on his bad stomach saying he wouldn't want to discuss that, he preferred to suffer with it rather than be mistaken for a malingerer. I had my reservations about that; I noticed that he was swallowing air regularly and then belching it up, presumably to back up his claim of stomach trouble.

Gordon was on the staff of the commissariat. His job was preparing speakers' outlines on current events for political discussions in the brigade. He guessed I would be assigned to the brigade's daily mimeographed news bulletin and he seemed relieved when he heard I had no intention of joining the staff of the commissariat, that I wanted a military assignment.

The next morning I reported to Doran at the brigade command post. Compared to his last appearance he was now smartly dressed in a tailored military uniform. We had met only a few times previously and although he had been friendly and courteous we had not established any personal relationship. He was a humorless dead-end kid grown into manhood during the extreme privations of the depression, leading the hobolike existence of the penniless Young Communist League organizer around the mining regions of Pittsburgh. He was about twenty-nine, elevated to his present post by a chain of fortuitous events. Arriving in Spain just before our Brunete offensive and assigned to the Brigade Commissariat as assistant to Steve Nelson, the Brigade Commissar, Doran happened to come across a propaganda truck equipped with a loudspeaker just when the assault on Belchite reached its critical stage. With quick presence of mind Doran brought the truck up and talked a pocket of resisting Fascist troops into surrender. A few days later, when Nelson was wounded, Doran became acting Brigade Commissar. After Nelson was sent back home the Party decided that inasmuch as most volunteers in the brigade were young and members of the Young Communist League, the post of brigade commissar in the future should be held by a member of the Young Communist League, and since Doran was already acting commissar, the post went to him.

As it happened, in Doran's case this worked out fine; he took to military life like a duck to water. Brigade Commander Lieutenant Colonel Vladimir Copic, himself a former commissar, was an old-time Yugoslav Communist well versed in the rules of playing the party game—grab all the credit but make sure to have someone on hand to blame when things

372

backfired. Dave was a fighting man by instinct and he was happy to devote his time to military matters. Lieutenant Colonel Copic was eager to encourage that trait; he wasn't much of an organizer and two heads were better than one. Dave did most of Copic's military work which left Copic time to build up his political fences with the Russian military advisers and other higher-ups in the I.B. Doran was a strong disciplinarian and did not hesitate to employ measures from which Copic would shrink. Copic was essentially a very vain person, a one-time aspiring opera singer; he demanded applause and much of it. Dave had no such limitations to curb his drive—he was the more determined military man of the two.

Doran eyed me steadily while I explained why the brigade book was late. I blamed it all on the paper shortage. He charged I had violated his orders, I should have stayed in Madrid until the book was finished. I refused to be thrown off balance, I told him I had stayed until we ran out of paper. Captain Ryan was there, no purpose would have been served by both of us idling away our time in Madrid. I wanted to be with the brigade where I could be of more use.

Dave now switched to a conversational tone, asked me what I thought of Bill Laurence, and a number of other leading comrades in Spain—the regular double-edged party trick to size up where a man stood and perchance obtain some derogatory information on one's rivals. I spoke well of Laurence and of all the rest, which seemed to satisfy him. He then informed me that Johnny Gates had also transferred to the brigade, he had come up last night, what was my opinion of him?

I spoke of Gates highly and said Gates had an air of modesty about him that had a good effect on the men. Doran was very much interested when I related how I had located Gates at the Cordoba front, how well his Brigade Commander and his Brigade Commissar spoke of him. I must have given a higher opinion of Gates than Doran apparently would have preferred—they were both of the Y.C.L., hence potential rivals—because Doran quickly retorted that popularity with the men was not necessarily a desirable trait in a commissar, that he personally wasn't interested in winning popularity contests but in building the XV Brigade into the best fighting unit in the I.B. He then rose abruptly before I could ask about my assignment and told me to go down to the brigade ammo dump, pack a mule, and take a load of munitions up to the Mac-Paps who were under attack.

The ammo depot was not very busy. The mule then being loaded with cases of rifle and machine gun bullets was for someone else who, to my surprise, turned out to be Johnny Gates. He waved and was on his way before they even started loading my mule.

The front line was about five miles away on a mountain top with only a single trail leading to it. At first I had difficulties with my mule. He was poorly loaded and I had to readjust the cases that shifted. Then the mule became balky. I goaded him in English, then in Spanish, but without result. Finally in exasperation I cursed him in Hungarian. For some inexplicable reason that struck a responsive chord in him, he pricked up his ears and got going. I wondered what ancestral memories those Hungarian curses had awakened in him; one of his remote progenitors must have accompanied the Huns, Tartars, or Turks on their invasions of Hungary.

The Fascists, who had been taken by surprise by our night attack, rallied by the time I was halfway up and opened up with artillery. They started shelling the trail and as each shell screamed in I instinctively ducked or flung myself to the ground. This was not the first time by any means that I was under fire in Spain, but on those other occasions I had exposed myself to it voluntarily. Those other times I had been a visitor to the fronts, always knowing in the back of my mind that I could withdraw at will. This was different. Now I was under orders and had to walk into it. I was now afraid and reluctant to move, I had to force myself to get to my feet. Luckily the range wasn't too accurate, the closest explosion missed me by about twenty yards, and by figuring percentages I soon persuaded myself to ignore the shelling and pretend unconcern. I steeled myself not to duck when I heard a shell overhead and soon learned to distinguish between the near ones and those passing over. The trouble with the mule also helped. The mule, not being a reasoning animal and ignorant of percentages, stupidly refused to advance into danger. He tried to bolt and drag me back every time he heard a shell—it took all my physical strength to pull him forward. I caught up with Johnny Gates and we made our way together to the Mac-Pap battalion command post. On the way we encountered stretcher-bearers evacuating shellfire casualties. They were young boys rather badly mangled, one of them seemed dead.

We discovered Major Cecil E. Smith, a former Canadian Army sergeant now Battalion Commander, and Frank Rogers, Battalion Commissar, with a small group of officers standing under an olive tree. We headed there with our mules. They started shouting to us to stop and get the hell under some other tree. The battalion Command Post was being shelled and we were under direct observation. We tied our mules to an olive tree and crossed to the battalion staff.

The atmosphere was tense. Our night *golpe de mano* (a surprise attack, literally "strike with the fist") had caught the Fascists by surprise. The battalion took the Fascist trenches with but few casualties and then braced itself for the inevitable counterattack. The morning had been comparatively quiet. The Fascist command, preparing for its spring offensive, had not anticipated any Loyalist attacks, particularly in that quiet sector. They needed time to react. But their reconnaissance planes had been busy since daybreak and by noon they had already managed

375

to move in sufficient artillery to subject us to heavy fire. Fascist bomber and fighter planes were due any moment, for the Fascists were observed getting ready for a counterattack.

Frank Rogers whom I hadn't seen for months wanted to know what the hell I was doing, picking that time for a visit. When I proudly informed him that I had finally managed to transfer to the Brigade and had just brought up some ammunition, he wanted to know who in hell asked me to do that, they had plenty of ammo, the battalion had its ammo supply well organized. I told him those were Doran's orders. This made him frown and he told me in a quiet aside: "Doran is testing you and is doing the same with Gates. The bastard ought to know better, you've both been around."

That thought had not occurred to me and I did not like it. I was happy to take that ammo up feeling I was contributing to the actual fighting right from the start; this made me feel like a foolish schoolboy. I told Frank I would like to transfer to his battalion. He said they sure could use me and that he would discuss it with Major Smith.

On the way back the Fascist planes became more numerous. I noticed more and more formations coming up from all directions, mostly fighting planes concentrating for an attack. They struck just as I was leaving the trail for the highway to Segura de los Baños.

The Fascist planes came in fast and low, lower than I had even seen them, the air throbbed and the ground vibrated with the roar of their motors. I watched them with rising tension, still the visiting observer but nonparticipant, when I saw the first bombs fall. They exploded sufficiently far from me not to make me too apprehensive although the concussion set my ears ringing and I had to open my mouth to equalize the pressure. Then came the strafing and I was no longer a bystander. Planes with their machine guns wide open came swooping down the road. I yanked the halter frantically but the mule stood braced with its four legs wide apart. I let go and dove down the embankment as plane after plane with hurricane force swept by so low that their propellers almost sucked me up, the ta-ta-ta of their machine guns approaching like ugly ogres in hundred-league boots rattling iron sticks on a giant fence. When the planes were gone, I climbed up the embankment. The mule was on his side, dead, his belly ripped wide open, his eyes glazed; the steam from the big mound of excrement at the base of his tail was mingling with the steam from his entrails. I felt very sorry for the mule but had no time for contemplation, another large formation of planes was coming up. I rushed down the embankment, ran across the *barranco,* and dove into a stone hut on the other side just as the bombs began dropping.

The hut shook, loosing clouds of dirt and dust from the rafters and stirring up the dry straw on the floor. I was choking and rolled under the stone trough, rising and falling with the trembling ground while titanic smoking fists beat down outside. The immediate strafing that followed was somewhat of a relief; by contrast the hardest part was over. As soon as my eyes cleared a bit I ran out. The air was hazy with smoke and dust and I heard screams. I ran toward the sound and saw other dim figures rise and run in the same direction. The screams seemed to come from a large smoking crater and a number of men, all Spaniards, were running around yelling in panic, not seeming to know what to do. I rallied a couple of them, shouted to the others to come around, and set them digging with their bare hands.

We had just got the first man out, he was limp with no visible wounds but he seemed dead, when a major came running down the hill yelling at the top of his lungs in half-German, half-Spanish that the division observation post in the church tower had been hit trapping General Walter, the Division Commander, inside. He wanted us to go back with him. The men hesitated and looked at me. I told them to go on digging, and directed the major down the road to get other help. I had met Walter a few times; he was a general with a large staff and I knew that in a minute or two he would have all the help he needed and then some, while if we left, the men here would surely die, no one would hurry back here to get them out. The German major demanded my name and I told him Juan Gomez; the dust and smoke was too thick for him to recognize me later. He left cursing and on the run. Later I learned I had been right in my decision. We rescued five men. General Walter's post had not collapsed, he had suffered no damage outside a few minor scratches.

When I finally returned to the Commissariat I found a bit of excitement. The hut in which I had slept the night before had been hit by a shell. I found my musette intact under the debris and recovered it; it was good to see that faithful companion again.

That evening I went back to Dave Doran about my assignment. I asked for a military post and told him about my military background. Dave did not see it my way. He explained that the Brigade had changed considerably since the early days in Jarama. The days of battle-green officers, untrained commissars and men were long past. Most of the officers were graduates of the I.B. Officers' Training Schools, the others had gained their experience in the field; in short, the Brigade had developed its military leaders out of its own ranks. I had not undergone any basic training, I was too old for a rifleman and had no field experience in command. He had other plans for me. The British needed a battalion commissar and had asked for Bob Cooney but he had no one capable of taking Cooney's place until Gates and I came up. Gates was younger; he was sending him to the Lincoln to assist the battalion commissar. He wanted me to replace Cooney as Chief of the Brigade Commissariat. The Commissariat needed reorganization badly and also to be turned into an efficient political staff. He was too busy with military work; he needed an assistant who knew how to act on his own without running to him for a decision every time something came up.

I resented being considered old, although I had to admit my heart did no longer take kindly to the mountainous terrain. I asked him just what exactly was the function of the Chief of the Commissariat? Doran answered that it was something like the Organizational Secretary to the District Organizer, to work closely with the Brigade Commissar and see that the political directives were implemented and carried out throughout the Brigade. It was a position parallel to the Chief of Staff to the Brigade. When I asked for particulars, exactly what I and the commissariat were expected to do, he told me to talk it over with Bob Cooney, work out a plan and program on the basis of our talk, and report back to him the next day. I still wasn't keen on it and asked him how about assigning me to the observers or military intelligence but he cut me short; it was a decision and those were his orders. He was curt and formal about that—he made me know that was where informal discussions ended and official relationships began.

Cooney's dour face lit up at the news. It was obvious he was eager to get away, he must have disliked working with Doran very much. I had a difficult time keeping him with me long enough to give me a few pointers. He must have approved of my approach in his fashion, for later, when I was with the British battalion during our Ebro counteroffensive, he was about as friendly to me as the British were capable of being to any American.

The next morning I typed out a proposed departmentalization and a program of work for the Commissariat. My party experiences came in handy.

I found Dave free, lolling in the forenoon sun on the hillside in front of the Brigade Command dugout, and took my plan to him. I read it to him and we discussed it point by point, Dave generally approving, making suggestions here and there. We were about a third finished when the Fascists began sporadically shelling us and a shell landed on our hillside less than a hundred feet away. Naturally I looked up and found Dave affecting unconcern, his eyes fixed on me. I took the cue, if the sonofabitch was still testing me, I could play it as well as he. I read on placidly even though the shelling became more regular, they were 75-mms. and came in at about two-minute intervals, exploding at random. I would look up after every sentence awaiting his comments but as the shelling continued his comments gradually ceased and I saw him getting tauter, watching me with eyes narrowed to a slit. He wanted me to make the first move but I wouldn't oblige. The shells now landed in more rapid succession, I guessed two batteries were firing. There was no sense to this idiotic game but he had called it, it was up to him to halt it. I kept reading on when a shell struck one of our observation posts about thirty feet away. I saw men running toward the struck post but I went on reading. Dave now rose abruptly and said my plan was fine, he was in full agreement, I had full authority to go ahead, and stalked into the dugout. I stood there in seeming unconcern until I saw him disappear and then took to my heels, running as fast as I could until I found a hollow to dive into. When the shelling ceased I went back to the commissariat.

The first man I bumped into was Dave Gordon who congratulated me. I didn't know what for and he told me he had heard I was going to be appointed Chief of the Brigade Commissariat; the comrades in Ohio would be proud of me.

I was a long way from Ohio and was proud of nothing. The games Doran seemed to like to play were too sadistic for my liking. I walked away from Gordon and without being aware of it I found myself humming a song I had picked up from the seamen in the Almansa battery, those "bad elements" the battery commissar was forever trying to suppress.

> We're a bunch of bastards,
>   Bastards are we;
> We'd rather f . . . than fight
>   For Liber-teee!

> Aye, Brother, aye, and up your arse!

53   WHEN sleep doesn't come some people count sheep, others resort to sleeping pills. I have an inexhaustible supply of the latter, I brought them back from Spain. I possess a large variety of them but I don't take them orally—they float into my consciousness on their own volition. Here are a few samples:

TRANQUILIZERS—TAKE ONE TO FOUR

After a spell of bad weather the sun is out; it reflects blindingly from the snow. I am on a mountaintop, exulting in the warmth. I spread my poncho on the snow and start undressing slowly, peeling off layer after layer of clothes that haven't been off my body in weeks. Finally I stand stark naked amid all that snow soaking up the sun, methodically searching the seams for lice and snapping those ugly gray bodies, sluggish with my blood, between my thumbnails. It's wonderful to be alive. The supply of lice is limitless and as I crack them endlessly one after the other, I gradually fall asleep.

✦ ✦ ✦

We are resting between actions, slowly recovering from the crippling blows. New reinforcements have come in, mostly Spanish and Catalan. We are camping in the open in a valley under the beautiful Spanish night sky. The new recruits are apprehensive and homesick, they converse in whispers. I call Julio over and ask him to sing. He is one of those Spanish volunteers in whose development we take great pride. He is a village cobbler, father of four children, an *analfabete* before he

382

volunteered. He learned to read and write in the brigade—the result of our campaign to wipe out the high degree of illiteracy among our Spaniards. He has a beautiful lyric tenor voice and great nobility of bearing—born in the United States or in Italy he would have become a famous opera singer. As his gold-spun voice rises in song after song, the Spaniards draw closer and closer; it takes them back home to their beloved; some are silently crying. I am also caught in the mood but this is not what I have originally intended. I whisper to Julio: *"Era una noche . . ."* I have heard him sing that one before, it starts out as melancholy as only a Spanish folksong could, but the ending is explosive. Julio winks and begins.

> It was one of those beautiful nights
> In the balmy Spring scented with flowers;
> The sky sprinkled with stars sparkling brilliant
> Over the silvery sea. I was strolling along the shore
> Listening with aching heart to the soft murmur
> Of the gently lapping waves when I heard
> The plaintive lament behind a dune:
>
> "Don't you squeeze my breast, you bum—let go
> my tit!"

That breaks the spell. The new recruits are clapping and bellowing, repeating that chorus over and over. Others come forward with their favorite songs and we are all merry, singing far into the night. The young recruits are no longer strangers and alone, they have been fused into one group of comrades. The songfest goes on and on and I float off into sleep.

✦   ✦   ✦

After days of riding and choking with dust in the bouncing Russian-made open Ford trucks we set out on foot to take up new positions. We're well equipped and full of the spirit of offensive. We start out late in the afternoon, the sun is still shining but its heat is gone, her rays bathe the wild mountain scenery in a friendly welcoming smile. The unpaved serpentine road winds gently up the mountainside and we march in an endless line, happy and gay, exulting in our strength. The road climbs steeper and steeper and conversation dies out; breath comes laboring and soon the heart pounds. The sun has long set yet we march on, plodding far into the night, dragging grimly up one mountain, stumbling down another, on and on: lift one foot, pick up the other, this foot here and now the other, the other, the other . . . until it wearily blurs out in sleep.

↗ ↗ ↗

From Barcelona to Madrid is a long distance—it takes a day by truck. The road leads through some of the most breathtaking mountain scenery in Spain and I dread every foot of it. I know it is fear, nerve-wracking fear that I find impossible to mask— worse than any battle. Fear in battle comes and goes in spurts, relief follows tension. Here tension is constant and increases with every twist and turn of the narrow road as it winds its way along the precipice. Some of the curves are so sharp that the truck has to back and fill with half of its body over the abyss, misjudgment by an inch would spell the end. I travel these roads often. The Spanish chauffeur is grinning over my funk and as he reaches the mountaintop he cuts the ignition and coasts down with ever-increasing speed, avoiding going over by a hair at each turn, proud of how much gas he saves that day. It doesn't bother him that these mountain gorges are dotted with trucks and cars that have missed, that we are losing more trucks and cars to these mountains than to Fascist aviation. I squeeze down on the floorboard until I am half lifted out of my seat, hold my breath till my lungs are ready to burst, and relief comes only when the Fascist planes come into sight. The chauffeur then brakes frantically and dives into a ditch. It is his turn now to show fear and he can't figure this crazy Americano who has been so scared when sitting safely in the cab and who now stands on the roadside watching the planes without taking

384

shelter. He yells to me to join him and when I refuse to take shelter, he makes circles around his ear with his little finger: *"Loco, está muy claro."* ("He's crazy, for sure.")

I ride those trucks on and on, veering around those turns with demoniac speed, squeezing my eyelids tight when the truck sways until I doze off fitfully. . . .

SEDATIVES

It is a beautiful spring morning, sunny but not hot, early March, 1938. We're in defensive position in Belchite, have moved in late last night. The Commissariat is set up in a large court-yard fenced in by a thick stone wall. An almost straight, wide highway leads to the lines about five miles ahead but oddly there is no traffic on it. There is unusual plane activity, greater than any of us has seen before, the sky is never clear for a moment of Fascist planes. We have no planes of our own at all. It is still very early in the morning and the front is quiet, apparently the anticipated Fascist spring offensive has again been delayed. The planes are all over the sky, flying high in individual formations of three, each formation sweeping over and over its own patch of sky. I am still very tired, I have had only two hours of sleep. I stretch and yawn while considering what I should do first. I decide to wait until the truck returns and then drive up to the Brigade Command Post; I have lent the truck to Lieutenant Biegelman of the observers and it still hasn't come back.

I am waiting for some other car or truck to come along on which to hitch a ride but no vehicles are on the road, which is rather strange. Two other International Brigades besides ours are in the line and there should be a steady stream of supplies moving up to them. A disheveled staff major from the division arrives on foot asking if I can lend him transportation, he has lost his fifth car that morning on his way up from Army Corps. The major doesn't know what's going on, no vehicles seem to get anywhere this morning, the Fascist planes pounce on anything that moves on the roads and bomb and strafe it out of commission. Every road he has traveled is dotted with destroyed transport. "I can't figure it out," he laments over and over, still unnerved by his narrow escapes.

I'm no longer eager for a ride. I strike out on foot, cutting across the newly plowed field, deciding to drop in on the Brigade Medical Post on the way to see if they are all right before reporting to the Brigade Command Post. The furrows are deep, it is rough going, the reflection of the sun on the dried-out lime-white ground is beginning to make my eyes smart. I pause to rest, scanning the planes circling high; the field is flat and my eyes can travel for miles. A formation of three planes keeps circling high overhead but it never occurs to me to take cover. I even speculate on why it is so difficult to convince our men, particularly the newer recruits, that they don't have to freeze to the ground the minute a plane appears, that just because they can see a plane anywhere in the sky doesn't prove the plane can also see everyone on the ground.

The planes are moving away. I resume my trek. Suddenly the lead plane peels off, makes a turn, and plunges into a screaming dive coming right at me. That's impossible, a plane won't attack a single man, I reject the concept, while flinging myself to the ground, burrowing my head into a furrow, pressing my body into the earth. The rapid tattoo of the strafing machine gun swells into a furious crescendo, the bullets advance, hop-skipping to me from the rear. Each strike is louder as it rushes up, four . . . three . . . two . . . SKIP! I will it desperately, my body tensed like a bow. The bullet skips and strikes ahead, and further ahead and ahead, and it is fading away now. My pent-up breath leaves me, I sit up and there comes that second plane and the third with their machine guns wide open, and then again, then two go away and one comes back dropping small personal bombs, they sound like mortars, they explode offside; outlined in my black poncho on that gray-white field I am a perfect target, and those planes make two more strafing runs on me all alone in that field, in my black poncho, before they finally leave me. Joe Dallet's black poncho outlines me starkly, and as the machine gun bullets strike closer and closer I arch and make them skip and skip and skip until they are past and hop away, fading out, fading out, and I am fading into sleep.

✓ ✓ ✓

We are marching again all night, troops of all units disorganized and intermixed. This is not an orderly withdrawal but a near rout, Belchite is lost. It took us almost two weeks of fighting to capture Belchite in the Brunete offensive last year; the Fascists with their blitz attack have recaptured it from us in one day. The Brigade is cut up and scattered. The Fascists with their concentration of planes have immobilized our transport and while the planes keep our men pinned to the ground, their armored columns slice through our lines encircling us unit by unit. Whatever is left of the Lincoln is heading towards Hijar; the British are fighting toward Caspe; the Spanish are dispersed in all directions. All we have is what's left of the Mac-Paps, two to three hundred men. In the morning we make a weapon-count. We have no mortars left, no machine guns, we find only 153 rifles in the entire Mac-Pap battalion, a few cases of grenades, and small arms ammunition. We halt in a *barranco*. I find a culvert about three quarters of a mile ahead of the Brigade Command Post, twenty feet under the road, almost high enough to walk erect inside, the perfect bomb shelter, and I set up what's left of the Commissariat there. We have just about enough room, I have only about nine men with me now, the rest have scattered during the retreat. The culvert is dry, there is no water in the gully leading from the mountaintop into the deep *barranco* way down below which runs parallel with the road.

I walk back to the Brigade Command Post set up on a hill

at right angles to the road. It is not much of a Post. Major Nicolai, acting Brigade Commander, is sitting hunched over his knees, with Ivan at his left. Bob Merriman, Chief of Staff, is lying stretched out on the ground, a few other staff officers are sprawled out here and there. No one feels like talking, everyone is exhausted. I ask Nicolai what the situation is, he doesn't know, he is waiting to hear from the division. He looks apathetic, a hell of a commander to have in a time like this. I ask Merriman where our new lines are. He points to the mountain ridge above the road where the figures of a few men are outlined. His reply is startling, he speaks in a low tone.

"There is nothing between us and the Fascist except those few scouts on that ridge." He watches the impact of that sink in, then arises. "Come, Voros, let's take a look."

We climb to the ridge and look. The terrain stretches for miles, all we see are mountains and valleys and glimpses of an empty road in the distance, but no movement anywhere. The beauty of the scenery doesn't register—the sinister presentiment of danger and menace does. We talk with the scouts, they hearten at sight of us. They are weary and sleepy, but dependable; they are all party members. They have seen nothing suspicious, no sign of pursuit at all. Merriman and I go back. The descent is worse than the climb, we slip and stumble on the trailless way down. We rejoin the group and sit around, no one shows any sign of initiative. We're waiting for news from the division and there is little inclination for talk. Finally a motorcycle messenger rides up and reports to Nicolai. He jumps up excitedly, speaks rapidly to Ivan who translates, we are to withdraw to kilometer stone 70 on the Alcániz Road and await further orders there. We have but one map between us but I remember the road. The officers are all getting to their feet, I wave a salute to Merriman and go back to get my staff started on the twelve-mile march.

When I enter the culvert the men are anxious to know what

the situation is. I tell them, "Let's eat first." I don't want to get them more jumpy, some of them are too jittery as it is. We get out some cans when a sudden clamor erupts on the road above, shouting and yelling. The cries are incoherent and the culvert reverberates with the pounding of running feet overhead.

The shouts are now closer and more articulate.

"Fascisti! Fascisti!" comes the panicky cry.

My men rush out and I follow them. The road above is full of men running, screaming "Fascisti!" and they point back. My men are already clambering up to the road and I follow after. I am not as limber as they and they outdistance me quickly. I call to them to wait but none of them will stop. They yell back "Fascists!" and keep running. I see them joining the fleeing horde, even forging ahead with a fresh burst of speed.

"Stop! Stop!" I yell but no one pays heed, the panicked mob soon disappears behind the bend.

The road is now clear of all life both ahead and behind except for one straggling figure who approaches painfully. He can barely run, he staggers and stumbles, falls, gets up on his feet, slips again and lands sprawling on the hard road. I walk back toward him, his eyes are bulging with terror, his wide open mouth is gasping desperately for air.

"Dejaté! hombre!" "Calm down, man," I call to hearten him.

He doesn't hear, he clambers to his knees and hands, pushes himself up and runs again, his strained breathing loud like a locomotive. He staggers on a few more yards, then collapses. By the time I reach him he no longer breathes, his mouth is still wide open, his face is frozen in agony. He is a Spaniard. I see no wound on him, he has died of panic and exertion.

I am alone on the deserted road. I strike out ahead and as I round the curve I see everyone is fleeing the road, rushing down into the *barranco,* while the Mac-Paps who have been posted there are already out of it, scaling the mountain on the far side, disappearing over the ridge. I am usually quick to get excited but in moments of crisis my mind perversely goes into reverse and makes me abnormally calm. That's what happens to me now and I walk back to the culvert for my poncho and musette. I am about to take along a few cans of food also but change my mind, they would weigh me down too much in escaping over the mountains. I go through the packs abandoned by my men, take all the cigarettes I can find and one loaf of bread.

I climb back to the road and start out toward kilometer stone 70 on the road to Alcániz. Not a soul in sight anywhere. I look across the *barranco* and watch a straggler painfully making for the mountaintop. He is stumbling and crawling on, he looks like a small puppet from the distance. The mountains pull me, "Come my way, everybody else is." I have a dread of mountains, my heart acts up in high altitudes, I'd rather risk walking through fire than climbing them. The dread of wandering around those mountains all alone and lost brings a decision; I set out on the road. The impulse to break into a run is overpowering but I hold it down, I must conserve my strength.

I pass the bend and walk on in measured steps. I don't fully believe in the break-through, no more than a half-hour could have passed from the time I was up with the observers, the Fascists couldn't have moved that fast with any sizable force.

Logic is a comfort but it is a fickle one. Suppose the Fascists have infiltrated, unobserved by those scouts? Suppose I'll be surrounded and captured? As a Communist I'll be killed on the spot, most likely tortured first. I pull out my wallet to tear up my identification papers and documents. My Spanish party membership book is red with stiff covers. I am about to rip out the pages, then stop. I am not going to let them capture me alive, my last bullet will be for me, let the bastards know that a Communist will fight to death, that it was a commissar they killed. This defiance somehow cheers me. I am still all alone in creation, there is still danger lurking all around but the road now leads downhill, another cheerful sign. I round another

390

curve and stop dead in my tracks. There is a tank ahead with a man in the open turret watching through binoculars.

"*Nuestros!*" ("Ours!")

It is our tank and I could shout with joy. Everything is not lost after all, I was right in sticking to the road.

I walk up to the tank with a cheerful greeting. The Lieutenant does not respond. He is a Russian. I speak to him in Spanish, then try German and French, but he doesn't say a word, he keeps surveying the terrain. I stop there, I am now safe. Let the Fascists come, they'll be in for a hot surprise. Suddenly the Lieutenant curses, I follow his direction and there on the mountain ridge on the left, the far side of a gully, I see two horsemen outlined against the sky, then four more trotting up. They stand silhouetted against the sky, Moor cavalry scouts. The Lieutenant shouts an order into the tank, this is perfect. We're in the shade and the Moors can't see us, it's close range and we can get them all with one shell! The tank shifts into gear but the gun barrel is not turning, it is the tank that is turning, a full 180 degrees, to move back.

"Shoot!" I yell to the Lieutenant, but the tank has completed its turn, it is retreating without firing a shot. I clamber up on the tank to go with them, the Lieutenant yells at me to get down, I yell I am a comrade and hold on. He swings at my hands with the barrel of his long Russian machine pistol and I instinctively release my grip before he shatters my fingers. I fall on my face on the road just barely away from the iron treads that are now crunching by, a few inches closer and they would crush me. I get to my feet cursing that Russian comrade, the tank is churning away at top speed, I look up the ridge and the Moors are gone.

I walk down the road cursing that Red Army lieutenant, that lousy Russian sonofabitch of a bastard, and their crappy tanks. Those lousy tanks have never done us much good, they would pull out of battle at the first sign of danger, at the most critical points when we needed their support the most, leaving the troops demoralized. I keep cursing him and slowly the tension is gone, I feel I am safe, that I have outdistanced the pursuit. I break off a chunk of bread and eat it. I have been up two nights with only a short nap between but I am neither sleepy nor tired, it is great to be alive. I walk on alone on that deserted road for about a half hour and come to a village. The houses on both sides of the road are lifeless and deserted, the stores around the Plaza are shuttered and dead. I pass the Plaza and just before the road leaves the village I see a stalled truck ahead.

The truck is packed tight with civilians, men, women, and children, mattresses, pots, household wares, also a few unarmed Spanish soldiers in uniform. The chauffeur is a civilian wearing a black leather jacket; he is fumbling with the carburetor and ignition wires, his face is flushed and his temper is short. The people in the truck are shrieking at him to hurry up before the Fascists are on them, he curses and shrieks back. I go over to help him. I know nothing about his trouble and little about the engine but I see his carburetor is flooded and help him drain the glass jar that is full of sediment. The trouble fixed, he gets behind the wheel, the motor coughs and catches. I jump on the running board next to him, the people on the truck start screaming at me to get off, the truck is overloaded. The chauffeur orders me off, I refuse and he shoves me in the chest. I lose my grip and jump down livid with anger. I pull my pistol, stand back and say I am an International, if I don't go, no one else will. This is the first time in Spain I have raised a weapon, and then against the people whom I have come to defend. There is a murmur but no more shouts. Shame overcomes me, I speak to them in Spanish, tell them I have come all the way from North America to fight the Fascists, I came to help them, not to shoot them. Someone in the truck yells out, let him come, others take up the cry, the driver beckons me to get on. I smile and thank them, put away the pistol and take out three packs of

392

cigarettes, throw two up to the truck, another to the chauffeur and the others in the cab with him. There is a chorus of *grácias,* I climb back on the running board, and the truck starts. It is overloaded and topheavy, it sways, but it runs.

In less than an hour we reach kilometer stone 70 and I jump off. Everybody in the truck waves and wishes me *bueno suerto,* we are friends, the Spanish are really the most wonderful people on earth!

Kilometer stone 70 is a low concrete whitewashed post sticking out of the ground at the roadside. There is not a soul around, the road is empty except for the truck which is rapidly disappearing in the distance. I walk over to the stone to check it from close up, it says 70 km. in black on it, there can be no doubt. I am again alone in the world, the first to reach our destination. I cross the ditch to look around, the ground slopes and farther down I see a small cluster of men, ours.

I walk over, they are guards, four men with rifles guarding two prisoners, one of them is Wallach, the other a young English boy from the British Battalion. I am glad to see Wallach again. He is in rags, his khaki pants are torn, his khaki shirt has only one good sleeve, the other is in tatters. But he still has his pert little mustache which he keeps neat, his smile is the same friendly winning one. He tells me all the hospitals and jails in the rear are being combed and everyone who can walk is being sent to the front. He has been sent with the English comrade under guard to the Brigade, he doesn't know of what good he will be there. He claims he can hardly walk because of his double hernia but they won't believe him, they think he is a coward and antiparty renegade. I believe him and tell him to keep his spirit up, I'll see what I can do for him, maybe I can get Dr. Hene to help him. He remembers Dr. Hene from Paris and is happy. I ask the guards what they are doing here. They tell me they had been sent out by truck from Barcelona to take these prisoners up to the Brigade and someone at Division in Alcániz told them to stop here. I throw a pack of cigarettes to

Wallach to share with his English comrade and give another pack to the four guards to share among themselves. One guard grumbles that it isn't fair, the prisoners got more cigarettes than they. I ask the comrade would he rather be in their boots? He doesn't answer.

I walk a stretch down the road and see a culvert, it is a very low one, just barely room enough to crawl in. I am weary and sleepy and hot, the culvert is invitingly cool. I crawl in and stretch out to rest when I hear planes. I crawl back crabwise for a look, I see more and more Fascist formations coming up, circling, departing for Alcániz. I decide there is nothing I can do for the present, I may as well go to sleep, if the Fascists are to overrun us again I can run faster after I have slept a bit. I put my musette under my head for a pillow, turn it around and adjust it until it feels comfortable. I am worried that this is too risky, the Fascists may come upon me in my sleep. I argue that I am bound to hear the Fascists arrive, there will be bombing and shooting first. I stretch my arms and yawn, put my head back and I am off in an instant.

✓ ✓ ✓

Noises on the road overhead wake me, for a moment I don't know where I am. They sound like footfalls, there are many of them, I crawl back cautiously to take a look. It is dusk, I see men ahead on the road, alone and in groups of two or three, trudging on in the direction of Alcániz, more men are coming up from behind. They are from the Brigade. I stop the ones coming up, soon I have about fifteen, and more are joining as they see us in a huddle. The men are all from the Mac-Paps, they are heading for Alcániz. I tell them the orders are to assemble here. None of them knows me, I have no insignia of rank, only a tone of authority. Most of them stay, but a few go on, footsore and weary. I have no means to halt them and I make no issue of it, I tell the men who stay that those finks will be sorry, they will have to march back. Little by little I get the story of the rout—they claim Major Smith had yelled out: "Direction Alcániz! Every man for himself!" and took off. The men naturally scattered in panic. It sounds incredible, but all of them assure me it is true, some claim they heard him with their own ears. Later Major Smith is to deny having given that order and he retains his command. Still later Smith shoots himself in the foot while cleaning his pistol, he claims it was an accident. It is hushed up and he is sent to a hospital.

There is still no one from the staff at the assembly post Km. stone 70, even the guards and prisoners have disappeared. My group is growing, I have about fifty men now, none of them with rifles, and more keep straggling up. Most men from our Brigade stop but the Spaniards and other Internationals are still fleeing toward Alcániz and my men are getting fidgety. They are hungry and cold, there is a freeze in the evening chill. They are shivering in their thin, cotton uniforms, they have lost or thrown their blankets away in their flight. I am warm in my poncho, I am glad I went back for it.

An ambulance drives up from the direction of Alcániz, it is Dr. Strauss, I know him but slightly. He has come from the medical post in Alcániz for information and orders, he has questioned the fleeing men he met on his way, he can't believe either that Major Smith actually gave those orders. He is slim, blond, and very serious, a conscientious young doctor with a good reputation for steadfastness. I ask him to drive me to Alcániz, a distance of 20 kilometers, to dig up some food for the men. There are no commissars or officers in the group which now numbers close to a hundred, but I find a Canadian political delegate. I put him in charge and tell the men I am going to bring them food. I climb into the ambulance which is nothing more than a converted Ford station wagon, and Dr. Strauss drives me to Alcániz.

Just outside Alcániz I notice three brand new antiaircraft guns, their long, slim barrels arching gracefully into the sky in the moonlight. That sight makes me happy, now at last we have something to defend us against the planes. In Alcániz I make contact with the kitchen staff of the Lincoln Battalion but they have neither food nor stoves, their kitchen truck was lost in a plane attack. Finally I find the brigade staff kitchen and wake up the mess sergeant. He is a short, stocky Englishman, a good cook and a personal favorite of Lieutenant Colonel Copic, the Brigade Commander. He is well supplied with coffee and delicacies but he refuses to make his stock available to the men. He has strict orders from Copic that those supplies are for the staff mess exclusively, he is responsible for them. I finally prevail upon him to let me commandeer his supply by assuming full responsibility for overriding Copic, and give him an order to that effect in writing. He is dubious about my authority, he is a former regular British Army man and knows the ropes. I don't blame him, I myself fear Copic's wrath, but those men have to be fed. To overcome his apprehension I sign Doran's name also to the order.

We light a big fire and start making coffee and stew. The smell of cooking attracts a number of men to the fire, most of them Spaniards from the Brigade but many Internationals as well. While the food cooks I round up two trucks and after the men gathered around the kitchen are fed, I load them on the trucks and take them back to the post, with the kitchen truck following in the rear. About a dozen of them refuse to get on the trucks and some others jump off later on the way. That bothers me but there is nothing I can do about it, they wouldn't be much good in the line anyway. By the time I get back, officers have taken charge. Doran has established a position near Caspé, the men would be taken there as soon as they were fed. We have no more food left and I go back with the kitchen truck to Alcániz, sending word to Doran that I'll be bringing up food to them as soon as we can prepare it.

We drive back to Alcániz and I set the cooks to work again, they are mutinous but I shut my ears. We set out again with freshly cooked food and coffee just before dawn in search of the improvised new line around Caspé. The entire sector is in chaos, no one knows anything. The road is full of stragglers, most of them without rifles, wandering aimlessly about; empty trucks are driving up and down trying to connect with their lost units. The Fascist planes are absent so early in the morning, affording a respite for establishing some sort of liaison, yet no unit seems to know where Doran's group is. Finally we stumble on it.

I find them straddling a sunken road, in two hastily dug trenches thrown up overnight. They are a sad, dejected lot, the appearance of the food truck with warm food and coffee lifts their spirits somewhat. Including those men I have rounded up last night, less than 300 men are manning the line. Many of them are in tatters, their uniforms torn climbing the mountains. The trouser legs of one man are ripped in the seam from ankle to crotch, as they flap in the breeze his scrotum bobs comically. The men are shivering, more than half of them are without blankets.

Dave Doran reviews the situation for us. He feels confident we can hold. The Division has been promised reinforcements, the French People's Front Government is going to allow artillery and antiaircraft to come through; Moscow has promised fighter planes to contest the paralyzing Fascist superiority in the air: as Communists and anti-Fascists our job is to hang on by our teeth and hold out until that aid arrives. It is a good political talk and puts heart into the wavering.

I send the food truck back and Doran tells me to survey our needs. We seem to need everything, weapons, ammo, food, clothing, shoes, blankets, men. It is midafternoon by then, many planes are in the sky but so far we're not bothered. Doran asks me to go back and find the brigade *intendencia* and armory, they must be somewhere around Alcániz, and send back whatever I can. He is very sore both at the quartermaster and the armorer, they have made no attempt to get in touch with the brigade command. He feels the yellow bastards must have withdrawn half-way to Barcelona by now.

I am very weary, I have no transportation, and it is a trek of more than 30 kilometers. I haven't slept for three nights in a row except for two stretches of short naps, my eyeballs are dry in their sockets and inflamed, my eyelids keep closing down and I have to use my fingers from time to time to keep them propped up. I start out and I am less than a hundred yards away from the dugout when the planes discover us.

I look up and count about fifteen formations of three heading in our direction. I walk on until I see the planes going into a dive, then throw myself to the ground. The air again fills with the pulsing throb of the motors. I hug the trembling earth and mechanically count the explosions, five, six, eight, and I can count no longer, I try to open my eyes but the lids are glued down fast, I am losing count, the world is one stupendous roar and I lose consciousness. . . .

✯　✯　✯

"He's not dead, he's breathing," the voices say. I turn over and see three volunteers, two standing, the third one kneeling by my head. I rub my eyes, stretch and yawn, and I hear one of them exclaim in disbelief, "The sonofabitch has slept through it all!"

I get to my feet, the field is dotted with fresh craters.

"Many casualties?" I worry.

The news is good. The bombs missed the trenches, fell into this field, only a few are wounded. I couldn't have slept long, the sun is still in the sky yet I don't feel sleepy any more. I walk toward Alcániz. I hitch rides when I can, two of the trucks are lost to strafing but we have jumped out in time. I reach Alcániz still by daylight, learn the probable location of the *intendencia* from a brigade truck driver, and hitchhiking part way, walking the rest, I finally find it.

The quartermaster is a heavy-muscled New Yorker with light blond hair, he is familiar with my name from the *Daily Worker* yet he is suspicious of me. He is having his meal seated at a table, plates, forks, and everything. He doesn't invite me to join him. As I watch him eat I feel like one of the beggars of Madrid hungrily eyeing through the plate glass the diners stuffing themselves inside the luxury restaurants. The room we're in is stacked high with boots, uniforms, blankets, socks, underwear, every conceivable gear for which the men in the line hunger. Through open doors I see other rooms similarly piled to the ceiling. I am awed by this profuse wealth and move to the shelves to finger the goods. The *Intendant* watches my every move suspiciously, like a farmer with a hungry loiterer around his chicken coop. He doesn't stop eating for a long time. When he finishes, there is still some roast rabbit left on the plate. Only then does he ask would I want a piece. I am so hungry that my stomach pains, it takes effort to refuse. "No, comrade," I dismiss it, emphasizing the word "comrade."

When he hears that I want 150 blankets, a similar number of pairs of pants, tunics, about a hundred pairs of boots, canteens, 250 pairs of socks taken up to the lines at Caspé at once, he stares at me in outraged disbelief, a miser about to be robbed of his hoard. Then he starts fighting back, he won't do it, blankets, uniforms, and other gear will be issued only at proper times and according to regulations.

I explain the situation to him but this only confirms his stand, the men had been issued blankets and if they threw them away or lost them it was their hard luck, it would teach them to take better care next time. He is full of hatred against the men in the lines who are in a conspiracy to rob him of his property. I can't help being sarcastic, did he come to Spain to hoard goods, to keep shop, to undermine the fighting capacity of the others, or to be of help?

He has heard that one before and he is ready with the answer, his job is to help fight the Fascists by seeing that scarce supplies are not squandered recklessly.

By now we are both yelling and a number of his men crowd into the room to watch. He is on home territory, all his men are on his side—I am alone and outnumbered—outfought and outshouted.

"You win the argument," I concede, dropping my tone.

They all grin satisfied, their shopkeeper souls can again rest happily, they have been through many such battles before. The *Intendant* picks up a pair of knee-length heavy wool hose. He offers them to me as a gift and patronizingly asks if I want a pair of boots or anything else. I am ready to explode but I must control my temper. I pause a few seconds, then say:

"This is what I need and have come to get," and read off the list again. My voice is low but tense. "I want them loaded at once and taken to the Brigade Command Post. I want them there before 10 o'clock this evening!"

The *Intendant* is still belligerent, he won't give up. "Put a Communist in charge of a load of goods and you get a Capitalist," I reflect out loud. The *Intendant* casts off the insult like any trader and concentrates on saving what he can. He claims he hasn't half as many blankets as I want and he is short of everything else. I have counted nearly two hundred blankets with my eyes but I don't want to argue. I ask him for his inventory list. He claims he hasn't a new one and suddenly challenges my authority, demands a written order. I write him out one and sign it with my name and title. He refuses to accept it, he wants me to go back and get an order signed by the brigade commander or brigade commissar, that's the only order he would accept.

I write out a new order, sign Doran's name to it as per me. He refuses that one too. I lay it on the table and give him a last warning.

400

"There are your orders. If those blankets aren't there by 10 o'clock I'll be back again, but for you."

There is silence as I leave. At the door I turn back.

"And bring an inventory list with you, a new one!"

Let the bastard sweat over it, we should know what supplies we have anyway. I would like to ask him for transportation back to Alcániz but I know he would refuse. I am not even sure that he'll obey my order, but I feel I have scared him sufficiently not to disobey. Two days later he reproaches me bitterly that I made him lose 150 new blankets. I tell him wearily that we also lost those 150 men, but that doesn't register with him at all, he mourns those blankets.

I can't get a hitch back, I have to trudge on wearily, hour after hour, again alone in the night. This is one hell of a lonesome war, I wish I were part of a squad and moved only when the others did. By the time I reach Alcániz it is around three in the morning. The cooks are up, preparing breakfast; I am too numb to eat and refuse even coffee. The food should be ready in about an hour, I have almost a full hour to sleep. The night is bitingly cold but I find myself roasting close to the fire. I move a bit away, stretch out on the ground, pull the hood of my poncho over my face; this is heaven, and I am blissfully asleep. . . .

ϟ   ϟ   ϟ

The clatter of food kettles being loaded on the truck wakes me. Dawn comes early in Aragon in March. I wash my hands with soap and warm water for the first time in weeks, also bathe my eyes and face. The mess sergeant is preparing an omelet, I see him break six eggs into a pan, genuine real eggs that I haven't seen for months. I hope he'll share it with me. He brings all of it over, it is all for me. I fall to it greedily, wipe the last morsel out of the pan with a piece of bread, wash it down with cups of coffee, and we're ready to start. The brigade staff mess sergeant, a Lancaster man I believe, is coming with us. He is a fussy man around his kitchen but by no means lacking in courage. He doesn't have to take the risk, we may have to drive through fire. When I tell him that, he shakes his head, he wants to make sure that his truck gets back. There are three of us in the cab with the chauffeur, the four Spanish kitchen attendants are riding in the truck.

As we start there is little traffic, soon we encounter more and more trucks but the traffic is all one way, back to Alcániz; we're the only ones heading for Caspé. The significance of that does not occur to me for quite a while, not until we hit a crossroad. There is confusion at the crossroad. A number of trucks have pulled over to the side, a group of men arguing in the center of the crossing. I get out to investigate. They say the road on the left to Hijar has been cut and so has the road ahead to Caspé. I hear no firing, there are no officers around to confirm or deny this information. A motorcycle runner approaches at high speed from the direction of Hijar and skids to a stop. He is all out of breath, he was fired on by small tanks and armored cars blocking the road about 10 kilometers back but has managed to turn around and escape. The truck drivers are jittery, they don't know what to do. I leave them and decide to go on ahead.

We blow the horn and the men in the middle of the road give way, they stare at us and a few yell warnings; we shift gears and keep going. The men in the parked trucks eye us as we roll by. I feel queasy and my stomach tightens as we pass the last truck and see nothing ahead but the rutted road, ominous and deserted. We cross a railroad track and when we mount the embankment the vista is clear, we see or hear no sign of fighting. We should be near the line now and if the Fascists were advancing we ought to hear firing. We hear nothing. "You can't believe every rumor," I reassure the chauffeur and the mess sergeant, also myself. I am still on the alert but feel the tension easing. The road is very rutty now, the truck bounces hard as it hits the potholes, and by the time we hear the shells we also see them explode only yards ahead of us. The driver guns the motor and we bounce over the craters so hard I bump my head on the roof. We reach the cover of a thick olive tree by the time the next salvo explodes.

Three more shells come in rapidly one after the other, and then three salvos—they are searching for us but can't see us. I climb down and walk ahead crouched down, keeping close to the road, until I get to a knoll. I crawl up there and still see nothing, I stand up and see nothing, not a soul anywhere. I walk back to the truck and discuss it with the mess sergeant and the chauffeur. They are both party members, good, dependable men, they agree to chance it, the men must have food to fight, the least we can do is risk it. We can't figure where the shelling comes from, what stretch of the road is under fire. I take them for antitank guns. I guess we have about a mile to go, with luck we can make it in less than two minutes.

The chauffeur guns the motor and we're off in a rush and then we see them, small Italian tanks straddling the road ahead, firing directly at us. The chauffeur goes into a wide turn and we skid into the ditch, the rear wheels spin and then hold, we are out of the ditch now and back on the road in smoke and dust. The tanks are firing, the shells explode ahead and to both sides of the road, we drive through the smoke for dear life until there is no more shelling. The shells come again as we climb the railroad embankment but we are already on the other side, they explode behind us. The sergeant and the chauffeur talk about the narrow squeak, my mind is on Doran. They were not tied to the road, they must have cut through the encirclement.

The crossroad ahead is busy now, trucks at high speed converge on it heading for Alcániz. Foot soldiers are on the road trying to get on the trucks, the trucks do not slow down for them and they run alongside until they can grab hold and pull themselves up. A man ahead misses and staggers back, another truck is coming up but it won't slow down, it hits the soldier with a sickening thud and throws him flying ahead. Another truck follows by, it won't slow down either, it runs over the comrade without even braking, the other truck behind sees the body but won't slacken, runs over him too, then another. By the time we reach the comrade he is smashed to a pulp, our chauffeur gives him a wide berth but he won't slow down either. I do not know from what far land that comrade came in response to the call of international solidarity, nor what far country gave birth to those comrades of his who have squashed him into a smeary blob on the road without bothering to slacken their speed.

That speeding didn't help them any, a few minutes later we all slow down, then crawl, and then we're jammed solid. We sit in the trucks waiting, the road is packed with vehicles as far as the eye can see, front and back, no room to turn around. That road has been hewed out of the mountain with a steep drop into a *barranco* way below, not a chance to pull off to the side. We wait in the truck for the jam to clear, all eyes are scanning the sky. The sun is up high, the Fascist planes may turn up at any moment.

I think of Hemingway in Madrid in December, walking in on us without an overcoat, in a faded navy blue suit jacket and a scarf around his neck, asking Frank Ryan and me out for a drink, and my favorite book of his, *Farewell to Arms*. He is a great artist, his description of the panicky retreat at Caporetto in Italy in the First World War, the vehicles helplessly jamming the road, is more vivid to me even now than what I see spread in real life before my very eyes.

The waiting stretches out; not a vehicle is moving. I walk ahead picking my way in and out through those stalled trucks for more than a mile but all I see is an immobile column of vehicles stretching to the horizon. I walk back and as I reach the truck I see all eyes glued to tiny black specks in the sky circling around and around in the distance, then wheeling in our direction.

"*Aviacion!*" sounds the panicky cry, "*Aviacion!*"

The trucks come alive with men jumping off and swarming down in panic, they flee down into the *barranco,* many lose their foothold and roll down like logs. They don't look like planes to me, the formation is too irregular. I believe they are birds and sure enough, there is no mistake about it.

"*Pajaros! Pajaros!*" ("Birds! Birds!") I yell but no one pays attention.

The vehicles are all deserted now. My men did not run, they stand beside the truck. The Spanish comrades are laughing uproariously, yelling insults to those men who are still hugging the ground, calling them *coños, conejos, cobardes sin cojones* (cunts, rabbits, cowards without balls). Some of the men sheepishly reboard the trucks, but most of them keep running in panicky flight.

I have no idea when that traffic jam will clear, there is no sense in my staying with the truck. I tell the sergeant I am going back to Alcániz on foot. Alcániz is a strong town, I am sure it will be defended, that we'll halt the fascist advance there. That town is full of troops, I'll see what I can do there, I may find a lot of stragglers from the Brigade, get some news from the division.

It is difficult to walk on the jammed road. I leave it for a trail that I hope leads to Alcániz. There are other men on the trail heading in the same direction but they are not from our Brigade, again I walk alone. By now I am used to it. The books I have read about war have conditioned me to trench warfare, that's what I expected to find in Spain. This war is sure different, I wonder what Liddell Hart would say now.

I reach the outskirts of Alcániz late in the afternoon. The shiny antiaircraft guns are gone. Traffic is thick on the road, the jam has been unblocked. All the trucks are saved, a couple of Soviet Mosques patrolled the air while truckloads of volunteer civilian truck drivers were rushed up from Tarragona to drive the deserted vehicles away. Alcániz is being evacuated. The staff kitchen is gone, I wander around for information but find no one who knows about the XV Brigade. I strike out on the road. Soon it is dark and I have no idea where I am heading nor why when an ambulance pulls up, the driver leans out and asks in English, "You want a ride, comrade?"

It is Comrade Dicks from Cleveland!

We grin in recognition and we're both very happy. Neither of us knew that the other was in Spain. Dicks drives an old covered truck converted into an ambulance. He is a Negro, we are friends from way back. He feeds me with food and stories, he is on his way back to the Division Hospital. He sees I am groggy for want of sleep and insists I lie down. I protest I want to stay with him in front. He stops the ambulance and orders me inside. I lie down on a stretcher, Dicks pulls out his guitar and it is just like old times back home. He sings ballad after ballad, his voice sounds softer and softer, so soft I can no longer hear. . . .

HYPNOTICS

It is night again—the Brigade as a unified fighting force no longer exists. There is no chain of command, no liaison, no battalions, no companies, only isolated groups of men putting up last-ditch resistance, holding until surrounded, retreating to other posts, holding with diminished numbers, dispersed, falling back in isolated groups to rally again. The planes attack constantly; the greatest damage they do is to morale. Our poorly trained men panic at the appearance of the Fascist planes, they bolt and run leaving their equipment behind.

Dave Doran is the rallying point, the nerve center to which all impulses return and which alone serves as a clearing point for co-ordinated action. No matter who breaks and runs Doran can

406

be depended upon to withdraw no further than he must, to contest every foothold, to improvise some position. The task is to keep locating Doran, to bring him whatever help and supplies can be scraped together, to round up the fleeing men, to get them back to whatever new line Doran is trying to establish.

The night is dark, the line has been outflanked, and the men are scattered again. Jim, the Brigade party secretary, drives up with a beat-up small car. He is a tall Westerner in his middle twenties, I meet him now for the first time, he has quit the hospital abruptly at the news of the debacle and returned to the Brigade. We drive back to the field which was abandoned that afternoon by troops that broke under bombardment. We are searching for stragglers to take them to the new line that will be established during the night.

The field stretches flat for miles, scary and sinister under the ghostly moon. We meet a weary group of four, they've been wandering around for days since they were routed near Hijar. A few miles ahead, just at dusk, they were hailed in English by a small armored car. They approached happily thinking it was ours. They were less than ten yards away when they realized it was an Italian Fiat and bolted. The car fired at them, the four of them got away, but they don't know what has happened to the other five in the group. They still have their rifles, we send them back to an abandoned stable we have passed, telling them to stop others who may come their way; we'll take them all back later to the kitchen and feed them.

We drive on again, ever further into no man's land, expecting to run into an ambush at any moment, scanning the terrain for straggling men or wounded. Finally we meet two Germans from the Thaelmann Brigade. We learn they are still holding an improvised position to the right. They are our sister brigade, if we're to make contact with any of our men we must turn left. We take the left fork and drive on. We are tense, every second brings us closer to the Fascists. We see a flame in the distance, rising to the sky, we drive closer to investigate and soon we hear explosions. The explosions come from the fire, glowing tracers going off in every direction lighting up the sky. It is a burning ammunition truck blocking the road. We pull up as close as we dare and get out. As we advance on foot two men from the brigade hail us. There are two other men from the brigade stuck on the far side of the burning ammo wagon, they can't get themselves to pass the ammo truck fearful it will blow up at any minute. We wait for the truck to explode, but it keeps burning steadily, throwing forth bursting bullets in fiery stars at frequent but irregular intervals.

We can't wait any longer, we want those men. We get back into the car, Jim pulls his neck back into his shoulders, steps on the gas, and drives straight ahead. The heat is searing, the explosions deafen us as we shoot by that truck, sparks envelop us, then we can breathe again; we're through. We pick up the men on the other side and make the run again, this time it is easier, like jumping through a flaming hoop in the circus. I look back and see a great explosion, flaming shrapnel spurting like fireworks, a case of hand grenades going off.

We come to a group of abandoned, low stone huts and go through them; some stragglers may have taken refuge there. In the last one we hear breathing, five men are sleeping hidden in the straw, Americans. They wake, panicky, then seeing we're from the Brigade start cursing us for not letting them sleep. They refuse to budge, we prod them, kick the soles of their shoes: "Get up, get going, a line is being organized." They rise grumbling to their feet, they are fighting men we can tell, they still have their rifles. One of them complains, "That won't do my morale any good." We have drummed morale into them so long he now speaks of it as if it were a part of his body, a new organ that needed special care and attention.

Another volunteer farts with his mouth and gets on his feet. I recognize him, he is a good soldier, a party member. He ad-

408

justs his ammo pouch, slings his rifle on his shoulder and calls to the others; "Let's go, you bastards, today is as good a day to die for liberty as any." We direct them to the assembly point, promise that we'll hustle up some food, and leave. We can trust them; with that comrade to lead them they won't beat it.

We search through the night for stragglers, we round up about twenty. Jim goes on to make liaison, I lie down on the ground to catch a short nap, close my eyes. No man's land stretches again endlessly in the ghostly light of the moon, the ammo truck is burning, the bullets splutter in a shivering spark of fireworks, they arch and rise flamingly, blinding my closed eyes. I screw my eyelids tighter to shut out the sparks, they burst and erupt in flaming shrapnel, burst and erupt, burst and erupt and I am asleep. . . .

✓ ✓ ✓

The government is reeling, they shower us with panicky exhortations. Edwin Rolfe, editor of the *Volunteer for Liberty*, gets hysterical in Barcelona, he sends us truckloads of two-page special editions, one after the other, giving us not news nor information which we crave, but deluging us à la Pasionária, with shrill feminine screams of exhortation fathered by desperate fear.

DO NOT YIELD AN INCH OF GROUND
TO THE ENEMY!

DRIVE OUT THE INVADERS OF SPAIN

NOW IS THE TIME TO STRIKE BACK

The men in the Brigade receive these copies with sardonic laughter. They've been fighting, running, driven from position to position with ever-growing losses, short of rifles, ammo, food, reduced to small groups resisting in isolation only to be told that this is the time to drive out the invaders, to strike back.

409

Curiously, that back-ass propaganda lifts the spirits of the men. Their contempt for the rear-guard generals explodes into laughter, the best morale builder in the world.

We are reforming near Batea, we get rifles, ammunition, men. The Internationals sent up as reinforcements are a pitiful lot. They are men ruthlessly evicted from the hospitals, half-healed invalids, physically unfit for battle; the sweepings of the military offices in the rear, soft and flabby—many of them elderly comrades who should never have been sent to Spain. Finally there are the newest arrivals, volunteers sent up prematurely. Some have received a week or two of training, others none. This latest group, some hundreds in number, gives us the most concern. We are desperately in need of internationals to preserve at least the semblance of the Brigade being an international one but we need trained men, not such lambs offered up to slaughter.

We have but a few hundred internationals, Americans, British, Canadians, Cubans, and Mexicans left alive in the Brigade. We're an International Brigade in name only by now. Of the four battalions in our Brigade one is pure Spanish. In the other three, one company of the four is Spanish; in the companies, one section out of four is Spanish; in the sections, one squad out of four is Spanish. The Brigade has been so diluted with Spanish soldiers that the Internationals are acting mostly as noncoms which the Spanish lack. We have no time to integrate the new American volunteers into the units. Many of them sent up during the retreat are trying desperately to keep up with us, running along with no one to lead them as we are forced back from position to position; a great many of them are killed before they even have a chance to learn what is happening around them.

The terror in the International Brigades is on. To halt the Fascist offensive we need air power, artillery, tanks, armored cars, transport, trained officers, noncoms, and men. The Kremlin leaders think differently; although they supply us with some material they base their main reliance on terror. Officers and men are ruthlessly executed on their orders. The toll is particularly high among the Poles, Slavs, Germans, and Hungarians, especially among those who came to Spain from Moscow. These are summary executions, carried out in most cases secretly by the S.I.M.—a most convenient way to settle old political scores.

Dave Doran, too, catches the bug, he holds a series of courts-martial and condemns a number of our comrades to death for cowardice, for deserting their posts, for abandoning their duties, among them Captain Jack Cooper from Cleveland, commander of our machine gun company, a leading Young Communist League member from Cleveland. Doran is prosecutor and judge at the same time, he rolls the sentence "You're condemned to die before a firing squad" with great relish, lingering on the word "die."

He asks me what I think of the way he has conducted those courts-martial and he's taken aback when I tell him dryly, it was quite a ham Shakespearean performance. Next it is my turn to be taken aback when he informs me cuttingly it will be my duty to accompany the condemned men to the Division and witness their execution. Throwing all prudence aside I denounce Doran's act to his face as sheer madness, saying it will bring disaster to the party back home. I tell him none of those men are guilty of anything, they have simply been caught up in the maelstrom of retreat. I myself had encountered Captain Cooper and questioned him when he was heading for the rear. He was accompanied by only a few men, the last survivors of his company. Exhausted as they were, they were still carrying with them the few useless machine gun barrels they had managed to salvage from the holocaust; Jackie Cooper was nothing but a walking corpse intent only on saving the few survivors of his company until they could be reformed and re-equipped again. Doran threatens me, calls me a rotten bourgeois intellectual, the party would be better off with me dead, without my spreading my degeneracy in this critical moment. We're yelling at each other,

I'm definitely at a disadvantage being a subordinate of Doran, when Brigade Commander Lieutenant Colonel Copic, who had been on leave in Paris during the first part of the Fascist Aragon offensive, now rises unexpectedly to my defense. I do not know with whom Copic has associated in Paris but he affirms the power of the free press. He agrees that Matthews of the New York *Times,* Vincent Sheean, Sifton Delmar, and the others who visit us regularly are bound to find out about the executions and would report them no matter how much sympathy they have with Loyalist Spain. Copic also agrees with me that these executions would turn liberal opinion against us not only in America, but also in France. Copic and I are friends again but still distant, he has never forgiven me for dissipating his store of hoarded delicacies to feed the men. Doran reluctantly consents to give the condemned men another chance.

We move up in almost full Brigade strength, 6,500 strong, only the staff knows this is a gross illusion. More than half of our men are raw recruits with less than three or four weeks of training.

The Fifth Army Corps is entrusted to stop the Fascists from reaching the sea and cutting Loyalist Spain in two. Our Brigade is divisional reserve, we should be the last to be thrown in. The three Spanish divisions ahead of us are famed Communist crack divisions of the Spanish Loyalist Army. We are aware of our own weakness but have full trust in those Communist divisions. We are convinced they'll hold, we know that when our turn comes we'll hold also. *No Pasarán!* They shall not pass!

Our reserve position is far from the front lines, even the sound of bombing barely reaches us.

At nightfall we receive the disastrous news. The three Spanish Communist divisions ahead of us, glorified in the Spanish press for their death-defying courage, have pulled out against orders, leaving the front wide open to the Fascist advance. Our Brigade is ordered to defend a sector previously held by

412

a full division to safeguard the approach to Gandesa. The Brigade has to be divided into two, Copic to defend the northern fork, Merriman the southern one. Doran assigns me as commissar to Merriman, my first chance to act as commissar in actual battle. I have a number of final chores to attend to, by the time I am finished and go to see Major Merriman to discuss how I could best assist him, he has pulled out.

I start out before dawn hoping to catch up with Merriman. It is about 12 miles to his designated Command Post, a three and a half hour hike. After about an hour I see a group of men heading back from the direction of the front. They carry rifles, they are in squad strength. They are cutting through the field, avoiding the road, their direction is definitely to the rear. I cut across to speak to them, I have to shout a couple of times before they stop. They belong to the British battalion, they are lost and are looking for their unit. I don't know where the British battalion is, I tell them to come with me. They are undecided. As we parley I see a number of other men drifting back, some have rifles, some don't, they cut a wide circle through the field to avoid us. I ask the British squad leader to stop those men, I want his squad to act as a field guard to halt all men heading back and keep them from frigging off. They spread out at once and halt the drifters. I group them and take them along. We see more men drifting back; we stop them all. The British are tough about it, they threaten to shoot those who don't want to turn back. They mean business, they fire after two men who refuse to stop which quickly brings them around.

We have quite a few men now. As we march up I see an officer ahead, pacing up and down the road, it is General Walter. I greet him as he watches us pass and he calls me over. He asks me what troops we are, how many more are coming. He is disgusted when he hears these are only drifters I have corralled on my way up. I can see the disappointment in his face, he was expecting reinforcements. I ask him what the situation is, he shrugs his shoulders with a nervous jerk and turns away from me.

About a hundred yards further ahead I meet José Maria Sastré, Division Commissar. Before his promotion to Division Commissar he was Dave Doran's first assistant; we have worked together well and are friends. He is around 26, trim and slender, intelligent, serious, and loyal; he wants to be a professor after the war. He inquires about Doran. I tell him he is with Copic and ask him about the situation. It is not too good. Copic is under heavy fire and is asking for reinforcements. The Division has no reserves and General Walter has applied to the Fifth Army Corps, they haven't any either. Merriman is not at his Command Post, he can't be located. The divisional runners sent to the battalions have not returned.

As we talk General Walter comes striding up. I have met him a few times before, an uncommunicative, forbidding person, usually in a sullen mood. His forehead is furrowed in a deep scowl, he is tense and nervous. He ignores me, curtly informs José Maria that he is going to the Fifth Army Corps to see personally about reinforcements, and puts José Maria in command. The General tells him tersely that the line must be held at all costs and makes José Maria responsible for it. He strides away briskly, steps into his staff car, and disappears.

José Maria is startled. We both know that the Headquarters of the Fifth Army Corps is about ninety kilometers in the rear, on the other side of the Ebro River. We have been there together just two days before, at a meeting of the Division and Brigade Commissars; Doran took me along. José Maria knows that General Walter will be away for hours, maybe for the entire day, he is also aware that he is not qualified to command a division in battle. He is worried and instructs me to locate Merriman immediately, have him report to him in person at once.

The Command Post set up by Merriman is on the left side of a knoll which is bisected by a sunken road. I find about fifteen men there but not a single staff officer. I learn that having designated that spot as Command Post, Merriman had gone ahead with the troops to place them in position personally. By the time the last unit on the right flank had reached its position it was daylight, and it had to move in under fire. The runner sent back by Merriman told me that the last he saw of him, Major Merriman was leading the last troops personally into line under intense rifle and machine gun fire. No word had been received from him since.

I send the runner back to locate Merriman and another runner with him, the first one to stay with Merriman, the other to report back. Our position follows a low ridge about a mile and a half ahead and is outlined by light smoke and a hazy movement of air above. The firing is intermittent, mostly rifle and machine guns; I hear no artillery, only an occasional mortar. The sector is relatively quiet so far. I relax, the Fascists won't attack in force without strong preliminary bombardment by artillery, planes, and tanks. Merriman has the map, I try to orientate myself without it. The steep mountains, roadless and rugged, on the left flank are held by other elements of the army corps, Copic and Doran are on the right, while our sector is this valley guarding the road to Gandesa. I have only a general idea of our plan but I know we're stretched very thin. I missed the meeting where the plans were discussed and the instructions Dave gave me were very general. I am to assist Merriman, help him to enforce command, see that liaison is maintained, and do whatever is needed to maintain morale, to stiffen resistance; that Merriman is the best officer we have in the Brigade and although I am to be his Commissar, I should take my orders from him.

The runners I have sent after Merriman do not return. I must find Merriman, I can't just sit here without knowing what he wants me to do, nor can I leave that post or Merriman won't be able to get in touch with me. I send two more runners out, then two more to the other units asking for a situation report and whether they know the whereabouts of Merriman. Only one of the runners returns. Captain Hernández, Commander of the Spanish Battalion, reports two attacks early in the morning by the Fascists in company strength, both beaten back with heavy losses to the Fascists. His casualties are light, five men wounded, none of them seriously. He has been also trying to contact Merriman, his runners couldn't reach him. Merriman is reported to be pinned down on the extreme right flank which is under heavy machine gun and mortar fire, he has no liaison with him. Hernández is asking for mortar and artillery support. I go back to report that to José Maria. He is worried about Merriman. He is not a military man, now that General Walter is gone he wants Merriman with him.

Lieutenant Diggs comes up. He is our liaison with the Fifth Army Corps, a brave and capable officer. Diggs is a young Westerner of college age with handsome features, winsome smile, and erect military bearing which makes him look taller than he is; he is less than medium height. I ask him to get me some artillery and mortar support for Fernández. He promises he'll try but is not hopeful about it, the Army Corps is under very heavy attack in the northern sector. When I ask him how does it look, his usual cheerful smile vanishes into a frown. He doesn't like it, the Corps is stretched very thin, we have no reserves, little artillery, the promised Soviet fighter planes haven't come.

A little later the Fascists open up with artillery. As the shelling continues, I see men here and there leaving the line and heading for the rear. The guards stop them as they approach. They all obey but one, he continues in my direction. He is an odd sight, he wears a full wool uniform, a steel helmet, a rifle, a couple of hand grenades in his belt—full official battle equipment that I have seen no other man in the brigade to possess. I am puzzled. He is a husky boy, an American, broad-shouldered and athletic, I doubt if he is twenty. He walks unseeing, his eyes bulging and unblinking in a fixed stare, his mouth wide

416

open. I haven't seen him before, he must have come up with the last transport of volunteers fresh off the boat. He is in a state of shock, he won't respond to inquiries about his name and unit, only mumbles: "I wanttogohome, I wanttogohome." He makes a start to leave after each question but halts obediently when I tell him to stop, reacting like an automaton. I would like to get him out of here, it was patently wrong to have sent him into battle in the first place, and I wonder what I can do for him. I can't let him go to the rear—he would undoubtedly be shot for desertion and cowardice—nor would it be right to send him back to the lines. I keep him with me, tell him to lie down and rest. He does so automatically, but slips away unnoticed later when the artillery starts searching for the Command Post and shells begin exploding near us.

The Fascist shelling increases in intensity, the situation is grim. Capt. Hernández sends a runner again asking for artillery and mortar support, also for permission to withdraw a half mile to a better defensive line. I inform him he must hold and send the group of stragglers up to him as reinforcement. I walk back to José Maria, he is on his way to see me, we meet halfway. Hours have passed since General Walter left, no word has been received from him. I tell José Maria that Fernández must have artillery and mortar support. He frowns, he has no idea where to get them. He decides he'll go get in touch with General Walter. He tells me the line must be held at all costs, that I am responsible for it, and he is off.

The Fascist shelling grows very heavy, the line is ablaze with rapid rifle and machine gun fire. No new Fascist infantry attacks are reported, as yet. Our casualties are still light although increasing, and the line holds fast. I have liaison only with Capt. Hernández. None of my runners sent to the other units have returned. I do not even know where the other units are. I curse Merriman and his lousy egalitarian streak. As commander, he had no business to lead that unit into position personally and get himself pinned down right from the start, losing contact with the rest of his troops.

José Maria's order means that I am now responsible for holding the position without having any control over the fighting. I have lost all my regular runners; the ones I am forcing into service now do not know the positions of the units; I can and do send them out but they do not return. I have no contact with Copic and Doran who are with the other half of the Brigade; I no longer have contact with the division either since José Maria has pulled out and the rest of his divisional staff evaporated. General Walter passed the buck to José Maria, he has passed the buck to me. I have no one to pass the buck to. I am it. That's a hell of a way of being responsible for command when I don't even know what troops we have.

More and more men come drifting down from the line. We stop as many as we can. I keep them with me as a sort of reserve, by now I have about fifty or sixty of them again. Now I feel more like a commander although I know these men are not much good, most of them will try to frig off when we come under direct attack. A number of shells again land near-by, the Fascist observers must have noticed the concentration around the Command Post. A few shells burst very close and sure enough the men bolt.

"Stay put! Keep your head down! Stay where you are!" I shout, but only a few of them heed me, the others run on desperately with the Fascist artillery pursuing them.

Lieutenant Diggs comes up again; he is looking for José Maria. When I tell him he is gone he reports to me. Fascist columns in force are infiltrating both on the right and left, the Spanish regiment on our left has broken, he fears I am being encircled. He is on his way back to the army Corps to report it. I ask him what does he advise? He declines, his job is that of liaison not command. Since we're on close personal terms he confides he is glad that he can pull out in a hurry. I tell him I

418

feel we ought to pull back but I have been ordered to hold at all costs. Diggs agrees I have no choice, an order to withdraw might result in a disorderly, panicky rout. When he leaves, he shakes hands, an unusual gesture for him. After a few paces he turns and calls back.

"See you in hell, Voros, hold a place for me!" He grins and he is gone.

The shadows are lengthening, my Ingersoll wristwatch has stopped, no one has a watch. It must be close to five. Shells are now rapidly exploding all over the field and suddenly the line ahead of me becomes alive, figures are rising, and the entire line falls back. They are not running, only walking back, I guess Hernández has decided to pull back that half mile on his own. But the line doesn't stop, it keeps coming on. I walk ahead to intercept them, the road is full of men passing by me to the rear. I am the only one to walk against the tide and I am conscious of all eyes fixed on me.

Captain Hernández is in the middle of the column surrounded by a core of officers, his tanned face is streaked with blood, his forehead is bandaged. He tells me it was impossible to hold there any longer, they were receiving fire from both flanks, he had to pull out before being fully encircled. He has no further news about Merriman.

I explain the situation to Hernández. The orders are to hold at all cost; since Merriman is away the military command now falls on him. He accepts it grimly. I want to hold where we are but Hernández objects. We decide to fall back to a hill about two miles farther back, that hill commands the road and is a good defensive post, it provides a good view for miles. Hernández says they are very low on ammunition, unless I provide that in a hurry it will be impossible to offer much resistance. I recall having passed an ammo truck of ours that morning, just behind the fork of the road a few miles back. I see a station wagon field-ambulance that has pulled back with Hernández, it is empty. I ask the driver to take me back to pick up ammunition. The doctor in charge, a nonparty member, objects; I can't use an ambulance for transporting ammunition. I tell him to report me to The Hague when the Fascists, who have bombed our hospitals and massacred our wounded in the hospitals they captured, come up for trial before the World Court, and drive back. I locate the truck; it is still there but is nearly empty, only a few cases are left. The chauffeur is glad to get rid of those last cases, he is anxious to return to the armory. I am glad to learn he knows where the armory is located. I tell the chauffeur to wait until I return, that the lives of half of the Brigade depend on my reaching that armory and bringing up fresh supplies. He is a good party member, he needs no persuasion. He is nervous but I don't blame him; suddenly I realize I am also tense inside, perhaps even more than he.

By the time I return Hernández is busy placing his men into position. His command post is in a small cluster of heavy olive trees. He has less than three hundred men. He keeps a core of about forty hard-bitten veterans around his post as a mobile tough reserve, most of them Spaniards. He curses when he sees the few cases of ammunition I came back with; he wants to know how he is to hold with that. Besides, they also need food, his men are very hungry. I realize I am also very hungry. I haven't had a bite since supper last evening.

To quiet him I tell Hernández I have learned the location of the armory and the *Intendencia* can't be far away from that. The armory is just outside Mora La Nueva on the other side of the Ebro, little more than twenty kilometers away. I promise to bring up whatever I can, will also try to get reinforcements from the Division or the army Corps. Hernández urges me to hurry and I am about to leave when I remember something. I pull up formally.

"Captain Hernández, this place must be held at all cost, and you are responsible for it."

I feel silly as I say it, also a bit ashamed. I have passed the buck to Hernández, just as General Walter had passed it to José Maria Sastré, who passed it to me. I know very well that position cannot be held for long unless we get reinforcements. Now that I am pulling out, Hernández is it.

The Fascist planes catch the truck twice. The second time halfway past Gandesa, just as we are passing an antiaircraft battery. We jump off and run into the field, I see a small foxhole and dive in, right on top of Dave Gordon who has beaten me to it, stomach trouble and all. I took Gordon along with me intending to leave him at the armory when I went back to Hernández, to have him take over in case anything happened to me. Although Gordon is unable to mask his fear as a leading comrade should, he is enough of a Communist to stay put under fire.

The planes come diving in. Bombs burst all around, machine gun bullets and shrapnel whizz overhead, thud into the ground. The foxhole is narrow, short, and not too deep, I am practically kneeling on Gordon's back. We're safe from everything except a direct hit or a hit close enough to cave us in. The earth is so big, this trench is so small I no longer worry about being hit. In fact I feel exhilarated knowing that for the first time we're shooting back at those planes and after the bomb run ceases, I stick my head up to watch the antiaircraft guns in action. The field is hazy with blackish-blue picric smoke which shakes and shimmies in the wind, the gunners look like gnomes in the flashes of their guns. The bombers are back again and I drop back into the foxhole, a big fragment the size of a stove lid swishes by my head as I duck, this time I'm really scared.

The planes attack in waves, bombs follow bombs. When they finally depart they leave the field covered with a deep layer of choking dark smoke the eye can hardly penetrate. I cough and wipe the tears from my smarting eyes. Bomb craters are everywhere, some are huge, some merely scooped-out holes, smoke is rising from some, others look like freshly excavated earth. The fifty-odd bombs I counted caused not a single casualty. The anti-aircraft guns are intact; the crew are grimy with smoke and sweat, their faces distorted by strain. The gunners walk around weary and bent, their weepy eyes bloodshot from the acrid fumes.

We expect the truck to be riddled by shrapnel but we find it intact. We get on and get going, cross the Ebro River over the much-bombed steel bridge which had not received a single direct hit either, and locate the ammo depot without much difficulty outside Mora la Nueva. It is now sunset but with plenty of daylight left.

The Spanish captain in charge of the ammo dump, a tall, pale, flabby-looking man in his thirties, is antagonistic. He protests when I request a truckload of small arms ammo, rifles, and hand grenades sent up at once. He claims the truck will never reach there because of the Fascist planes. He wants to await the cover of night. I think of Hernández and his men facing annihilation after their few cases of ammo are spent and demand angrily that the truck be loaded at once. The captain does not answer back, goes into one of the houses to give orders to load the truck, I presume. I lie down on the ground to take a quick nap but sleep doesn't come. I am back with Hernández, getting set for a new Fascist attack. I wake with a start, it is getting dark. I walk over to the truck, it is as empty as when we pulled in, no activity around. I run to the house where I last saw the captain enter, I find him at a well-set table, eating his supper calmly. I storm at him why hasn't he loaded my truck, he answers unperturbed that the truck would be loaded after the men have finished their supper. I feel like murdering the bastard but that wouldn't speed up anything. I yell and curse and threaten until he quits his meal. I walk out with him, follow close on his heels as he issues his orders.

His men are all Spaniards. They go about loading the truck

among voluble discussions and arguments, too slow to suit me. I urge, plead, cajole, exhort them to hurry. I appeal to their patriotism and loyalty, praise extravagantly the glorious achievements of the Loyalist Army. They smile with pride, say *"Sí-Sí!"*, but the loading doesn't progress any faster. By the time the truck is loaded and we're pulling out it is night, the stars are bright in the sky.

Mora la Nueva is now deserted as we dash up to the bridge. We're halted by Spanish troops within fifty yards of it. They won't let us proceed, the bridge is about to be blasted. I plead with the Spanish major in charge to let us dash through. He insists it is too late, the dynamite charges are all in place, they will be set off *momencito*. We argue and fight, he becomes very excited when he learns that our truck is loaded with ammo. He yells at his men who watch me with rifles at the ready to get that truck turned around and driven back a distance.

A messenger rushes up from somewhere, the major screams "Everybody take cover," he sprints back, his men scatter and disappear as if swallowed by the earth. A tremendous explosion shakes the ground, followed by other detonations. A column of flame envelops the middle span of the bridge, a huge section of it rises, steel girders float into the sky riding on tongues of flame. I am impotent with rage, filled with shame and guilt. I see Hernández entrapped, I should be with him. My fists are clenched so tight they tremble. That buckling girder is closing the mouth of the trap as I watch, forgetful of taking cover. A large steel fragment whizzes by my head, the air is full of hissing shrapnel, I throw myself to the ground until the air is clear of flying fragments. Flames are still licking the frame of the bridge, they die out slowly one after the other. An awed hush settles on the night. My mind won't focus. I only sense that something indefinable has reached its termination, that an irrevocable finale has taken place before my eyes.

I walk back to the truck, tell the men to stay put until they hear from me, and wander around until I come across a wide dugout cut into the side of a hill. I walk inside, it is a high-domed large earth chamber excavated from the hillside with connecting chambers to the right and left. The dugout is lighted dimly by kerosene lamps hanging from the ceiling. I see a few divisional staff officers in the shadows arguing in Polish and German among themselves. I walk over to them, they know nothing or won't tell, they are waiting for news and orders themselves. I cross into a connecting chamber and unexpectedly see Lieutenant Colonel Copic there in his shiny black leather puttees striding fretfully up and down, talking in Russian to other officers whom I have never seen before.

"Comrade Copic!" I call to him, and he practically runs over to me. "Where is the Brigade?" he demands in a harsh tone, anxiety mingled with relief.

"That's what I want to know," I retort accusingly. He doesn't know; he had gone to the Army Corps for reinforcements and by the time he got back here they wouldn't let him cross the bridge. I tell him about Merriman and the position where I left Captain Hernández. He gets out his map, I show him our last position, he shows me where he left Dave Doran.

It is more than 25 miles from there to the Ebro. They are left deserted on the other side, cut off from all supplies, trapped by that premature, panicky blasting of the bridge. They should have let us withdraw and defend that bridge, hold it open until the last minute, until all the troops got back safe. The Ebro is too wide and deep to ford, too swift for most men to swim. Doran, Hernández, and the men with them will be hunted down by the Fascists like dogs. Neither of us says this out loud but we both know it. We also know that we have lost the Brigade. We glare at each other without uttering a word. Copic resents seeing me alive, my eyes full of accusations. I resent seeing him alive in his pressed uniform and shiny black puttees. It was Lieutenant Colonel Copic's duty as military commander to stay with the troops, it was Commissar Doran who should have gone to the Fifth Army. I turn my back on him without a word and stride outside.

The town is completely deserted. I walk around aimlessly when I see a light shining from a big garage. Some men from our Brigade Auto Park are busily stripping that garage of tools, parts, and whatever they can find, while the others are engaged in tearing down an inside brick partition. They are cheerful and happy about it, most of them are New York boys who take a great pride in "organizing" whatever they can lay their hands on, stealing whatever they can to keep our Brigade supplied with vehicles. They find that town a veritable treasure trove of abandoned army vehicles and they are busy towing away trucks, cars, motorcycles, everything with wheels on. They are tearing down that partition to get at a bus the owner had walled in there to hide it from the government. It is a beautiful luxury passenger bus, brand-new and shiny with red paint and chrome; we gape at this symbol of a long-forgotten peaceful civilian world. Even those cheerful scroungers are awed; taking that bus seems like out-and-out theft to them and they are not thieves. This bus is definitely a civilian vehicle, they feel they have no right to take it, nor can they bring themselves to leave it there for some civilian government officials to grab.

They want the bus very badly but are afraid of the possible consequences. They draw me into the debate. I, too, want that bus for our Brigade, but I'm similarly apprehensive. Finally we argue it out that the owner of the bus, by hiding it, is *ipso facto* a Fascist. He should have declared it to the government. The right thing to do is to take the bus into custody to protect the interests of the government, and turn it over to the civilian authorities later, if so requested. That sophist decision pleases everyone and the bus is towed away in triumph. By then it is getting along toward dawn. I go back to the dugout and find

425

about thirty men from the various units in the Brigade sleeping on the ground. I lie down too and close my eyes. Sleep is hovering around but won't settle: Hernández, the planes, the terrified boy with the bulging eyes, the exploding bridge all merge into a pinwheel that whirls around and around until I am dizzy and black out. . . .

NARCOTICS

The operating room is in a tent, the flaps are drawn tightly to prevent telltale gleams of light escaping into the night. The air is stifling hot under the bright gasoline lamp; amputated arms, hands, and legs overflow onto the packed dirt floor from the large wicker basket in the corner. Dr. Broggi, Division Surgeon, is operating on a bullet-perforated belly, his hairy arms are bloody past the elbows, his rubber apron is dripping blood on his shoes. He has been operating without a stop for more than twenty-four hours. It is now way past midnight, but there is still a line of stretchers with belly and thigh wounds awaiting emergency surgery outside. I am standing at his side feeding him cigarettes, placing them in his mouth for short puffs. Although he is totally exhausted, his quick, sure fingers move with precision. He sews up the incision, drops his instruments, and staggers out. I follow him and catch him as he is about to collapse, lay him gently on the first stretcher near-by which is sticky with blood. By the time I lift his legs on to the stretcher he is asleep. I go back to the tent. The tiny operating nurse who looks like a girl stunted in early growth is also groggy, but she stays to clean up. No orderly is around and she tries to carry the heavy can full of dead tissue, blood, and muck out of the tent all by herself. I run over and take it from her. My hand wraps around a slimy, snakelike object that slops over the handle. It moves under my grip, a piece of large intestine. I nearly drop the can in fright but stagger outside with it, lay it down and retch. I retch and retch until nothing comes up any more, yet I retch and retch until I wake up in the morning aching in every bone. . . .

✔   ✔   ✔

We have recrossed the Ebro in a counteroffensive, have fought our way back close to Gandesa. After a short rest we are moving back to the line again. Paul Wendorff, my former assistant on the Historical Commission, is on my staff now, he was sent to the Brigade when the Albacete base was moved to Barcelona. When the Brigade goes into action, the political members on the Commissariat staff are now divided among the battalions to assist the battalion commissars. I assign Wendorff to the Lincoln, the British is reserved for myself. The British are our shock battalion and I like to work with Bob Cooney.

This time the Lincoln is scheduled to attack. Wendorff, who had been at Jarama for many months, feels the odds are against him. We discuss that. I hold that the chances are the same for everyone every time he goes into battle regardless of how many previous engagements he has been through. Wendorff feels the cumulative chances work against a man, he is downcast and gloomy. Since the British battalion is to be in reserve in this engagement, I decide to change places with Wendorff and assign him to take my place with the British in the rear. Wendorff's eyes moisten, he mumbles words of gratitude. I shake that off brusquely. He is a big strapping fellow, I don't want him to feel embarrassed later for that temporary funk.

The Lincoln makes a surprise attack at dusk which collapses at the start because of poor training. The men lose contact with each other in the dark, they stumble around loosening rocks and alert the Fascists who meet them with mortars, grenades, machine guns; their artillery lays down a protective barrage and the attack has to be discontinued.

In the morning when Wendorff calls in his report, he sounds very cheerful. The battalion is ten kilometers behind the lines, the Battalion Post is well hidden and camouflaged against planes.

427

He is happy with the British, thinks they are wonderful comrades. An hour later the British Battalion calls—a stray shell exploded at their Command Post, one of those freak accidents of war. Comrade Wendorff was killed instantly, no one else was hurt.

I strike out at once for the British Battalion. One of the boys around Headquarters is a promising young Spanish YCL-er, I take him along for company. The boy chatters about what he plans to do after the war, asks me whether he should be a doctor or a lawyer, but I hardly hear him, my mind is on Wendorff, I keep seeing his large moist eyes. I become aware that I do not hear the boy's voice, I look around and see him half kneeling, tying the broken string of his rope-soled canvas *zapata*. I slow down but do not stop, let him catch up. He is running after me, we're going downhill, he has changed sides, he is in line with me but on my other side now, still a few yards back, when I am stunned by an explosion and hit by flying dirt.

I shake off the earth, rub the dirt out of my eyes, massage my ears to stop the ringing, and only then do I hear his screams. He is twisting on the ground with one leg gone, the other at a crazy angle, his stomach one big bloody wound.

"Help me, comrade, help me!" he moans. "Help me, Comrade Voros!" he murmurs, his eyes beseeching me. There is nothing I can do. I squat down beside him, lay my hand on his head. He whispers but I can't make it out, his pleading eyes are on me; his lips move and then he stops breathing.

I am still in shock, I keep stroking his forehead, his face dissolves into Wendorff's tear-moistened eyes. If I hadn't brought that boy along, if I had stopped when he was tying his *zapata,* he wouldn't have strayed to the other side of me, he would have remained on my left, if I hadn't been soft with Wendorff and traded posts with him ... "THAT ISN'T SO!" I scream inside. "Stop blaming yourself. The chances are one in a billion for you to have been in exactly the same spot where the shell that killed Wendorff landed, where this boy got hit instead of you!" That doesn't work, the boy and Wendorff now merge into one bloody mutilated corpse, four eyes are beseeching me for help. "NO!" my lips move, "no—No—NO!" My breath chokes in my lungs, my eyes fill with tears and the next morning when I wake my pillow is wringing wet, the sheets are twisted and damp with sweat, the muscles in my face are taut, my spine feels empty of marrow.

"Your old ague must be acting up again," I hear my wife say. I look up, she stands at my bedside, her voice filled with concern. "I had better call the doctor."

"No. It's all over," I assure her tonelessly. But I know it is not over, it will never be over. . . .

54 THE fascist Aragon offensive was the curtain raiser to World War II, but the democracies wouldn't believe that. Hitler supplied the blitz strategy and the Nazi planes, pilots, tanks, artillery, technicians that went with it; Mussolini contributed his Italian legions, more than 200,000 men, and a profusion of war material.

The God-fearing, Bible-reading democracies did not learn from the Scriptures. Instead of rushing to the aid of the rightfully constituted Loyalist government they fled every man into his tent and clamped an arms embargo on Spain preventing her from obtaining arms with which to defend herself, while closing their eyes to Hitler's and Mussolini's open support of Franco. British Prime Minister Neville Chamberlain, a pious manufacturer from Manchester, was trying to buy peace through a covenant with Hitler, refusing to recognize in him Nahash the Ammonite who like Hitler in his *Mein Kampf* spoke plainly in Samuel I: "On this condition will I make a covenant with you, that I may thrust out all your right eyes . . ."

Vincent Sheean, the famous liberal news correspondent, had a blind trust in President Franklin Delano Roosevelt. Driving down from Barcelona together with Lady Diana, he managed to contact us at the most critical phase of our retreat. Appalled by what he saw, that all we had were a few rifles, machine guns, and hand grenades with which to resist the mechanized Fascist troops, he reached for a pad and wrote out a passionate plea to his personal friend, President Roosevelt, asking me to cable it to the White House. It was way past midnight then, we were in a small crowded hut which was feebly lit, like the catacombs of old, by a single spluttering wick floating in a saucerful of olive oil. Sheean stood with head bowed as in prayer with Lady Diana proudly erect at his side; the rising and falling shadows in that cramped adobe hut heightened the effect of that moving scene. The drama of history touched us all and I did manage to find a way, against all odds, to send that cable out that same night.

F.D.R., the humanitarian and great liberal, read that cable and his left eye turned moist with tears over the agony of the Spanish people. President Roosevelt, the politician, scanned that cable with his right eye which stayed dry, being fixed on the strong Catholic bloc clamoring for all-out support of Fascist Franco and his Moors, those infidel defenders of the true Catholic faith. The provisions of the arms embargo were not lifted, they were tightened instead.

While the democracies, each man in his tent, awaited the very great slaughter, the Soviet Union acted, but in a most peculiar manner. The Great Red Father in the Kremlin, unlike Teddy Roosevelt, believed in talking loud yet he carried only a little stick—and all he sent us was slivers of it, one sliver at a time.

The matériel sent to Spain by the Soviet Union was fed to us in driblets, just enough to prolong the fighting but not enough to assure victory.

The Soviet fighting planes, the "Mosquitoes," were superior to anything the Fascists had, their Russian pilots were good and brave. But the Kremlin sent very few, and those only when Loyalist defeat seemed imminent. A hundred or so Soviet fighter planes sent in time might have wrested air superiority from the Fascists and defeated their Aragon offensive. They were not sent.

The Soviet tanks we received were so insignificant in number that the Russians in command of them were fearful to risk them in battle. Far from stiffening our resistance these steel monsters would turn tail just when we needed their support the most, leaving the defenders demoralized.

The Soviet rifle was a light and accurate weapon although its steel bolt was not sufficiently tempered; in rapid firing it had a tendency to jam because of heat expansion. The Soviet artillery we received consisted mainly of 75-mm. fieldpieces, at least I did not encounter any larger-caliber Soviet make guns on any front. Those 75-mms. were hard hitting, sturdy, quick firing, and easy to bring into action. But the Russians sent few of them, pitifully few.

Although most of us in the Brigade sensed the true situation, we would not admit it even to ourselves. Materialists as we all professed to be, at heart we were still romantic idealists who believed in the strife between Good and Evil as the eternal order of the universe; that by natural law Good is bound to win out over Evil for that was the evolutionary direction of mankind.

We just couldn't believe, and I was one who felt that way, that the democracies would actually abandon Loyalist Spain to the Fascists. I had firm faith that the reactionaries, Chamberlain and Sumner Welles, the socialist Blum, and the liberal Roosevelt would eventually awaken to the danger confronting the world from Fascism and act in time to forestall catastrophe. Blinded by our own propaganda I did not know then that it was the "reactionary" Sumner Welles who wanted to lift the embargo and it was the liberal F.D.R. who allowed it to stay clamped down.

Life in the Brigade following the Aragon disaster was comparatively uneventful and left no outstanding impressions in my memory. Only a few hundred of our men, out of seven thousand, escaped from that debacle—to my infinite relief Captain Hernández was among them. Some escaped by swimming the Ebro, Johnny Gates was one. Sam Goldman, the Cleveland attorney and my former roommate, came to a different decision.

432

After marching day and night to elude the pursuing Fascists he suddenly sat down on the road, telling his two pleading comrades to go on without him, he was through running. He took off his boots, spread his remaining few clips of bullets in front of him, and set about cleaning his rifle. His last stand was to be made right there; he was ready to go down but not without taking a few Fascists with him. I lived in hopes for weeks before I accepted that fatal news as final.

In the reorganization of the Brigade, John Gates, the ranking Y.C.L. leader after Doran's death, became Brigade Commissar. He was intelligent, energetic, and capable. I liked Johnny Gates, particularly his modest behavior in contrast with Doran's personal exultation in the power that went with his position.

Gates was about twenty-four years old then. He was born to poverty in New York and lived in semistarvation as a Y.C.L. organizer in Akron before he left for Spain. Where most Americans in Spain became debilitated from the monotonous diet of chick-peas cooked in plain water and rancid olive oil; where most Americans became nauseated even by the sight and smell of it, Johnny Gates would put away huge portions of it with gusto. Nearly all of us lost weight in Spain, victims to vitamin deficiencies. I went down from 175 pounds to 129, my skin broke out and oozed pus from innumerable boils, my knee joints were creaky and dry, my night vision became poor. But Gates's once skinny frame filled out from the *garbanzos* and took on blood and muscle. I had asked him about that on the Cordoba front as I watched him gobble up a large bowl of those foul smelling chick-peas (of which I could hardly get down a few spoonfuls), then go back for another helping, and still a third. Gates smiled sheepishly.

"I'll tell you, comrade, I have been so hungry all my life, I am happy that here I can eat all I want. I just love *garbanzos.*"

The Brigade also received a new commander. Lieutenant Colonel Copic had been recalled to Moscow and he left with

433

trepidation, not knowing what awaited him, fame or a bullet in the back of his head in some G.P.U. prison. The new Brigade Commander was an Asturian, a capable man of around thirty-two who had suffered a long term of imprisonment for his leading role in the revolt of the Asturian miners in 1934, Major José Antonio Vallador. In our counteroffensive across the Ebro River he soon proved worthy of our respect.

During that period of rest and reorganization the Brigade became Mecca to American and English visitors bringing anti-Fascist greetings and reassurances from home: "Carry on the magnificent fight, comrades, the people of the world are behind you." I shunned contact with the visitors as much as I could, by that time I'd had my fill of that self-deceiving propaganda. I particularly avoided meeting newspapermen, some of whom like Matthews, Sifton Delmar, Vincent Sheean I held in great respect. I didn't want to give them a chance to draw out of me the inside story back of those glowing accounts glorifying the leadership of the I.B. It also pained me as a Communist and as a former Guild member to watch the degrading behavior of our *Daily Worker* correspondents, first Joe North, later Edwin Rolfe, how they fawned on the representatives of the "capitalist press," currying their favor; the way they pleaded obsequiously with their every gesture, every act: please accept us as legitimate newspapermen, pretend to believe that the *Daily Worker* is a regular newspaper, not just a Communist propaganda sheet. They reminded me of whores at a block party— they had just as much right to be there as anybody else—after all, it was their own block giving the party—trying to erase the stamp WHORE by rubbing up to the respectable housewives.

I spent most of my free time in what was officially called "cementing our ties with the Spanish population." I found the Spanish most *simpático,* I delighted in their unspoiled simplicity, in their human dignity, and admired the fortitude with which they bore their wretched existence. Once, while leading a delega-

434

tion from the Brigade to the U.G.T. (*Union General de Traba-jadores*) in Barcelona to invite them to our May 1st celebration, it suddenly occurred to me that we had hundreds of recruits belonging to the C.N.T., the Anarchist Syndicalist Union, who had rather the worst of it in that Communist brigade, and I decided to invite some anarchist leaders also. In scanning the list of Anarchist organizations I came across the name *Mujeres Libres* ("Free Women"), which sent the blood coursing through my veins.

Visions of Emma Goldman, the uninhibited behavior of the girls I had known in Greenwich Village, the easy promiscuity of the female comrades in the Party in New York flashed through my mind; inviting Anarchists was surely a brilliant idea. These women were actually Anarchists and openly called themselves free. God, what a May 1st celebration that would make for the Brigade if I could induce them to come.

I located their office. The *Mujeres Libres* had an entire floor to themselves. This is a big organization, this is indeed marvelous, I exulted, and forgot all about my creaky knee joints and enlarged heart as I went bounding up those high Spanish steps. The girls in the office were young and pretty, the General Secretary of the organization was petite and beautiful. Her straight jet-black hair was combed severely back, emphasizing her enchanting classical features, her deep brown eyes shone like liquid pools, her olive skin was tantalizingly smooth. She received me with grave dignity and with evident reserve. She couldn't see how they could accept that invitation—in her experience the Internationals were mostly Communists and definitely hostile to the Anarchists. To break down that prejudice I first told her about my own personal interest in learning about Anarchism, then explained that American Communists were altogether different from other Communists; that it was in the American tradition to like Free Woman as well as, if not more than, all other kinds combined; and finally guaranteed that all volun-

435

teers in the brigade, regardless of their party affiliations, would receive them with open arms in a true united front spirit.

She was twenty-six, unmarried, and lived alone in her apartment. To make sure of their participation in that May Day celebration I intended to work on the Secretary General further that evening and invited her for dinner. At first she refused, claiming she had to go home to clean up her apartment and attend an important meeting that night. Her ultimate decision to skip both the meeting and the housecleaning was a political one. I was so eager to learn about Anarchism at first hand that I appeared a likely convert—if given sufficient personal attention.

I did learn many facts about Anarchism, the Anarchist movement in Spain, and about the plight of the Spanish women in particular, first over dinner, later sitting on a park bench in the Rambla. I suggested I could learn easier when not distracted by people parading up and down in front of us, say in her apartment, or in my room in the hotel, but the night was balmy and she enjoyed gazing at the stars. The stars were beautiful indeed although that was no time for such foolishness.

At last, to my delight, she sighed and said it was time we went home and we walked arm in arm blissfully for a good hour until we reached her apartment. At the door she pulled free, gave me the Anarchist salute, then bade me good-night. I pleaded earnestly there were still some points about Anarchists I wanted clarified; she countered gravely I had learned enough for one night, more than any *extranjero*. I couldn't very well dispute that, yet I did fervently but it was of no avail; she gave me no chance to learn the one fact about Anarchist women which to me seemed of the utmost urgency at the moment. Edifying as that evening was from the political point of view it still fell vexingly short of my expectations.

The *Mujeres Libres* kept their word. A busload of them, young and gloriously beautiful to our starved eyes, came to visit us that May Day and there was great rejoicing.

Those Anarchist girls were the friendliest lot, but it soon transpired all they were interested in was talking politics. Only Captain Hernández, alone in the entire brigade, managed to get one of them to go for a stroll to a far-off olive grove to continue their discussion there. His success was due to the fact that he was comparatively apolitical and as such he had discovered that his girl was also nonpolitical, that she was not a member of the *Mujeres Libres,* only her sister was; that she had come along for the ride and not to make converts.

This concludes the chronicle of my lamentable failure "to cement" over and above the call of duty "our relationship" with the Spanish civilians. Those Anarchist women, although far more provoking in appearance, were no more interested in sex than their politically minded sisters here in America in the League of Women Voters.

If that's damning with faint praise, I stand mute.

55 THE bright hopes raised by our successful offensive in recrossing the Ebro did not last long. The Spanish Loyalist Government lacked arms, supplies, trained manpower to exploit our initial success, and our advance soon bogged down. That offensive bled the Internationals white; we no longer had any manpower left to supply even the steel frame which kept our brigades together. Our usefulness as shock troops for the Loyalist Army was irrevocably past.

Recognizing this practical state of affairs Prime Minister Juan Negrin resorted to a master stroke. He publicly declared before the *Cortez* on September 21, 1938, that all Internationals on the Loyalist side would be withdrawn from the front at once and sent out of Spain as rapidly as arrangements could be made with other countries to admit them. In turn he asked that the Non-Intervention Committee compel Franco also to withdraw the Italian and Nazi troops fighting on his side—to let Spain decide her own fate without the aid of foreign interventionists.

It was a noble gesture although a rather feeble one and the Fascists knew it. By that time the number of all internationals in Loyalist Spain was way under 8,000. Of the over-all number of 50,000 Internationals who had gone to Spain, two out of every three or about 35,000 of them had been killed in battle or succumbed to their wounds later.

Hitler and Mussolini cynically responded by announcing they, too, would withdraw their forces, but man for man—one Fascist for each International, or a total of 8,000 out of their 200,000 foreign Fascist troops.

438

Shortly afterward I was summoned to Barcelona by Inspector General Luigi Gallo, Marty's deputy (at this writing the head of the Communist version of Hitler's storm troopers in Italy), to take over the editorship of the final issues of the *Volunteer for Liberty*. I objected to that assignment and proposed someone else in my place; I had had my fill of Party propaganda.

I was overruled. As it transpired the editorship of the *Volunteer for Liberty* was to be only an incidental part of my duties. I was wanted mainly to help complete the historical record of the International Brigades, that old assignment I had forgotten.

In the ensuing weeks, from the time of my transfer to Barcelona until the XV Brigade was formally disbanded, I only visited the Brigade twice, both times by official invitation; the first one proved highly distasteful, the second most depressing.

The first visit was at the urgent request of John Gates, transmitted by courier, but giving no reason for it. Although puzzled, I welcomed the excuse to get away from under the despotic eyes of Marty in Barcelona if even for a day or two.

When I entered headquarters I found Gates, that once modest and indifferently dressed young comrade whom I knew to be a nonsmoker now sporting a fancy tailored uniform, topped off with the highest officer's cap ever displayed in Spain. He was puffing on a fat, expensive imported cigar, sprawled back with his feet on his desk. When he saw me enter he swaggered over and instead of shaking hands he started to roar at me that I was in trouble, that I didn't know him well if I thought he would let me get away with it, that he'd have me court-martialed and so on. I was stunned; I had not the least idea what he was talking about until he finally bellowed at me, he wanted me to hand back at once the funds that belonged to the Commissariat, did I actually think he would let me get away with it?

I still did not comprehend it. That money had been deposited with the brigade's financial officer for safekeeping, all except the small petty cash that was handled by my clerk, José Civéra, an honest and trustworthy Spanish comrade. I had made a note of all that and given it to Dave Gordon to turn over to Gates because I had to hurry to catch my transport for Barcelona; Gordon knew that I had deposited that money. I told that to Gates but he was unbelieving.

We called in Dave Gordon. At first he disclaimed knowing anything about it, but after I hammered away at him he admitted I might have told him about the deposit and he might have forgotten to mention it to Gates but flatly denied having received that note. I recognized Dave Gordon's fine knife technique in that; he was going back to Ohio with a rather questionable record and had hoped to pull me down with him.

The brigade finance office was far away, it took more than two hours to locate the finance officer. I had never felt such acute distress even in the tightest situation in the field. I was in a perfect spot for a frame; in the Party the accusation of embezzlement is the first step to political liquidation, in Spain to physical liquidation as well.

The finance officer acknowledged having that money on deposit with him, every centavo of it. It was a considerable sum, as I recollect it, most of it the accumulation of the pay of those killed in battle whom the commissars would not report dead so their pay could be collected to swell the party's political fund, thus defrauding the Loyalist Government.

That put Gates in an embarrassing situation. At one time he might have apologized for such unwarranted behavior toward an old comrade but now he was Brigade Commissar; a party leader is infallible, he can't admit to mistakes. He tried to justify his attitude by blustering that I should have asked him for authorization before depositing the political funds with the military where it might be sequestered. I retorted since I was responsible for that money it was natural for me not to want to risk losing it by carrying it with me into battle.

On my way back to Barcelona I wondered why a rise in rank should so greatly change a Communist for the worse, turn

440

even that once-modest young man into a swaggering autocrat? I attributed it to character deficiency in Gates and to his overwhelming vanity which I myself had helped to nourish by writing a few flattering articles about him. I wasn't astute enough to realize that the major part of the blame rested with the totalitarian structure of the party. In a democracy the exercise of power is circumscribed and limited by law. In totalitarian societies, the leaders are the law and therefore their power is absolute. Of course they too share the risk of running afoul of someone higher up whose power over them in turn is again absolute—retroactively so, as many Soviet leaders have found out to their sorrow when it was their turn to be purged. . . .

The last time I was officially invited to return was to participate in the formal withdrawal of the Internationals from the Brigade. It was a weird farewell. The ceremonial speeches, the exchange of formal assurances and regrets between the departing Internationals and the remaining Spaniards could not mask the deep emotional chasm—the Internationals were jubilant, they were going home to the safety and enjoyment of civilian life; the Spaniards were despondent, they were left to face death by themselves.

After the official ceremony was over I found myself surrounded by a sea of Spanish comrades. We exchanged handshakes and embraces, some of them wept openly. I like to believe that I am not easily moved yet my eyes watered and my voice was husky. Captain Díaz, the Nationalist, looked deep into my eyes.

"Deserting the sinking ship, eh, Voros?" He said it in a soft voice, so low that no one around could hear him.

"This is the Communist fulfillment, ¿Verdad?"

I could not answer in words, merely put my arm around him. I felt lower than a ship's rat. Captain Díaz and I would often argue Communism in private but I had not been able to convert him.

Now I knew why!

56 WHILE the Americans rejoiced, the volunteers of many other nationalities faced the prospect of withdrawal from Spain with grave concern.

The Americans had nothing to fear from returning to their homeland. The only charge that could be raised against them was violation of a passport regulation, at worst a minor offense, and the wide anti-Fascist, pro-Loyalist sentiment in the U.S.A. made prosecution for it extremely doubtful.

However, the Germans, Italians, Yugoslavs, Hungarians, Greeks, Bulgarians, Austrians, Poles, etc.—many of them with a blood price on their heads—could not possibly return to their own Fascist or semi-Fascist countries without facing long-term imprisonment, torture, and even death. Many of those exiles had had hopes of settling in Spain after the war, of finding a haven there after existing for years like hunted animals, hiding out with forged passports only one step ahead of the police, imprisoned for false entry time after time, and shunted from one unwelcoming country to another. Men without a country, the crippled among them even dreamed of a modest government pension, of living out their lives in their newly adopted country as honored citizens.

These dreams were now shattered. By the terms of Negrin's unconditional withdrawal no volunteer was permitted to remain on Spanish soil even if he wished to stay and become a Spanish citizen. That left these volunteers with but one country to go to—the Soviet Union. I considered that a cheerful alternative, this was the preferred choice of most of them anyway.

"They have fought the Fascists, the foes of mankind; now they will have a chance to help build Socialism in the only socialist country in the world—the fulfillment of the Communist dream! History is working out well for them, the only reward worthy of aspiration." I wrote a warm farewell to them in an editorial for the *Volunteer for Liberty,* congratulating these Internationals on their good luck in going to the Soviet Union.

My first intimation that there was something wrong with that concept came when I was unexpectedly summoned by Marty. Waving the proofs of that editorial with its Spanish translation in my face he began to scream: Who gave me the right to formulate policy for the Soviet Union? He tore those proofs to bits and ordered me out of his sight, raving that although he knew all Americans were arrogant and stupid, yet he hadn't expected to encounter such colossal political idiocy in a leading comrade.

I left in a daze. I did not have the faintest idea what was wrong. Basically that editorial was nothing more than a friendly, run of the mill expression of solidarity with the Soviet Union and the international working class, such as any Communist editor would write year in and out, by the ream.

The next day I found a note on my desk addressed to all editors announcing the new official line we were to follow, i.e., the volunteers who were the finest and most experienced anti-Fascist comrades in the world were badly needed in the democratic countries to lead the fight there against Fascism; hence that is where all of them must go.

I must indeed have been a political idiot as Marty had charged because I didn't catch on even then. In fact, I approved of that new line and thought it logical until a German colleague enlightened me. He was witheringly sarcastic, deriding me as a self-righteous, insensitive, smug American and finally turned on me furiously.

"Don't you see what this line actually means?"

I didn't, even though I tried hard. That line sounded solid to me.

"It means the Soviet Union has shut her doors in our face, you fool!" he almost hissed in hate. His long-practiced party-leader mask was gone, his face was writhing with emotion.

"We have no place to go, can't yet understand that! Which country would permit us, seven-probe Communists, to enter her gates? Would you expect the capitalists to invite us in and say, 'please cut our throats and ring the death knell of capitalism over our tomb!' We are the battle-tested, battle-scarred Communists who have fought to the death at the call of the Comintern, and now the Soviet Union is refusing us asylum. We're doomed, doomed by the Soviet Union, we may even end up by being handed over to Hitler!"

He turned away from me, his face buried in his hands. Up until then I knew him only as one of those close-mouthed, secretive Germans who rebuff all attempts at friendship and intimacy, careful not to show any emotion. Now that hard-bitten revolutionary actually sobbed. The enormity of that revelation affected me greatly. I found there was nothing I could do or say; I tiptoed out of his office. I did not know then how prophetic his words were—that many of them would indeed be handed over to Hitler by Stalin after the Nazi-Soviet Pact in 1939 to celebrate that love feast. . . .

When we crossed into France the men went wild over the sight of real milk and white bread with which we were greeted at the French railroad station. At Le Havre we were held up nearly a week because of a strike by the French seamen. Although we were confined to the grounds I managed to slip out and mingle with the population.

When we finally sailed from France we made strange pas-

444

sengers. Even though we had been deloused, most of us out of sheer habit were still scratching our armpits, rectums, and genitals in full view of the other passengers who, alarmed, understandably would have no traffic with us. Few if any of the volunteers were aware of this rebuff. They, too, preferred to keep their distance, contemptuous as they were of those "lousy capitalists."

57 WE landed in New York some time in December, 1938. The customs did not delay us long, most of us had nothing of value to declare. My possessions consisted of my notebooks, some historical documents and photographs I had managed to retain for souvenirs, a few handkerchiefs, two pairs of spare socks, an extra shirt and one extra set of underwear, all packed in a cheap paper suitcase. The customs inspector gave it one disgusted look, poked a wary index finger into the contents, nodded to me to close the top, scribbled a hasty cross on it and I was through, back in America, alive. Of the approximately 4800 American volunteers about 3500 had served with the combat troops, according to my reconstruction. Nearly three out of every four of the latter had been killed fighting Fascism in Spain. I doubt the accurate figures will ever be ascertained for no full record was kept either here or in Spain.

After we were through the customs the party organized us into a parade. I marched for about a block and then pulled out only to find myself surrounded by a number of admiring comrades; some I recognized, the rest seemed only vaguely familiar. I was a hero!

We walked east on Fiftieth Street and I paused three times to buy frankfurters. I ate five of them and was on my sixth when we entered a cafeteria. I had a couple of hot roast beef sandwiches there and drank glass after glass of beer. On my way out I saw a penny scale and stepped on it. Beer, hot dogs,

446

sandwiches and all, I was still a skinny bastard; weighed only 137 pounds.

My proud friends escorted me in triumph to the office of the Friends of the Abraham Lincoln Brigade which was over-crowded with waiting friends and relatives. The air was festive and jubilant. Tacked on the wall were all kinds of mimeographed invitations to receptions by the various party branches in honor of "these brave sons of the toilers, the conquering heroes of the revolutionary working class who slew the ugly beast of Fascism. Donation Fifty Cents."

When my turn came to register, the girl comrade took my name, address, the party unit to which I belonged, which was Ohio. I had no New York address. When she heard that she offered me a room way out in Brooklyn belonging to a comrade who was temporarily out of town. I could use that for a couple of days until I found a place of my own. She then informed me the Friends of the Abraham Lincoln Brigade were desperately short of funds, I would understand that with all the expenses they were having, but she could let me have a couple of dollars if I needed assistance desperately, five dollars, she eyed me speculatively, ten dollars! That was absolutely the limit, but the party would get me on relief before I spent that ten if I was careful with it. I told her I didn't want any money, which made her happy.

She asked me to wait, she would see if there were any mes-sages for me, she came back with three, her voice and entire attitude changed. She was a hairy witch with warts all over her face. She didn't know I was *the* Comrade Voros, she used to read my articles in the *Daily Worker* and she loved them, she smiled at me coquettishly, handing me the slips. One was from the editor of the *Daily Worker,* the other two from the Central Committee, all of them requesting me to report there at once.

The girl comrade asked me to give back the key, she had just recalled that a comrade had offered her apartment which was much closer, it was in Manhattan just outside the Village. I could have it for two whole weeks, it was a very modern apartment beautifully furnished, she had been there once to a most wonderful party. She also asked me was I sure I didn't need any money, she could let me have twenty dollars for the time being. I accepted the apartment but again refused the cash, the very thought of accepting money collected by the party for Spanish aid made me feel unclean.

As I was leaving I was again met by friends, new ones. They were discussing the shameful betrayal by Daladier in Munich who had thwarted the burning desire of the French people to go to war against Hitler in defense of Czechoslovakia.

I listened to them in wonder. They were intelligent, educated men and women, most of them in the learned professions, how could they be that ignorant? I explained to them that the French people did not want to fight, Daladier was a hero to them for averting war. Now it was their turn to be incredulous, hadn't I read this article in the *Daily Worker,* or that one in the *Inprecor?* How stupid of them, of course I couldn't know what was going on in the world, after all I had just come from Spain, I had been isolated.

I retorted acidly I had just spent six days in France, had met all sorts of people in Le Havre, including the striking seamen— the French were completely demoralized, they would rather make a pact with the devil than go to war.

That broke up the party. Some of the comrades gave me quizzical looks, others began to soothe me:

"Don't get worked up. We know what you have been through, after a good rest you'll be back to normal."

By now it was late afternoon, there was still time to go up to the *Daily Worker* and the Central Committee, but I thought to hell with that. I wandered around taking in the familiar sights of New York without absorbing much. My thoughts were revolving hazily without any clear ideas emerging. Now and then I stopped for another hot dog, another cup of coffee, then went to the apartment that unknown comrade had so trustingly offered to the party.

The apartment was full of modern prints and books and smelled of perfume and powder, making me wish she were there, whatever she looked like. I felt low and in strong need of feminine companionship. I considered going to one of those party receptions to pick up a woman, yet the thought of the stupid adulation to which I would be subjected repelled me, nor was I in the mood to take any more of that cocksure party spouting to which I had been exposed since I stepped off the boat. I went out, located a liquor store, bought myself a fifth and went back to the apartment.

I drank myself stupid that night, the first and only time I ever went on a solitary drunk. I hummed to myself all the Spanish revolutionary songs I knew until I came to the *Internationale*. I sang that in English, and loud. I repeated the chorus over and over until the words actually became animated and leered at me: "THE INTERNATIONAL SOVIET SHALL BE THE HUMAN RACE." They wouldn't go away and I got mad. I smashed the glass against the fireplace, tore off my clothes and went to bed.

58 THE editorial offices of the *Daily Worker* were much neater, cleaner, and better equipped than when I had last seen them nearly two years before. The comrades also were better dressed, their shirts were clean, their collars were not frayed, they all wore ties and most of them were shaved. The party and the paper had evidently prospered. They gave me a good reception. I was still a hero, albeit a smaller one—having had a hand in the making of many a proletarian hero those comrades had a better perspective.

The *Daily Worker* wanted to put me to work right away— they were trying to build up the circulation of the *Sunday Worker* and claimed I was just the right man for it. I was to take over the editorship of the *Sunday Worker* Supplement and turn it into a popular literary magazine written in a non-party style that every worker and housewife could understand. Such a magazine circulated by the party throughout the country in hundreds of thousands, even millions of copies, would have a tremendous impact and influence on the people. It was an alluring project yet I refused, as I did the alternative offers to join the New York staff of the *Daily Worker,* or to revive the *Daily Worker* Ohio Bureau again. I told them I had a year of absence coming and intended to take it.

My reception at the Central Committee was also good. Here I was no hero, only a leading comrade returning successfully from an assignment.

Joe Peters, in charge of the organizational department of the

Central Committee (the head of the Party's spy apparatus as I learned later from Whittaker Chambers' testimony), had grown a potbelly since I last saw him. Although politically we had been on opposite sides in the Hungarian factional struggle there was no enmity between us. After I insisted I was definitely not going back to the *Daily Worker*, Peters offered me a number of positions in the party apparatus, to send me to any place in the country I wished on special assignments. I declined those offers, too, agreeing only that I'd see him after my leave of absence.

When finally I had myself announced to Alpi, known as Comrade Fred Brown, he came flying out of his office. A Latin, he embraced me, a long-lost brother back from the war. He felt my arms, checked me all over, asked me, his eyes sparkling, how his special assignment had worked out? He was happy when I grinned and told him I did manage to get around. He asked me to wait until he could get rid of a few of his appointments, then he would close shop and we'd go to some small Italian place where we could talk without interruption. Minor and Gates had already made their reports to the Central Committee, he was now most eager to hear my account to get a real perspective.

The small *bodega* in the Village was quiet and restful, the *paisan* left us discreetly alone after our meal, silently replacing the empty bottles with fresh red vino from time to time. As my story unfolded Alpi grew more and more downcast and depressed, and only when he heard me conclude that the Fascist victory was a matter of a few months at the most, did he rouse himself to argue against it.

He told me that my account was entirely contrary to the reports given by Gates and Minor whose unanimous conclusions were that Loyalist Spain was absolutely determined to fight to the death and if the party concentrated all its efforts on lifting the arms embargo in the U.S., the victory of the Loyalists was certain. He was in agreement with them.

451

My reaction was bitter. Minor was a senile idiot, Johnny Gates an overambitious careerist hell-bent to make his way into top party leadership by whatever means. Alpi was a military man, I reminded him, let's forget politics, let's forget the Comintern thesis on the Spanish situation, let's hold in abeyance the analyses of the Soviet military experts, what the hell else would they say except to confirm the party line. Let's look at facts as I had found them. I ticked them off, one by one, many in the form of questions.

What good are planes, howitzers, even battleships and destroyers, without trained personnel to man them?

How long does it take to train artillerymen? How long does it take to train enough pilots, navigators, ground crews, artillery officers out of men who, no matter how determined and brave, often lack primary, not to mention secondary schooling? Those were the youth we had on our side in Spain—the Fascists had most of the educated ones.

Who would man those arms and weapons even if they were to reach Spain in time, read the instruments, figure the artillery tables, when one of the greatest weaknesses of the Loyalist Army was the lack of soldiers sufficiently literate to be developed into competent noncommissioned officers, without whom no modern army can function efficiently?

I told him about a recent shipment of brand-new heavy machine guns I had heard about, stored away in the military warehouses in Barcelona, lying there unused because it takes men with good training to operate heavy machine guns and Loyalist Spain did not have even a fraction of those.

Alpi listened in silence, his head bowed over the table, his fingers playing with the crumbs from the breadsticks on the red-checkered tablecloth, maneuvering them as if an army.

"Take the Loyalist Army!" The Spanish were brave and self-sacrificing, excellent troops where they had good leadership in the field, but essentially they were soldiers of mood. They would

452

rush enthusiastically into fire when pepped up with calls to their courage and loyalty—they would break just as fast when met with unexpected resistance. Furthermore, the withdrawal of the Internationals had broken their spirit. They felt we had abandoned them because their ship was sinking, leaving them to drown. I quoted him what some of the bravest and the best of their officers and men had told me after we officially withdrew from the brigade. I also told him about the general attitude of the nonparty Spanish populace, nationalists, trade unionists, socialists, anarchists whom I had met in person.

Next, the Spanish Party itself was guilty of a grave error in policy. True, it had gained an immense following but still not sufficient to sway the majority. Because of the soft-pedalling of its revolutionary aims, its failure to call for the expropriation of the capitalists and the distribution of land its own followers were getting dissatisfied, while the nonparty majority was beginning to resent more and more the party's ruthless drive for absolute control.

That was the picture. The Loyalist government could not possibly resist for long. At this stage it wasn't arms alone that Loyalist Spain needed for its survival, but also armed assistance: trained French Divisions under French military commanders, and since the French could definitely not be counted upon to intervene, a hundred thousand or more Red Army trained Soviet volunteers transported by sea like Mussolini's Fascist Legions, experienced flyers and technicians like those flown in by Hitler.

Alpi's response was low. "You know that is impossible, that would involve the Soviet Union in war."

I wasn't ready to concede that fully. However, I told Alpi there was one thing the party and the Soviet Union could safely do—come out for some sort of negotiated settlement between the Loyalists and Franco, along the lines the British had recently proposed. Make a world-wide drive for armistice, am-

453

nesty, and plebiscite, enlisting the support of all democratic nations for international guarantees of no reprisals by either side. That was the only way left to save the millions in Loyalist territory from the savage, bloody reprisals openly threatened by Franco.

Alpi was dejected. My report was contrary to all reports from the Comintern, contrary to the party line, to the policy of the Soviet Union, he murmured.

"Let me write a detailed report, a true and factual one," I pleaded. "I could get that out in a few days. You submit that to the Central Committee and cable it directly to the Comintern. We must save what we can of Loyalist Spain, the least we will accomplish is staving off a massacre. The civilized world will support us in that drive."

Alpi was in anguish.

"You know, Voros, that's impossible, you know I can't do that. You know the Comintern line is the line of Moscow. You know I can't go against that."

His usually deep, resonant voice was now a low whisper, I detected a tremble in it. He wasn't talking to me, he was talking to himself.

We rose without a further word. This was Alpi, the one-time fearless leader of the armed Italian revolutionary bands, the most sincere man among all the top leaders of the various Communist Parties I had come across. He understood the Spanish situation, my report merely confirmed what he had surmised was the truth. He was appalled by the savage reprisals that awaited the Spanish people, yet—even he wouldn't dare act contrary to the party line, tragically wrong as he knew it to be.

As we shook hands, he asked me what I wanted to do, he would find the kind of a party position best suited to my inclinations. I said I would call on him as soon as I was ready but I knew that would be never.

I walked the streets of New York all the rest of that day, more

454

depressed than I had ever felt in my life, cursing the party and the party leadership from Stalin down to Alpi. They were all a bunch of bastards, stooges every one of them. I cursed and swore they would never again trick me into accepting any party function, they would never again maneuver me into a position where I could not say what I thought, where I would have to subordinate my principles to a line handed down from above. Had I been more coherent, I could have expressed it succinctly:

"No more thought control for me!"

Why didn't I quit the party then?

That's just exactly what I thought of doing. As I passed the headquarters of the New York Newspaper Guild I felt like going up to the club, stepping up to the bar, ordering up a drink for everyone and then offering the toast:

"Here is to Stalin, and the Communists, may they all burn in hell!" and then tearing up my party card.

It was a most gratifying emotional outburst and I kept relishing that picture in my mind, until reason took over. What was I trying to do, play into the hands of the Fascists?

Fascism was marching victoriously toward world domination, its confidence in victory growing with every new appeasement. The Fascists were the *Herrenvolk,* openly proclaiming themselves the Master Race predestined to rule with blood and iron over the enslaved masses. The democracies were burrowing in cowardly fashion every man deeper in his own tent awaiting the very great slaughter. The only hope of standing up against Fascism lay in the Soviet Union, the only country that could be counted upon not to appease Hitler. Much as I hated Stalin my place was still on his side; much as the ideals of Communism were violated in actual practice in the Soviet Union and by the Communist Parties everywhere, they still paid at least lip service to them, holding out the hope for a better and more just society.

Yet I found no comfort in my reasoning. As I paced street after street in a greatly depressed state some lines by a revolu-

455

tionary poet suddenly came to my mind. I did not recall his name, nor the actual wording, only the content of what he said.

"We, Communists, are condemned men. We live in a prison, whether in or out."

That poet meant the prison of capitalism. But I knew better, Communism was a prison, too. Since I couldn't choose to live in the prison of Fascism, all I had left was the prison of Communism. What the hell choice was that?

Condemned men have no choice. And I was one of them.

59 I HAD one last official piece of business to attend to. I went back to Ohio for my formal leave of absence from the party. I was a hero again, a great hero with mass meetings and public receptions scheduled. I ducked them all, including the big ceremonial banquet given by the Hungarians in my honor—I couldn't bear to be toasted in celebration of a nonexistent victory while Hernández, Díaz, and the rest of my comrades were left fighting to the death.

I did agree, though, to address a meeting of the Cleveland Newspaper Guild. It was a cautious talk; I skirted the party line about Spain and parried questions about it. It wasn't a good lecture—the newsmen sensed I was holding back but were sympathetic enough not to press me.

The next day, Paul Bellamy, editor and publisher of the *Cleveland Plain Dealer,* sent a message: would I come and see him? The party was excited about it. What a wonderful break for propaganda in the capitalist press!

Bellamy received me with cordial informality. He put me at ease quickly with a few remarks of sympathy for Loyalist Spain and then the interview began. It was off the record and by the time I finished answering him I saw the Spanish Civil War in a far clearer perspective than at any time in Spain. His questions organized my unassorted facts, my undefined thoughts and conclusions into a coherent whole and I answered him truthfully.

At the close of the interview Bellamy unexpectedly offered me a job on the foreign desk.

"But I am a Communist," I gulped.

Bellamy didn't mind that. He was gambling that I would continue to maintain the same objectivity I had manifested in our talk. My understanding of Communist aims might even be an asset in appraising the international situation which showed signs of boiling over at any moment.

My heart leaped at his answer. Here was an opportunity to do real journalistic work for a change, also financial security. This was still the depression and all I had between me and starvation was a few travelers checks, less than $200, all that was left of my life's savings. Bellamy was waiting for my decision.

I took a deep breath, thanked him, and regretfully declined his offer. After refusing to work for the *Daily Worker* I couldn't have taken a job on a capitalist newspaper, that would have been interpreted as a betrayal of the party.

Back at party headquarters the comrades were disappointed with my sketchy report. All I would say was that Bellamy personally showed sympathy with Spain. They wanted to know whether I could persuade Bellamy to lead a fight for the lifting of the arms embargo. I answered in the negative. I couldn't tell them that my answer to Bellamy concerning the embargo was the same that I had given to Comrade Alpi, that it was too late for that, that the best way the U.S. Government could help the Spanish people at this stage would be by negotiating for an armistice with guarantees of no reprisals on either side.

John Williamson, Ohio District Organizer, recognizing I was deaf to all offers of party jobs, tried to bargain with me to stay on temporarily to reorganize party finances. He thought I could do a wonderful job at raising money; with my record in Spain and my wide circle of acquaintances I ought to be able to tap sources that had never contributed. As a start I ought to hit up Bellamy for a big contribution for Spanish aid. That really settled it. I told him I wasn't well, I had to have time off to get back in shape. The final agreement was that although I was entitled to an official leave of absence, I still had to attend party meetings in order not to lose touch with the party but I was exempted from carrying out assignments—released on parole, so to speak.

I was free at last! "No more orders and regulations for me," I kept repeating to myself as I boarded the bus to New York. It had taken ten years from the time I accepted that temporary assignment to the *Uj Elore,* but I was finally free.

It was a great letdown. I should have been elated but I wasn't. I was free to do what? To go back to my old life? That was impossible. I couldn't escape into the past—my blessed ignorance and indifference to politics was gone forever. My past associations, even my family ties were severed—we no longer lived in the same world or talked the same language.

I was free—or was I? What was freedom? I was casting myself off from the ship on which I had sailed for ten years to navigate alone on a solitary raft with no clear destination in mind. Was that freedom?

It didn't seem so. A free man is supposed to be a happy one. Which I was definitely not!

60 ADDICTION to Communism is like addiction to drugs—the victim resists the cure and is reluctant to admit the destructive side of his habit.

My withdrawal symptoms manifested themselves in prolonged periods of mental anguish which made me shun contacts with the outside world. My companionship was limited to my wife— my old-time girl friend from the days long past. She had consented to marry me even though she knew I had no prospects of a job, that in the months until the fur season opened up we'd have to exist on my remaining savings from my foreman days which by then had shrunk to less than two hundred dollars. She had no job either and we lived in a furnished room on a carefully planned subsistence level, limiting ourselves to a strict budget of ten dollars a week out of which rent took four, to a diet of soup and cheap staples with an occasional splurge of a Sunday meal at Stewart's Cafeteria. For newspapers I depended on the trash baskets of the near-by subway station, spent money only on the *Daily Worker*—no comrade threw that away, his instructions were to leave it on the subway seat in the hope that some bored passenger might pick it up.

Since the subway cost a nickel I stopped riding it. I walked about sixty blocks each way to the few party unit meetings I forced myself to attend. Those units were called branches now. My branch met in a fencing studio around Twenty-third Street and the comrades were mostly professional people, men and women in their late twenties and early thirties. I didn't know

460

them and they knew me only by my party name which was Douglass. I was content to leave it that way and they didn't make much effort to know me better, either. I sat through those meetings without participating in their earnest discussions about changing the fate of the world which, as far as their own role was concerned, usually revolved around the question whether to sell the *Daily Worker* on one specified corner in preference to another. Little had changed in party routine in those ten years since my first attendance at a party meeting in New York; assignments were as seriously debated and as little carried out as then. The main difference that I saw was that these comrades were arguing dialectics with a choicer vocabulary and with less of an accent.

The last party meeting I was ever to attend happened to fall on the day the afternoon papers headlined the outbreak of an army revolt in Madrid, and reported that Negrin and other government and party leaders had fled Spain in their private planes. I was brooding over those developments, distressed over the fate of those faithful in the ranks who had no private planes in which to escape, when the voice of the literature chairman brought me sharply to my senses. He was holding aloft a party pamphlet just issued, written by Joe North, former *Daily Worker* correspondent in Spain, former editor of the *New Masses,* then the *Daily Worker's* special expert on Spain.

"It is a most important pamphlet," the chairman intoned, "everybody should buy as many as he or she can afford, it explains the party line on Spain. This pamphlet refutes the lies of the Fascist provocateurs, it proves why the Loyalist Army will continue to fight on for years until victory is assured. It must be distributed in quantity to reach the greatest masses of people."

The comrades each dutifully bought several of them. I picked up a copy and leafed through it. Incredible as this may seem it bore the title "Why Loyalist Spain Will Win!" or some such words. Joe North did not hog all the credit for that brilliant

461

dialectical forecast of history. He modestly acknowledged that his analysis had merely confirmed the correctness of the party line and the previous reports made by those other two eminent researchers and objective scholars, Robert Minor and John Gates.

I lifted my eyes and saw that the noses of all comrades were buried in the pamphlet. Then the silence was broken by a comrade on my left commenting with loud satisfaction:

"This pamphlet sure came just in time. Now we'll know how to answer the lies of the Fascist Hearst and the other capitalist newspapers." His words were greeted with spontaneous applause. I got to my feet and walked out without giving them a further glance; what the hell was I doing there among those political cretins?

Other incidents of similar idiocy followed in quick succession, making it more and more difficult to put off resolving the issue. Like the time I attended a new Theater League performance somewhere around Fiftieth Street off Broadway.

It was an anti-Nazi play by Bertolt Brecht, the famous German revolutionary playwright. It was the tragedy of an honest, upright German Reich justice who had retained his position on the bench even under the Nazis, although deep in his heart he was still devoted to the principles of true justice as they existed in Germany before Hitler. The play opened with the justice and his wife fearfully discussing their horrible suspicion that their own beloved only son, a loutish boy of 14 who belonged to the Hitler Youth, might be capable of denouncing his own father as being disloyal in thought to the Nazis. True enough, exactly that was to happen to him. Few eyes remained dry at the conclusion of the play as that German judge was led away by brutal stormtroopers wearing swastika armbands while their son, that monster product of Nazi training, proudly declaimed from the stage that no true Fascist must ever hesitate to denounce his own father and mother if they were disloyal, if only in thought, to the Nazi Reich.

462

There was tremendous applause and many curtain calls. The party comrades were cashing in on the play by loudly hawking their literature when one of the leaders of that theatrical group turned to me with pride: what did I think of the performance, wasn't Bertolt Brecht a genius? I praised the performance and told her how it moved me; as to Brecht, he was obviously a man of great talent but in this instance, unquestionably also a dishonest plagiarist. Those were fighting words. I was immediately challenged to prove that and in no time became the center of a large crowd, mostly hostile. I asserted that the play was based almost verbatim but without acknowledgment on a Soviet news report. Hostility now gave way to perplexity and I was asked to elucidate.

I related how, early in 1935, following the assassination of party leader Kirow in Leningrad when the first big Soviet purge began, the Party had called on the Young Pioneers to ferret out the hidden counterrevolutionary sentiments of their parents and report it to the G.P.U. We at the *Uj Elore* once published a report on one such trial sent to us by the official Soviet News Agency which gave details of the exemplary Communist behavior of a young boy of 14, a leading member of the Young Pioneers, whose suspicion became alerted when he saw his father abruptly stop talking to his mother the minute he entered the room.

This incorruptible product of Soviet upbringing had not only denounced his father to the G.P.U. but also blazingly repudiated his father's cowardly denial of the charge. He denounced him in open court as a barefaced liar, demanded that his father pay with his life for his traitorous sentiments, and called upon all Young Pioneers to overlook all sentiment and follow his example. In conclusion that news report proudly noted that this outstanding Young Pioneer leader was the first one to applaud in court when he heard his father pronounced guilty and sentenced to death.

When I finished my tale the group around me hastily dissolved except for a few innocents who stayed on to argue that I really couldn't be serious in maintaining that there was any analogy at all between those two cases? Couldn't I see that the theme of this play was the bestial corruption of youth under Hitler? Wasn't it also clearly evident that the story I quoted was about the trial of a bourgeois counterrevolutionary traitor in the pay of the imperialists? No, the only thing evident to me was that I had overstayed my welcome and I left in the glare of hostile eyes.

Then came signs.

Within a period of two days three letters came to me unexpectedly from France. One was from Alexander Cseresznyes, the other from that German commissar, the third from a Spanish youth leader formerly on my staff in the Brigade. They were from different concentration camps in France, but containing the same heart-wringing tale of misery and ill-treatment to which those remnants of the defeated Loyalists who crossed into France were being subjected. They were sleeping in the open in midwinter without blankets, clad only in their filthy summer rags. Those concentration camps were but bare ground surrounded by barbed wire, without even wells or latrines, and only the cold winter sky for roof. They were forced to sleep rolling in their own excrement in holes scratched out of the ground with their bare fingers, drinking the human-sewage-infected water that accumulated in the shallow, handscooped holes in the ground. Besides being starved they also suffered from their Senegalese guards who sadistically enjoyed using their whips on them. They were begging me for help, to organize for them food, money, used clothing, cigarettes, anything. In closing they affirmed anew their loyalty to the Communist Party and emphasized that what they desired above all was political asylum in some country willing to receive them.

I took those letters up to the Friends of the Abraham Lincoln Brigade demanding that we act at once. "Yes, it is too sad, we know all about it, but there is nothing the Friends can do right now, collections are slow in coming in, we need all the funds to run the office and to take care of the wounded and needy veterans here."

I lost my temper and demanded an emergency meeting, what those comrades wanted most was a chance to leave France. Pasionária was not suffering in those camps. She had been transported with other Communist leaders by boat and special plane to the Soviet Union to be feted there as the last-ditch fighter of Fascism, even though her son, the offspring of this fiery speaker who passionately demanded that every last Spaniard fight to the death, had sat out the Spanish Civil War in Moscow where his mother had prudently sent him for safety.

I drew up a resolution on the spot and thumbtacked it on the wall:

BE IT RESOLVED: that the Friends and Veterans of the Abraham Lincoln Brigade petition the Soviet Union to offer asylum to all the exiled victims of Franco now languishing in the French concentration camps.

Be It Further Resolved: that copies of this resolution be sent not only to the *Daily Worker* but also to all capitalist newspapers and wire services, for widest dissemination.

By that time there was quite a commotion, my resolution was hastily removed from the wall, and I was upbraided by the paid office staff. Didn't I know what I was doing? How could the Friends and Veterans of the Abraham Lincoln Brigade be asked to sign such a petition, how could I possibly ask the Soviet Union to admit those people? Wasn't I aware who those people actually were? Did I know how many actual spies, saboteurs, counter-revolutionists, imperialist and Fascist agents and spies were among those "so-called veterans"? Why, most of those people were international wreckers trying to worm their way into the Soviet Union.

"You bastards really believe that? Believe that those comrades

465

in arms of ours, who gathered from all corners of the world at the call of the Comintern, who risked their lives over and over in the fight against Fascism, are really Fascist agents?"

I must have become overemotional for they started to soothe me. "Now, now, take it easy comrade, we know how you feel. Do you think we enjoy thinking of those comrades suffering in those French concentration camps? We are working very hard to get them admitted to Mexico. . . ."

I stalked out telling them to cross my name off their list, pronto!

The signs came more rapidly now. Upon his return from Moscow Gil Green, National Secretary of the Young Communist League, commented admiringly on the loud, prolonged applause and standing ovation afforded to the party leaders in the Soviet Union. He contrasted it scathingly with the informal, almost indolent attitude with which the membership received its leaders here and demanded a change. His orders were that in the future the Party and Y.C.L. leaders were to be greeted by the same loud cheers and standing ovation whenever they entered a meeting hall.

The focus became sharper:

> FRANCO! FRANCO! FRANCO! SIEG HEIL!
> HEIL GIL GREEN, BROWDER, STALIN!
> Arise ye prisoners of starvation;
> Goosestep ye wretched of the earth!
> Damnation shall be your salvation;
> Sovicts to bring the new rebirth!

Next Stalin spoke and Molotov echoed him.

"The Soviet Union does not consider any imagined or real ideological differences a barrier to establishing friendly and cordial relationship with any other nation."

"Fascism is a matter of taste."

I needed no further signs. My recovery was complete. Cured by the hair of the same dog . . .

61 Once my eyes recovered their sight I was galvanized into action. This was the spring of 1939 and there was no time to waste. The Nazi war machine was getting ready to roll. People all over the world were pinning their hopes on the great Soviet Union with its mighty Red Army to forestall the Hitler juggernaut—that illusion needed to be blasted. I sat down and wrote day and night until I finished the draft of a short book which was aimed to shake the American people into awareness that the Soviet Union was just as totalitarian and equally as imperialistic as Nazi Germany.

That draft was titled "Chronicle of the Second World War," as set down by a young reporter with the last surviving American troops hiding out in a mountain post, awaiting the last assault. It was a projection of the coming World War II as I visualized it then, with Stalin villainously making war inevitable between Fascism and the democracies, and when they were both sufficiently exhausted falling first on Hitler, next on the democracies, ultimately taking possession of a devastated world.

When I was finished with it I thought of just the right organization for it—the World Peaceways, a group of pacifists who were not involved with any of the peace fronts of the Communists.

When Mr. Wise, Secretary of the World Peaceways, read that first draft he became enthused. He was thinking of an initial printing of 100,000 copies to be followed by a second printing of 200,000 and as many more as public interest in it warranted.

He wanted changes though; his suggestions were good and I agreed to them instantly.

After that first draft was finished I rejoined the furriers union. Fur shops were still sweatshops and I would get home too fatigued physically to do much writing at night; by the time the manuscript was ready for editing it was late August. Two days later came the news of the Nazi-Soviet pact and my appointment with the World Peaceways set for the following week was canceled by silent agreement. No one needed my book any longer to warn him of Stalin's treachery, Hitler had already invaded Poland.

I followed with sardonic glee the gyrations of the party, the desperate flip-flops of the comrades to justify that Soviet-Nazi alliance. Yet even I couldn't foresee their ultimate degradation —that the remaining members of the Communist Party would openly work for the victory of Hitler. Thorez, the leader of the French Party, deserted the army and the French Communist Party issued leaflets calling on all other French soldiers not to fight Hitler but desert. Harry Pollit, the Secretary of the British Party, with whom I once spent a whole night in Madrid, called for making peace with Hitler even while Britain was being devastated by falling Nazi bombs. The Communist Party of America ordered my one-time Cleveland comrade Wyndham Mortimer to call a strike against the North American Aviation Corporation to keep our own country from producing planes in our defense. My former favorite Y.C.L. friend, Al Balint in Cleveland, led a steel strike to cripple our preparedness while my former colleague, devout Louis Budenz, the Catholic managing editor of the *Daily Worker,* was openly supplicating for the defeat of the democracies.

In 1940, I incurred the hostility of my Communist union by joining the Volunteers for Roosevelt for a third term, and on December 8, 1941, the day after Pearl Harbor, I kissed my wife and infant son good-bye and went downtown to enlist.

The line was long, it stretched around the block. More and more people came to join it; there was shoving and jostling; it was difficult to keep the slowly moving line in order. A couple of young fellows thought I was an easy mark and tried to elbow me out of my place. Naturally I fought back and the Marine sergeant came up to investigate. "What's the trouble, Pop? What are you doing here?"

"I came to enlist, what else?"

I was indignant. Here I was, leaving my wife with my six-month-old son to fend for themselves because principles take precedence over family obligations; now some young squirt, who as likely as not had no real conception what this war was about, was trying to push me out of line.

"Come on, Pop, quit it," said the Marine sergeant with a friendly grin. He was tall, broad-shouldered—a trained, healthy specimen. "Be a nice guy, Pop, and give a chance to the young fellows. You don't belong here, Pop. When we need grandfathers, we'll call you," he coaxed.

The line rocked with laughter. The sergeant was not being sarcastic, he was humoring me, to the delight of those young men.

I left the line and walked away.

"Pop," they called me, and "Grandfather!"

I stopped in front of a plate glass window and took a good look at my reflection. My face was haggard and deeply etched; my cheeks sunken over the missing teeth I had lost in Spain and had no money to replace; I was still more than twenty pounds underweight because of a souvenir from Spain—chronic diarrhea. I was only forty-one, but Pop indeed; my soldiering days were over. The best a man of my age could expect in modern warfare would be guarding bridges. I went back to work utterly deflated.

Less than a month after that incident, on a sunny Sunday morning, I encountered Peter Chaunt, the Party boss of the

I.W.O. Hungarian Section. I was wheeling my infant, he was walking his sleek wolfhound. We stopped to talk. When he asked how I felt about the war I told him about my frustration, about being too old to join in the fighting. Chaunt became most serious and told me I was in a position to make a very great contribution to fighting Fascism. The *Uj Elore* was no longer a Communist newspaper, it had changed its name and had been turned into a united front organ to rally all Hungarians in America regardless of creed or political beliefs behind the war effort. The Hungarian Horthy troops fighting alongside the Nazis were then deep in the Soviet Union, yet many Hungarians in the United States were still secretly sympathetic to Horthy. These men were traitors to their adopted country, the United States, yet were able to influence the ignorant Hungarian masses. Chaunt proposed that I come back and take over editorship of that paper; my name was popular with Hungarians; my past record as a fighting anti-Fascist would make me the ideal champion to rally the patriotic Hungarian masses around me.

That offer appealed to me. In the mobilization of our national resources for war I considered certain steps dangerous for the welfare of our nation, like the order that froze wages while leaving profits uncurbed. I expressed those thoughts to Chaunt, adding the Leninist slogan: "We mustn't allow the capitalists to profiteer and place the burden of the war on the shoulders of the working class."

"You've really been away too long, you've really lost touch," Chaunt replied condescendingly.

Nothing mattered in this war but one thing, to save the Soviet Union, Chaunt explained the new party line. Let the capitalists make all the profits they can, let them raise prices, do anything they pleased as long as they turned out the war materials the Soviet Union needed. As Marx said, "The greater the profits, the greater the capitalist incentive." We had to spur on this capitalist incentive by preventing strikes; by using all our influence to drive the workers to greater productivity, to make them work double shifts and to hell with time and a half for overtime. The interests of the Soviet Union were the supreme guide; if that interest was best served by helping American capitalists to greater profits, then dialectically that was what we had to do, that was Leninism.

I was too amazed to speak. Chaunt took my silence for agreement. "Come see me tomorrow morning and don't forget to bring your statement with you."

"What statement?"

"A statement confessing your errors, admitting that the party line is always right. Stress particularly how right the party was in making that nominal pact with Hitler; explain how you became a victim of the warmongers by not realizing that that pact was the greatest contribution by the Soviet Union to maintaining peace, which only failed because of the Chamberlain and Blum imperialist warmongers."

Chaunt was petting his dog. It was a sleek, aristocratic wolfhound—Russian, not Soviet. Chaunt himself looked more prosperous than I had ever seen him.

"Is it a real united front paper?"

"Sure. That's why you're needed so badly, that's why I want you to start tomorrow."

"I am ready to start tomorrow. But I want to publish my statement as a two-column signed editorial on the front page."

"Why on the front page?"

"Because I want it there. And I want it published as written."

Chaunt was now wary. "Of course the Central Committee will have to go over it and pass on it before publication. They may want some changes made."

"Not if it is a united front paper."

I still played it straight, noting with delight the beginning of a doubt in Chaunt's eyes. Now it was my turn to assume the long-familiar Communist tone of lecturing, to count off the points one by one on my thumb.

Number one: My statement would open with the announcement that I was no longer a party member, that I was assuming editorship of the paper only because of my firm belief in the need of united effort to bring this war for the survival of democracy to a successful conclusion.

Number two: Next I would explain that I had quit the party because I was opposed to the tyrannical and despotic practices in the Soviet Union which permeated all Communist Parties in the world.

Number three: I have reached the conclusion that ever since Stalin came into power the Communist Party Line has been wrong in all its major decisions beginning with the policy in China in 1927 up to and including the criminal adventure of the Nazi-Soviet pact which exploded the Second World War.

Chaunt did not hear me all out. He yanked the dog viciously to his feet and stalked away, his freckled face livid with anger.

There may have been no connection but shortly afterward I began to experience trouble in the fur market.

I would go on a new job in the morning; there would be a whispered conversation between the shop chairman and some workers who recognized me; the boss would call me in later and I would be dismissed without explanation or, where the boss needed me badly, with a despondent shrug—"I like your work but I can't afford to have trouble with the union." One day I became embroiled in a physical fight. I was called a paid Nazi spy, sharp furriers' knives flashed. Had it not been for the timely appearance of two policemen I might have been carved up or crippled, a fit punishment for an anti-Communist.

That made it obvious both to my wife and me that sooner or later I would be forced out of a job in every fur shop, that we had to leave New York.

We counted our resources—a few hundred dollars in cash savings, some used furniture—a pitifully small stake to start a new existence. Never mind. We settled on a small town, half rural, half urban, which was most unlikely to harbor any Communists who knew me.

We moved there convinced that the trail had come to an end; that my life as a Communist would be but a memory of my past, that nothing would hinder me from adjusting myself to the normal life of a citizen.

It did work out except for the stigma.

Epilogue

COMMUNISM creates its own antibodies. There is but one group of people in the entire world who are totally immune to all threats and blandishments from Moscow or Peking —the former Communists. Paradoxically, there are far more of us inside the iron curtain than out and our numbers are growing by the day. The red rulers fear us more than all other of their foes combined; more of us have suffered death and torture at their hands than all the Communists executed by Hitler, Mussolini, and other Fascist dictators. The people who participated in the demonstrations in Poland; the men, women, and children who manned the barricades in Budapest in 1956, were led by our political blood brothers, the former Communists. Because of our experiences we are the most implacable foes of totalitarianism and the greatest allies in the fight for liberty— a fact recognized in all lands yet blindly ignored in the United States.

It is an axiom that the demands raised by the revolutionaries of yesterday may well be but the low norms of the morrow. The revolutionary demand of $15 a week unemployment compensation for which my skull had once been nearly split in two is by now way below the standard established in most states. The revolutionary demand of fifty cents an hour minimum wage, for which I had been roughly handled and driven out of town at pistol point in Yorkville, Ohio has long been raised to one dollar an hour by a Republican administration, no less.

All nations need their quota of rebels to goad them into enacting those social reforms that are essential to their progress. Stagnation and decadence invite disaster, for the Goths and Vandals are forever lurking outside the gates in search for the breach in the crumbling walls.

For having been such a rebel as I was, about a million of my countrymen in all walks of life were made into whipping boys by every demagogue and professional patriot who deals in hate to further his political ambition; branded subversives by opponents of all progressive measures who are hell-bent to restore all evils of the past in their selfish greed. I have never committed a crime or been charged with one; nor was I ever arrested. I was never involved in spying nor even knew about it—and that applies to all but a minuscule percentage of us. The few involved in spying have either gone to jail or glory depending on who told on whom first. The Communist Party which I quit over twenty years ago has by now all but disintegrated. Yet, I and my fellow former rebels have been degraded to second-class citizens, denied even the right of serving our country in the capacities we are best fitted for because of a panicky law that demands a negative answer to this question:

"Are you now *or have you ever been a member of . . . ?*"

Panicky laws do not make for national security, especially when they themselves smack of totalitarianism. Nor can we depend for our national defense on the strength of our arms alone. We need ideological weapons also and trained men to use them—experts that are plentiful among former Communists.

Basically there are only three great revolutionary proclamations that exert the most profound influence on the mind. The *Communist Manifesto* is but one of them. The other two in historical order are:

476

The Sermon on the Mount;

The Declaration of Independence.

As a nation born of revolution and a professed Christian one we have a special claim on both of these. Why on earth should we panic when faced with the incendiary cry of revolt.
Arise ye prisoners of starvation . . .
Of all nations in the world we have the best claim to respond:
Peace on Earth; Good Will toward Men;
All men are created equal with the unalienable right to life, liberty, the pursuit of happiness!

In this struggle of ideologies the odds are two to one in our favor if we are but bold enough to take advantage of it. Let us devote our diplomacy, our surpluses, our technological skill with our traditional democratic forbearance to the above aims. Let us persist in this endeavor for another few decades. We will then discover that we no longer have to fear the rising of those proletarians who, according to the *Communist Manifesto,* have *nothing to lose but their chains.*

There won't be any of them left!